The Free Black in
Urban America 1800–1850

Leonard P. Curry

The Free Black in Urban America 1800–1850

The Shadow of the Dream

The University of Chicago Press
Chicago and London

FOR FLETCHER AND JUSTIN

The University of Chicago Press, Chicago 60637
The University of Chicago Press, Ltd., London

Library of Congress Cataloging in Publication Data

Curry, Leonard P
  The free Black in urban America, 1800–1850.

  Includes bibliographical references and index.
    1. Afro-Americans—History—To 1863.   2. United
States—Social conditions—To 1865.   I. Title.
E185.9.C87   973'.049673   80-27811
ISBN 0-226-13124-6

LEONARD P. CURRY is professor of history at the
University of Louisville.

Contents

List of Figures

List of Tables

Acknowledgments

Of the obligations incurred by historians there is no end. Without libraries and archives—and, hence, librarians and archivists—we cannot function, and such talents as we may possess are lodged with us, useless. During the past decade and a half I have spent the equivalent of five years as an almost daily user of the facilities of the Library of Congress or the National Archives. Consequently, I owe enormous debts of gratitude to members of the staffs of both these institutions. Without their conscientious commitment to making a wide variety of materials readily available to inquiring scholars—and their richly informed assistance when requested—it would have been impossible to begin, let alone complete, the explorations upon which this volume rests. Equally helpful on a continuing basis has been the staff of the University of Louisville Library and that of the Filson Club.

Funds for the support of historical research are—as all practitioners of the art know to their sorrow—both limited and difficult to obtain. I am, therefore, deeply grateful to the following organizations and university bodies that have provided some measure of support for my investigations of antebellum urban America: the Smithsonian Institution for an appointment as a postdoctoral research associate in 1970–71; the American Council of Learned Societies for a research grant in 1976; the American Philosophical Society for grants in 1972 and 1976; the University of Louisville Graduate Faculty Research Fund for grants in 1977, 1978, and 1979; and the University of Louisville Arts and Sciences Faculty Research Fund for funding in 1966, 1967, 1973, 1974, 1975, 1976, 1977, 1978, and 1979.

I would be remiss if I did not also record my appreciation of several friends and fellow historians whose comments contributed to the evolution of this study. In addition to dozens of professional colleagues who have, with patience and enthusiasm, discussed with me various aspects of my work, I would especially single out Ira Berlin, whose comments on a much earlier version of chapter 2 stimulated me to address specifically several additional questions; John Duffy, who kindly consented to read and evaluate a late draft of chapter 9; and Jon Wakelyn, who read and commented on a near-final version of the entire study. All these people—named and unnamed—were extremely helpful, but they bear no responsibility for the finished product.

My greatest debts, however, are owed to those who, except for the author, lived most intimately with this work—my children, who accepted with equanimity the irregular hours and the intricate juggling of schedules necessitated by this lengthy project, and especially my wife, who endured so much, and contributed so much, and, ultimately, without whom there would have been little done, and nothing worth the doing.

Preface

It is now more than a decade since I first began the exploration of the antebellum American city of which this volume is the first fruit. I was attracted to this area of study by a purpose and a hope. I intended to produce a work that would treat synthetically the American urban experience in the first half of the nineteenth century and thus fill substantial voids in both the literature dealing with urban development in the United States and that related to antebellum America. Study had convinced me that the urban dimension of life in the United States during the period 1800–1850 had been insufficiently appreciated (and probably insufficiently understood) as a factor shaping pre–Civil War society, and it appeared to me unlikely that this circumstance would change until at least some effort was made to treat in more general fashion, but in some detail, the nature of that urban dimension. In the literature of the city it was also clear that the synthesizing efforts of Carl Bridenbaugh[1] for colonial cities and Blake McKelvey[2] for the post–Civil War urban centers had no counterpart for the period between 1776 and 1865. It was almost as though historians of Jeffersonian and Jacksonian America had agreed that the era could be meaningfully perceived only from the viewpoints provided by agriculture, transportation, and slavery, and urban historians had concluded that no significant changes took place in urban structures, forms, populations, or functions between the Revolutionary and the Civil wars. Historians being fractious, stubborn, and idiosyncratic by nature, there was, of course, no such conscious consensus, or "establishment," view, let alone an ideological or intellectual conspiracy of silence. But it remained true that the paucity of urban materials and the slightness of concern for city life in either interpretative or synthetic examinations of the antebellum era were appalling to a student of the era consciously looking for such elements.

The purpose of producing an accurate synthesis of the antebellum urban experience was coupled with the hope of accomplishing this task in a truly comparative fashion. That is, I wished the findings, analyses, and interpretations to rest not on an array (however large) of materials drawn from any urban experience occurring in the era and extrapolations from such not demonstrably related evidence, but rather on information consciously collected on the same topics from a stable universe of urban centers. The major problem with such an approach is one of scale. As Bridenbaugh discovered, as early as the 1760s the scholar can no longer confine his investigations to an urban universe of five cities or generalize accurately and cogently about the urban experience on the basis of evidence drawn from so small a sample. And in the early nineteenth century this problem is compounded by the great increase in both the populations of the major cities and the number of urban places of substantial size. Obviously, an analytical universe appreciably larger than the five cities Bridenbaugh used for most of his work is essential.

Almost from the beginning of research on this project it was evident that an examination of the free blacks in the cities was badly needed, and it soon became clear that the materials existed to support such a study. That was the genesis of this book. It is governed by the considerations outlined above—the presentation of a synthesis of the results derived from the study and analysis of data collected in a truly comparative manner. I am concerned with exploring the elements of both commonality and diversity in the free black experience in these cities in the antebellum era.

After some preliminary exploration and consideration I resolved to limit the years for investigation to the period 1800–1850. There were several reasons for this decision. Admittedly, traditional practicies would have suggested the year 1860 as a terminal date, but the more I examined the evidence, the more I became convinced that the urban experience of the free blacks in the last antebellum decade was different from that of the previous half-century. The rising antislavery agitation of the late 1840s and '50s, the reaction to the Fugitive Slave Act of 1850, and, especially, the increasing support that the antislavery crusade attracted in the North had great impact on the white response to the presence of free blacks in the urban environment (and, of course, elsewhere) and also sparked even more assertive activity on the part of the black leadership in the North. The end result was greater repression in the South and the relaxation of some restrictions in the North. These circumstances perturbed the "normal" development patterns of black urban life and clearly suggest that the sixth decade of the nineteenth century should be viewed as a part of the succeeding era, which extended (with the exception of the Reconstruction interlude in the South) for at least sixty-five, and perhaps even a hundred, years beyond 1850.

The choice of 1850 as a terminal date was also influenced by the extent to which the urban environment in which the free blacks operated was dramatically altered in the subsequent decades. Rising slowly after 1820, and much more rapidly in the late 1840s, the rate of urban growth in the United States reached a level that it would sustain with only minor variations until 1930—during the ninety years after 1840 the percentage of the nation's population that was urban increased by about five percentage points per decade. This continued high rate of urbanization doubtless significantly affected the urban black populations that remained, for some time, relatively stable (except in southern cities which attracted more black residents after the emancipation of the slaves). Almost certainly the increased demand for housing, coupled with the widespread construction of multifamily dwellings that occurred almost entirely after 1850, forced blacks in northern (and some southern) cities into tighter residential concentrations and almost totally eliminated the intermixture of the races that had been universal in these areas before 1850.

Recent arrivals from abroad made no small contribution to this growth as the great upsurge of immigration that began in the late 1840s continued almost unabated until well into the twentieth century. It appears likely that this steady modification of the urban populations adversely affected (relatively, though not necessarily absolutely) the conditions under which urban Negroes lived and labored. Certainly the foreign born appear to have been among those who confronted black urbanites most directly in the competition for housing and employment. Such competition, though present, seems to have been of very limited importance before 1850.

Additionally, the economic structures of the cities began to shift with considerable rapidity after 1850. The explosive expansion of the nation's rail networks, which began in the late 1840s and accelerated sharply in the 1850s, gave rise to a greatly increased concentration of commercial enterprise in the major urban areas, and also stimulated the concentration and rapid growth of manufacturing in those metropolitan centers. Thus, new urban occupational patterns replaced the old, and blacks were often ill prepared to adjust to the changes. These same forces fostered the creation of larger work force units, which made increased occupational discrimination against blacks easier, more thorough, and (given the climate of opinion) probably inevitable.

For all these reasons it appears to me that 1850 is the appropriate terminus for this study of the urban free black experience. The 1850s themselves, I have become convinced, constituted an atypical decade when viewed from the perspective of the patterns of urban free black development in the first half of the nineteenth century.

The research universe employed consists of fifteen cities—the largest fifteen in the nation in 1850 (if we exclude the Philadelphia suburbs of Spring Garden, Northern Liberties, and Kensington, which are covered in some of the Philadelphia data in any event)—Albany, Baltimore, Boston, Brooklyn (not incorporated into New York until 1898), Buffalo, Charleston, Cincinnati, Louisville, New Orleans, New York, Philadelphia, Pittsburgh, Providence, St. Louis, and Washington. This array has the advantage of including a good mix of characteristics: eastern, western, northern, southern, early-developing and late-developing, small (five with populations of less than fifty thousand) as well as large.

These cities are not the fifteen with the largest free black populations in 1850, though all fall in the top twenty-five, and the list includes the top seven as well as thirteen of the top sixteen. Some elements of diversity in this respect are desirable when exploring the free black experience in urban America, for it is important to determine to what extent (if at all) that experience differed in cities with different proportions of blacks. If only the cities with the largest number of free black residents were selected, we would learn nothing about the development of smaller black communities in genuine urban centers, and, additionally, the research universe would be more heavily tilted toward the Southeast, imparting some measure of regional bias to the conclusions.

Whenever possible I have avoided a discussion of urban slavery, believing that the work of Richard C. Wade[3] and Claudia D. Goldin[4] (though I am not always in total agreement with all their views) has already supplied the most pressing needs of the historical profession in this area. Occasionally, however (as in chapters 1 and 9), the nature of the data or the constraints of the analytical framework have necessitated the inclusion of slave materials.

No sensible scholar would claim to have been able to examine all the multitudinous and frequently obscure materials that might relate to this awesomely massive, multifaceted, and often unwieldly topic. The attempt to explore in depth fifteen cities for half a century necessarily imposes some constraints on the types of sources employed, if the study is to be completed in one lifetime. But I have spread my research net as widely as possible in a dozen years of intensive effort. Nor would any investigator who has handled large amounts of numerical material assert that no error has crept into the extensive collection and analysis of statistical data. To cite but a single example, the pervasiveness of human error will always prevent any two researchers collecting information from the manuscript census or from city directories from ever producing identical results save by accident. But as far as possible these analyses have been crosschecked and verified, often beyond the point of diminishing returns.

My intention has been to explore the concerns, the agonies, the successes, the failures, the weaknesses, the strengths the isolation, the unity, the sacrifice, the hopes, and the struggles of the free black in urban America in the first half of the nineteenth century. As might be expected, the urban free black shared the nineteenth-century version of the "American Dream"—a compound of beliefs in the possibility (indeed, the likelihood) of achieving freedom, individual economic success, and personal, institutional, and societal improvement. Though the reality was always less than the dream—especially for individuals starting at the bottom of the ladder—there were also elements of truth in the images, especially in comparative terms within Western culture, even for urban free persons of color. Many (a larger percentage in 1800 than in 1850, admittedly) had been born in slavery but were legally free; some attained economic success; and the churches, schools, and associations that they created doubtless contributed to the intellectual and social "improvement" of the urban black population throughout the half-century. But in important respects the free blacks found themselves unable to share fully in the "American Dream" or the benefits of the relatively free, open, and affluent American society. Their educational advancement was limited, their social development was thwarted, occupations were closed to them, housing was denied to them, personal safety eluded them, and basic human dignity was begrudged them. Because they were black, freedom was always and everywhere for them cruelly incomplete. In striving for the "American Dream" they were destined always to fall short. Some things were gained, to be sure, and many were gains by no means devoid of substance, but to most urban free blacks it must surely have seemed that they had been able to grasp but the shadow of the dream.

1 The Spreading Shadow:
The Growth and Nature of
the Urban Black Population

The first half of the nineteenth century was a period of dramatic growth of America's urban population. The numbers dwelling in urban places (i.e., those with twenty-five hundred or more inhabitants) increased by just under one thousand percent between 1800 and 1850—a growth rate almost triple that of the whole population. Since seven of the fifteen cities examined in this study were already substantial in size at the beginning of the century, their growth rates were, in percentage terms, somewhat smaller, but still consistently more than twice that of the general population. When free to do so blacks, too, joined this migration cityward. Between 1800 and 1850 the number of blacks residing in these fifteen cities quadrupled. The shift is even more pronounced among free blacks—the number in 1850 was almost six times that of 1800.[1]

The black population, as might be expected, did not increase in all of the cities at the same rate. The numerical increase during the half-century was less than one thousand in Albany, Boston, and Providence, for instance, but greater than ten thousand in Baltimore, Charleston, and New Orleans, and almost that great in Washington (see table A-1). Nor was the pattern of increase consistent in individual cities, though each showed some increase during the fifty-year period. In Albany more than one-half of the modest growth in the black population between 1800 and 1830 was wiped out by declines in the 1830s and '40s. After quadrupling in the first twenty years of the century and more than doubling in the next two decades, the black population of New Orleans declined precipitously by almost a fifth in the 1840s. Substantial, if unremarkable, increases in New York's Negro population between 1800 and 1840 were eroded by a decline of more than twenty-five hundred in the fifth decade of the century. Charleston's nonwhite population declined somewhat in the 1830s, as blacks sought housing outside city boundaries, only to rebound in the 1840s when annexation brought them back inside the corporate limits. In some other cases the black growth patterns were more consistent.

Despite this very substantial increase in the absolute number of blacks residing in these major American cities, the rate of growth was, in general, smaller than that of the white population. Consequently, in almost all of the metropolitan centers blacks constituted a smaller and smaller percentage of the urban population as the half-century wore on. By mid-century, for instance, blacks comprised less than one-half their 1800 percentage of the Providence population (see table A-2). Comparable figures for other cities were less than a third in Boston, a little more than a quarter in New York, slightly more than one-seventh in St. Louis, less than an eighth in Albany, and something below one-tenth in Brooklyn. In Cincinnati, Charleston, and Washington, on the other hand, the percentages were minutely greater in 1850 than half a century earlier. The proportion of blacks in the population was unusually stable in Charleston, Washington, and Philadelphia; in some other cities the fluctuations were both larger and more erratic. A decline in the black percentage of the urban population was almost universal at the end of the half-century, with only Pittsburgh showing an increase in the 1840s. For ten of the fifteen cities the black percentage in 1850 was the smallest reported for the half-century (see tables A-2 and A-3).

The declining proportion of Negroes in the metropolitan populations did not reflect an avoidance by blacks of the urban environment. Rather, such trends resulted primarily from the fact that the nation's black population, unlike the Caucasian elements, did not receive sizable accretions from abroad. There were, to be sure, a handful of black immigrants from other countries, but even these were rather heavily concentrated in the first quarter of the century rather than the 1830s and '40s, the years of heaviest European immigration. Additionally, most slave blacks were not free to follow their own inclinations in the matter of residence.

The black population in these cities was, of course, divided into two parts—the slave and the free. When the second federal census was taken in 1800, slavery had been fully abolished or prohibited only in a handful of northern New England states and in the area lying north of the Ohio River. Consequently, federal census enumerators, at one time or another during the antebellum era, reported slaves in all of these fifteen cities except Boston and Cincinnati (see table A-4). In 1800 more than one-fifth of the slaves residing in these metropolises were in the New York urban centers. Indeed, only in Charleston were more slaves reported than in New York (2,868), and Negro bondsmen constituted more than a tenth of the whole population in Albany and almost one-fifth in Brooklyn (see tables A-4 and A-5). As a practical matter, slavery had disappeared from the nine northern cities by 1830, when census officials found only twenty-eight slaves in all of them put together; by 1840 the number had shrunk to four. Despite the rapid disappearance of human bondage in the northern cities (where it declined more rapidly than in the rural areas), the number of slaves reported by census marshals in all fifteen increased in every decade during the first half of the nineteenth century, rising from 19,018 in 1800, to 24,960 in 1810, 28,175 in 1820, 39,605 in 1830, 47,998 in 1840, and 49,690 in 1850. Their total slave population was, thus, more than 2½ times as great in 1850 as it had been fifty years before, despite the fact that bondsmen were reported in only six of them by then. Obviously this occurred only because of very large increases in the slave populations of the southern cities (see table A-4).

Despite the addition of more than ten thousand bondsmen in Charleston and New Orleans, however, the percentage of population enslaved declined in all these cities (see table A-5). In 1800 slaves constituted over ten percent of the population in more than one-half of them; fifty years later this was true of only one-fifth. And in every city the percentage of the population that was slave was lower—in most cases, much lower—in 1850 than it had been a half-century earlier. In the combined population of the six southern cities alone, the slave component declined from more than a quarter to just over one-tenth, despite the trebling of the actual number of slaves. Meanwhile, the rate of increase of the urban slave population had declined almost to the vanishing point. The decennial rate of increase, which in earlier decades had ranged between one-eighth and three-eighths, had by the 1840s shrunk to about 3½ percent. By the middle of the nineteenth century, then, urban slavery, in numerical terms, would seem to have reached a point of absolute stagnation and relative decline.

Free persons of color, unlike the slaves, were to be found in all fifteen cities throughout the first half of the nineteenth century. Moreover, in each there were more in 1850 than at the beginning of the century.

The major sources of this continuing growth of the free black population were emancipation, manumission, and natural increase. There was also a small amount of immigration from abroad, and internal migration within the United States played a significant role in a few cases.

By the beginning of the nineteenth century a modest free Negro population of slightly over one hundred thousand existed in the United States. About one-eighth lived in these fifteen cities. Although reliable figures for the free black population in the Revolutionary era are not available, it would appear that the free Negro population of 1800 was largely the product of actions taken within the last quarter of the eighteenth century. Of these cities, only Boston and Cincinnati were located in states (or territories) in which all slaves had been freed (or slavery prohibited) before 1800; the additions to the small colonial free Negro element in the others had been made almost entirely by individual manumission. Individual manumissions in the northern ones were doubtless much encouraged, however, by the legislative acts providing for the eventual freeing of the children of slaves that were passed in Pennsylvania (1780), Rhode Island (1784), and New York (1799).[2] Many more such individual manumissions obviously took place in the South without the incentive of such legislative provisions, however, for by 1800 almost fifty-five percent of the free persons of color in the United States resided in the slave area, which also contained just under one-half of the total population.[3] The six southern towns contained, in 1800, almost twenty-nine percent of the whole population of the cities in this study and more than thirty-two percent of the free blacks.[4]

No purpose would be served by belaboring the question of the reasons why such manumissions took place, for a detailed description of randomly surviving data on a handful of cases has no greater validity than two or three generalizations of varying relevance. The Revolutionary human rights rhetoric perhaps moved some masters to free their slaves, and others probably anticipated declines in both slave values and the economic utility of the slave system in the post-Revolutionary era. A few slaveowners doubtless manumitted their own or their relatives' slave mistresses and children, and many urban slaves unquestionably purchased, either directly or through intermediaries, their own freedom and, in a substantial number of cases, that of their families as well. Moreover, an unknown number of persons classified as free persons of color in the cities were probably fugitive slaves or their offspring. Though technically slaves, they could, by submerging themselves in the urban free Negro populations, secure most of the benefits of freedom.

In addition to emancipation, manumission, and natural increase, a small amount of immigration contributed to the growth of the free black population in the late eighteenth and early nineteenth centuries. The most significant element among black immigrants consisted of persons fleeing from Santo Domingo in the 1790s. These new arrivals went mostly into the Lower South cities of Charleston and New Orleans.[5]

The continuing operation of the gradual emancipation acts after 1800 had greater impact in Albany, Brooklyn, and New York than in the other northern cities. Slaves constituted almost half the black population in New York in 1800, more than two-thirds in Brooklyn, and over three-quarters in Albany. By 1820 these figures had declined to substantially less than a quarter in Brooklyn, barely over one-seventh in Albany, and under one-twentieth in New York. By the end of the next decade, census enumerators found only seventeen slaves in New York and none in the other two towns.[6] In all three, emancipation thus accounted for a large part of the growth of the free black population in the early nineteenth century. Indeed, a comparison of the total black populations in the six northern cities east of the Appalachians in 1800 and in 1850 shows increases so small as to suggest that a major portion (except, perhaps, in the case of Brooklyn) could be accounted for by emancipation (including in-migration of freed slaves from the surrounding countryside) coupled with natural increase (see table A-1).

Some contemporaries, however, argued that the reported growth in the free black population in some northern cities, far from being the result of emancipation and natural increase, was almost wholly the product of in-migration and census errors.[7] Unfortunately, data on internal migration are very sparse in the first half of the nineteenth century. In 1850, however, the census marshals inquired into the nativity of each person listed. An analysis of nativities of free blacks in 1850 can yield some suggestive data about the importance of both internal migration and foreign immigration in the growth of the free black populations.

It is obvious (see table A-6) that in-migration played an overwhelming role in such cities as Cincinnati, Buffalo, St. Louis, and Boston—where between two-thirds and six-sevenths of the adults were born outside of the state in which they resided—and a predominant role in Philadelphia and Pittsburgh as well. The case of Washington is not so clear, for although only about three-eighths of the adult free blacks were natives of the District of Columbia, another three-fifths had been born in Virginia and Maryland. In fact as much as 80–90 percent of Washington's free Negro population in 1850 may have been drawn from a contiguous area no larger than the state in which any one of the other cities was located.

Indeed, Negroes from these Upper South states formed large components of the in-migrants in almost all the major cities. Virginians comprised over forty percent of all out-of-state natives (excluding the foreign born) in the free black populations of Baltimore, Buffalo, Cincinnati, New Orleans, Pittsburgh, and St. Louis, and the figure rose to over sixty-five percent in Louisville. Maryland natives made up over twenty percent of this population segment in Albany, Philadelphia, and Providence and over forty percent in Pittsburgh. Additionally, Kentuckians constituted roughly one-seventh of such out-of-state natives in Buffalo and Cincinnati and more than one-fifth in St. Louis, while Delawarians were almost two-fifths the figure in Philadelphia.

Only in New Orleans did foreign immigrants constitute as much as one-tenth of the free persons of color. The reported figures for Boston (9.42%) and Buffalo (5.72%), where more than one-half of the adult blacks listed as having been born outside of the United States claimed to be natives of Nova Scotia, New Brunswick, or Canada, may well be inflated. While the total number of individuals involved (eighty-three in the two cities) is not so large as to render such migration impossible, the advantages that an assertion of British citizenship would confer upon a fugitive slave are so obvious as to suggest that at least some of these claims were probably fictitious. It is also worthy of note that these two cities had the largest percentages of blacks of unknown nativity—almost one-seventh of the total in Boston. Such vagueness may have been another method of avoiding identification as fugitives. The presence of numerous runaways in Boston was noted as early as 1814, and there is reason to believe that a third of a century later a number of fugitives were still to be found there and in Buffalo as well.[8]

Thus, it would appear that the contemporary observations about the importance of in-migration in the modest growth of the black population in several northern cities were, on the whole, accurate.[9] In combination with emancipation, manumission, and natural increase, such migration had by 1850 produced a free Negro population in the United States that was almost exactly four times as large as it had been fifty years earlier.[10] In these fifteen urban centers, the growth in the number of free persons of color was more substantial—from 14,719 to 87,086—though still well below the growth rate of the whole population (see table A-7).

The rates of increase were, as might be expected, very uneven. In absolute terms, the growth was smallest in Albany, Buffalo, and the New England cities, where the combined increase between 1800 and 1850 was barely over three thousand. At the other extreme, six cities—Baltimore, New York, New Orleans, Washington, Philadelphia, and Cincinnati—each added more than three thousand to its free black population during the half-century, with Baltimore's growth of 22,671 being greater than the combined increase in eleven of the remaining fourteen. Generally speaking, the number of free persons of color increased in each decade in each city. But in six cases during the half-century—Albany and Charleston in the 1830s and Albany, Boston, New Orleans and New York in the 1840s—the census figures showed absolute declines.

In two instances—Charleston in the 1830s and Boston in the 1840s—the census figures do not accurately reflect reality. The 1840 census appears grossly to have overstated the number of free persons of color in Boston; there were probably very small increases in the black population in both the 1830s and 1840s.[11] The decline in Charleston in the 1830s was real, but not entirely relevant. A virulent outbreak of cholera in 1836 and yellow fever epidemics in 1834,

1835, 1838, and 1839, and the concomitant increase in the mortality rate (to four percent in 1838), doubtless depressed the population growth. But more importantly the disastrous fire of 1838, which destroyed about one thousand buildings in the third and fourth wards (where more than seventy percent of the free persons of color resided in 1830), stimulated both free blacks and slaves to change their residences to the area lying just beyond the city boundaries—Charleston Neck—"where the class of houses suited to their condition are numerous, and obtained at moderate rents." This area was subsequently annexed by the city in 1849. Hence, both the large decrease shown by the census figures of 1840 and the enormous increase shown in 1850 are misleading.[12]

The other four instances of absolute declines in the free black populations—Albany in the 1830s and '40s and New York and New Orleans in the 1840s—were apparently real losses, though there would seem to be no specific explanation for the reductions. The 1850 census figures for both states show absolute declines in the free black populations.[13]

Although there were only a few instances when the number of free blacks in a city actually declined, the rate of increase of the free Negro population—as was the case with the slaves—was considerably lower than that of the whites in most of these cities, and indeed in the nation. Consequently, the general trend was for free blacks to form a smaller and smaller proportion of the urban populations as the half-century wore on. Of course, the pattern was not regular, and in four southern cities (and possibly in two northern ones) free blacks made up larger percentages of the population in 1850 than at the beginning of the century. In Washington and Louisville the pattern was directly contrary to the general tendency, with free persons of color constituting a larger proportion of the populations in each succeeding decade, with two exceptions. Consequently, in 1850 free blacks made up more than one-fifth of the population of Washington, compared with less than 4 percent fifty years earlier. The change in Louisville was much less spectacular—from about one-quarter of a percent to just over 3½ percent. In Baltimore and Charleston the patterns were irregular, but the ratios of change were about the same—from 10½ percent to 15 percent in Baltimore, and from 5 percent to 8 percent in Charleston. Buffalo and Cincinnati may have shown some slight increases, but this is not certain, since the 1800 figures are unavailable in one case and estimated in the other; the shift was, in any event, minute.

The actual size of the free black populations varied more widely than the growth trends. In 1800 the number of free persons of color exceeded 1,000 in only four of the fifteen cities examined— Philadelphia, New York, Baltimore, and Boston. By 1850, however, the free blacks numbered more than 5,000 in one-third of the cities—Baltimore, New York, Philadelphia, New Orleans and Washington. Baltimore's total of 25,442 constituted almost thirty percent of all free persons of color living in the fifteen cities.

The urban black population differed from the white in that it was—almost wholly for the slaves and partially for the free blacks—in some measure selected rather than self-selecting. One might expect, consequently, that it would not necessarily have all the same characteristics as other population groups. One difference—more pronounced among slaves than free blacks—was the disproportionate number of females in the black populations (see tables A-9 and A-10).

The preponderance of females in the slave populations doubtless reflected both a heavy demand for house servants and a pervasive fear on the part of whites that adult black males were not to be trusted in the urban, and more nearly free, environment. This is not to say that male slaves were rare in the cities, for they were not. In only six instances recorded in table A-9—Baltimore and Washington in 1840 and 1850 and New Orleans in 1820 and 1830—did males constitute less than forty percent of the slave population, and in almost a third of the instances the figure was over forty-five percent. But every census report for the six cities in the slave area during the period 1820–50 showed a predominance of females in the slave population, although the same was true for the white population less than one-half of the time. Moreover, the *highest* ratio of white females to males—1.0892:1 in Baltimore in 1840—was only minutely greater than the *lowest* ratio of female to male slaves in any instance. It is also true that the female dominance in the urban slave populations was increasing during these years, with the average female-to-male ratio rising from 1.2887:1 in 1820, to 1.5172:1 in 1850 (see table A-12). This trend was primarily the result of very heavy increases in female dominance in the border cities of Baltimore and Washington, where the percentages of males in the slave population declined by thirteen and almost ten percentage points, respectively.

Two considerations may have influenced masters there to reduce the number of male slaves in their urban holdings. Both cities, and especially Baltimore, were more subject to riots than the other southern cities, and masters may well have feared the impact of such outbreaks of violence on the male slave psyche. Additionally, their geographic locations doubtless caused many masters to feel that their slave property was less secure than in cities farther south or in less densely populated rural areas.[14]

Among urban free negroes the female preponderance was by no means so great as in the slave populations, and by 1850 the average female-to-male ratio for urban free blacks was almost precisely the median between those for whites and slaves (see table A-12).

Although there were, over the thirty-year period, substantial fluctuations in individual cities, the average proportion of females remained remarkably constant in both the white and the free Negro populations of the fifteen urban centers—there were between 95 and 98 white females to each 100 white males and from 124 to 132 free black females to each 100 free Negro males. But within these rather narrow limits the trends over time were reversed in the two urban population elements—in 1850 the average female proportion was the largest during the period for whites and the smallest for free blacks. The magnitude of the sex differentials constituted another obvious difference between whites and free blacks. In only eight of fifty-eight possible cases (one of which—that of Boston in 1840—was almost certainly the product of census error) did the census figures show more males than females in the free black population, though males were dominant in the white populations in twenty-six cases. Only twice did the figures show a lower proportion of females among free blacks than among whites (see table A-10).

The presumed tendency of masters to manumit female slaves cannot fully explain these sex differentials, for northern urban free black populations that were much more heavily the product of mass emancipation displayed sex ratio characteristics similar to those observable in the southern free Negro populations created by selective manumission. In both slave and nonslave cities, the census data show female-to-male ratios of more than 1.2:1 in the free black population in more than three-fifths of the cases examined (see table A-10).

The search for satisfactory explanations is further complicated by the fact that the national free Negro population was also predominately female throughout this period (1820–50), while both the white and slave national populations contained a majority of males. This circumstance would appear not to be the result of significantly different sex ratios at birth, for the proportion of females among young white, slave, and free Negro children during these years fell within a very narrow range, though it was slightly higher among blacks than among whites. Moreover, the sex ratios in the whole populations of whites and slaves conformed very closely to those among white and slave children, while this was by no means true among free persons of color (see tables A-11 and A-12). It is difficult to escape the conclusion that the preponderance of females in the national free black population was primarily the result of an unusually high mortality rate among males, especially from the mid-teens onward.

But the proportions of females in the free black populations of these cities (see table A-10) clearly were not mere reflections of similar conditions in the larger national population. It is obvious that the percentage of females was usually much greater in these urban free black populations than in the free black populations of the states (and the District of Columbia) in which they were located or in the national free Negro population. In fifty-one of fifty-seven cases (if we exclude the erroneous 1840 Boston figure) the percentage of females in the urban free Negro population exceeded that in the state (or District) population.[15] Clearly this concentration of females (and, especially, adult females), in the free black component of the population was an urban phenomenon. It was, moreover, a phenomenon not shared by the remainder of the free population, for sex ratios among whites were substantially the same in the cities as in the national population (see table A-12).

A variety of reasons—none of them wholly convincing—can be advanced to explain this peculiarity. In the southern cities—especially the Deep South urban centers—selective manumission doubtless had produced, by the 1830s, a decidedly female-dominant population which could be "normalized" by natural increase only over a period of several decades. It may also be true that northern cities, in particular, offered relatively better employment opportunities to black women (primarily as house servants and hotel employees) than to black males and, hence, encouraged a highly sex-differentiated in-migration. Census enumerators may also have failed to report significant numbers of free black male urban residents, though the extent of such under-reporting is impossible to determine.[16] It is possible, of course, that the free black male mortality rate in these cities was dramatically greater than that for the rest of the population. And, finally, the preponderance of females may have been, in part, a statistical fiction produced by urban economic segregation—the concentration of affluent residents in the center city creating a similar concentration of female live-in servants, while these same economic conditions drove free black families (with their more "normal" sex distribution) beyond the city boundaries in search of cheaper housing.

There can be no doubt that such economic segregation did, in fact, exist, and it probably contributed to the female-dominant nature of the urban free black populations. But the impact was by no means sufficiently great to explain the magnitude of the existing sex differentials. Table A-13 compares the 1850 female-to-male ratios for free Negros in twelve cities and in the counties (or districts) in which they are located.[17] It will be noted that in ten of the twelve counties the female-to-male ratio was lower than in the corresponding cities. But in only three cases was the differential as much as 0.10 and in seven instances it was less than 0.05. Hence, economic segregation (by forcing blacks beyond the city bounds) probably increased the apparent magnitude of the female dominance, but it cannot be seen as a major causative factor.

With such heavy preponderances of females, it might be expected that children should constitute considerably larger proportions of the black populations—slave and free—than of the white in these cities. But such was not the case. Indeed, an analysis of the census data for the six slave-area cities during the years 1820–50 shows that although the percentage of women in the slave population was in every case greater—sometimes more than twenty percentage points greater— than in the white population, in almost three-quarters of the instances children constituted a larger proportion of the white than of the slave element. An extreme example is New Orleans in 1820, where the white population contained less than forty percent females while well over sixty percent of the slaves were women and girls. But despite these enormous sex imbalances, children under fourteen years of age made up a larger percentage of the white than of the slave element (see tables A-9 and A-14).

In the free Negro populations, too, the preponderance of females was not matched by an unusually high proportion of children. Indeed, the percentage of children was lower among free persons of color than among whites in more than three-quarters of the cases between 1820 and 1850 (see table A-15). The differences between whites and free blacks may be stated most succinctly in the form of the average percentage of children in the urban population of each group. In 1820 the average percentage of children aged under fourteen was a little less than three percentage points lower for free people of color than for whites, and between 1830 and 1850 the proportion of children aged under ten in these two population groups was consistently $1\frac{2}{3}$–2 percentage points lower for free blacks (see table A-16). While such differences appear not to be of great magnitude, they must be viewed in the context of urban free black populations that were, except in a bare handful of cases, predominantly female (especially adult female), with the female-to-male ratio occasionally exceeding 1.6:1 (see table A-10).

There are several possible explanations for this apparent anomaly in both the slave and free black urban populations. Perhaps urban slaveowners or hirers sent all but the youngest slave children out of the city if they also owned a plantation, but there would appear to be no way to determine if this practice was common. It is possible, of course, that blacks simply had lower fertility rates than whites, or higher infant mortality rates, or both. The national population data for the years 1820–50 appear not to support this conclusion for the slave population, despite the fact that the extremely unsatisfactory national mortality data for 1850 show slave death rates about a fifth higher than those for whites.[18] For the census reports show the proportion of children among slaves to be substantially the same as in the white population in 1820 and $2^1/_3$–$3^1/_6$ percentage points higher than among whites in 1830, 1840, and 1850. There are some data that suggest that slave mortality rates may have been considerably higher than those for whites in urban areas by the end of the half-century (see pp. 145–46), but whether that differential was sufficiently concentrated in the under-ten-years category to explain the discrepancies is extremely doubtful.

The free black national census data for this same period, however, suggest that this population element did have a lower fertility rate than either whites or slaves, or a higher infant mortality rate, or both. In each of these censuses the percentage of children in the national free Negro population was lower than that in either of the other two elements despite the fact that only the free black component showed a preponderance of females nationally (see table A-16). Mortality data (pp. 137–38) clearly indicate that free black death rates in urban areas were significantly higher than those for whites during this period but, as in the case of slaves, there is no evidence that the incidence of deaths was concentrated at the lower end of the age spectrum.

Another alternative explanation should also be considered. It may well be that in all but the most primitive populations the proportion of women of childbearing age has less impact on the birthrate than the relative number of family units established. If this is true, then the birthrate in a monogamous society would be negatively affected by any significant imbalance in the sex ratio—whether male-dominant or female-dominant—in a given population. In the case of the urban slave populations the data would appear to support such a conclusion, though with diminishing strength in each succeeding decade. The rank-order correlation (Spearman) between percentages of females and of children in the urban slave populations was always negative, declining, however, from − .90 in 1820 to − .60 in 1830, − .37 in 1840, and − .14 in 1850 (see tables A-9 and A-14). Thus, this discrepancy between the proportion of women and that of children in the urban slave populations may speak volumes about the importance of the urban slave family.

The data for the urban free black populations suggest a similar conclusion, though the indications are considerably less strong than for the slave component. In three of the four sets of census data (1820, 1830, and 1840) the rank-order correlation (Spearman) between the percentages of children and females in the populations were negative, but at levels below −.17, but for 1850 there was a moderately strong positive correlation of + .53. All that can be stated with confidence is that usually the percentage of children in the urban free black populations appears to have been somewhat adversely affected by high percentages of women, especially if we except from this analysis the Lower South cities of Charleston and New Orleans.[19]

This caveat serves to highlight some dramatic differences in the figures displayed in table A-15. In only thirteen of the fifty-six sets of data (i.e., white and free black percentages for a given city in a given year) is the percentage of free Negro children greater than that of whites. In all but two cases (Brooklyn and Pittsburgh in 1820) these high-percentage cities were located in the slave area—Charleston and New Orleans in 1820, 1830, 1840, and 1850; Louisville in 1830; and St. Louis and Washington in 1840. Conversely, in fourteen of the fifty-six sets of data the free black percentage is more than five percentage points below the white figure. These cities are, in every case, located in the northern states. The differentials are, in some instances, enormous. New York in 1820 and Charleston in 1830 each had populations with roughly 103–4 white females to each 100 white males, and more than 140 free black females to each 100 free Negro males. But in Charleston the proportion of children among free Negroes was more than thirteen percentage points greater than among whites, while in New York the white percentage was more than ten percentage points larger than among free blacks.[20]

Mortality rates for free blacks in general and infants in particular may have been higher in northern than in southern cities (see p. 139). but differential infant mortality could hardly account for such differences as these. It seems more likely that two other factors influenced the fertility rate of the free black population in these Lower South cities. First, an unknown number of family units were established by male slaves and female free blacks. And second, white male/black female sexual liaisons, which were more widely accepted in the slave area, extensively supplemented the monogamous family as a factor influencing the natural increase of the free black population.

This, then, was the urban black population of the first half of the nineteenth century, still containing a substantial number of slaves in the six southern cities, but increasingly composed of free blacks. These free persons of color were, as a group, disproportionately urban. In 1850 more than one-fifth of all free blacks in the country lived in these fifteen cities, as compared with less than one-twelfth of the whites.[21] They shared a number of the demographic characteristics of other urbanites, such as geographic mobility and low birthrates, but differed in other respects (e.g., the high proportion of females in the population) from urban whites. It was a population diverse in skills, in intellect, in ambition, in self-perception, and in ability to cope with the urban environment. Doubtless they sought the same things as other urbanites—a less intensive social oversight and control than was prevalent in smaller and less complex communities; access to urban educational and cultural activities; association with a larger and better-developed community of one's "own kind"; occupational specialization; and economic opportunity. In the hope of finding what they sought they endured congestion, poor housing, filth, discrimination perhaps less personal but no less pervasive than in nonurban areas, segregation in some ways more pronounced than elsewhere, and fear that never slept. They came in such numbers probably not because they had greater hope for success than other Americans, but because they had less to lose. They neither expected nor sought complete freedom, a significant measure of equality, or a dominant political, social, or economic role in urban life. They sought merely the closest approach to freedom, opportunity, comfort, and safety that America offered to a despised, suppressed, and excluded people. They sought the city.

2 The Most Laborious and Least Profitable Employments: Urban Free Black Occupational Patterns

Cities, in all ages, have been the vital centers of economic activity. As such, they have made insatiable, though frequently erratic, demands for human labor and have offered enormously varied opportunities for human enterprise. Their commercial operations not only absorbed the energy and imagination of merchants, bankers, brokers, and related entrepreneurs, but also swallowed daily the labor of thousands of clerks, shipyard workers, stevedores, seamen, draymen, coopers, blacksmiths, day laborers, and the practitioners of hundreds of other trades. Their workshops required the services of additional thousands of skilled and unskilled workers laboring under the direction of hundreds of capitalists and aspiring capitalists. Perhaps of greater importance still was the demand for labor generated by the mere gathering together of some thousands of people into urban communities. There were houses to be built, clothes to be made, streets to be cleaned and paved, foodstuffs to be distributed, and a multitude of human needs and desires to be satisfied. Some of these needs were, indeed, created by the urban environment—the necessity of providing in some organized fashion for the distribution of water and the disposal of waste, for example— but most were nothing more than the aggregating of individual human requirements and yearnings. This process of aggregation, in turn, created markets for particular services that could not have existed in less concentrated populations, and these conditions made possible, and potentially profitable, the increasingly narrow economic specialization long considered to be inextricably connected with the process of urbanization. Thus, numerous urban residents found it possible to devote their energies wholly to such wildly diverse occupations as bootblack and opera singer, feather cleaner and restorer of oil paintings, rag picker and silk dyer, because they could not or did not wish to do anything else. Hence, F. J. Kingsbury stated little more than a truism when he observed in 1895 that one of the explanations for "The Tendency of Men to Live in Cities" was that "a large part of the work of the world must be done in cities, and the people who do that work must live in cities."[1]

To these needs and opportunities the free black in antebellum

America responded as did other native-born residents and the increasing immigrant population. They bore, however, an additional burden, for racial prejudice was no less prevalent in an urban than in a rural environment. This prejudice made itself felt in a most bitter form in the field of occupational opportunity.

The restrictions and disadvantages under which urban blacks labored in this area of their lives were of two kinds—legal and societal. The restrictions imposed by law were less numerous than has sometimes been assumed. The most widespread occupational limitation had to do with the sale of liquor, and probably resulted from the fear that free black tavern keepers would serve whiskey or gin to slaves who might then be emboldened to rise up against their masters. To prevent such social disruptions, various southern governments enacted laws prohibiting free blacks from trafficking in spirituous liquors. When the Kentucky legislature, in 1833, established a minimum fee of forty dollars for liquor licenses to be issued by the city of Louisville, it further provided that no free person of color might obtain such a license. Though city governments frequently ignored state legislation dealing with free Negroes because the laws emanating from the rural-dominated legislatures were often inappropriate to the urban experience, in this instance the city council supplemented the state act by an ordinance prohibiting the issuance to any free black of a license to operate a grocery—the most usual source of liquor for the urban poor.[2] At about the same time (1835) the St. Louis councils provided that no Negro might be licensed as the keeper of an ordinary (that is, a retailer of food and drink to be consumed on the premises) and a Charleston liquor license ordinance of the next year clearly assumed that free blacks were not to be licensed—a prohibition enacted by the state legislature in 1831—since they were prohibited from remaining on the premises of a licensed establishment longer than necessary to make a purchase.[3] A Washington ordinance of the same year (1836) was somewhat broader, prohibiting "any free negro or mulatto, or . . . any person acting for any negro or mulatto," from selling any alcoholic beverages (including beer and cider) or from keeping "any tavern, ordinary, shop, porter cellar, refectory, or eating house of any kind, for profit or gain."[4] Neither Baltimore, New Orleans, or St. Louis, nor the states in which they are located, appear to have established such prohibitions before 1850.[5]

Another continuing fear of whites in the slave area was that free Negroes—especially urban free Negroes—would offer slaves an avenue for the profitable disposal of agricultural products stolen from the surrounding farms and plantations, and thus encourage such pilferage. To inhibit these activities the Maryland legislature, in the first half of the nineteenth century, passed a number of progressively more stringent acts designed to prevent free persons of color from trafficking in agricultural produce. The city councils of Louisville and St. Louis struck at the occupations offering greatest opportunity for "fencing" farm produce, and, instead of attempting to prevent the sale of such materials, in the mid-1830s they took the much more clearly discriminatory action of prohibiting the licensing of any free black as a hawker, huckster, or peddler.[6]

In a small number of instances, however, legal restrictions appear to have had no other purpose than to limit black employment opportunities for the benefit of white competitors. The whites were not slow to seek through legislation the economic dominance they seemed unable to obtain through competition. The Maryland legislature, for instance, received a petition in 1827 from Baltimore residents asking for legislation to prevent Negroes from owning or driving hacks, carts, or drays. This was followed by a request in 1837 to prohibit blacks from engaging in any artisan trades and another in 1844 asking for their exclusion from the trade of carpentry. This latter communication also urged that a tax be levied on all free blacks employed in any other artisan capacity.[7]

No such legislation was passed in Maryland (indeed, the 1827 petition produced an immediate counterpetition from Baltimore merchants),[8] and in Charleston repeated petitions from white artisans in the late 1830s could not move the city councils—dominated as they were by employers who wished to keep wages low—to limit competition by excluding blacks from any of the trades that they then followed. Charleston's ordinance of 1811 (in effect until 1846) forbidding any Negro "to keep or mark the game at any Billiard Table" can scarcely have weighed heavily on the black community.[9] But in Washington, Louisville, and New Orleans a few prohibitory ordinances were enacted. The New Orleans city council, in 1822—in an action of little practical economic importance to blacks—directed the "municipal labor manager" to employ only white workers.[10] The limitations were potentially somewhat more severe in Louisville, where, in 1839, the city councils enacted an ordinance forbidding any black resident to "keep a confectionary or victualling house or cellar, or a fruit store or cellar, or sell fruits or melons out of any store, house, or on any street or any other place."[11] But it was in the nation's capital that the most extensive legal restrictions on free black employment were imposed. That portion of the ordinance of October 29, 1836 relating to liquor sales (previously mentioned) clearly went well beyond the bounds necessary to control the traffic in alcoholic beverages. More significant was the fact that by the terms of another section of that same ordinance, as amended some two weeks later, free persons of color would not be issued licenses "for any purpose whatsoever ... except licenses to drive carts, drays, hackney carriages, or wagons," and those entering the city after November 9, 1836, would be granted no licences at all.[12] It is difficult to imagine any legitimate regulatory purpose—even based on the most prejudicial assumptions—to be served by such restrictions. There are, however, two very obvious results envisaged: first, the immediate one of increasing the scope of white occupational opportunity by limiting the trades that blacks might follow and by limiting the number of blacks eligible to engage in authorized occupations; and, second, the more important ultimate one of discouraging further free black in-migration to the city and encouraging the departure of those already there.

All evidence available about free black employment in the cities suggests that such governmental restraints were largely ineffective. The manuscript returns of the 1850 federal census record the existence of a free black tavern keeper in Charleston and 135 free men of color in Washington following prohibited artisan trades, as opposed to 73 employed in the occupations specifically authorized in the 1836 acts.[13]

Much more effective than legal prohibitions were societal restraints. While legal restrictions on black employment were few and confined to the southern cities, societal limitations were many and more onerous in the North. In New York, for instance, there was no legal barrier to prevent Negroes from acting as carters, but their inability to obtain the necessary licenses from the city authorities was notorious. It seems clear that in the 1830s Anthony Provost and William Hewlett were denied cart licenses solely on the ground of their color, and the *Colored American* was moved to demand in the fall of 1837 that Mayor Aaron Clark use his authority to prevent physical attacks on black carters and porters and to ensure "that city inspectors issue licenses to all regardless of race."[14] Little improvement took place, however, for free persons of color rarely found employment as carters or draymen in the nation's largest city throughout the first half of the nineteenth century. City directories of the 1840s recorded fewer than ten Negroes following these occupations and the more thorough canvassing by the federal census enumerators in 1850 located only thirty-one (less than one percent of the employed free black males reported).[15] Cartage and drayage were services in continuing nonseasonal demand in all of the cities and were, consequently, potentially lucrative occupations. Moreover, they required little training and relatively slight capital investment and (though the rates were strictly regulated) offered the energetic drivers the opportunity to increase their incomes by increasing the number of loads carried during a working day. Hence, employment in these capacities was coveted by poor, untrained, but ambitious urbanites.

It was not only in New York that free blacks were denied competitive access to these trades. Though there is little evidence of specific complaint in other cities, the 1850 census data strongly suggest that such discriminatory practices were widespread in the North. Among the nine northern cities examined, it was only in Philadelphia (40) and Cincinnati (18), aside from New York, that the enumerators found more than ten free persons of color engaged in drayage and cartage. Only in Cincinnati and Providence did the number of black carters and draymen constitute as much as two percent of the employed black males (the figures were 2.01% and 2.14%, respectively).[16] By comparison, in the six southern cities investigated, the number of free black males following these vocations ranged from 2.27 percent in New Orleans to 9.88 percent in Baltimore.[17]

Free blacks encountered much stronger opposition when they attempted to enter artisan trades in the northern cities. In 1830 "A Colored Philadelphian" asserted, "If a man of color has children, it is almost impossible for him to get a trade for them, as the journeymen and apprentices generally refuse to work with them, even if the master is willing, which is seldom the case."[18] Conditions did not improve in the years that followed and, indeed, may well have deteriorated. Despite her violent proslavery prejudice, Mary H. Schoolcraft was only slightly in error when she declared in 1852, "There are no professional black gentlemen here in Philadelphia, and very few who are even mechanics."[19] Indeed, the discrimination was even greater than the small number of black artisans would suggest, for, as Benjamin C. Bacon pointed out in 1859, "Less than two-thirds of those who have trades follow them. A few of the remainder pursue other avocations from choice, but the greater number are compelled to abandon their trades on account of the unrelenting prejudice against their color."[20] Twenty-one years before, it had been estimated that about thirty percent of Philadelphia's black artisans were excluded by discrimination from practicing their trades.[21]

Nor were the residents of the City of Brotherly Love peculiarly renowned for their prejudice. The president of the Mechanical Association of Cincinnati was tried before the society in 1830 for having accepted a black apprentice, an error few other master workmen apparently made, then or later. In New York no Negroes were employed in shipbuilding until after the War of 1812, and throughout the entire half-century free persons of color obtained very little access there to the artisan trades. And the Cambridge don Edward S. Abdy, speaking of free persons of color in Boston in 1833, noted that "with the exception of one or two employed as printers, one blacksmith, and one shoemaker, there are no colored mechanics in the city." He added, "Even a license for keeping a house of refreshment is refused, under some frivolous or vexatious pretense, though the same can easily be procured by a white man of inferior condition and with less wealth."[22] Nor did Abdy much exaggerate the deplorable condition of Boston's blacks, for the 1835 city directory listed only 7 black artisans and no Negro proprietors of any establishment remotely classifiable as a "house of refreshment," and in 1836 the agent of the Boston auxiliary of the American Union for the Relief and Improvement of the Coloured Race found that of 111 black males aged 11 to 20 living with their families only 3 were "learning mechanical trades."[23]

Even when engaged in the most menial of occupations, the urban black was not free from employment discrimination. Efforts to force Negroes out of unskilled jobs have frequently been attributed to the increasing immigrant population after the late 1830s, and doubtless there were many incidents such as that in New York in November of 1850, when Irish laborers walked off the job when an employer refused to discharge all nonwhite laborers. The attack on black laborers by Irish coal heavers on the Schuylkill docks on the second day of the 1842 Philadelphia riots was probably motivated, at least in part, by similar considerations.[24] But discrimination, even in unskilled occupations, had been obvious well before the swelling waves of Irish immigration began to break upon the American shores. As early as 1823 the Pennsylvania Abolition Society noted that even "in the most laborious and least profitable" occupations, "prejudice and pride" pursued the free persons of color. "Turnpikes, Canal, Coal-Mines, Brick-Making, Street Paving and Cleaning, which engage so many thousands," the report of the society observed sorrowfully, "give no employment to them; let their situation at least engage our sympathy, if we can afford them no relief."[25] And in the winter of 1831 a black resident of Philadelphia complained bitterly that "during the late snow storm, thousands of persons were employed in cleaning the gutters, leveling the drifts, &c. Among the whole number, there was not one man of color to be seen, when hundreds of them were going about the streets with shovels in their hands, looking for work and finding none."[26]

Free blacks in southern cities undoubtedly felt, in some measure, the pressure of similar societal restrictions, but the evidence is much more spotty and, occasionally, suspect, and the effects were minimal and, in some instances, transitory. Before the mid-1830s, certainly, black and white artisans worked peacefully side by side in Baltimore shipyards, and when, in the late 1840s, white craftsmen forced their erstwhile black compatriots off the docks, the black caulkers, as a countermeasure, organized successfully and refused to work with whites. In 1851 J. H. B. Latrobe painted a dismal picture of the decline of free black employment opportunities in Baltimore, ending with the words, "The white man stands in the black man's shoes, or else is fast getting into them." But this assertion must be viewed with suspicion, for Latrobe headed the Maryland Colonization Society and his observations were printed in its official journal. Colonizationists were notorious for exaggerating the plight of free blacks, in the hope of encouraging them to immigrate to Liberia.[27] In the years following the War of 1812, J. C. Brown, a black mason residing in Louisville, complained about threats by "white mechanics" jealous of the fact that he "was more successful in getting jobs," but he seems not to have been molested, and he was able to enlist prominent white employers to support him.[28] It is by no means clear that the English geologist Sir Charles Lyell's widely cited repetition of hearsay about the displacement of blacks by whites as servants and draymen in New Orleans in the 1840s had reference to free persons of color, and it is certain from the context that Frederick L. Olmsted's equally renowned comments of a decade later on the same subject referred primarily to slaves. Such loss of employment as did take place (and it appears likely that most of those affected were slaves) was, in any event, temporary in nature before 1850.[29]

Clearly the best evidence about free black occupational opportunities is to be found not in the sporadic complaints and unsubstantiated assertions about discrimination and exclusion sprinkled through contemporary accounts and secondary works alike, but rather in a careful and comprehensive examination of free black occupational patterns in all of the cities studied. The most nearly satisfactory data upon which to base such an analysis are those collected by the United States Census Office in 1850 (see appendix B).

The most obvious point demonstrated by the census figures is the extent to which the legal and societal restrictions and prohibitions were effective in limiting the employment opportunities of urban free blacks. In all of these cities except Charleston and New Orleans, more than one-half of the black males were employed in the low-opportunity (group A) occupations. In fact, the number exceeds three-quarters of the employed blacks in four of the cities (Boston, Providence, Pittsburgh, and Washington) and is greater than two-thirds in five others (New York, Brooklyn, Albany, Cincinnati, and St. Louis). Indeed, contemporary observers in most American cities would have found the appearance of a black in any capacity other than that of a laborer, servant, or similar menial worker surprising and, perhaps, unsettling. In 1851 George S. Appleton published in Philadelphia an attractive little volume for the juvenile trade, designed to introduce upper-middle-class children gently to the rest of mankind. Bearing the title *City Characters; or, Familiar Scenes in Town,* it depicted in word and picture the activities of twenty-three individuals who might be encountered in the streets of Philadelphia. The woodcuts illustrating four of the occupations—those of laundress,

whitewasher, woodsawyer and rag picker—clearly show Negroes.[30]
This view of the "place" of the free black in the urban economy was
equally prevalent in other cities, as is shown by comments about
"sable laundresses" in Boston, black chimney sweeps in New York,
and the large number of Negro servants encountered in various northeastern cities.[31] The disproportionate number of free persons of
color employed as servants is illustrated by the fact that more than
one-sixth of the 15,540 applications for positions as house servants
processed between 1826 and 1830 by the New York Society for the
Encouragement of Faithful Domestics came from Negroes, although
they constituted less than seven percent of the city's population.[32] It
was generally thought by contemporary observers that the influx of
Irish in the next two decades resulted in the displacement of large
numbers of free persons of color in this occupational category, especially those who had been in the less menial, better remunerated jobs,
such as waiters and stewards.[33] Even so, the occupations of waiter,
steward, and servant still accounted for about one-sixth or more of all
employed free black males in St. Louis, Washington, and five northern
cities in 1850, with the figure rising to roughly one-quarter in New
York and Philadelphia.[34]

The effects of racial vocational limitation are also readily apparent at
the upper end of the occupational scale. Only in New Orleans, in
1850, were as many as five percent of the free men of color to be
found engaged in those activities classified as professional, managerial,
artistic, clerical, and scientific, and the total in all fifteen cities was
fewer than four hundred—less than two percent of all employed free
black males. Even those figures exaggerate the importance of the black
professional element. More than one-quarter of the total resided in
New Orleans, and many of these Negro "professionals" had the most
marginal claims to that classification. In New York there were James
McCune Smith, who had taken his M.D. in 1837 from the University
of Glasgow, and the twenty-three-year-old Thomas J. White, to whom
Bowdoin had awarded a medical degree a dozen years later, but they
had few counterparts among the thirty-nine black physicians reported
in the fifteen cities by the census office, some of whom were listed as
"Indian doctors" or "colored doctors," and others recorded as illiterate.[35] As a rule, the free persons of color recorded in the census as
doctors and dentists are not included in the professional lists in city
directories, and some are shown in the directories with other occupations, which strongly suggests that their practice of the healing arts was
irregular, in more senses than one. In Philadelphia, for instance, the
census marshals entered Henry Glees's occupation as doctor of
medicine and that of William Higgins as dentist, but the 1852 directory shows Glees as a cabinetmaker and Higgins as a barber.[36] The

training and abilities of Negro teachers and ministers, too, varied enormously, and many clergymen earned their livelihood in other employments. On the Philadelphia census sheets William Harman is entered as a Methodist minister and David Scott as a Baptist minister, but in the city directory they appear as a cordwainer and a laborer, respectively. And even the renowned Bishop Richard Allen, founder of the African Methodist Episcopal Church, operated a boot and shoe store "in his latter years."[37] It should also be noted that the number of black ministers was directly related to the degree of religious segregation, as well as to the size of the Negro population. Hence, in New Orleans and Charleston, where separate black churches were few (and sometimes served by white pastors), the census marshals in 1850 found only a single free black serving as a minister, but in the other thirteen cities the eighty-seven ministers constituted almost thirty percent of those blacks in the professional category.[38] Additionally, outside of the two Deep South cities, musicians accounted for almost a quarter (23.55%) of the entries in this occupational category. Very few of these, however, could be compared to Philadelphia's famous Francis (Frank) Johnson. A prolific composer, skilled conductor, and virtuoso performer on trumpet and bugle, Johnson dominated the field of military and dance band music in Philadelphia in the second quarter of the nineteenth century. His reputation was widespread and his European tour of 1837 was apparently a huge success.[39] The only other employment in this category followed by any significant number of free men of color was that of clerk, and more than seventy percent of those so classified in these fifteen cities resided in New Orleans. These five occupations—physician, teacher, minister, musician, and clerk—accounted for more than eighty-five percent of all black males in the professional category (336 of 391).

It is clear from even the most cursory examination that in most instances these occupations did not offer likely avenues to economic success. With the exception of some of the musicians, those who dispensed their services on a fee basis found their clientele restricted to the most economically deprived segment of the urban population. Clerks were notoriously poorly paid, regardless of race or condition, and these positions were often filled by ambitious young men, still living with their parents, who viewed their current employment as the first step in a prosperous mercantile career. Needless to say, few free men of color were permitted to follow that path. The salaries paid to ministers, if any, were frequently insufficient to support the incumbent. Teachers suffered economically from the fact that Negroes were wholly excluded from the public educational system in many of the cities, forcing black educators to rely for support on parental tuition payments, the level of which was, of necessity, realistically related to the client group's ability to pay. And in those cities that provided public funds for Negro education, the black teachers were paid less than their white counterparts.

The very few practitioners of entrepreneurial occupations had, if anything, even less likelihood of achieving any significant degree of economic success. The percentage of free men of color engaged in these vocations exceeded five percent of the total in only New Orleans (8.00%), Boston (7.36%), Buffalo (6.04%), and Cincinnati (6.14%). Less than 3½ percent of all employed free black males were engaged in activities classifiable as entrepreneurial or mercantile. This figure, small as it is, is both inflated and misleading. Almost one-sixth of those so classified were listed as farmers. Many of these were elderly, and, given the nature of the urban economy, almost all were probably unemployed. A more realistic figure for the size of this occupational category, therefore, would be something less than three percent of all employed Negro males. Of this reduced number (576), almost thirty percent were classified as peddlers, traders, hucksters, market men, dealers, and oystermen—all of which offered only a minute chance of moving from the lowest rung on the economic ladder.[40]

A few black mercantile operators, to be sure, achieved a significant measure of success. Thomas Downing's oyster bar just off Wall Street in New York was not only elegant and well patronized but was also, in the three decades before the Civil War, a favorite resort for mercantile, legal, financial, and political leaders. In the 1830s the autocratic Thomas M. Jackson catered almost all "important" New York weddings. In Cincinnati the slave-born Robert Gordon's shrewd operation of his coalyard enabled him not only to overcome the efforts of his white competitors to drive him out of business but also to accumulate sufficient wealth to permit him to invest heavily in Cincinnati real estate at a later date.[41]

It appears, however, that, aside from hucksters, peddlers and similar marginal mercantile operators, black entrepreneurs outside of the Lower South depended almost exclusively on a black clientele for support, and suffered all of the difficulties that such dependence entailed. Indeed, north of the slave states, the development of black entrepreneurial activity seems to be directly related to the degree of racial residential segregation. It is no accident that Boston reported a higher percentage of blacks engaged in these occupations than any other of the fifteen cities except New Orleans; Boston was also, beyond a doubt, the most thoroughly segregated city in the nation in its residence patterns. Moreover, more than one-fifth of Boston blacks in this category were clothes dealers, and another one-eighth operated boardinghouses—both occupations offering little promise of upward economic movement. Finally, more than one-half were traders, and subject to all of the economic uncertainty and limitation that that term implies.[42]

Thus, of the three occupational categories placed in group C (high occupational opportunity and achievement), the artisan component clearly incorporates those occupations offering the urban black the greatest real opportunity to achieve a measure of economic success. Free men of color avidly sought out every artisan opening available, but, tragically, those occupations offering the greatest possibility of success were, as has been noted, the very ones from which Negroes were most likely to be excluded.

This exclusion was not uniform across the country, however. The most striking and immediately apparent pattern observable in a city-by-city analysis of free black male employment is the geographic clustering of the high-opportunity and low-opportunity cities. Of the five cities with the lowest percentages of blacks in group A occupations, four are located in the slave area; of the five with the highest percentages, only one is from that region. Conversely, the five urban centers with the highest percentages of black artisans are all southern cities, while only one city from that area is to be found among the five with the lowest black artisan employment (see tables B-1 and B-2). When the cities are ranked by the more comprehensive index of occupational opportunity, once again the regional grouping of the centers offering blacks the most favorable and the least favorable employment opportunities is strongly marked. All but one of the "top" five cities are located in the slave area, and all five of the "bottom" urban centers are northern (see table B-3).

This pattern of geographic distribution of urban black occupational opportunity actually possesses an even greater degree of regularity than these obvious differences suggest. If the fifteen cities are divided into five regional groupings and the census entries for employed free black males in all of the cities in each block are combined into single universes and analyzed in the same manner as the individual city data (see appendix B), it is easier to observe the extent to which black occupational opportunities differed among the subregions.

The progression of the resultant figures is striking. The percentage of blacks engaged in the low-opportunity group A occupations was lowest in the Lower South cities, increased dramatically in the urban centers of the Upper South, and continued to rise in the cities of each successive subregion to the north. The examination of the artisan trades shows a similar progression in reverse, with urban black artisan employment at its highest level in the Lower South, delining precipitously in the Upper South, and decreasing continuously in each succeeding subregion. The figures for the index of occupational opportunity, combining, as they do, data indicating similar trends, show a substantially identical progression in slightly more pronounced form

(see tables B-4, B-5, and B-6). These patterns are shown graphically in
figures 1 and 2.

Analyses of occupational categories not treated here in detail show
the same regional differences in black employment patterns. The occupations grouped under the heading Transportation constitute a case
in point. In every southern city more than one-half of all blacks following occupations included in this category were employed as carters, draymen, carmen, hackmen, cabdrivers, or carriage drivers—the
occupations in this grouping that offered the greatest promise of economic advancement—and the figure rose to more than three-quarters
in Washington (76.04%) and Charleston (75.68%). But only in Cincinnati (36.00%) and Buffalo (33.33%), among the nine northern
cities, did as many as one-fourth of the Negroes in this category follow
these more desirable occupations, and in Boston the number dropped
to zero. At the other end of the economic opportunity scale among
transportation occupations was that of porter. Among the southern
cities, it was only in St. Louis (41.46%) and Baltimore (27.07%) that
as many as one-quarter of the black males in this category were employed as porters. Conversely, only in Providence (16.22%), Albany
(33.33%), and Boston (44.44%) among the northern cities were
fewer than one-half of the free men of color following transportation
occupations so engaged.[43]

Similar differences are observable even in the entrepreneurial category, despite the small number of blacks engaged in these occupations. The unpromising distribution of Boston's black entrepreneurs
among the specific occupations included in this category has already
been discussed, and conditions in New York and Philadelphia were
almost equally depressing. In the City of Brotherly Love, as in Boston,
about one-half (48.65%) of the black males following entrepreneurial
occupations were engaged in huckstering and related activities. In
New York the figure was only about three-tenths (29.87%), but
another tenth operated boardinghouses and another one-fifth
(20.78%) were employed in a variety of prepared food vending operations, only a few of which appeared likely to prosper. The 141 free
Negro entrepreneurs in New Orleans, on the other hand, included 23
merchants (this term was normally applied to wholesale, not retail,
operators), 1 commission merchant, 10 brokers, 10 builders (as opposed to carpenters, bricklayers, and related craftsmen), 17 landlords,
4 capitalists, 1 agent, 2 livery stable operators, 2 coffee house keepers,
32 grocers, and 15 operators of other retail stores. These occupations
offered substantially greater chances of economic success than did the
marginal activities previously discussed, and the 117 blacks so employed constituted more than four-fifths (82.98%) of the total number
in this occupational category in New Orleans. Nor was the position of
free black entrepreneurs there without some counterpart in other

southern cities. Well over one-half (58.33%) of Charleston's free men of color engaged in entrepreneurial activities were wood factors—an occupation that brought modest prosperity to the Dereef family and others so employed—and the one-half of Louisville's black entrepreneurs who were tobacconists could also hope for at least some measure of financial success.[44]

It is always possible, of course, that these pronounced regional

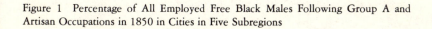

Figure 1   Percentage of All Employed Free Black Males Following Group A and Artisan Occupations in 1850 in Cities in Five Subregions

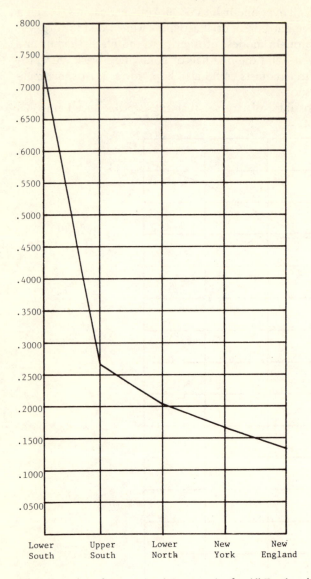

Figure 2 Index of Occupational Opportunity for All Employed Free Black Males in 1850 in Five Subregions

differences in free black male occupational patterns do not result from the action of circumstances related to the geographic location of the cities, but, rather, from the operation of variables whose influence is cloaked by the apparent strength of these regional patterns and by the persistent tendency to examine all national data for the antebellum period in relation to North-South sectional controversy.[45] The importance of such concealed influences (if they exist) can be revealed by a system of analysis that identifies potentially influential variable and examines the black employment patterns in relation to those variables.

Since it has been repeatedly suggested that recent immigrants had, by 1850, displaced large numbers of blacks from occupations in which they had earlier had substantial footholds, it is tempting to suggest that the pattern of regional differences in black employment is only a reflection of the higher percentages of foreign-born residents in the populations of the northern cities. Such an assertion rests, initally, on a false assumption—that few recent immgrants resided in the southern urban centers. Washington and Charleston, it is true, had a smaller proportion of foreign-born residents than did any other of the fifteen cities. St. Louis and New Orleans, on the other hand, ranked first and second in this respect, and the percentages of foreign-born residents in the whole population were substantially the same in Louisville as in Boston, in Baltimore as in Providence. Free black males, it is true, suffered under severe disadvantages in St. Louis, which ranked last among the cities in percentage of blacks employed as artisans and a poor tenth in the index of occupational opportunity, but no city provided more favorable employment opportunities to free blacks than New Orleans. Indeed, the two cities with the most favorable black occupational patterns—New Orleans and Charleston—ranked second from the top and second from the bottom in percentage of foreign-born residents. Even within regional groupings, it is difficult to detect any influence exerted by the presence or absence of immigrants. The proportion of foreign-born residents in New Orleans was almost $2\frac{1}{2}$ times that of Charleston, but the free black occupational pattern was marginally better in the former city. Louisville's foreign-born residents amounted to almost a third of the entire population, while in Washington the figure was less than one-twelfth, but blacks clearly had superior employment opportunities in Louisville. Recent immigrants constituted less than one-third of Pittsburgh's population and almost one-half of Cincinnati's, but Pittsburgh ranked last among the fifteen cities in employment opportunities for blacks while Cincinnati stood just above the median position. But it should not be inferred from these examples that a strong positive correlation existed between the presence of recent immigrants and favorable black employment patterns, for such was not the case either. All analysis indicates that there was no discernible relationship between these two variables. For the fifteen cities, the coefficient of correlation (r) between the black index of occupational opportunity and the percentage of foreign-born residents in the population is $-.0134$, or about as close to a zero relationship as it is possible to obtain.[46] It would appear that in 1850 racial occupational discrimination in American cities was neither a recent nor an alien importation.

Nor do detailed analyses of other potentially influential variables prove much more helpful in suggesting explanations for the differences in black occupational patterns among the cities. There are wholly insignificant negative correlations between the black index of occupational opportunity and both population size (−.1268), and percent of population growth between 1830 and 1850 (−.2547).[47] There is an equally unimportant positive correlation with the percent of free persons of color in the whole population (.2913).[48] There is a modest negative correlation (−.5945) with the per capita annual value of manufactured product—that is, the higher the level of manufacturing activity (as indicated by this figure), the less favorable was the pattern of black employment.[49] The coefficient of correlation between the black index of occupational opportunity and geographic location of cities by subregion was .6956—greater than that resulting from the analysis of any other variable.

Thus, the general pattern of urban black male employment in 1850 is quite clear, and, indeed, almost any element in that pattern can be rather precisely defined. It is desirable, however, to broaden the inquiry to determine the extent to which the 1850 data is representative of the entire half-century under consideration. But to accomplish this temporal extension of exploration it is necessary to incorporate different kinds of data. The seventh census (1850) was the first in which the marshals recorded specific occupations, though in 1840 male occupations were aggregated under seven broad (and largely useless) heads.[50] For the larger cities, however, there exists another source of information about free black occupations extending, in some instances, over a considerable number of years—the city directory.

The first and most obvious impression to be derived from a separate analysis of the directory data is that the geographic distribution of black occupational opportunities among the cities in the subregions, which was so notable in 1850, prevailed throughout the entire period (see table B-7). Employment opportunities for blacks were clearly superior in the Lower South cities, worst in those of New England, and better in the urban centers of the Upper South than in those in New York and the Lower North (though the distinctions between these last two regional groupings is less pronounced than in the case of the 1850 census data). In the mid-1830s, for example, about fifty-nine percent of the free black males in Charleston and about sixty-two percent in New Orleans were artisans, while the number did not reach five percent in either of the New England cities.

A close analysis of this directory data suggests that in several cities there was no appreciable shift in the patterns of occupational opportunity for free persons of color. In Boston, Baltimore, and Charleston the movements were so minute and (to some degree) counterbalancing as to be insignificant. The case of St. Louis is more complex. Between 1842 and 1854 there were substantial declines in the percentages of free black males employed both as artisans and in group A occupations, and the end result left the index of occupational opportunity essentially unchanged. But within some of the categories there was an observable movement during the period from higher-opportunity to lower-opportunity occupations. It appears likely, therefore, that free Negro occupational opportunities were declining in St. Louis during the 1840s and '50s. In Washington the increase of the percentage of blacks in group A occupations and the decline in those employed as artisans between 1822 and 1853 were both pronounced and make it clear that occupational opportunities for free black males deteriorated substantially in the nation's capital. Similar shifts took place in New York in the 1840s (though the changes were of much smaller magnitude), indicating that there, too, free black occupational opportunities decreased from an already depressed base.

In three of the nine cities for which acceptable directory data have been obtained, the occupational patterns reveal improving employment opportunities for free persons of color. The changes in New Orleans were slight and in Providence and Brooklyn more substantial, but in each city the percentage of free blacks following group A occupations declined and the percentage employed as artisans increased. But these improvements still left urban blacks with extremely limited opportunities. Between 1832 and 1844, for instance, the percentage of Providence's blacks following group A occupations declined by almost thirteen percentage points, and the percentage employed as artisans increased by almost four percentage points. But the end result was to move the index of occupational opportunity from an unbelievable .0348 to a deplorable .1178. In Brooklyn between 1838 and 1851, the directory data shows a decline of almost fourteen percentage points in the portion of blacks engaged in low-opportunity group A occupations and an increase of almost three percentage points in the number of artisans, with a resulting increase in the black male index of occupational opportunity from .1265 to .2096.

The directory data suggest, therefore, that in most major American cities in the decades before 1850, free black employment patterns remained stable or were marked by declining access to the more promising occupations. In a third of the cities Negro employment conditions improved, but the favorable shifts wre either slight or, if more substantial, operated from such a dismally low base as to make the resulting improvement largely insignificant. Directory data must be used with caution, especially when comparing conditions in different cities, but the general thrust of the analysis of this material would appear to be unmistakable. Table B-7 displays, in condensed form, some of the results of this analysis.

It is, of course, possible to establish the nature of the correlation between the census data and the directory data (see appendix B). This correlation appears to be very strong, but even if the directory and census figures are assumed to be. wholly comparable, and shifts in urban black occupational patterns are computed on the basis of the 1850 census data enumeration and earlier directory data, remarkably few (and small) differences from the earlier generalizations emerge. This approach does make it possible to add Philadelphia and Cincinnati to the list of cities in which black employment trends can be analyzed. The improvement in Negro occupational opportunities appears somewhat smaller in Brooklyn and slightly larger in Providence. At the other end of the. scale, this joint data base analysis indicates more pronounced declines in employment opportunities for free persons of color in Washington, New York, and St. Louis than were suggested by the examination of the directory data alone. In all of the other cities (including Philadelphia and Cincinnati) the change in employment opportunities was insignificant in magnitude (never exceeding .0400 on the index of occupational opportunity scale).[51]

An assumption strongly implied in much of this discussion of black male occupational patterns has been that the employment opportunities of urban blacks were enormously more restricted than those of the rest of the urban population. But is it not possible, alternatively, that these employment patterns were representative of those of the entire urban population in the antebellum era, and that the differences in black occupational opportunities among the cities were only accurate reflections of regional differences in employment? With more than two-thirds of the free black males in three-fifths of the cities engaged in low-opportunity group A occupations, such a conclusion appears inconceivable. Fortunately, data are available for six of these fifteen cities that make it possible to seek the answer to this question in a less impressionistic fashion. State or city censuses produced detailed aggregations of employment for Boston (in 1845), Charleston (in 1848), and New York and Providence (in 1855), and there are detailed contemporary listings for Louisville and Cincinnati that were obviously taken from the 1850 manuscript census returns (see appendix B).

An examination of these compilations quickly dispels any lingering doubts that might exist about the extent of discrimination in employment. In Providence, Boston, and New York the percentages of blacks following low-opportunity group A occupations was roughly

2⅖, 2⅘, and 3½ times as great, respectively, as the percentage of all employed males engaged in such activities, and the proportion of free blacks employed as artisans was only about one-seventh of the comparable figure for the whole male population in Boston and New York and little over one-ninth in Providence. The relative occupational position of free persons of color was somewhat better in Cincinnati and Louisville. In Louisville the percentage of free Negroes engaged in group A occupations was a little less than three times as great as the figure for the total free male population, and in Cincinnati about 2⅓ times as large. But more important shifts occurred in the artisan category, where the free black percentage of the figure for the total population rose to more than one-sixth in Cincinnati, and to almost one-third in Louisville. It is in the lower South, however, that the most dramatic differences are observable. In Charleston just over twenty-three percent of the free men of color followed low-opportunity group A occupations, and the comparable figure for the whole free male population was almost sixteen percent. This constituted a ratio of about 3:2 and was notably more favorable to Negroes than the 3:1, 7:2, and 7:3 ratios existing in the other five cities. The artisan category showed more remarkable differences still. Roughly one-sixth of all free males were employed as artisans in Charleston, but more than one-half of all free men of color were so engaged (see table B-9).

These figures certainly reveal some differences in free male occupational distribution among the cities. This is not too surprising, since Boston, Louisville, New York, Providence, Cincinnati, and Charleston ranked first, second, third, fourth, seventh, and fourteenth (in that order) in per capita annual value of manufactured product.[52] But these differences appear to be unrelated to free black employment patterns. In Louisville and New York, for example, roughly the same percentages of the male population were employed as artisans, but the percentage of free men of color so employed was almost 2½ times as great in Louisville as in New York. Indeed, insofar as there is any relationship between general male employment patterns and those of blacks, that relationship would appear to be inverse, rather than direct. For it is in the city with the most limited opportunities for artisan employment (Charleston) that one finds the largest proportion of free men of color engaged in artisan occupations.[53]

Three broad generalizations about urban free black employment patterns in the first half of the nineteenth century have been conclusively established. First, free blacks suffered from widespread discrimination in employment in the cities, which resulted in the development of occupational patterns that made significant black economic advancement highly unlikely. In no city—not even Charleston or New Orleans—did free men of color enjoy truly equal access to all occupations, restricted only by individual ability. Second, throughout the half-century these discriminatory conditions persisted. There is evidence of modest imporvement in employment conditions in only two or three cities, while deterioration or stagnation of opportunity is apparent in the others. Third, occupational opportunities for free black males were much more extensive in the Lower South cities than elsewhere. These opportunities were much reduced in the cities of the Upper South, and the deterioration continued progressively in the Lower North, New York, and New England. Moreover, these conditions appear not to be closely related to any of a variety of potentially influential variables whose effect might be cloaked by the more obvious pattern of subregional differences.

This last item requires some further examination. Though these regional differences have remained largely unexplored, they were apparent to contemporary observers. Charles Lyell commented in the 1840s upon the greater prevalence of employment discrimination in the North, and in the preceeding decade the New York-based *Anti-Slavery Record* noted poignantly that "in Kentucky, prejudice does not forbid master mechanics to teach colored men their trades."[54] Certainly there was no lack of racial prejudice in the South, but it does appear that this prejudice did not make itself felt in the form of discrimination in employment to the degree that was common in the northern cities.[55]

It might be tempting to speculate that southern whites avoided all employments involving manual labor and thus abandoned to the free blacks the fields of drayage, cartage, and many potentially lucrative artisan trades. But this supposition does not survive scrutiny. In every southern city both the directory listings and the manuscript census returns include many whites engaged in every occupation followed by free Negroes. Further evidence is provided by the 1848 Charleston census, which divided the population into three groups—whites, free persons of color, and slaves—and recorded the occupations of the males in each group, thus permitting a more detailed analysis of comparative occupational patterns than is possible elsewhere (see table B-10). Clearly, although Charleston whites (and free blacks, too, for that matter) were underrepresented in the lower-opportunity occupations, they were by no means absent from them. There were, in fact, ten times as many whites as free blacks in unskilled jobs. Additionally, white artisans outnumbered free Negro artisans by a ratio of more than 3:1. While the figures available for Louisville are less precisely comparable than those for Charleston, it would appear that white laborers outnumbered free black laborers by a 19:1 ratio and that in the unskilled occupations the white-to-free Negro ratio was almost 17:1. In drayage and related activities, whites outnumbered free blacks by a ratio of 14:1. And despite the fact that more than a sixth of all employed free black males were artisans, they were outnumbered by whites by a ratio of more than 100:1.[56] Clearly southern whites did not abandon the more laborious occupations to the free men of color, whatever their occupational preferences might have been.

Two factors that possibly help to explain the pattern of regional differences in free black employment might be considered. First, well before the creation of the free black communities in the post-Revolutionary era, southern urbanites were fully accustomed to the presence of black artisans. In southern cities, more than in their northern counterparts, slaves had always been extensively employed as skilled workers, in part because of an urban free labor shortage that was more pronounced in the South than in the North. Hence, by the antebellum era southern whites did not perceive free black artisans as either strange or threatening elements in the urban population. This may well account (in part) for the fact that racial prejudice, which was undoubtedly strong in the South, did not manifest itself in the form of occupational discrimination in the southern cities nearly as often and pervasively as in northern urban centers. Additionally, the existence of black artisans in these southern towns meant that young black males were much more likely to secure apprenticeships that would enable them to enter these same trades. Second, the southern urban free black communities were created by selective manumission, not by mass emancipation. Moreover, this was more pronouncedly true in the Lower South than in the Upper South, for there were many fewer cases of masters freeing all of their slaves (usually by will) in the Gulf and South Atlantic areas than in the border states, and in a number of such cases the slaves were sent or taken north. Later, of course, more extensive legal barriers to voluntary manumission were enacted in the Deep South. Among southern slaves who were manumitted, therefore, many earned the money to buy their freedom, some were freed as a reward for their labor or loyalty, and not a few were manumitted because of a familial relationship with their masters. Hence, it is apparent that many of the southern free blacks were drawn from the most able, energetic, and talented of the slave population, while many others had familial ties that were likely to make it easier for them to acquire education, training, and capital. It is hardly strange that such selectively manumitted slaves—many of whom had already successfully competed with free workmen—should exhibit a higher incidence of continued occupational achievement than a northern free black population that, to a much greater degree, included the weak as well as the strong, the indolent as well as the energetic, the inept as well as the able, and the unprepared as well as the experienced.

The black occupational experience in American cities was thus in some measure, kaleidoscopic, though the more somber hues prevailed. For every flash of brilliance of a James Forten in Philadelphia, or a James McCune Smith in New York, or a Thomy Lafon in New Orleans, or a John F. Cook in Washington there was an endless procession of drab portraits in gray and tan of the "many thousands gone," without hope in life and without remembrance after death. This was, of course, true for the great mass of whites as well, though for the urban Negro there was also the ever-present and all-important stark confrontation of black and white. But each made his contribution, however small, to the building of the city, and for many there was doubtless some measure of satisfaction and gratification. For a small number—larger in some cities than in others—there was the certain knowledge that they had achieved a measure of economic and occupational advancement for themselves, their children, and, perhaps, their people.

3 A Stake in Society:
Property Ownership among Urban Blacks

In one respect, at least, the English settlements in the New World were a near-perfect embodiment of the spirit of capitalism. Nowhere else did the zeal for private property ownership and the opportunity for the acquisition of personal wealth (especially in the form of landed estates) march more harmoniously together. After having fought for independence at least in part to prevent the imperial government from acting in such a fashion as to inhibit their highly individualistic property accumulation, and created a national government which would foster but hardly regulate those impulses, the American people, in the first half of the nineteenth century, surged hungrily across the continent ingesting one and a third billion acres of land, which they proceeded, by the application of labor and technology, to exploit for private gain as rapidly as their own resources and those they could attract from abroad would permit. The result was an extraordinarily broad dispersal of property ownership, both real and personal. This circumstance, in turn, fostered a belief (not always closely related to reality) that individual property ownership was within the reach of almost everyone. It was no accident that property qualifications for voting and officeholding began rapidly to disappear during those years when the perception of the imminence of universal male property ownership was strongest. Even if one still believed that a "stake in society" was prerequisite to political participation, it could nevertheless be logically argued that the retention of such property qualifications was anachronistic in a society in which almost every adult free male (or, at least, almost every adult free *white* male) could meet the requirements.

The tendency in the eighteenth and nineteenth centuries to speak of property ownership primarily in agricultural terms should not be permitted to lead us into error. The economy of the era was no more manorial than its government was feudal. In a mercantile society, commercial cities play an important—perhaps even dominant—role, and in these urban centers the opportunities for property accumulation are certainly more diverse and apparently greater in magnitude. People came to the cities perhaps primarily because they perceived there the greatest opportunities for economic advancement, especially for those with little or no capital, and in an aggressively capitalistic society economic advancement was seen as closely tied to property ownership. Certainly the cities offered a multitude of examples of economic success, and, even in the narrower context of real estate ownership, nowhere had land values increased more dramatically than in the urban areas.

Many free blacks were doubtless drawn to the cities by these same impulses. Certainly they found there greater employment opportunities, which they no less than the whites hoped would make it possible for them to accumulate property. It may be that, because of their great economic deprivation, their expectations were, in absolute terms, lower than those of white urbanites, but there is no evidence that they were proportionately less.

Reliable evidence of property holdings by urban blacks (and others as well) is exceedingly difficult to obtain. Real estate, to be sure, was likely to appear on the tax rolls, but the relationship between the assessed value and the actual value of such property varied greatly from city to city and from year to year and, indeed, from ward to ward and from lot to lot, within individual urban centers. Real estate owned outside the city boundaries was, of course, not included on the municipal tax roles. For a number of urbanites, and a few blacks, this circumstance resulted in a significant understatement of their property holdings. For example, Stephen Smith, a black lumber merchant whose wealth was estimated at $100,000 in 1846, owned fifty-eight brick houses in Philadelphia. His mercantile operations, however, were in Lancaster County, and he owned a number of other buildings in the towns of Lancaster and Columbia.[1]

Personal property was, in general, much less likely to appear in any public record. It is clear that assessors, in accordance with law and practice, routinely excluded household goods from the list of taxable property. Additionally, the well-to-do usually tried to avoid paying taxes on such intangibles as corporate stocks and bonds and frequently strove to minimize the tax paid on merchandise in warehouse as well. The poor, of course, had less personal property to conceal, but even small taxes bore so heavily upon their limited resources that they, too, seldom reported any property not readily apparent to the assessor. Free blacks were among the poorest of the poor, and they appear rarely to have been credited with any personal property except retail merchandise, horses, carts, and, in southern cities, slaves.

The 1850 federal census was the first to report real estate holdings; the data in the returns for that census, with all their drawbacks (see Appendix C), are probably the most nearly comparable available, and conclusions derived from them can be viewed as at least suggestive, though certainly not conclusive. As might be expected, the data show enormous differences from city to city in the levels of real estate ownership, however measured, among free persons of color. The $2,354,640 worth of real estate held by free blacks in New Orleans, for example, amounted to almost three-fifths of all reported free black holdings of real estate in the fourteen cities considered (census marshals reported no real estate holdings in Providence; see appendix C) and was considerably more than fifty times as great as the total free black holdings ($41,900) in Boston (see table C-1).

It is obvious that some of the figures derived from the census data are not clearly comparable from city to city. The enormous relative magnitude of the free Negro real estate holdings in New Orleans, it is true, establishes beyond any doubt the advantages enjoyed there by free blacks. The relative positions of free persons of color in the other thirteen cities, however, are by no means so apparent. The gross value of black real estate holdings would, for example, almost certainly be strongly affected by radically different land values and probably by the size of the free black population as well. It is clear, for instance, that the fact that the census returns show the gross black real estate holdings to be lower in Washington than in seven other major urban centers, despite its having the second largest number of free Negro real estate holders, is largely a reflection of extremely low land values. Conversely, the very high average value of holdings in Philadelphia was a product of very high property values combined with a low incidence of black landholding.[2]

Hence, a more meaningful figure is probably the percentage of real estate owners in the free Negro populations (see table C-2). There are great variations in this respect among the fourteen urban centers, ranging from less than one percent in four of the cities (Baltimore, Boston, New York, and Philadelphia) to more than six percent in two (Buffalo and New Orleans). Even if these figures are accurate—and in some cases they almost certainly are not—they do not, standing in isolation, reveal very much about the relative incidence of property holding among blacks. What is needed, obviously, are figures showing the percentage of real estate owners in the whole populations of the major cities, with which the data on Negroes could be compared. Unhappily, such figures are not universally available. The superintendent of the United States census for 1850 estimated (very roughly) that 7½ percent of the free persons in the nation owned real estate.[3] But it would be anticipated that the incidence of landownership would be considerably higher in rural than in urban areas. It is also likely that such holdings would be more common in the smaller, newer, less heavily built-up towns than in the older and more densely occupied cities. Most state census aggregations are as silent on this subject as the federal census reports, but the New York state census of 1855 does include data from which the percentage of landowners in the urban populations can be calculated. Fortunately, four of the fourteen cities under consideration are located in that state and these four include two newer and expanding towns—one large (Brooklyn) and one small (Buffalo)—and two older and more heavily built-up urban centers—one large (New York) and one small (Albany). It is thus possible not only to make direct comparisons in four cases, but also to derive a figure (the average percent of landownership in these cities) which may have some general relevance to all fourteen urban centers.

The percentage of real estate owners in the whole populations of these four cities (see table C-3) ranged from about 2⅓ percent in New York to about 8¼ percent in Buffalo. It is also readily apparent that the ratio between the proportions of landowners in the whole population and among blacks is, in three of the cities (Albany, Brooklyn, and Buffalo), not only very consistent, but not particularly unfavorable to the black population. In the city of New York this ratio rises dramatically to more than three times that in the other cities.

The average percentage of landowners in the whole populations of these four cities is 5.19 percent. As the data on the New York urban centers clearly demonstrate, this figure cannot be assumed to be representative for any given community and, hence, cannot serve as a base with which the percentage of black landowners in any of the ten remaining cities can be compared. It is, however, not unreasonable to suggest that the figure of 5.19 percent—derived as it was from an analysis of the data in four very different communities—probably represents fairly accurately the average percentage of real estate owners in the entire group of fourteen cities. The average ratio of black landowners to real estate holders in the whole urban populations can then be computed. The average percentage of real estate owners in the free black populations of the fourteen urban centers is 2.65 percent, and the ratio (adjusted for size of populations) of landowners in the whole populations to those in the free black populations is 1.96:1.[4]

On the basis of these data, then, it would appear that in 1850 urban free blacks were roughly one-half as likely as American urbanites in general to own real estate. Given the level of general economic deprivation of blacks and their limited employment opportunities (see chapter 2), it is remarkable that the relative number of black landowners was as great as this analysis suggests. Indeed, this level of real estate ownership must be considered a monument to the energy, enterprise, and frugality of the free persons of color, especially in view of the strong likelihood that the census enumerators in a number of cities significantly underreported both the number of black landowners and the value of the property that they held.

In several cities, to be sure—e.g., Boston, New Orleans, Philadelphia, Cincinnati, and Baltimore—the census data appear to conform moderately closely to those derived from other sources (see appendix C). But in at least two cities one suspects that the census enumerators significantly understated black landownership. The reported holdings in New York are so low as to challenge credibility, even giving due consideration to the severe deprivation under which blacks were known to labor in the nation's largest city, their extremely limited occupational opportunities, and the remarkably low incidence of general landownership in New York. It must be acknowledged, however, that reports of higher levels of black real estate ownership are both undocumented and of doubtful reliability.[5] The evidence of under-reporting in Charleston is much stronger. The 1859 list of Charleston taxpayers included 303 free black real estate owners holding real property assessed at about $3/4 million. It is possible that the dramatic increase of well over $1/2 million in the reported value of black-owned real estate in this nine-year interval can be explained in part by un-realistically low estimates in 1850 coupled with the admitted strong inflationary pressures during that decade, but nothing save gross error in 1850 can explain the addition of more than 250 blacks to the list of landowners in a period of declining free Negro population in the city. The 1859 figures are further supported (if confirmation is needed) by the city census of 1861, which enumerated over four hundred pieces of black-owned real estate, despite the fact that a number of free persons of color were not designated as such.[6]

Incidentally, other sources suggest that free black landownership in Providence (in which no real estate holdings were recorded by the 1850 census marshals) was roughly comparable to that in the other cities. The 1840 tax list contained the names of forty-two Negro real estate owners, plus twelve landholding estates of deceased blacks. These forty-two owners constituted 3.23 percent of Providence's black population.[7]

Many of the urban black landholdings were, as the figures in table C-1 suggest, of slight value. In seven of the fourteen cities more than one-half of all the blacks reported as holding real estate by the 1850 census enumerators held property valued at $1,000 or less, and almost exactly one-half (49.87%) of all the black holdings in all the cities combined were of this level of value. The figure rose to more than ninety percent in Washington (with its very low land values) and was three-quarters or more in Albany and Baltimore and greater than two-thirds in Brooklyn, Buffalo, and New York. At the other end of the scale, just under five percent of the reported holdings were valued at $10,000 or more, and in only two cities—New Orleans (51) and Cincinnati (9)—was the number of such holdings greater than four.[8]

A few of these holdings were substantial. In these fourteen cities the census marshals found nineteen free persons of color who owned real estate worth more than $20,000 in 1850. Thirteen of these were residents of New Orleans and two were Philadelphians. The other four lived in Baltimore, Brooklyn, Charleston, and Louisville.[9] The largest holdings, as well as the greatest number of such holdings, were to be found in New Orleans. Elsewhere, only Stephen Smith of Philadelphia was reported as owning as much as $50,000 worth of real estate.[10] In New Orleans, however, Erasme Legoaster, Leon Sindoz, and Theodore Thomas (all of whom were listed as landlords) were shown as owning property valued at $150,000, $60,000, and $50,000, respectively. Additionally, merchant Bernard Soulié and grocer Edmond Dupuy were credited with holdings of $50,000 each.[11]

Again, the underreporting of black landholdings in Charleston must be noted. The 1850 census data show only three free persons of color with real estate holdings of $10,000 or more—confectioner John Lee ($30,000), hotel keeper John Lee ($15,000), and Jane Wightman ($10,000).[12] The 1859 tax list, however, showed three times as many black landholdings of $10,000 or greater, including four valued at more than $20,000. Indeed, Maria Weston's real estate holdings, assessed at $41,575, were exceeded in value by those of only thirty-six white individual landowners in the city, and two other members of the same family held real estate valued at another $21,000.[13] Certainly in Charleston a number of free black families were in comfortable circumstances in the mid-nineteenth century. The Dereefs, the Holloways, the Matthewses, the McKinlays, the Smalls, the St. Markses, and the Westons were numbered among those free persons of color holding real estate assessed at $5,000 or more. They tended to follow entrepreneurial and artisan occupations—R. E. Dereef was a wood factor, Richard Holloway and T. R. Small were carpenters, and William McKinlay and Samuel and Jacob Weston were tailors—and obviously invested their surplus funds in real estate holdings in various sections of the city. In 1861 members of the Dereef family owned thirty-nine pieces of property in four of the eight Charleston wards. The Westons held twenty-eight parcels, and a half-dozen other black families (e.g., the Smalls, the McKinlays, the Dacostas, the St. Markses, the Matthewses, and the Holloways) had multiple and dispersed holdings.[14]

Obviously real estate holdings did not represent the whole wealth of urban blacks. It is extraordinarily difficult, however, to find reliable data on other property holdings. At no time during the first half of the nineteenth century were the federal census marshals instructed to inquire into the ownership of personal property other than slaves, and in the case of this single exception, the data collected related to numbers, not value. In many cities (e.g., Providence and Charleston), public officials clearly did not attempt seriously to assess household goods or, indeed, any other form of personal estate except such visible and valuable items as slaves, mercantile stocks, horses, and carriages. Assessors in some other urban centers doubtless inquired much more minutely into the value of personal property holdings making strenuous efforts, for instance, to subject even such intangibles as corporation stocks to taxation.[15] It is possible, consequently, to speak of total urban black property holdings only in a very general fashion or in specific cases. An 1846 listing of "some wealthy citizens of Philadelphia"—that is, those whose estates were estimated to be worth $50,000 or more—contained four identifiable black entries in its eighty pages. Joseph Casey, a hairdresser, the estate of sailmaker James Forten, and Robert Purvis, Forten's son-in-law, were credited with holdings of $50,000 each, while the value of lumber merchant Stephen Smith's property was estimated at $100,000.[16] In Buffalo, on the other hand, an addendum to a list of over seven hundred "men of prominence" contained the names of six "colored men worthy of mention"—"Peter West, town crier (odd character)," three barbers, a clothing renovator, and "Henry Hawkins, a noteworthy and handsome man."[17] Such a listing hardly argues for a pattern of extensive black property ownership in that city. Diverse and impressionistic (and, doubtless, frequently erroneous) sources suggest that property accumulation was more common in Cincinnati. There wholesale grocer Samuel T. Wilcox was credited with $59,000 worth of property in the 1850s, and bedstead manufacturer Henry Boyd with $26,000. Additionally, coal dealer Robert Gordon had apparently amassed a substantial estate by the Civil War.[18]

Toward the end of the antebellum era, as savings banks were established in the major cities, black wealth accumulation came to include money on deposit. Reliable information on the extent of such deposits is, if anything, more difficult to obtain than data on personal property ownership. James M. Wright has found that in 1860, black accounts in the Eutaw and Central savings institutions in Baltimore totaled $20,827.75, but most reports rest on little save impressionistic evidence. New York Negroes were supposed to have held $50,000–$80,000 on deposit in saving banks in 1837, and deposits of blacks in Philadelphia (and vicinity) ten years later were "stated on good authority to exceed two hundred thousand dollars."[19]

Of the total property holdings of urban blacks in antebellum America, one can say only that though they were substantial in a few cities, they clearly constituted a very small proportion of the total held by urban residents. Only in a few isolated instances can any reliable comparison be made. In 1811, black-owned property accounted for just over half a percent of the total assessed in St. Louis. Comparable figures were barely over a fifth of a percent in Providence in 1840 and slightly more than a third of a percent in Baltimore in 1860.[20] In every case the proportion of property held by free persons of color can be characterized only as minute.

One interesting aspect of urban black landownership is the extent to which Negro women owned such property. As has been previously noted (see chapter 1), in 1850 females outnumbered males in the free black populations of all of these cities except St. Louis, by ratios ranging from 51:49 in Buffalo to about 61:39 in Charleston. Obviously the proportion of women among black real estate owners never approached these ratios, but considering the fact that only rarely could married women (black or white) exercise control over property, surprisingly large percentages of reported black real estate holders in some cities were women (see table C-4). This percentage approached fifty percent in New Orleans, exceeded thirty percent in Louisville, and was 15–20 percent in four other cities. A rather pronounced regional alignment is apparent in this analysis. In all but one of the cities in the slave area, women constituted one-eighth or more of the black landowners; in all but two of the northern cities they were less than one-eighth. It appears likely that this distribution reflects both the concubinage system that existed openly in New Orleans and more clandestinely in other southern urban centers, and a closely related practice of settling property upon slave mistresses when emancipating them.[21]

It might mught be noted that in the city with both the highest incidence of black landownership and the highest percentage of black female real estate owners (New Orleans), the level of female property holding was relatively constant at all levels of estate value. Women, for example, owned 47.97 percent of all black real estate holdings valued at $500 or less, 48.52 percent of those worth $1,000–$2,500, and 49.02 percent of those worth $10,000 or more, as compared with 46.46 percent of the black holdings of all sizes. Though the variations are greater, there was a fairly general distribution of female holdings across all value categories in Charleston, Louisville, Philadelphia, Cincinnati, and Washington, as well. In the other cities, however, black women's holdings were heavily concentrated at the lower end of the value scale. No black woman was reported as holding real estate worth more than $2,500 in Albany, Baltimore Brooklyn, Buffalo, Pittsburgh, and St. Louis, or more than $3,000 in New York.[22]

Free blacks in southern urban centers held another species of property—slaves. Free persons of color became slaveholders for a variety of reasons. Most frequently, it appears, the slaves were the slaveholder's own spouse, children, or other relatives. In the absence of much more data than exist one can only speculate why free blacks continued to hold family members in slavery in the first third of the nineteenth century. It may be that they believed that their children, in particular, were, as slaves, better protected from kidnaping and sale than they would be as free persons. Certainly the officials of slaveholding communities viewed slave stealing as a serious offense. It is possible that in some cases the money for the purchase of family members had been borrowed, and that the slaves purchased constituted the collateral, or that ownership had simply been transferred in consideration of a note secured by the slave property involved. Or its may have been that the free black slaveowners—understandably desirous of avoiding conact with a government that viewed slavery as the normal condition of blacks—simply did not wish to involve themselves and their families in the legal process necessary to obtain "freedom papers." In the 1830s and '40s, changes in the legal code in all southern states made it more difficult to free slaves, and in some of the states of the Lower South emancipation was almost impossible.

Not all slaves held by blacks were family members. Some free persons of color purchased slaves to permit the bondsmen to accumulate money to purchase their own freedom. In the mid-1830s a black clergyman in St. Louis held a sizable number of slaves for this purpose, and there were doubtless many other such cases less well known.[23] And, finally, some Negroes undoubtedly purchased and held slaves for their labor in the same manner as white slaveholders, though this would appear to have been more common in rural than in urban areas. In Natchitoches Parish, Louisiana, in 1830, for example, Louis Meytoier and Augustin Meytoier held 54 slaves each, and eleven other members of the Meytoier family in that parish held another 109 slaves.[24]

The detailed examinations of the 1830 manuscript census data relating to the free Negro carried out in the early 1920s under the direction of Carter G. Woodson make it possible to examine urban black slaveholding rather minutely (see table C-5). In the six southern cities, the number of black slaveholders ranged from none in St. Louis to 753 in New Orleans. The total number of slaves held by Negro owners in these cities (excluding St. Louis) ranged from 8 in Louisville to 2,363 in New Orleans. These figures do not reveal the incidence of slaveholding by blacks, however, for they do not take into consideration the size of the free black populations in these cities. The percentage of slaveholders in the free black populations varied greatly; the figure was less than two-thirds of a percent in Baltimore, about 2⅙ percent in Louisville, roughly 2⅔ percent in Washington, a little over 6½ percent in New Orleans, and just under 12½ percent in Charleston. Since Woodson and his investigators also produced data on the free black heads of families, and since his listing of free Negro slaveowners actually records the number of families containing slaves rather than the number of individual slaveholders, it is possible to calculate the percentage of free black families that held slaves in each of these cities (see table C-6). On the basis of these computations it would appear that more than three-fourths of all free black families in Charleston held slaves, and that the figure was over forty-five percent in New Orleans.

Free black slaveholding was, by any measure, more important in the Lower South cities of Charleston and New Orleans than in the Upper South cities. Though the free Negro population of Charleston was only about two-thirds that of Washington, Charleston had more than three times as many black slaveholders as the nation's capital; they held almost eight times as many slaves; and Charleston free black families were almost six times as likely to hold slaves. Similarly, New Orleans' free Negro population was less than two-fifths that of Baltimore, but New Orleans had almost eight times as many free black slaveholders who owned over fourteen times as many slaves, and its free Negro families were more than ten times as likely to hold slaves as those in Baltimore. Additionally (see table C-7), individual free black slaveholdings of larger size were also heavily concentrated in Charleston and New Orleans, where were found not only more than ninety-two percent of all black holdings of five or more slaves reported in the five cities, but all holdings of greater than nine slaves as well.

These dramatic differences in the scale of black slaveholding between Upper South and Lower South cities doubtless reflects both the greater general affluence of the free persons of color in New Orleans and Charleston and the greater difficulties in manumitting slaves encountered in the Lower South. Some slight impact may have been made by the presence of a number of free black immigrants from Santo Domingo, some of whom had owned slave-operated plantations before being driven out by the success of the slave uprisings of the 1790s.

Women constituted an even larger percentage of black slaveowners than of black real estate holders (see table C-8). In four of the five cities—Charleston, Louisville, New Orleans, and Washington—women made up two-fifths or more of all black slaveholders, with the figure rising above two-thirds in Charleston. In fact, in Charleston women constituted a higher percentage of black slaveholders than of the free black population as a whole. The proportion of women was much smaller among Baltimore's black slaveowners—about two-ninths. Moreover, the percentage of women remained high among black holders of larger numbers of slaves. Indeed, Lydia Burnie, with forty-one slaves, and Cécëe McCarty, with thirty-two, were, in 1830, the largest black slaveholders in Charleston and New Orleans, respectively—the two Lower South cities where larger holdings were substantial in number.

It would be almost impossible to state with certainty whether free Negro slaveholding in these five cities increased, decreased, or remained constant during the remainder of the antebellum period. The 1850 manuscript slave schedules do not identify slaveholders by race, and short of cross-checking each slaveholder's name against the voluminous free inhabitants schedule there is no way that the necessary data can be obtained.[25] One suggestive piece of evidence might be cited, however. In 1859 the Charleston tax list included the names of 109 free persons of color who held a total of 281 slaves.[26] By that date the city boundaries had been extended to include the area known as Charleston Neck. Woodson and his associates extracted from the 1830 census the names of 394 black slaveholders living in the city and the Neck; they held a total of 2,245 slaves. If both the 1830 and the 1859 figures are accepted as valid, they indicate that during a period of about three decades the number of free black slaveholders declined by almost three-quarters, and the number of slaves held by blacks by about seven-eighths. As has been previously noted, the 1830 census figures—as interpreted by Woodson and as employed in this chapter—contain a high potential for error.[27] If, as one suspects, some considerable portion of the slaves included in the 1830 figures produced by Woodson and his associates were not owned by blacks, then the reduction in free Negro slaveownership in the decades that followed would be proportionately less. Additionally, since the 1859 compilation was produced for the purpose of levying taxes, it is logical to assume that a number of individual slaves might not have been listed if their status was not obvious. But unless one or both of these deviations were enormous it is difficult to escape the conclusion that slaveholding by Charleston's free blacks—and perhaps by those residing in other cities as well—declined dramatically in the 1830s, '40s, and '50s. Indeed, it may well be that the general reduction in the number of urban slaves during these years was largely the result of this pronounced shift in the incidence and magnitude of free black slaveownership.

Clearly urban blacks shared the capitalistic zeal for property acquisition. They strove earnestly—and in some instances with pronounced success—to obtain real estate, personal property, and, sometimes, slaves. If, as was true in most cities, they lagged far behind the rest of the urban population in the accumulation of such property, it was not because they had different values, but rather because their employment opportunities were so severely limited and they were so nearly universally excluded from speculative activity by the limited acceptability of their notes-of-hand. It was no accident that blacks acquired the greatest amount of property in those cities in which they had the most favorable patterns of employment. And as they sought broader employment opportunities they stretched out yearning hands not only for the immediate benefits of an easier existence but also with the ultimate hope of achieving property ownership and, with it, a measure of economic stability and security in a society in which the most consistent elements might well seem to be the reverence for property and the pervasiveness of prejudice.

4 Lofts, Garrets, and Cellars, in Blind Alleys and Narrow Courts: Urban Black Housing and Residential Patterns

The poor have rarely been well or even adequately housed in any society; certainly they were not in any Western society in the nineteenth century. Though this circumstance prevailed equally in rural and urban areas, the disparities between the housing available to the poor and that occupied by the rest of the population were certainly more obvious, and perhaps absolutely greater, in the cities. It is true that even as late as the middle of the nineteenth century American cities contained little to match the worst of the slums in the major European metropolises. An English visitor in the early 1850s, Isabella Bishop, observed that the poor were, in general, much better housed in New York than in London (and might have added that New York's slums were almost without parallel elsewhere in the country). Even so, she thought the Five Points area no better than St. Giles' in London or the Saltmarket in Glasgow and found a group of Negro dwellings identified only as the "mud huts" almost equally bad.[1]

It was indisputable that the housing occupied by blacks tended to be decidedly inferior to that of the poor in general. This was so not only because free people of color were, as a group, the poorest of the poor, but also because many landlords either preferred to rent to whites or absolutely refused to accept black tenants. This discriminatory attitude was particularly prevalent outside recognized black districts and was strongly encouraged by the occupants of neighboring houses. In the early 1830s when a black family attempted to move into a white residential area in Boston, local residents threatened to demolish the house rather than permit it to be occupied by Negroes. The result of this pervasive prejudice was that, as George G. Foster observed of Philadelphia's blacks in the late 1840s, they were often "crammed into lofts, garrets and cellars, in blind alleys and narrow courts."[2] Foster's impressionistic opinion was eminently correct. A decade earlier, in 1838, the Pennsylvania Society for the Abolition of Slavery compiled a list of black artisans in the city that included the names of 612 Negroes for whom addresses were listed. Of these, 133, or more than one-fifth, lived in alleys, courts, or at the rear of other buildings. Even among the master·workmen, between a sixth and a seventh had residences in these areas. As high as these figures are, they understate reality, for it is obvious that a number of the addresses listed are those of business establishments, not residences. Additionally, many Philadelphia alleys were not designated as such. Another fifty of these black artisans resided on Bedford, Bonsall, Gaskill, Little Pine, and St. Mary streets, all of which were actually alleys two blocks or less in length. The people of color whose names appear in this compilation constituted the economic elite of the Philadelphia black community, including such notables as the Fortens, the Bustills, Peter Richmond, James J. G. Bias, the Douglasses, and James McCrummill. The rank and file of the city's Negroes were doubtless much more likely to occupy buildings in such locations as Eagle, Davis, and Bird's courts and Current, Middle, Paschall's, Hog, Twelvefoot, and Prosperous (!) alleys.[3]

Nor should it be thought that Philadelphia's blacks were atypical in regard to housing. An analysis of a sample of entries in an 1835 Baltimore directory shows three-eights of the listed blacks living in structures situated in alleys (without reference to those dwelling in courts, places, and rear buildings)—a figure almost precisely ten times as great as that for whites. The actual housing conditions of this city's free persons of color, it is true, may not have been quite as bleak as these figures suggest, for a number of Baltimore's alleys (e.g., Apple Alley, Strawberry Alley, and Petticoat Alley) were rather wider than was common in most cities and divided blocks of unusual breadth. Four Providence directories in the 1830s and '40s show $\frac{1}{7}$–$\frac{1}{12}$ of the listed blacks residing in alleys or in rear buildings, and even in a less crowded western city such as Cincinnati, more than one in fourteen of the Negroes listed in the 1843 directory had alley addresses. The Negro housing situation in Boston was probably roughly equivalent to that in Philadelphia in this regard. The 1833 directory shows precisely one-third of all blacks living in alleys, courts, places, and rear buildings.[4]

Such alley and rear structures were likely to be found in greatest number in the older and more heavily built-up northeastern cities, where higher land values tempted owners to place the maximum possible usable structural space on each lot or square. Nevertheless, the location of a house—whether in an alley or on a main street—was, of course, by no means a certain indication of its quality as a residence. The structures located in courts and alleys, or built on the rear ends of lots, were, to be sure, usually small, flimsy, and devoid of sanitary facilities, but these conditions could be found elsewhere as well, and occasional sound and comfortable dwellings existed in the most unlikely situations. In all the major cities a handful of blacks—usually artisans or professional men—occupied decent, sometimes even substantial, residences. A good example of the better sort of black dwelling—perhaps not in the best one percent but almost certainly well within the top tenth—was the building rented by William J. Brown's parents in Providence in the 1820s. The house—occupied before the Browns by Thomas Reed, "considered the upper crust of colored society"—was of frame construction and consisted of a cellar and four rooms, two on each floor. It seems to have been unusually well supplied with windows, having at least five and possibly more, and a brass knob embellished its front door. Reed, a barber, had conducted his business and housed his family on the ground floor and employed the upper story "as a genteel boarding house. He did not accommodate sailors." Its location was hardly ideal, since it adjoined a sailors' boardinghouse on the east, but its spaciousness and amenities doubtless outweighed that consideration. For the first six months after the Browns took up residence they had the use only of the second floor, but they could hardly have considered this a great hardship. "Two rooms was considered quite a genteel tenement in these days for a family of six, especially if they were colored, the prevailing opinion being that they had no business with a larger house than one or two rooms."[5]

A larger number of urban Negroes struggled unceasingly to maintain moderately clean and healthful homes in marginal buildings. But many others, forced into some of the poorest housing the city had to offer, eventually stopped striving or caring for anything save survival. In city after city the worst Negro housing attracted the horrified attention of city officials, medical authorities, reformers, and travelers alike. By the beginning of the second quarter of the nineteenth century Cincinnati's black residential area along Columbia Street and Western Row was solidly built over with flimsy frame tenements which, though unsightly and dangerous to their black occupants and to the city as a whole, were undeniably profitable to their white owners. When, over the next decade and a half, the concentration of black residences moved to beyond Fifth and Sycamore streets in the city's East End, it seems unlikely that their housing dramatically improved. Such buildings aroused the ire of local whites not only because they bred epidemics and posed a major fire hazard, but also because they were affordable to blacks and, consequently, made it possible for them to remain in the city. "Heaven preserve the shanties," commented one editor bitterly in 1830, "and supply the proprietors with tenants from whom the rent can be screwed, without respect to color or character."[6]

Conditions were similar elsewhere. In Albany in 1830, "one of the worst localities in the city" was near the Capitol "on the south side of State street," which was "covered by the cheapest buildings, and occupied by people of the 'baser sort' both black and white."[7] In 1820 it was reported that more than one-fifth of the people of color living in the Banker Street area of New York occupied cellars, and three decades later William M. Bobo commented on the rickety, filthy shacks housing Negroes in the city's fifth ward.[8] In Charleston in the late 1830s, officials spoke of "negro huts" and pointed to Clifford's Alley, "occupied principally by small houses, inhabited by negroes," and "perhaps one of the greatest nuisances, within the limits of the corporation." As early as 1820, Baltimore's health officials singled out as a major health hazard a "nest of houses" near the Centre Market "tenanted by Negroes, and divided by an alley, very appropriately called *'Squeeze Gut!'*" which they described as "a collection of huts and filth," and thirty years later the board of health condemned the "cellars, wretched hovels, [and] crowded and lothsome rooms" occupied by blacks and characterized them as "replete with all that was calculated to engender disease."[9]

It was in the largest and densest of the cities of the Northeast, however, that the worst Negro housing was to be found, and the only mitigating circumstance was that only a minority of blacks (together with a few whites) were ever housed in these barbaric quarters. By the middle of the nineteenth century the unrestrained zeal of property owners to obtain the greatest return for the smallest investment had produced in New York and Philadelphia conditions whose vileness and depravity were unmatched in America either before or after that period. W. E. B. DuBois would write at the close of the century, "The present [1899] slums at Seventh and Lombard are bad and dangerous, but they are decent compared to those of a half century ago."[10]

In 1847 a visitor to the most abominable slums along the Philadelphia-Moyamensing boundary described the standard dwellings there as

> small wooden buildings roughly put together, about six feet square, without windows or fire places, a hole about a foot square being left in the front along side of the door. . . . These desolate pens, the roofs of which are generally leaky, and their floors so low, that more or less water comes in on them from the yard in rainy weather, would not give comfortable winter accommodation to a cow.

At one point, "turning into an alley between two of the buildings on Baker street," itself nothing more than an alley less than two blocks long, he "followed through a dirty passage, so narrow, a stout man would have found it tight work to have threaded it." The yard at the rear contained

> a long range of two story pens, with a projecting boarded walk above the lower tier, for the inhabitants of the second story to get to

the doors of their apartments. This covered nearly all the narrow yard, and served to exclude light from the dwellings below. . . . Here were dark, damp holes, six feet square, without a bed in any one of them, and generally without furniture, occupied by one or two families. . . . Some . . . had six, and even eight persons in them, but more generally two to four.[11]

For these accommodations the residents paid 8–10 cents a night. The cost of erecting the double row of pens was estimated at $100, and two men who questioned each inhabitant as to the amount of rent paid calculated that they produced an annual income of $1600. Small wonder that the owner had, a few years before, declined to part with so lucrative an investment![12]

Miserable as these conditions were, they had their counterpart in New York. Dr. B. W. McCready reported that in 1842 he had attended typhus patients in a rear buildings reached by a "covered alley-way" on Elizabeth Street in the lower fourteenth ward, a few blocks from the notorious Five Points area. "This was a double frame house," he observed,

three stories in height. It stood in the centre of the yard. Ranged next the fence were a number of pig styes and stables, which surrounded the yard on three sides. From the quantity of filth, liquid and otherwise, thus caused, the ground I suppose, had been rendered almost impassable, and to remedy this, the yard had been completely boarded over, so that the earth could nowhere be seen. These boards were partially decayed, and by a little pressure, even in dry weather, a thick greenish fluid could be forced up through their crevices. The central building was inhabited wholly by negroes.[13]

All evidence suggests that by the middle of the nineteenth century not only had the poorest free black housing touched a minimum in comfort and a maximum in misery, but also that black housing, in general, was becoming increasingly crowded as the incidence of multiple-family residences increased. This latter trend was observable only in a few of the more densely populated cities, and doubtless affected poorer whites as well as blacks. But other factors, perhaps economic and perhaps cultural, doubtless influenced the incidence of black multifamily housing.

As might be expected, the greatest proportion of dwellings with multiple black residents was found in New York, where the 1852 directory showed 1,344 listings of Negroes at 479 locations, an average of 2.81 listings per address. Only one-seventh of those listed resided at addresses for which no other black occupant was recorded, while forty-five percent lived in buildings each of which housed five or more blacks included in the directory, and one-eighth shared addresses with at least nine other blacks in the directory. The incidence of multiple Negro directory listings at the same address was much lower in Boston, despite the fact that it too was heavily built up. Of 151 addresses listed for blacks, 101, housing almost forty-two percent of the blacks included, were listed only for a single person of color. Another forty-two percent resided at addresses listed for two or three blacks, while only four addresses were shared by five or more. The average number of listings per address in Boston in 1845 was 1.60— much lower than in New York in 1852. In other cities the incidence of multiple black occupancy of buildings appears to have been still lower. The average number of listings per address was 1.36 in Albany in 1850, 1.31 in Providence in 1844, 1.14 in Charleston in 1859, and 1.03 in New Orleans in 1852, while addresses shared by four or more blacks were recorded only in Charleston (2), Providence (1), and Albany (1). In New Orleans all but 10 of the 302 addresses were listed for only a single black. These figures understate the extent of black residence in multifamily dwellings, for many Negroes shared build-ings with whites, but they do suggest that there were significant dif-ferences among the cities in this regard, with black multiple-family dwellings being much more usual in New York than elsewhere, and relatively common in Boston and probably in Philadelphia as well.[14]

The Boston figures suggest less use of multifamily housing by blacks than one would expect in that crowded city. But the directory figures are further supported by the Massachusetts state census of 1850, which shows the sixth ward (which contained almost sixty percent of the city's blacks) to have had the third lowest ratio of families to inhabited houses (1.27:1) of all the wards. Doubtless the ratio for blacks alone in this ward was considerably higher—the 1845 directory data show 1.89:1—but still well below the 4.05:1 ratio in Boston's eighth ward. It is probable that in such long-established areas of black residential concentration the existing small buildings were not sus-ceptible of being further subdivided, nor were they replaced by larger structures.[15]

The residential patterns of urban blacks and the degree of residen-tial concentration, however, show still greater variations from city to city. There is, regrettably, no way to show accurately and concisely either the absolute or the relative extent of the concentration of black housing in the nation's major cities. A very crude measure is the index of dissimilarity, i.e., the percentage of the white and nonwhite popu-lations that would have to be shifted to achieve a random distribution across all the geographic units within which the measurement takes place.[16] This index has two major weaknesses which derive from the fact that population figures are not available for units smaller than wards. First, the degree of racial residential concentration is inevitably—sometimes drastically—understated because the geographic extent of the wards tends partially to conceal areas of high-density Negro population within them. A larger number of units smaller than wards will invariably produce a higher index of dissimilarity. The Baltimore data for 1840 and 1850 provide a clear example of this phenomenon. There is no indication from any source that Baltimore's free persons of color were becoming increasingly residentially concentrated during the fifth decade of the nineteeth century. Nevertheless, the index of dissimilarity as derived from the census figures more than doubled between 1840 and 1850—increasing from 9.92 to 21.47 (see table 4-1). It seems clear that this shift resulted solely from the increase in the number of wards from twelve to twenty. Secondly, ward boundaries can—and frequently do—bisect areas of black residential concentration, dividing the numbers, and their impact, between two or more wards. A third difficulty is unrelated to the use of wards as analytical units, but, rather, derives from the use of census figures. Because the census marshals enumerated—or intended to enumerate—all persons, the census data include relatively large numbers of Negro live-in servants, who were frequently, though not always, concentrated in wards with few black domiciles. The presence of such servants in these wards was in no way reflective of black family residence patterns. For all these reasons, indices of dissimilarity derived from census data and based on the whole populations of wards as analytical units tend to understate the extent of black residential concentration.[17] This is admittedly somewhat less true of the southern cities where live-in free Negro servants were much less common, since such service was usually provided by slaves, whether owned or hired.

For all its drawbacks, the index of dissimilarity, even when so computed, can sometimes serve as a very crude *relative* measure of racial residential concentration. Table 4-1 displays the indices of black/white residential dissimilarity for the fifteen major cities, in 1820, 1830, 1840, and 1850. It is immediately apparent that in none of these cities did the degree of racial residential segregation approximate that prevailing in many American cities in the third quarter of the twentieth century. Karl and Alma Taeuber computed the indices of dissimilarity for 207 cities from the 1960 census data (including all fifteen of the urban centers examined in table 4-1, though the Brooklyn and New York data are now, naturally, combined). They reported the index of dissimilarity to be in excess of 60.0 in every case; above 90.0 in seventy-eight instances; and below 75.0 for only thirteen cities.[19] These findings cannot be directly compared with those for 1850, for

Table 4-1   Free Black Indices of Dissimilarity for Fifteen Cities Rank Ordered
for 1850

	1820	1830	1840	1850	FPC in 1850 Number	% of Population
Boston	46.26	44.23	51.10	59.20	1,999	1.46
	(12W)	(12W)	(12W)	(12W)		
Philadelphia	35.64	31.02	34.42	49.39	10,736	8.85 ·
	(14W)	(15W)	(15W)	(17W)		
Pittsburgh	10.29	15.27	18.76	46.56	1,959	4.20
	(2W)	(4W)	(5W)	(9W)		
New Orleans	n.a.	11.55	29.24	45.18	9,905	8.51
		(4W)	(8W)	(16W)		
Cincinnati	24.55	43.97	37.93	37.53	3,237	2.80
	(4W)	(5W)	(7W)	(11W)		
New York	16.86	17.82	28.19	37.26	13,815	2.68
	(10W)	(14W)	(17W)	(19W)		
St. Louis	n.a.	n.a.	17.39	35.89	1,398	1.80
			(4W)	(6W)		
Brooklyn	n.a.	n.a.	16.59	31.89	2,424	2.50
			(9W)	(11W)		
Buffalo	n.a.	n.a.	22.12	25.16	675	1.60
			(5W)	(5W)		
Albany	6.68	14.74	23.21	25.08	860	1.69
	(5W)	(5W)	(5W)	(10W)		
Providence	n.a.	21.57	26.31	24.29	1,499	3.61
		(2W)	(6W)	(6W)		
Baltimore	13.12	11.59	9.92	21.47	24,442	15.05
	(12W)	(12W)	(12W)	(20W)		
Charleston	n.a.	10.00	8.20	20.57	3.441	8.01
		(4W)	(4W)	(5W)		
Washington	17.97	16.65	n.a.	20.48	8,158	20.39
	(6W)	(6W)		(7W)		
Louisville	n.a.	n.a.	n.a.	15.86 n.a.	612	1.34
				(8W)		

Source: See note 18. The figures in parentheses indicate the number of wards
or subdivisions.

the Taeubers' analysis is much more precise, being based on block,
rather than ward, data, and on households rather than individuals. But
it is probably safe to suggest that in the 1850 data an index of dissimilarity of 25.0 or less represents insignificant residential concentration
by race; an index figure of 25.1–33.3 indicates moderate segregation;
and one in excess of 33.3 suggests a high level of racial residential
concentration, at least in relative terms.

These rough categorizations are supported by examinations of the
extent to which blacks were concentrated in a few wards (or a single
ward) in the various cities in 1850. Boston's sixth ward contained

more than three-fifths of the city's blacks and about one-eighteenth of the whites. Similarly, the Spruce and New Market wards in Philadelphia's extreme southeastern corner housed almost four-ninths of the city's blacks and just over one-eleventh of the whites, and in Moyamensing's second ward, just south of the Philadelphia boundary, lived another large concentration of blacks (almost one-half of that suburb's Negro residents). In like fashion Pittsburgh's adjoining sixth and seventh wards contained almost two-thirds of the blacks and less than one-fifth of the whites, and New York's contiguous fifth and eighth wards housed more than two-thirds of the black residents and barely over one-tenth of the whites, while in three of Cincinnati's eleven wards (the first, fourth, and ninth), all adjoining, lived more than five-ninths of all the city's blacks and something over two-ninths of the whites. New Orleans' concentration of free Negroes was heavily in the fifth and seventh wards at the north end of the first municipality and in the contiguous first ward of the third municipality. These three wards housed more than one-half of the free people of color and roughly one-seventh of the city's white residents. By way of contrast, the entire second municipality (the "American" sector) contained only about one-ninth of the city's free blacks and over one-half of the whites. The high index of dissimilarity for St. Louis results primarily from the very small number of free persons of color in the first and sixth wards—the second and third most populous in the city. These wards contained well over a third of the white population and something over one-sixteenth of the free blacks. Free Negroes were relatively evenly distributed among the other wards.[20]

At the lower end of the scale, Louisville's index of dissimilarity is doubtless somewhat below actuality because of the gross skewing of the data from which it is computed. But, indeed, any analysis based on ward data would be even less satisfactory for Louisville than for most other cities because its wards were long and narrow, stretching from the Ohio River to the city's south boundary, and cutting across diverse socioeconomic zones and concentrations. Other data suggest that the black residential patterns in Louisville were roughly similar to those in Baltimore, Charleston, and Washington—somewhere in the 20.0 to 22.0 range. Thus, these four cities are clustered very tightly at the bottom of the list when ranked by index of dissimilarity, with Providence slightly above them, just below the arbitrary point of division between "insignificant" and "moderate" residential concentration by race. In the three southeastern cities (excluding Louisville because of the unreliability of the data), not a single ward could be found whose free black percentage was double the proportion in the whole city population. And only in Baltimore's first and ninth wards, Washington's sixth ward, and the first ward in Charleston were the free black percentages less than half those for the city as a whole. In Providence, only in ward two was the black percentage more than double the city percentage, and only in ward five was it less than one-half the percentage for the whole city population. At the other extreme, one or the other of these conditions existed in nine of Boston's twelve wards, in thirteen of Philadelphia's seventeen wards, and in seven of Pittsburgh's nine wards.[21]

Several things are apparent from an examination of table 4-1. First, larger cities tended, in general, to have higher indices of dissimilarity. Of the five largest cities in 1850, four were in the "high" range (i.e., above 33.3), while the other was in the "insignificant" block (i.e., below 25.0). Second, the indices of dissimilarity are much higher for northern than for southern urban centers. Of the six southern cities only two (New Orleans and St. Louis) had indices in the "high" area, while the rest occupied the four lowest positions in the "insignificant" range. Of the nine northern cities, five were in the "high" category, three were "moderate," and only one had an "insignificant" index of dissimilarity. Third, there would appear to be no clear relationship between the number or percentage of free persons of color in the city's population and the index of dissimilarity.

On the matter of trends in residential segregation during the half-century, the data are inconclusive. It is true that for every city except Cincinnati and Providence, the 1850 index figure was the highest for the years examined. But in almost every case the number of reporting units (usually wards) had increased as well, and, as previously noted, the index of dissimilarity will almost always rise as the reporting units become geographically smaller and more numerous. In those instances in which the number of units remained unchanged, the trends were not consistent. The index of dissimilarity rose in Boston (1820–50), Philadelphia (1830–40), Buffalo (1840–50), and Albany (1820–40), and declined in Providence (1840–50), Baltimore (1820–40), Charleston (1830–40), and Washington (1820–30). These data suggest that racial residential concentration was increasing in northern cities and declining in southern urban centers, but the figures are by no means determinative.

A more careful examination of the data shows that during the fourth and fifth decades of the nineteenth century, residential segregation was on the rise in all the cities with the probable exception of Washington, Providence, and Baltimore; the possible exception of New Orleans and Albany; and the tentative exception of Cincinnati. (No conclusions can be drawn from the Louisville data.) The Washington increase of less than four index points between 1830 and 1850 is less than might be expected with an increase of one-sixth (from six to seven) in the number of reporting units and may well indicate a decline in residential segregation, and Cincinnati's index of dissimilarity declined despite a 120 percent increase (from five to eleven) in the number of wards. But in this latter instance the figures may be deceptive, for the new ward boundaries intersected the black residential area in Cincinnati's East End (see pp. 66–67). In Providence, the trebling of the number of reporting units between 1830 and 1840 might be expected to produce a much larger increase than the less-than-five index points computed for those years, and the index of dissimilarity actually declined slightly between 1840 and 1850. The Baltimore situation is more complex. Between 1820 and 1840 the index of dissimilarity declined at a rate of 12–14 percent per decade, but it suddenly gained 11½ index points (an increase of 117 percent) in the last decade of the half-century. The number of wards increased from twelve to twenty in the 1840s, however, and the apparently dramatic jump in the index probably did not represent a real increase (certainly not a significant increase) in racial residential concentration.[22]

It is difficult, on the basis of the available data, to determine the trend of New Orleans' residential patterns. It is true that the index of dissimilarity almost quadrupled between 1830 and 1850, but (because of the extreme sloppiness of the census marshals) so too did the number of reporting units, which doubled in each decade. Under such circumstances it is impossible even to guess whether the rapidly escalating index numbers reflected a genuine increase in free black residential concentration or were merely the product of more nearly satisfactory reporting procedures. In Albany there was clearly an increase in residential segregation between 1820 and 1840—indeed, the increase in the index of dissimilarity was very constant at 8–8½ index points per decade. But the less-than-two-point increase in the last decade of the half-century was much smaller than would be expected with a doubling of the number of wards. It seems likely, therefore, that the pattern of increasing racial concentration so clearly established in the 1820–40 period was reversed in the 1840s.[23]

Some slight mention might be made of Charleston, which shows an opposite trend. But since the Neck area had been annexed between 1840 and 1850, and since the Neck housed more than two-fifths of all Charleston's free persons of color (compared with about two-ninths of the whites) in 1850, it is tempting to suggest that the rise in the index of dissimilarity in the final decade of the half-century resulted wholly, or almost wholly, from this annexation and did not reflect a real increase in racial residential concentration. Fortunately it is possible to test this hypothesis by extracting the data for the 1840 wards from the 1850 census, since their boundaries were not changed in the interim. An analysis of these figures produces an index of dissimilarity of

14.37—still more than six index points (and seventy-five percent) above the 1840 figure. There can be little doubt, then, that racial residential concentration in the South Carolina metropolis, though still at an "insignificant" level, was increasing in the last decade of the half-century.[24]

City directories offer another avenue for exploring black residential patterns in antebellum American cities, but their use presents both advantages and disadvantages. The major disadvantages are the incompleteness of the data (which varies widely from year to year, from city to city, and from compiler to compiler) and the virtual impossibility of comparing white residential concentrations with those of free blacks. The advantages are the directories' listing of adult heads of families (few others are included) rather than whole populations; the almost complete exclusion of live-in servants and transients; and the greater precision with which the residences are usually located. Thus, it is possible to examine the black residential patterns within wards, though, as a practical matter, not in a comparative black/white fashion.

The disadvantages inherent in the incompleteness of the directory compilations can be minimized by selecting for analysis only those directory listings that include relatively large numbers of free persons of color. But there remains the possibility that directory compilers may have consistently underreported blacks (and probably whites as well) in certain sections of the city. A careful comparison of directory listings for Boston (1845), New York (1852), and Washington (1850) with the corresponding federal census returns suggests that such underreporting usually occurred only in wards with relatively few Negroes. Only one other consistent pattern of nonrandom underreporting is observable. Proprotionately fewer black directory listings are included for the "out wards"—those lying farthest from the city's center. The wards south of Fourteenth Street in New York, for instance, contain almost ninety-five percent of the black directory listings but only eighty-six percent of the Negroes reported by the census marshals. In part this circumstance doubtless results from the fact that the "out wards" contained substantial numbers of live-in black servants, but it probably also reflects less scrupulous canvassing on the part of the directory agents. The only cases of significant unequal underreporting in sections with relatively large numbers of black residents were in New York's sixth ward and Boston's sixth ward. The former contained the infamous Five Points slum area, and the deplorable and dangerous conditions may well have discouraged thorough investigation by the directory agents. Boston's sixth ward contained fifty-four percent of the black directory listings and sixty-one percent of the blacks reported by the census enumerators. But since the sixth ward also included the affluent Beacon Hill neighborhood, this discrepancy may have reflected little more than the presence of numerous live-in black servants. When the wards are arranged in rank order by the percentage of reported black residents, there are few discrepancies between the directory and the census data, and such differences as do exist are usually of a magnitude of one position on the rank-order list (if we exclude New York's sixth ward, and the tenth ward where there was *apparent* overreporting of black residents in the directory).[25]

The directories' exclusion of live-in servants and transients also causes these listings to show heavier concentrations in the wards with the largest Negro populations than do the census listings. The 1850 census shows New York's fifth and eighth wards to have contained forty-one percent of that city's blacks living south of Fourteenth Street, while the figure computed from the directory data is fifty-nine percent. In the nation's capital the census enumerators found forty-one percent of the free persons of color living in wards one and two, but sixty-four percent of the free black directory entries are located there.[26]

The major contribution that the directory data make to a better understanding of black residential patterns, however, is the identification of concentrations of black residents inside of and across ward boundaries. This can be accomplished only by plotting directory listings on city maps—a tedious activity, to be sure, but sometimes rewarding. There are three major problems (tedium aside) associated with this type of analysis. First, almost none of the directories published before the 1830s included any significant number of free persons of color. Consequently, only three directory residential analyses were made for this study for years before 1830—Boston in 1818, Brooklyn in 1823, and Washington in 1822—and in each case the number of locatable residences was less than one hundred. This was true also for six later analyses—Louisville in 1836 and 1841, Pittsburgh in 1839, Washington in 1830, and St. Louis in 1838 and 1847. Such analyses must be used with care, although the numbers involved constituted from fifteen to over forty percent of the estimated number of the city's adult free black males (but it must be noted that a number of listings are of females). Second, some directory compilers either did not include or did not identify free persons of color. It is not possible, consequently, to prepare analyses for Philadelphia or Buffalo or for some other cities late in the half-century. Third, in some cases free black residences are unlocatable on the city maps because of the vagueness of the directory information or the labyrinthine street-numbering practices. For this reason it has not been possible to prepare directory residential analyses for New Orleans or Baltimore.

A total of twenty-three residential analysis maps were prepared, each of which includes all locatable black directory listings. A number of these merely confirm the free black residential patterns shown by the census data, though they do reveal some clustering even in such minimally residentially segregated cities as Albany (see figure 3) and Charleston (see figure 4), though not, to any significant degree in Washington (see figure 5). In a number of cases, however, the analysis of directory data shows a significantly higher incidence of racial residential concentration than is apparent in the census statistics. Thus, although the indices of dissimilarity calculated from ward census figures for Brooklyn, Providence, and Louisville (for which the data are extremely unsatisfactory) show levels of racial residential concentration ranging from "moderate" to "insignificant," an examination of

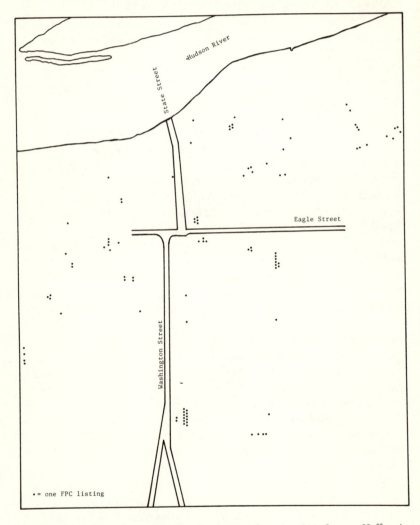

Figure 3   Free Black Residential Distribution in Albany in 1850. Source: *Hoffman's Albany Directory for 1850, 1851*

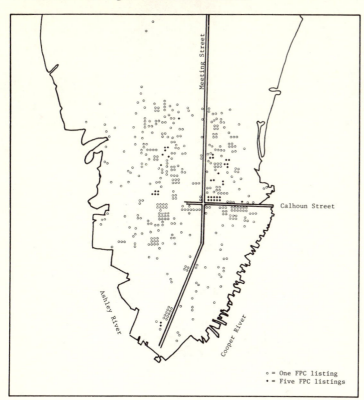

Figure 4   Free Black Residential Distribution in Charleston in 1859. Source: Mears and Turnbull, *Charleston Directory* (1859)

the distribution of directory listings suggests a different conclusion. In Louisville (see figure 6) an analysis of the very full listing of free persons of color in the 1851 directory shows almost one-sixth of the locatable free black residents living in a four-block area bounded by Ninth, Chestnut, Eleventh, and Walnut streets in what was then Louisville's West End, overlapping wards seven and eight. If the free persons of color in the five blocks lying adjacent to these four on the north and west are included, the figure rises to almost one-quarter (24.88%). While figure 6 also shows free black residences to have been widely distributed across all eight wards (and on a north-south axis within them as well), this cluster suggests that Louisville was somewhat more residentially segregated by race than the index of dissimilarity indicates.

An analysis of the 1844 directory data in Providence reveals a somewhat similar situation. In that city, as in Louisville, the index of dissimilarity derived from the 1850 ward census figures indicates an "insignificant" level of residential segregation. But when the black

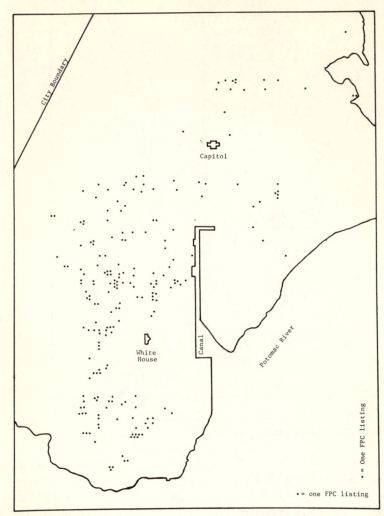

Figure 5   Free Black Residential Distribution in Washington in 1850. Source: Waite, *Washington Directory for 1850*

directory listings are plotted on a map of the city (see figure 7) areas of concentration emerge, despite a very wide distribution of blacks in almost all residential areas of the city. Almost a fifth of all blacks included in the directory were listed as living in Olney Street, "Snowtown" (a designation for the Olney Street area), or "Hard-scrabble"—a term that appears to have been used to designate the same area after the destruction of the original "Hardscrabble" in the riot of 1824 (see figure 7).[27] Since the built-up area extended only about two blocks along Olney Street, this indicates a very heavy con-centration of Negro residences in this section of the first ward.

Moreover, another one-ninth of the listed blacks resided in a two-block section of Benevolent Street in the second ward (see figure 7). Thus, these few blocks contained almost thirty percent of all the black residents included in the 1844 directory.

The index of dissimilarity derived from the 1850 census data places Brooklyn in the high "moderate" range of racial residential segregation. But an analysis of the directory data for 1851 reveals a considerably heavier concentration of black residents. More than fifty-five percent of all blacks included in the directory lived in an area five blocks square, comprising barely over one-tenth of a square mile (see

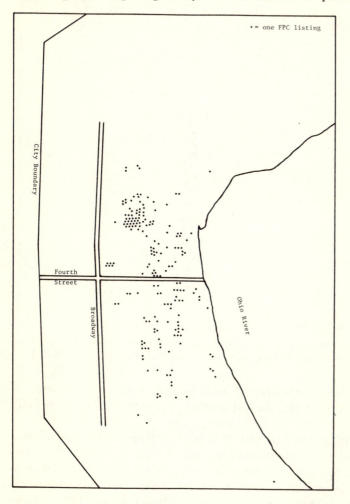

Figure 6 Free Black Residential Distribution in Louisville in 1851. Source: John B. Jegli, *A Directory for 1851–1852 . . . in the City of Louisville* (Louisville: J. F. Brennan, 1851)

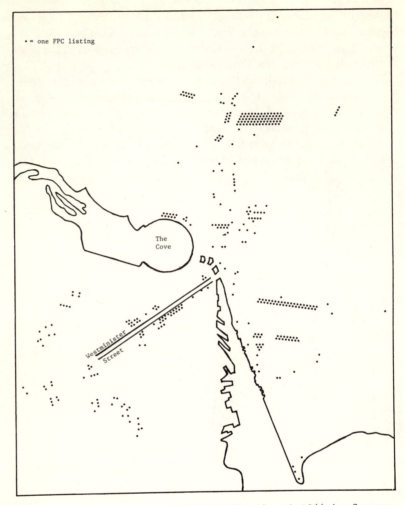

Figure 7   Free Black Residential Distribution in Providence in 1844. A = Snowtown. B = Benevolent Street District. Source: *Providence Directory* (1844), pp. 193–202

figure 8). This concentration overlapped the northwestern quarter of the fourth ward and the extreme southeastern section of the fifth ward.

Even cities with "high" levels of residential segregation as indicated by the index of dissimilarity are found, on examination of the directory data, to have a greater degree of racial residential concentration than the index figures suggest. An analysis of the 1850 census data shows Cincinnati to have had an index of dissimilarity of 37.53—at the bottom of the "high" range. But the 1843 directory data reveal that well over a quarter of all listed blacks resided in a five-block area in the city's East End bounded by Sycamore, Fifth, Culvert, and Seventh streets, and another five percent were located in a single adjacent block south of this area (see figure 9). Hence, over thirty-one percent of the city's black residents were clustered in six blocks straddling the boundary between the first and ninth wards. Though the remainder of the Negro population was somewhat more widely dispersed, a southeastern concentration is observable—less than one-sixth of the listed blacks lived in the portion of the city lying north and west of a line along Main, Seventh, Vine, and Fourth streets.

The 1850 index of dissimilarity for New York, calculated from the

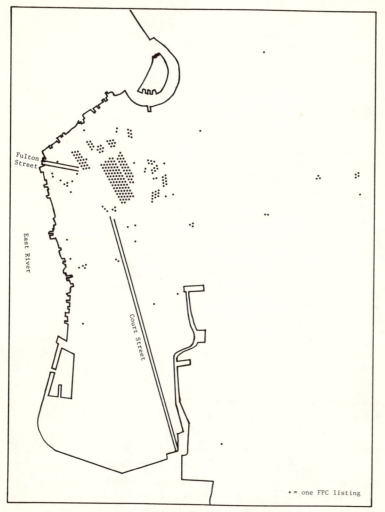

Figure 8   Free Black Residential Distribution in Brooklyn in 1851. Source: *Hearne's Brooklyn City Directory, 1851–1852*

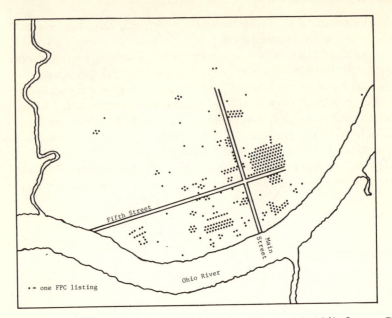

Figure 9   Free Black Residential Distribution in Cincinnati in 1843. Source: Cist, *Cincinnati Directory for 1843,* pp. 391–99

census data, is almost identical to that for Cincinnati. But again, an examination of the directory materials discloses considerably more intensive concentration of black residences (see figure 10). Well over half (53.2%) of all blacks reported by the 1852 New York directory as living south of Fourteenth Street were located in a fifty-block area comprising the southeastern third of ward eight, the eastern half of ward five, and two blocks in the extreme northeast corner of ward three. This section was roughly a quarter of a square mile in extent and constituted approximately one-eighteenth of the area of the city south of Fourteenth Street. Even in this section there were a dozen blocks with no recorded black residents and several more with only one. Moreover, another one-twelfth of the Negroes living south of Fourteenth Street were located in three widely separated single blocks in wards ten, fourteen, and seventeen.

An analysis of directory data also reveals that the index of dissimilarity understates the extent of racial residential concentration even in the most obviously segregated of the major cities—Boston. The 1845 directory listings, it is true, show only fifty-four percent of the Negroes in the first eleven wards living in ward six, as compared with a figure of sixty-three percent derived from the 1850 census data. But *all* of those sixth ward black directory listings were located in the northern half of the ward, and another tenth lived within one block of the sixth ward boundaries (see figure 11). By way of contrast, only a little over one-fourteenth of the listings were located in wards seven through eleven, at the southern end of the city, a percentage very similar to that reported by the census marshals.[28]

It is more difficult to determine whether or not urban free black residential patterns changed significantly during the first half the nineteenth century, either in intensity of concentration or in the location of such concentrations as existed. As has been noted (see p. 58), the indices of dissimilarity as computed from the federal censuses are inconclusive because of the changes in the number of wards for which data were reported, though the apparent trend was toward more resi-

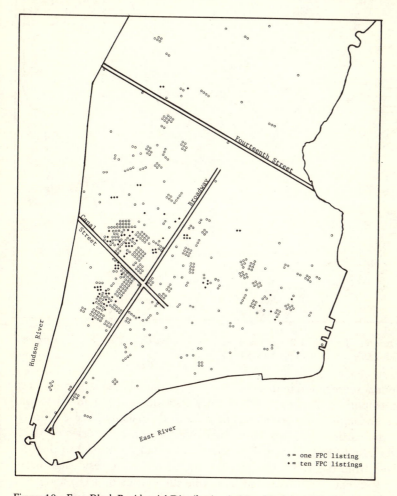

Figure 10   Free Black Residential Distribution in New York in 1852. Source: Wilson, *Directory for New-York for 1852–1853*

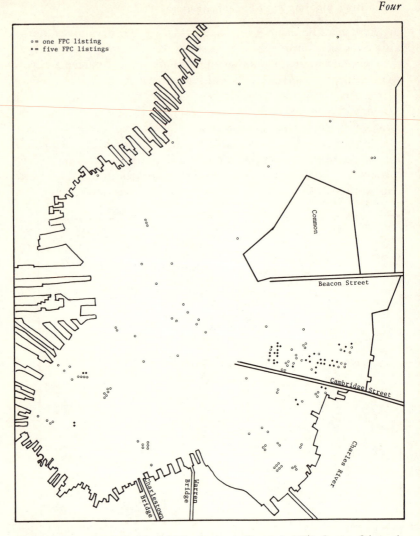

Figure 11   Free Black Residential Distribution in Boston in 1845. Source: *Stimpson's Boston Directory* (1845), pp. 543–50

dential segregation in most cities, and especially in the larger northern metropolises. Analyses of directory data do not add much to our understanding of these trends because of the paucity of black listings in the earlier compilations, though Washington directories of 1822, 1830, and 1834 all reveal patterns substantially identical to that derived from the 1850 directory (see figure 5).[29] The residences listed for free persons of color in Louisville directories of 1836 and 1841 were widely scattered across the city, revealing no hint of the concentration in the Seventh Street area shown by the later data (see figure 6). This suggests that this clustering was of recent origin in 1851, but the number of black listings in earlier directories is too small to support a definitive statement.[30]

In Boston the earliest concentration of black residences was apparently in the extreme North End, opposite Charlestown. Before the end of the second decade of the nineteenth century, however, the movement of the city's blacks into the West End, behind Beacon Hill, was well established. By 1818 fifty-three percent of the Negroes listed in the Boston directory lived in the area bounded by Charleston, Hancock, and Pinckney streets (see figure 12), and by 1835 the figure was fifty-seven percent. Consequently, by the mid-nineteenth century

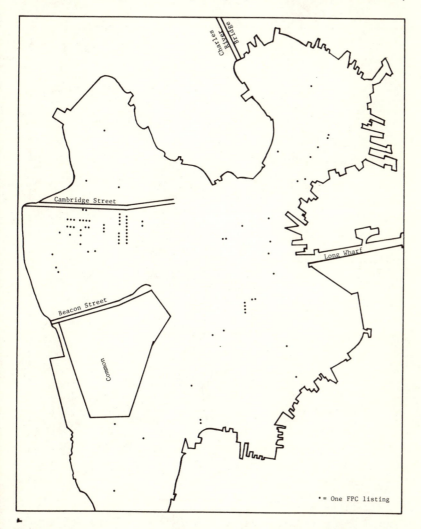

Figure 12   Free Black Residential Distribution in Boston in 1818. Source: *The Boston Directory* (Boston: E. Cotton, 1818), pp. 252–54

the major element in Boston's black residence patterns, as shown in figure 11, was at least a third of a century, and perhaps a half-century, old.[31]

In other cities it would appear that the black residential patterns existing in 1850—whether heavily concentrated or not—were more recent in origin. In Albany, for instance, there was clearly a shift away from the area east of Eagle Street in the late 1830s and '40s (cf. figures 3 and 13), as was true of the population in general. The distribution of blacks was widespread in the late 1830s as well as in 1850, and there is no evidence of an increase in the clustering of black residences. In

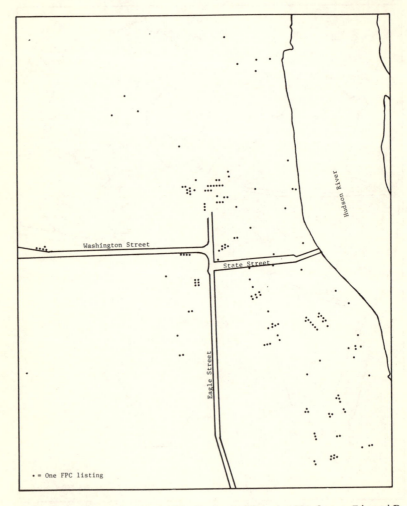

Figure 13   Free Black Residential Distribution in Albany in 1835. Source: Edmund B. Child, *Child's Albany Directory and City Register, for the Years 1835–36* (Albany: E. B. Child, 1835)

Brooklyn and New York, however, the concentration of black residences would appear both to have increased in intensity and to have shifted geographically in the second quarter of the century. In New York, though there was a foreshadowing of the later concentration in the fifth and eighth wards, the 1835 directory data show a fairly general distribution of black residences across at least five wards (see figure 14; cf. fig. 10). A dozen years earlier, though seven-twelfths of the blacks included in the 1823 Brooklyn directory resided in the second ward (bounded by Bridge, Sands and Fulton streets and the East River), there were several discernable clusterings within that ward.[33] The major black residential areas in Brooklyn in 1823, however, were both less heavily concentrated and (like the whole popula-

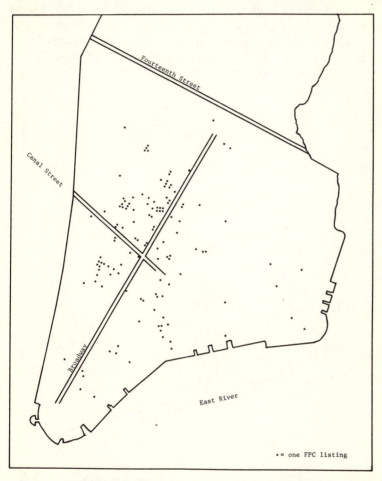

Figure 14   Free Black Residential Distribution in New York in 1835. Source: Thomas Longworth, *Longworth's American Almanac, New-York Register and City Directory* (New York: Thomas Longworth, 1835)

tion) located farther to the west than their counterparts in 1850 (see figure 15; cf. fig. 8).

The absence of Negro directory data for Philadelphia is particularly unfortunate in view of that city's very large black population and its relatively high and obviously increasing level of residential segregation as indicated by the index of dissimilarity. But because most of Philadelphia's ward lines remained relatively stable throughout the half-century, a careful examination of the ward census data can reveal in a fairly precise manner the shifting patterns of black residential concentration.[34] These data show that the black population was already rather heavily concentrated south of Spruce Street in 1800, when the census enumerators found almost a third of the city's free Negroes in that area. In the years that followed, Philadelphia's blacks were pushed west and, much more heavily, south, away from the city center (see figure 16). Between 1800 and 1820 the percentage of the city's blacks living in the six wards lying along the Delaware River

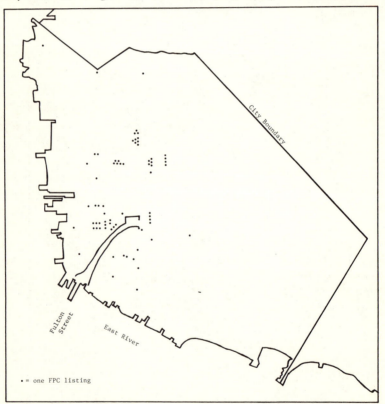

Figure 15   Free Black Residential Distribution in Brooklyn in 1823. Source: Alden Spooner, *Spooner's Brooklyn Directory, for the Year 1823* (Brooklyn: Alden Spooner, 1823)

north of Spruce Street and east of Fourth fell from 25½ percent to
10¾ percent and the number of Negroes in that area actually declined
by almost a quarter, despite a nearly eighty-percent increase in

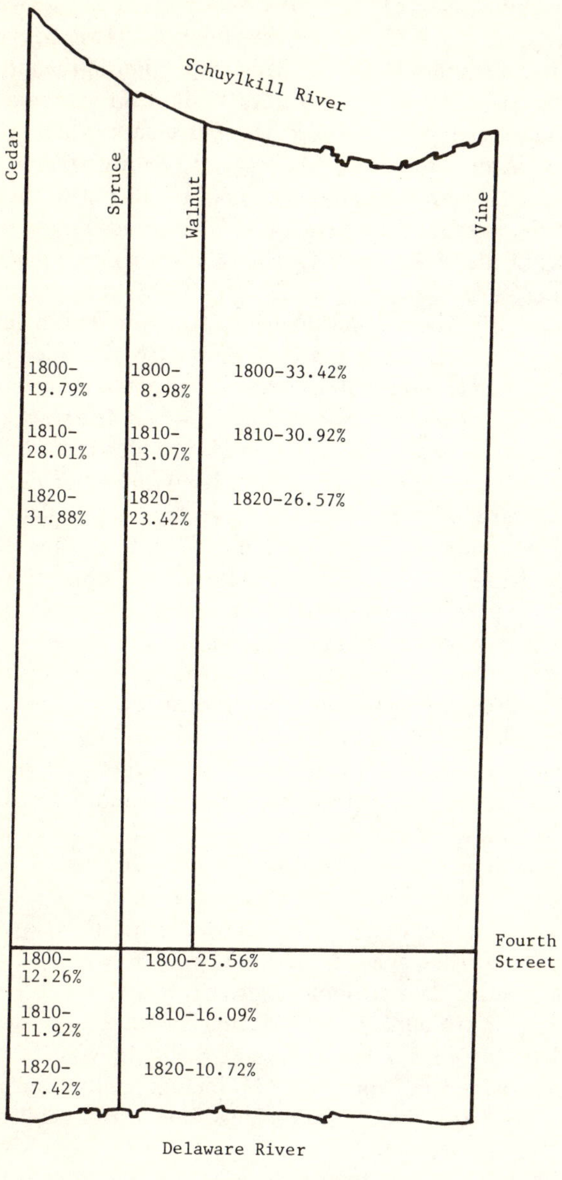

Cedar

Spruce

Walnut

Schuylkill River

Vine

1800– 19.79%	1800– 8.98%	1800–33.42%
1810– 28.01%	1810– 13.07%	1810–30.92%
1820– 31.88%	1820– 23.42%	1820–26.57%

Fourth
Street

1800– 12.26%	1800–25.56%
1810– 11.92%	1810–16.09%
1820– 7.42%	1820–10.72%

Delaware River

Figure 16   Shifts in the Free Black Population of Philadelphia, 1800–1820: Sectional
Percentage of Total Free Black Population. Source: U.S. censuses for 1800, 1810, 1820

Philadelphia's black population. The westward shift was apparent even in New Market ward, south of Spruce, where about one-eighth of the city's Negroes had lived in 1800. By 1820 this figure had dropped to a little over one-fourteenth, though the number of black residents had increased slightly. The west wards along the Schuylkill River showed proportional increases in black population, but the growth was heavily concentrated in the southernmost wards. The proportion of the city's blacks residing in the five west wards north of Walnut Street actually declined from about one-third in 1800 to somewhat more than one-quarter twenty years later, while the percentage of the city's blacks in the two remaining west wards—Cedar and Locust—increased from 28¾ percent to 55⅓ percent. These two wards alone accounted for almost eight-ninths of the increase in Philadelphia's black population during these two decades.

This trend continued in the second quarter of the nineteenth century (see figure 17). The years between 1830 and 1850 saw a decline in the percentage of Philadelphia's blacks living in eleven of the twelve wards (both east and west) north of Spruce Street—the sole exception was the extreme northwest ward (North Mulberry), which recorded a very slight increase from about three percent in 1830 to 3⅖ percent in 1850. Even Locust ward, with its relatively large Negro population, showed a small reduction of the percentage of the city's blacks within its boundaries. The largest decline came in the east wards, where the proportion of the city's free persons of color in residence dropped from rather more than a fifth to one-tenth. The figures for the area south of Spruce Street (which by 1850 included Pine, New Market, Spruce, Lombard, and Cedar wards), on the other hand, reflected an increasing concentration of blacks at the south end of the city. In 1830, 41⅓ percent of Philadelphia's Negroes lived in this section; by 1850 the figure had risen to over fifty-nine percent. A more detailed examination of the census data after the 1825 modification in the north-south dividing line and of the returns from the new wards created in 1846 clearly indicates that the black population was concentrated in the western sections of the east wards and the eastern sections of the west wards—that is, between Fourth and Twelfth streets. In fact, the census data strongly suggest that in 1850, 55–60 percent of Philadelphia's Negro population resided in a thirty-four block area bounded by Cedar, Fourth, Spruce, Seventh, Walnut and Twelfth streets (the shaded area on figure 17), including all of Spruce ward, the western halves of New Market and Pine wards, and the eastern quarter of Locust ward.

It must be noted, however, that nowhere did racial residential segregation remotely resemble that common in American cities in the second half of the twentieth century. Even in such areas of con-

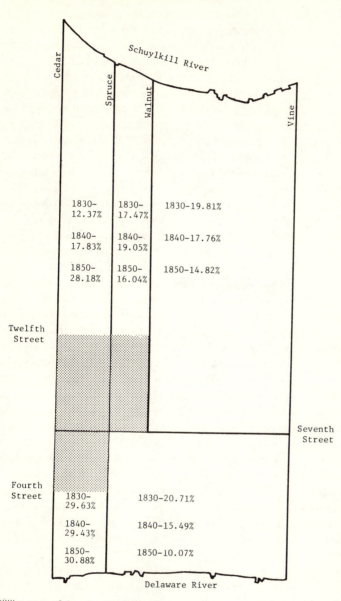

Cedar

Schuylkill River

Spruce

Walnut

Vine

1830–
12.37%

1830–
17.47%

1830–19.81%

1840–
17.83%

1840–
19.05%

1840–17.76%

1850–
28.18%

1850–
16.04%

1850–14.82%

Twelfth
Street

Seventh
Street

Fourth
Street

1830–
29.63%

1830–20.71%

1840–
29.43%

1840–15.49%

1850–
30.88%

1850–10.07%

Delaware River

▦ = area of heaviest concentration

Figure 17   Shifts in the Free Black Population of Philadelphia, 1830–50: Sectional Percentage of Total Free Black Population. Source: U.S. censuses for 1830, 1840, 1850

centrated black residences as those in Boston, New York, and Philadelphia, the separation of black and white residents was by no means complete, while in the cities in which free blacks were widely dispersed, the races appear to have been intermixed even in the smallest subunits. There were frequent mentions of white residences interspersed with the most deprived of Baltimore's free black population, and the seamen's boardinghouses, even when operated by whites, were not segregated.[35] In Albany, whites were found within the cluster of black residences that had developed near the Capitol early in the second quarter of the nineteenth century, and at about the same time a Providence citizens' committee noted that though a number of houses in "Snowtown" were tenanted by blacks, "some of them were occupied by whites, and some by an indiscriminate mixture of whites and blacks."[36]

In some cities more detailed analysis is possible. In 1805 Matthew Flannery produced a street-by-street listing of the residents of New Orleans, and his report showed free persons of color living on 40 of the 43 streets then in existence and usually dispersed widely along them.[37] Similar conditions existed in Charleston more than a half-century later. The 1861 census reported 210 streets with one or more residents. Of these, only 15 (with less than one percent of the white population) housed no blacks, and 7 (with less than one percent of the slave population and about two percent of the free black population) were without white residents. Free black residences were located in 137 streets, only 5 of which were all black. Whites and free blacks were, moreover, heavily intermixed, with numerous property owners renting indiscriminately to both races. In at least ten cases a free person of color who owned two or more adjacent dwellings lived in one and rented another to a white tenant, and white householders with adjacent free black tenants were more than twice as frequent. A typical pattern existed in Water Street—a short street between East Bay and Meeting streets in the city's first ward. Of the nineteen dwellings, twelve were occupied by white owners, one by a free black owner, two by white tenants, three by free black tenants, and one by slaves. Throughout the city many whites rented from free Negro landholders and a large number of free blacks rented houses owned by whites.[38]

Though there was a much higher degree of racial residential segregation in New York—in its seamen's boarding houses, unlike those of Baltimore, blacks and whites did not mix—whites were to be found even in the areas of heaviest black concentration.[39] George Foster, in 1849, described the residents of the Five Points district as "of all colors, white, yellow, brown, and ebony black," and the 1855 state census, as Rhoda Freeman discovered, showed "that Negroes and whites resided in the same houses even in the areas of greatest concentration of the Negro population and often as boarders in the same apartments."[40] This is also the pattern revealed by John Doggett's 1851 street directory, which listed the resident owners and renters of each house or apartment. An analysis of the listings in this volume shows almost forty-five percent of the blacks living in buildings also occupied by whites. Of the 372 streets listed by Doggett, only one (with just over two percent of the Negro listings) was all black.[41]

Even in the most heavily concentrated black residential area in urban America—the northern half of Boston's sixth ward—whites were to be found in considerable numbers. The proportion of black residents was highest in Southac and Belknap streets (together with their adjoining courts), but thirty-seven percent of those living in the former street and fifty-eight percent in the latter were white. Nor should it be assumed that only the most recent immigrants lived in such close proximity to the despised blacks. In the nine streets with the heaviest black residential concentration (containing ninety-seven percent of all sixth ward Negroes), native-born whites outnumbered immigrants in all but one, usually by substantial margins.[42]

In antebellum American cities, thus, free persons of color, like their ancestors and their posterity, were poorly housed in small building or tenements, badly built and maintained, that were much more likely than the residences of whites (especially in northern cities) to be located in alleys and on closed courts, or crammed onto the rear portion of narrow lots. Increasingly, in most of the nation's major cities, growing numbers of the free black residents lived in ever tighter residential concentrations which were pushed toward the periphery of the city. If, however, a recognizable black district had developed in a city by the beginning of the second quarter of the nineteenth century, it tended to remain relatively stable geographically, like the black districts on New York's Lower East Side and on the northwest slope of Beacon Hill in Boston. The degree of this residential concentration varied greatly from city to city, with the levels being highest in the large cities in the Northeast and almost undiscernable in some southeastern metropolises. But nowhere did the degree of residential separation of the races approach the levels of the twentieth century. Even so, there was an important difference between the blacks and the whites who lived in the areas where the concentration of Negro residents was highest. For the whites, such districts were (at least potentially) temporary steps on a residential pilgrimage that might lead anywhere; for blacks they were both the beginning and the end of the road. For three-quarters of New York's streets, avenues, lanes, courts, and places were utterly devoid of black residents, and in Boston the figure was probably at least eighty-five percent. The comparable figure

for the Irish—the next-to-the-lowest population group on the socioeconomic scale—in Boston was less than ten percent.[43] Dragged from
the church on the Sabbath, forced from the workbench during the
week, shoved from the sidewalks and driven from the streets on any
day, the urban black in many cities was dogged by pervasive racial
antipathies to his very doorstep.

5 A Wholly-Distinct and an Outcast Class: Discrimination, Subordination, Segregation, Oppression, and Exclusion

White superiority—and, hence, the "innate" inferiority of Negroes—was, in antebellum America, a concept requiring neither scientific nor theological justification, nor documentation by evidence. It was a given, a timeless verity applicable to all societies in all ages. Nor was it a belief peculiar to Americans. In the late 1830s Frederick Marryat—English naval officer, novelist, and accomplished snob—condemned the "unjust prejudice against any taint of the African blood," which he found "extraordinary, in a land which professes universal liberty, equality, and the rights of man." He was moved to these comments primarily by his contact with Philadelphia blacks, whom he found "very superior" to those in the West Indies. "Not," he carefully added,

> that I mean to imply that they will ever attain to the same powers of intellect as the white man, for I really believe that the race are not formed for it by the Almighty. I do not mean to say that there will *never* be great men among the African race, but that such instances will always be very *rare,* compared to the numbers produced among the white. But this is certain, that in Philadelphia the free coloured people are a very respectable class, and in my opinion, quite as intelligent as the more humble of the free whites.[1]

A quarter of a century earlier Daniel Drake, Cincinnati's candidate for Renaissance man, indicated doubt that the free blacks of that city were as uniformly vicious and criminal as was generally thought. "They are," he wrote, "a thoughtless and good humored community, garrulous and profligate; generally disinclined to laborious occupations, and prone to the performance of light and menial drudgery."[2]

These were the comments of individuals more favorably disposed toward the urban blacks. The generality of the white population would have found such observations erroneous, unconvincing, or irrelevant. The only development within the black community that would have won their unqualified approval would have been its disappearance. An early historian of New York found the "composition of the population" in that city in the first decade of the nineteenth century "highly gratifying" because "the colored population, which, for a hundred years before the Revolution, had constituted a sixth part of the whole . . . had declined relatively nearly one-half." Even relative decline, if not dramatic in magnitude, did not secure to the black community that which it most desired—anonymity. In the second decade of the nineteenth century the number of Massachusetts blacks had increased by only three while the white population had grown by more than fifty thousand. Nevertheless, that state's legislature, in 1821, "alarmed" by the "increase of a species of population which threatened to become both injurious and burdensome," appointed a committee, chaired by Boston's Theodore Lyman, Jr., to investigate the matter. In its report the committee did "not think it necessary to make particular mention of the evils which will accompany this description of population," assuming, apparently, that they were well known, but it did note, as obvious matters, an increase in crime and pauperism as well as the accumulation in large towns of "an indolent, disorderly and corrupt population." These were common views. Less than three years later the grand jury of Washington County, in the District of Columbia, headed by Samuel N. Smallwood, recently mayor of Washington, reported to the court, "We . . . do on our oaths, present the rapid increase of Free People of Colour, within said county, as an evil which requires the interference of the Legislative authority."[3]

Such views were well-nigh universal, and even the blacks themselves felt compelled, in some circumstances, to acknowledge their inferior status. "Your Memorialists," wrote a group of Charleston free blacks in 1791, when petitioning the South Carolina legislature for a repeal of discriminatory legislation, "do not presume to hope that they shall be put on an equal footing with the Free white citizens of the State." Even James Forten, who, when roused, rarely sugarcoated his bitterness toward his fellow Philadelphians, thought it necessary, in a slashing attack on proposed legislation in 1813, to make reference to "the white men, whom we should look upon as our protectors," and to declare, "We wish not to legislate, for our means of information and the acquisition of knowledge are, in the nature of things, so circumscribed, that we must consider ourselves incompetent to the task."[4]

While few have denied the universality of this racial prejudice, many have argued that its intensity varied among different groups of Americans. Though more recent scholars have tended to think it more prevalent among "the lower and rougher classes of white people," New York's Peter Williams, a black Episcopal minister, believed it to be greater among the rich. He added that it was also stronger in the city than in rural areas. Englishman Edward S. Abdy, to whom Williams confided his opinions in the early 1830s, thought them valid on the basis of his subsequent observations. But Abdy further perceived a wide range of other variations, asserting "that the feeling, however suppressed or disguised, was more bitter in women than in men—in the clergy than in the laity—and in the north than in the south." While there is little or no evidence to support several of these generalizations, a number of observers agreed that the signs of prejudice were more in evidence in the North.[5] It would appear that some travelers (and some northern blacks) reached this conclusion on the basis of the stringent occupational discrimination and widespread aversion to any contact with blacks that were so prevalent in northern cities and largely missing in their southern counterparts, without taking into consideration the fact that prejudice took other forms in the urban centers of the slave area.

But even if there were variations in the intensity of manifestation of racial prejudice, none could deny its universality. "Though they have long since ceased to be slaves," wrote "a New-Yorker" in 1853, "they are still a wholly-distinct and an outcast class in the community."[6] "The negro and colored population," observed an English traveler in New Orleans rather more than a decade earlier, "are here, as everywhere else throughout the United States, the proscribed class."[7] A Providence black recalled that a white teacher at a Negro school threatened to flog any of his pupils who greeted him in public. "The feeling against the colored people," this writer noted, "was very bitter."[8] And the position of the black had, on the whole, actually improved somewhat when an English artisan working in New York during the Civil War wrote: "I have often heard the nature and condition of the coloured people discussed by my shopmates in America. I have met with a few well-conditioned men who look upon the blacks as rational beings; but the strongly expressed opinion of the majority was, that they are a soulless race, and I am satisfied that some of these people would shoot a black man with as little regard to moral consequences as they would a wild hog."[9] Similar comments might be added almost endlessly, but perhaps the English phrenologist George Combe summed it up succinctly when he wrote from Philadelphia, "So intense is the aversion even of many humane and educated persons in this city to the colored race, that apparently they would shrink back from the gate of Heaven, if it were opened by a colored man and showed colored people within. Only the warmly philanthropic view them as men."[10]

Doubtless motivated themselves by such views, as well as urged on by the populace, the executive and legislative officers of the cities and the states in which they were located passed a variety of laws and ordinances designed to prohibit or discourage the in-migration of blacks and to limit the freedom of those already resident or who might immigrate despite legal inhibitions. Only a few southern cities and Boston were located in jurisdictions that forbade all or some blacks from beyond the state boundaries to establish residence therein. These prohibitions, because they transcended the power of the municipal corporations, of necessity emanated from the state legislatures. But because of the concentration of free blacks in the urban areas, the cities and their residents were frequently in the forefront of those urging the passage of such legislation.

In 1820 the South Carolina legislature prohibited free blacks from entering the state and, to slow the growth of this portion of the population even further, permitted manumission only by legislative act. These provisions were not sufficiently comprehensive to satisfy the residents of a city deeply shaken by the Denmark Vesey "plot" to foment a slave uprising, and fifty-four Charlestonians petitioned the legislature to expel recently arrived free persons of color and to make manumission almost impossible. Though the legislators were unwilling to go that far, over the next three years they did extend the prohibition to prevent the return of black residents who had left the state and to require the jailing of black sailors while their ships were in port. Transgressors could be—and in the period immediately following the passage of the acts, at least, were—seized, imprisoned, and (if the offense were repeated) flogged.[11]

The legal provisions in Baltimore and New Orleans were similar, if somewhat less thorough. As early as 1807 the Maryland legislature limited the residence of free blacks entering the state to a period of two weeks, though an exception was made for sailors, wagon drivers, and messengers. In the 1830s, after the Nat Turner uprising and the publication of David Walker's *Appeal* (see pp. 226–27), these restrictions were strengthened and extended to include black residents of Maryland who left the state for over thirty days, unless they had received prior permission to return or were delayed by illness. In 1840 an additional exception was made for free persons of color who had visited Trinidad or British Guiana to examine the possibility of emigrating. There is, however, less evidence of rigorous enforcement than in Charleston.[12]

In Louisiana, the territorial legislature, perturbed by the influx of blacks from the West Indies in 1806, forbade the immigration of all free black males over fifteen years of age from that area, and the next year any immigration of free blacks from abroad was prohibited. But Governor W. C. C. Claiborne and other officials were unwilling to enforce these restraints, especially against those refugees from Santo Domingo who had fled to Cuba, only to be ousted from that island in 1809. In an attempt to ensure that their residence in Louisiana would be short, the legislature required free black male immigrants aged over fifteen years to post a bond to depart as soon as possible, but it appears that very few of the hundreds who arrived did so. As elsewhere, this restriction was extended to black residents who had left the state, but that prohibition was almost entirely eliminated by further legislation in 1831. Additionally, efforts to prevent the immigration of blacks born outside of Louisiana had been wholly ineffective, as the state acknowledged by the passage of legislation in 1830 and in 1843 permitting free blacks who had been in the state for more than five years to establish legal residence. Incidents of enforcement, despite the more stringent legislation of the 1840s, were so rare as to attract widespread attention.[13]

The situation in Boston was less clear. A Massachusetts law of 1788 provided "that no person being an African or Negro, other than a subject of the Emperor of Morocco, or a citizen of some one of the United States (to be evidenced by a certificate from the Secretary of the State of which he shall be a citizen) shall tarry within this Commonwealth, for a longer time than two months." The problem, of course, lay with the method specified for establishing citizenship in another state, for few if any blacks could have obtained such certificates even if they had known that they might be needed. Consequently, when the Boston selectmen, in 1800, warned 239 free persons of color (presumed to be in violation of the act) to leave the town, only 60 were listed as having arrived from outside the United States. This "warning out" affected between a fifth and a quarter of the adult blacks, and more than one-half of those listed had come from states contiguous to Massachusetts. In that same year the selectmen petitioned the legislature to amend the act so as to prohibit black immigration more successfully—a proposal that was again considered by the general court twenty years later.[14]

For St. Louis, the prohibition on free black immigration came late in the half-century. The original constitution of the state, in 1821, had, to be sure, contained a provision relating to the exclusion of black migrants that had sparked extensive debate in Congress. That document had stated it to be the "duty" of the legislature, "as soon as may be, to pass such laws as may be necessary . . . to prevent free negroes and mulattoes from coming to and settling in this State, under any pretext whatsoever." But the furor in Congress over this article apparently convinced Missouri legislators that "as soon as may be" must be construed as admitting of considerable delay, for it was not until 1843 that prohibitory legislation was finally enacted.[15]

Blacks were not absolutely prohibited by law from establishing residence in any other of the nation's fifteen largest cities, but that was not necessarily because of any great good will on the part of white urbanites. In the nation's capital in 1828 a grand jury urged (unsuccessfully, as it turned out) the passage of legislation to prevent the further entry of blacks, both slave and free, into the District of Columbia. More than a decade earlier, in 1815, Philadelphia members of the Pennsylvania legislature, pressured by private citizens and local officials, secured the appointment of a committee to consider the advisability of barring such immigration, and the issue was again raised after the Nat Turner revolt, but the necessary legislative support for the proposal could not be obtained. And early in 1842 the *Cincinnati Post* reported white residents mounting an organized effort that would "effectively prohibit negroes and mulattoes from purchasing or holding real estate" within the city limits.[16] On the other hand, as has been noted, no amount of ill will on the part of city residents could change the realities of urban life which made it difficult, if not impossible, to enforce restraints on black settlement. Consequently, this legislation remained, for urban blacks, more a threat than a barrier.

Not only were efforts made to prohibit entirely the in-migration of blacks into various states and cities, but laws were passed requiring all free blacks to register with local officials and, in some cases, to post bonds for their good behavior and to ensure that they would not become a charge upon the community. Bonds were generally required only of new arrivals. Such acts were designed both to make black immigration almost impossible and to discourage native blacks from remaining in the jurisdiction.

Washington's ordinance of April 14, 1821, may be cited as a particularly oppressive example of such legislation. It required all resident free blacks to register annually and

> to enter into bond with one good and responsible free white citizen, as surety, in the penalty of twenty dollars, conditioned for the good, sober, and orderly conduct of such person or persons of color, and his or her family, for the term of one year following the date of such bond, and that such person or persons, his or her family, nor any part thereof, shall not, during the said term of one year, become chargeable to the Corporation in any manner whatsoever, and that they will not become beggars in or about the streets.

Only after the bond was posted would the mayor issue a license to permit such free blacks to reside in the city for one year. The mayor might, at his discretion, demand additional bonds for the good behavior of children, and the bond for newly arrived free blacks was five hundred dollars, "with two good and responsibile free white citizens as sureties." Additionally, free Negroes were not permitted to change their places of residence until after such changes had been entered on their licenses by the registrar.[17] But such stringest legislation was difficult to enforce, as is shown by repeated council resolutions in-effectually attempting to secure compliance.[18]

Other cities had similar experiences with licensing laws. St. Louis had provided for registration of all free blacks as early as 1835, but fifteen years later fewer than one-half were apparently enrolled, and that was probably an unusually large number. In Cincinnati, as noted elsewhere (see pp. 104–5), the announcement in 1829 of the inten-tion to enforce the registration and bonding laws of 1804 and 1807 was sufficient to produce a furor in the community.[19]

As was the case with legal efforts to prevent or discourage the immigration and continued residence of free persons of color, other specific legal restrictions on blacks were frequently the product of state law and were, consequently, by no means peculiar to the urban areas. Black testimony against whites as well as jury service by free persons of color was prohibited in the sourthern states containing the major cities and in Ohio as well. In other northern states whose laws did not prohibit the empaneling of Negro jurors, black residents were, nevertheless, never summoned for jury duty. The Ohio legis-lators went further still, resolving in 1839 that "the blacks and mulat-toes, who may be residents within this State, have no constitutional right to present their petitions to the General Assembly for any pur-pose whatsoever, and that any reception of such petitions on the part of the General Assembly is a mere act of privilege or policy and not imposed by any expressed or implied power of the constitution."[20]

The restrictions and limitations on night meetings by Negroes, which were universal in the southern cities, and the curfews requiring blacks to be off the streets by nine or ten o'clock, which were almost as common, were often established by state law, although such legisla-tion was frequently supplemented by city ordinances. Although legis-latures and city councils in the free states did not enact such racially discriminatory curfew laws (which were admittedly intended primarily to control the slave population), the attitudes of northern white urban-ites were probably accurately reflected in a Philadelphia mayor's order of 1837 which specified, "Every colored person found in the street after [the posting of the] watch should be closely supervised by the officers of the night." The meeting restrictions were apparently enforced only spasmodically in the cities, where they were a matter of far less concern than in the countryside. Still, the prohibition could be, and was, invoked in times of perceived danger. In 1838, the mayor of St. Louis, disturbed by "the recent extensive distribution" of "in-cendiary abolitionist newspapers, tracts, and pictures," announced that the "usual permits from this office to colored people for social parties and religious meetings after night will be withheld until information is given of the hiding-places of the incendiaries, which must be known to

some of our colored people." In Charleston, at least, curfew regulations seem to have been rather rigorously enforced, but there would
appear to have been considerable laxity elsewhere, though a theater
entrepreneur in Washington in 1833 found the laws sufficiently in-
hibiting to black playgoers to petition the city council to relax their
application.[21]

As a practical matter, suffrage was controlled entirely by the state
constitutions or state (or federal, in the case of Washington) statutes,
including the city charters. In the cities of Charleston, Washington,
New Orleans, St. Louis, Louisville, and Cincinnati black voting was
prohibited by the earliest constitutions (or, in the case of Louisville,
the Kentucky constitution of 1799). Free blacks who could meet other
requirements, however, voted in Baltimore until the constitution was
amended to restrict suffrage to whites in 1810. In Philadelphia and
Pittsburgh they were apparently entitled to vote—though it is not
certain that they did so—until barred by the 1836 court decision in
Fogg v. *Hobbs* and the 1837 constitution. A vigorous protest of
Philadelphia blacks against this disfranchisement was unavailing. In
the New York cities no distinction by race was initially made among
voters, but this equality was gradually eroded. Blacks were first required to present certificates of freedom and later to meet property
qualifications higher than those established for whites; finally, when
the constitutional amendment of 1826 abolished the property
qualification for all other voters, it was retained for blacks. The
number of black voters was never very large in any of the New York
cities and became less significant as the half-century wore on. Providence blacks were entitled to vote until prohibited by law in 1822,
but, as a practical matter, the highly restrictive Rhode Island constitution effectively excluded Negro voting until it was replaced by a new
document in 1842. There is clear evidence that free persons of color
voted in considerable numbers after that date. Only in Boston, of the
nation's fifteen largest cities, were free blacks entitled to vote on equal
terms throughout the first half of the nineteenth century. There were
about 250 qualified black voters in that city in 1838 and rather more
than 350 seven years later, though only about forty percent of those
qualified apparently voted.[22]

A variety of state laws and city ordinances made it illegal for blacks
to do many things that were not prohibited to whites. In a number of
southern cities blacks might not purchase or possess (or sell) liquor,
guns, or powder, or might do so only with the permission of certain
persons, or at certain hours. In Charleston blacks might be flogged
for "whopping or hallooing . . . or . . . making a clamorous noise, or . . .
singing aloud any indecent song." They were also forbidden to smoke
a pipe or "segar" in "any street, lane, alley or open place," or to

walk with a cane or stick unless "blind or infirm." Not only would violaters be whipped, but they also should "forfeit every such pipe, segar, cane, club, or other stick, to any white person seizing the same." In the same city any blacks, including women and children, found in the vicinity of a fire were to be taken up and flogged unless actually assisting to extinguish the blaze. In Baltimore a Negro might own no more than one dog, and none at all after 1844 in Charleston. Blacks were not permitted to gamble with cards or dice in the latter city, or to play any game with whites in New Orleans. In 1829 free blacks without business requiring them to be there were prohibited from entering the grounds of the Capitol in Washington, and nine years later the new garden and promenade on the Charleston Battery were also declared off limits after 5 P.M. to all blacks not attending whites. Nor were these enactments empty threats, for a black school-master was twice physically expelled from the Capitol grounds in the 1840s. And in St. Louis all black primary education except private tutoring would appear to have been rendered illegal by the act of February 16, 1847, which provided, "No person shall keep or teach any school for the instruction of negroes or mulattoes, in reading and writing."[23]

Additionally, blacks were occasionally punished differently from whites for the same offense. In several southern cities free blacks, as well as slaves, might be whipped for violation of ordinances prescrib-ing only fines for white offenders, and in Baltimore, after 1839, a black arrested as a vagrant might be sold for a period of one year. In 1829 the governor of Louisiana ordered the sheriff in New Orleans not to "expose *white* criminals, condemned to hard labor, to the gaze of the populace on the public streets." There was a great deal of local opposition to this direction, for it was thought to be designed solely for the benefit of one Louis Gayare, a wealthy and well-connected Creole who had recently been convicted of stabbing his mother-in-law to death. Because of the very considerable public pressure the order was revoked almost as soon as it was issued. More lasting was the 1836 act of the Maryland legislature permitting free blacks, who had pre-viously been confined in the penitentiary, to be sold outside of the state for a term of years upon conviction of a second serious crime. Given the impossibility of monitoring the status of these individuals, the result would doubtless be the permanent enslavement of the of-fender. In other cases the legal distinctions involved no offense at all, but simply prescribed or permitted different treatment of blacks and whites. In Baltimore black apprentices need not be taught to read and write and, unlike whites, might, with the approval of the orphans' court, be sold to any other person in the county for the remainder of their apprenticeship. In Charleston in the late 1840s a free person of color who failed to pay his taxes might be sentenced to work on the treadmill for up to one month. A decade earlier blacks, bond or free, who contracted smallpox in Louisville were (unlike whites) required to enter the smallpox hospital, and the authorities were authorized to use force to accomplish the transfer. To prevent concealment of black victims, the ordinance also provided that any householder who failed to report a case of smallpox contracted by a Negro should be fined fifty dollars. And in Maryland an unsuccessful effort was made to exclude free persons of color from the benefits of the insolvency laws and, instead, require them to be sold (for a period of time) for the payment of their debts.[24]

The determination to maintain the subordinate status of the black population was also obvious in the widespread exclusion of blacks from many facilities and their segregation in others. "In most of the Free States," wrote James Freeman Clarke in 1859, "they are not allowed to vote, nor admitted into the public schools, are driven from places of public amusement and from public conveyances, and are not permitted by social sentiment to engage in more than ten or twelve out of the three hundred and more occupations set down in the census for the white male population." While Clarke's statement contains some slight hyperbole, it is far more notable for its omissions than its exaggerations, and conditions were considerably worse before 1850 then they were a decade later. Discrimination in employment was extreme in the northern cities; segregation in churches was well-nigh universal; and blacks were segregated in the public schools of every city from which they were not excluded (see chapters 2, 10, and 11).[25]

The refusal to admit blacks to public conveyances would appear to have been usual but not universal. They were seated in the Brooklyn cars, for instance, but in New York were wholly excluded from the omnibuses and permitted to ride only on the outside platform of the horsecars, despite the fact that they paid full fare. These conditions persisted until the mid-1850s when Elizabeth Jennings, a black teacher, and the Heidelberg-educated J. C. W. Pennington, a black Presbyterian minister, boarded the cars, brought suit against those who removed them, and secured access to public transportation. In New Orleans, free persons of color were carried on the Lake Pontchartrain Railroad, but only in separate cars. Black efforts to end these discriminatory practices met with little success in Louisiana, however. In the summer of 1833 a dozen or so free Negroes boarded a car reserved for whites, and a melee followed in which the blacks fired upon their assailants. The trespassers were overpowered, however, and their leader was beaten and jailed.[26]

Clarke was not quite accurate in saying that blacks were universally "driven from places of public amusement." They were, to be sure, excluded from most of the "public gardens," museums and galleries, and from some individual theaters. In Charleston they were prohibited by law from attending theaters unless serving as attendants to whites, and in Cincinati exclusion by custom appears to have been almost universal. It was reported that over the door of one Cincinati theater were inscribed the words, "Niggers and dogs not admitted." In most of the urban theaters, however—from New York to New Orleans and from Washington to St. Louis—blacks were admitted but required to take seats set aside for them in the galleries. If there were no galleries, other arrangements might be made; in the second decade of the nineteenth century the proprietors of the Washington Gardens in Boston announced, "SEATS are likewise partitioned off for *People of Colour.*" Even such segregated facilities might be denied to blacks on occasion if the play presented was thought to be "unsuitable." Washington newspapers in 1838 criticized one theater for admitting Negroes to performances of *Othello,* and later in the same year public clamor moved the management to bar blacks from performances of *The Gladiator*—a drama based on the revolt of Spartacus. Separation of the races in theaters was required by law in New Orleans, where free blacks taking seats reserved for whites were subject to a stiff fine. But in most cities custom and the force of public opinion were sufficient to ensure the preservation of the pattern of segregation.[27]

Penal, reform, and humane institutions were also usually segregated. In Philadelphia there was such public opposition to admitting black juveniles to the house of refuge—and very few were, in fact, received—that the managers launched and carried through a campaign to build a separate facility for Negroes, arguing that the only real alternatives were racial segregation or black exclusion. In the New York almshouse the lying-in wards for blacks and whites were placed in different wings, and though both black and white women were assigned to oakum picking, they worked in separate rooms. The New Orleans city council, in 1827, provided that black and white criminals sentenced to hard labor should be separated and differently clothed. It was at about the same time that a traveler noted that black prisoners in the Philadelphia County jail were not permitted to sit on the same benches as white prisoners, and about a decade later the visitors of the Baltimore jail expressed gratification that an expansion of facilities had made possible the completion of cells for Negroes, permitting the warden "to keep the black men . . . entirely separate from the whites." It is not clear that inmates in New York's city prisons were rigidly segregated, but when Charles Dickens, in the early 1840s, commented on the "unwholesome" condition of the lowest level of cells in the "Tombs," the jailor acknowledged the accuracy of the observation by replying, "Why, we *do* only put colored people in 'em. That's the truth." And in 1848 the commissioners of the asylum assured the Washington city officials that white and black paupers "are not permitted to mingle together," and that the same was true in the workhouse, "so far as we are able to control the matter." Even those who were ill were separated, by virtue of the fact that two rooms could now be set aside for the care of the sick.[28]

In death, as in life, the urban black was likely to be set apart. Even blacks who were members of the congregation could not be buried in the graveyard of Philadelphia's St. James Episcopal Church at the end of the first half of the nineteenth century. In Baltimore segregated interments were only slightly less universal. There, in 1818, of 574 reported black burials, 427 were in the segregated public burial grounds (East Potter's Field, West Potter's Field, and the almshouse) and 105 more Negroes were laid to rest in the cemetery of the African Methodist Church. Only 42 Negro bodies were interred in other church cemeteries, and some of those may have been segregated. Needless to say, blacks were almost always excluded from the new garden cemeteries, such as Laurel Hill near Philadelphia, when they began to be established late in the period. In Louisville, though the public burial ground was not designated as a pauper cemetery and whites were encouraged to purchase lots, all "Africans and their descendents" were interred in a single segment of the field, and similar circumstances existed in Washington early in the century. The superintendent of the city burial ground in Charleston was required not only to segregate the dead but also to record their interments in separate books. In New Orleans, at the beginning of the second third of the nineteenth century, the public burial grounds were first divided between Catholics and Protestants, then between whites and blacks, and, finally, between free Negroes and slaves. It was probably not so much the fear of being found in undesirable company when the last trump sounded as the fact that black graves attract black mourners that inspired such regulations.[29]

There seemed to be no end to the forms prejudice took. Though a graduate of the University of Glasgow, Dr. James McCune Smith was refused membership in the New York Academy of Medicine, and he and the Reverend Charles B. Ray were both ousted from the World Temperance Convention. When the "National Exhibition of American Manufactures and Products of Mechanical Arts" was held in Washington in 1846, the managers graciously set aside a single evening when people of color would be permitted to view the exhibits. And the Zoological Institute in New York not only excluded Negroes from membership but advertised that fact in the apparent belief (probably correct) that such exclusion would make membership more attractive to whites. In the 1830s the white bands which were to supply music for some of Philadelphia's volunteer fire companies in their annual parade, offended by the fact that some companies had secured black bands, refused to participate. As a result, separate parades were held. It may be, of course, that the white musicians shrank from having their performances compared with that of some of their Negro competitors, for Francis Johnson's black band was certainly the leading musical group in Philadelphia at this time. But when Johnson's band accompanied the Pennsylvania State Fencibles to a muster of elite militia units in Providence, it was not permitted to participate. Earlier still, in the summer of 1818, a proposal by a group of young black men to form a volunteer fire company provoked a vigorous response from the white "fire laddies." Representatives of twenty-five companies approved a resolution which observed ominously that "the formation of fire-engine and hose companies by persons of color will be productive of serious injury to the peace and safety of citizens in time of fire," and urged all Philadelphians to withhold their support. More than two-thirds of the companies in the metropolitan area eventually associated themselves with this protest, and a meeting of black leaders, chaired by James Forten, publicly urged that the plan be abandoned. In the face of such negative reactions, the members of the African Fire Association met and, after declaring that they "did not expect dissatisfaction," and observing sorrowfully that they had been "influenced solely by a wish to make themselves useful," voted to disband.[30]

The view of the Negro as grossly inferior to the white (and perhaps, in some measure, subhuman), which both inspired and was reinforced by these discriminations, gave rise to a variety of slights, insults, and assaults that served no conceivable social purpose, however twisted and malign, save that of bolstering the ego of the participating whites. When blacks were brought before magistrates on any save the most serious charges, the court reporters made them figures of fun—exaggerating (or fabricating) their mannerisms, dialect, and ignorance of legal forms. On the street and at work the ridicule was even more apparent, and ridicule easily escalated to insult and to violence. Around any corner and down any street—at work, at play, or at prayer—urban blacks were apt to be met by curses, missiles, and physical assault. They were pushed from the sidewalks in Boston and Providence, stoned in Providence and Philadelphia, and casually cuffed aside almost everywhere. In the City of Brotherly Love their worship services were disrupted—and two persons killed in the panic—by "a party of young, well dressed white men" who threw into the stove substances that gave off noxious and choking fumes. In the same city and in New Orleans nearly identical incidents occurred that speak volumes about the pervasiveness of both racial prejudice and human depravity. In each case a half-grown Negro boy was seized by workmen and thrust into boiling tar for little apparent reason save that the child and the tar were both available.[31]

This is not to say that blacks were never treated fairly by individuals or accorded justice by city officials, for such was clearly not the case. In the 1850s the horsecars of New York and the schools of Boston were desegregated. Though the culprit who thrust a black child's hands into hot tar in New Orleans escaped justice, he did so only by evading a determined white pursuer. Even when it was clear that an ordinance had been violated, unusual efforts were sometimes made to effect more perfect justice. In 1826 Charles Buchanan, a free black of Washington, ran afoul of the law. The act in question required a heavy tax to be paid on slaves of nonresidents residing in the city without their owners. Though he had such a slave in his household, Buchanan had failed to pay the tax and was charged and convicted under the ordinance and assessed a fine, a portion of which was forfeit to the constable and the informer in the case. The city council, however, not only remitted the portion of the fine accruing to the city, but also ordered that the constable and informer be paid from city funds, and added a final section to the ordinance, an addition that makes clear the reasons for the council's actions: "That the said Charles Buchanan and his wife Fanny, a slave, the property of Mrs. Sally Duval, who resides beyond the limits of this Corporation, be, and they are hereby authorized to reside and keep house together, without liability to the provisions or penalties of the acts heretofore passed imposing taxes on slaves the property of non-residents."[32]

Doubtless many blacks in the nation's largest cities lived out their lives without ever having been the victim of an assault by whites or excluded from any place they tried to enter. But the price by which this peace was purchased was a careful conformity to discriminatory law and custom, a scrupulous avoidance of certain portions of the city at certain times of the day, an assiduous cultivation of acceptable mien and carriage, and a fair amount of luck. But not one sentient black in antebellum American could escape the knowledge that he lived in a white land under a white government that administered white law for the benefit of a white population, and that in the eyes of all these he was a being inferior to all but the most base and degraded of the whites, and that no amount of conformity to white mores and customs or acceptance of white values could change that reality. Henry Bradshaw Fearon had hardly overstated the case when he wrote:

There exists a penal law deeply written in the *minds* of the whole white population, which subjects their coloured fellow-citizens to unconditional contumely and never-ceasing insult. No respectability, however unquestionable,—no property, however large,—no character, however unblemished,—will gain a man whose body is (in American estimation) *cursed* with even a twentieth portion of the blood of his African ancestry, admission into society!!! They are considered as mere Pariahs—as outcasts and vagrants upon the face of the earth![33]

6 Race Riot:
Prejudice Explodes

The antebellum American city nurtured violence. Crime rates were high, assaults common, riots frequent, and the men and organizations charged with preserving the peace were constitutionally and legally weak, usually timorous and frequently palsied to the verge of inactivity by the agonizing possibility that the gibber of the mob was the voice of the people, which (being also the voice of God) it was heresy and sacrilege, as well as treason, to oppose. The result was that when riots erupted, the constabulary, the police, and the watch were usually ineffectual, often dilatory, sometimes unlocatable, and occasionally even supportive of the purposes of the mob. A bank failure, an election, a jailbreak, a labor dispute, opposition to technological change, an increase in bread prices, a struggle for possession of a hydrant at a fire, anti-Catholicism, opposition to foreign-born residents, or racial prejudice—any of these or something else entirely might aggregate individual antipathies, fears, and anger into a mob bent on violent action.

If the riot was the ultimate expression of the city's violent nature, to the urban black (when he was the target) it was the ultimate expression of racial prejudice. In the cities as elsewhere, the free blacks met with degrading restrictions and exclusions. Though these sprang from a pervasive and often institutionalized racial antipathy, the Negro encountered and endured them as an individual, and by playing an assigned role or by skillfully manipulating the elements of the society and the economy, he could in some measure minimize their impact upon him. But the mob raging through the black ghetto made no distinction save those of color and availability—it was the ultimate expression of racial prejudice in that nothing else mattered.

In a discussion of riotous assaults upon urban blacks, one of the major problems is that of determining which incidents to include. In some instances, for example, although the formation of a mob was sparked by racial antipathy and its intentions probably were to initiate assaults upon blacks and upon identifiable black institutions, it did not, in fact, carry out the envisaged attacks. Charleston and New Orleans offer cases in point. In New Orleans on the last Sunday in August, 1835, two or three hundred white mechanics assembled in the Place d'Armes to protest the employment of "slaves in the mechanical arts" and, it appears, with the intention of engaging in some sort of aggressive action. But the militia was mustered with alacrity and the notoriously inept city guard (police) rose to the occasion. The quick arrest of the leading spirits, including "the drunken spokesman of the assembly—a ragamuffin named Lee," and the threat of further action brought a speedy termination to the affair.[1] The intended target of the Charleston mob which assembled in July of 1849 is more certain— they hoped to destroy a new Episcopal church structure on the corner of Beaufain and Willson streets, which was to be occupied by blacks, free and slave. It is doubtful, however, that the assembled whites were offended by the religious activities of the Charleston Negroes. More likely the structure was merely a convenient physical object upon which to vent their racially oriented anger and frustration, which were probably generated by a number of irritations and dissatisfactions, including the extensive employment of free black and slave artisans. In the event, the timely intervention of the authorities dispersed the mob and prevented an attack upon the church, though not without some difficulty.[2] In each of these instances racial antipathies and perceived threats from the black population sparked the assembling of a mob which was apparently prepared to perform some act of physical force, but because of the effective exercise of the police power, no riotous assault upon the black community occurred.

The activities of the Baltimore mob of June 20–21, 1812, display, perhaps, an even greater degree of ambivalence. There can be no doubt that the assemblage was essentially anti-English in spirit and directed specifically against the political opponents of the Madison administration.[3] There is no evidence that, in the initial formation of the mob, racial antipathies played any role, but after destroying the *Federal Republican* offices and dismasting a number of ships, "in the wantonness of their cruelty the unfortunate blacks attracted their attention." Some houses owned by John Briscoe, a free man of color who was "charged with expressions of affection for the British nation," were destroyed, and it was rumored that an attack would also be made upon a Negro church. The arrival of a troop of horse prevented this action if it was, in fact, even contemplated.[4] It would appear that this mob was not antiblack and that the attack on Briscoe's property was not racially motivated, but it is possible that the existence of the riotous assembly permitted actions to be taken and others proposed which had their origin in pervasive racial prejudice.

In other cases mob action was taken against individual blacks, doubtless at least in part because of their color, but there was no general assault upon the Negro population, as, for example, in the case of the St. Louis mob action in April, 1836. Francis L. McIntosh, a black steamboat hand from Pittsburgh, forced a deputy constable to release another steamboatman taken into custody. When peace officers attempted to arrest McIntosh for this action he resisted, killing Deputy Sheriff George Hammond and wounding Deputy Constable William Mull. Subsequently overpowered and incarcerated to await trial, McIntosh was taken from the jail by a mob and burned alive. In the next month a prominent local judge with the wonderfully appropriate name of Lawless dismissed all charges against the ringleaders of the mob on the ground that they were caught up in an "electric frenzy" produced by abolitionist agitation![5]

Somewhat analogous, though much less violent, was the action taken in Albany on May 14, 1832. Continually disturbed by the noise and disorder emanating from a house of Lodge Street between Beaver and Howard occupied by several families, both black and white, a number of residents of the locality determined to eliminate the nuisance. They wholly destroyed the structure, apparently without injury to any of the occupants. The mayor, the high constable, and several watchmen were on the scene, "but were unable to quell the disturbance until the building was razed to the ground."[6] It is quite likely that the building was considered a "nuisance" because (in addition to other complaints) it housed blacks. It seems almost certain, therefore, that both the Albany and the St. Louis mob actions were racially motivated but very narrowly focused. In each city the black community doubtless felt some trepidation, but in neither case does it appear that there existed any impetus for or likelihood of further or more indiscriminate assault.

In at least seven of the fifteen cities studied, however, there occurred one or more incidents that can unquestionably be characterized as race riots. The mobs were racially motivated, their attacks on Negroes appear to have been almost entirely indiscriminate, they almost always invaded black residential areas, and the targets of their violence were, with a bare handful of exceptions, only blacks. The cities in which these riots occurred were Philadelphia, Cincinnati, Providence, New York, Boston, Pittsburgh, and Washington, and the few nonblack mob targets were whites associated with (or accused of) abolitionist activity.

The Snow Riot (or "Snow Storm") that erupted in Washington in August 1835 was somewhat more limited in scope than some of the other episodes. A series of unrelated events was thought to have contributed to the outbreak of violence on the nights of August 11 and 12. Dr. Reuben Crandall (rumored to be the brother of the notorious Prudence Crandall) was arrested on a charge of disseminating seditious (i.e., abolitionist) literature, and some of the residents of the capital, convinced that such publications were designed to encourage slave insurrection, seem to have connected Crandall's alleged activities with the attack made upon Mrs. William Thornton (a prominent Washington matron) during the previous week by a slave whom she surprised in the act of burglarizing her house. The raw material for the formation of a mob was available in larger than normal amounts because the civilian artisans at the Navy Yard were on strike as a result of a dispute with the commandant involving the disappearance of a large quantity of copper bolts and an edict barring lunch pails from the facility. When the size of the crowd collected before City Hall on the morning of August 12 caused the authorities to postpone Crandall's trial, a number of the workingmen assembled recalled (or were reminded) that Beverly Snow, a free black who operated a restaurant at Sixth Street and Pennsylvania Avenue much favored by well-to-do Washingtonians, had (it was rumored) spoken of the wives and daughters of "honest mechanics" in a disrespectful and belittling fashion. The mob of some two hundred, joined by another two or three hundred boys and other onlookers, then surged down Louisiana Avenue and Sixth Street to Snow's establishment. The proprietor, however, escaped through a sewer and left the city. The authorities were ill-prepared to deal with this threat to the peace—there were only three officers (aside from the small night watch, that was intended primarily as an animated alarm system) and the militia organization had wholly collapsed in recent years. For some eight hours the mob, unmolested and unmolesting, milled around the restaurant. The members of the crowd were apparently unwilling to take further action by daylight, but at about six o'clock a marshal attempted to disperse the remnants of the dwindling body with the assistance of an unarmed posse and was repulsed. The mob now began its work of destruction. After wrecking Snow's premises, the rioters commenced their assault on the black community (mostly in the Capitol Hill area), severely damaging the Cook and Smothers schoolhouses and breaking the windows of one Negro church. The mob was finally dispersed by a substantial body of armed citizens under the command of Major General Walter Jones. Although there were some isolated episodes on the thirteenth, the reassembly of over a hundred of Jones's forces inhibited further riotous activity. Amazingly, no deaths or serious injuries appear to have occurred.[7] A number of arrests followed, and, despite some threats from persons purporting to speak for "the mechanics of the city," the judicial process proceeded without interruption.[8]

These events have been recounted in some detail because they illustrate the interrelationships and reinforcement patterns among various elements of motivation contributing to the outbreak of racial violence. In most riots the evolution was admittedly less complex, but

the resentment of abolitionist agitation and the ill-defined belief that
the antislavery movement in some way constituted a threat to the
white workingman were persistent (though sometimes unstated) components of much antiblack mob activity. The Snow Riot appears to
have followed a rather precise step-by-step pattern of development
from antiabolitionist protest, to a determination to punish (or perhaps
only frighten) an individual Negro for unacceptably assertive behavior, to a more generalized movement against the city's free blacks,
focusing particularly on those symbols of black advancement and instruments of black community development, the school and the
church.

The anatomy of other riots may well have been equally complex,
but the paucity of information about them prevents firm conclusions.
Many, indeed, are known only from passing, oblique, or cryptic references. Of the several racial mob actions in Pittsburgh in the 1830s, the
only one for which there is even limited data is that of April 27, 1839.
This riot was apparently an uncomplicated act of general racial aggres-
sion (sparked by an interracial fistfight) which left a number of Negro
dwellings damaged, including that of John B. Vashon, a leader of the
Pittsburgh black community. Its most notable result was the formation
of a unique interracial peacekeeping force.[9] About the Boston riot of
July 14, 1826, nothing is known save that a white mob invaded "Nigger Hill"—the north side of Beacon Hill and the most concentrated
black ghetto in the United States—and destroyed several houses.
There had been rioting in the Broad Street area (involving Irish
workmen) for several days prior to the fourteenth, and the incursion
into the Negro section may have been in some way related to those
events. It could hardly have been a direct spillover, however, for
Broad Street is on the opposite side of the peninsula from "Nigger
Hill."[10]

Antebellum Boston's other major racial clash occurred near North
Square on Sunday, August 27, 1843, and was sparked by an assault,
physical and verbal, by a handful of white sailors on four blacks. But
when the Negroes defended themselves a crowd of several hundred
quickly gathered, and, in the spirit of the Sabbath, the cry of "Kill the
niggers" was raised. Within minutes the rioters were "breathing out
threatenings against the colored people, and every colored person that
appeared in the street was beset and beaten, some of them nearly to
death." The mob was finally dispersed by the joint efforts of the police
and fire personnel. There were a number of injuries, some of them
quite serious. It is interesting to note that there were no sailors or
blacks among the persons arrested, and that all were Irish, which
(together with the rapidity with which the mob assembled) strongly
suggests that though the altercation may have furnished the occasion

for the outbreak of violence, the real causes lay closer to race hatred.[11]

Though the decade of the 1830s in New York was apparently marked by numerous racial assaults by crowds of whites, most were too small-scale and short-lived to reach riot proportions.[12] And of the extensive riots in New York in the first half of the nineteenth century, only that of July 1834 was strongly marked by racial conflict. The violent election riots that spring had been followed by spasmodic mob actions on a smaller scale, all of which doubtless contributed to the creation of a climate conducive to violence. The targets of the July riots were both abolitionists and blacks. The initial clash came on July 7 when a predominantly Negro audience listening to an abolitionist sermon delivered by a black minister was ousted from Chatham Street Chapel. This event was followed by two days of antiabolitionist meetings, newspaper agitation, and complaints about black "insolence." On July 10, violence again erupted, and for the next three days mobs estimated at up to twenty thousand persons attacked white and black churches, the Bowery Theater, whose stage manager was English and, hence, presumed to be an abolitionist sympathizer, and the houses of both blacks and abolitionists. "The cabin of the poor Negro, and the temples dedicated to the service of the living God," one New York newspaper lamented after the first night of renewed rioting, "are alike the objects of the blind fury." The determined, but reasonably restrained, intervention by the militia on the night of the eleventh and twelfth and the arrest of about one hundred fifty of the ringleaders effectively ended the mob violence. Except for the assaults connected with the clearing of Chatham Street Chapel on July 7, the rioters appear to have committed remarkably few personal attacks, but at least twenty blacks suffered property loss, and two Negro churches were heavily damaged.[13] One of the most notable aspects of the riotous activities was the extent to which the rioters appeared to respond to directions from recognized leaders and the manner in which the different segments of the mob (sometimes widely separated) kept in constant communication through runners.[14] In few riots were antiabolitionist and anti-Negro sentiments more inextricably interwoven. Unlike the "Snow Storm" mobs in Washington in the following year, the New York rioters of 1834 did not abandon their attacks on abolitionists when they began to assault Negroes, but continued to direct their violence against both targets at the same time. The attacks on black property and black churches, therefore, did not constitute a separate and later stage in the evolution of mob activity, reached by progression only after the mob had exhausted its ability to assault its initial target; rather, antiblack sentiment and action constituted an integral part of both the origin and the continuing activity of the mob.[15]

In contrast, the riotous assaults on free blacks in Providence appear to have resulted from unalloyed racial antagonisms. The Hardscrabble Riot of October 18, 1924, was apparently sparked by an earlier controversy over right-of-way on the city's sidewalks. On the night of the eighteenth a mob descended on Hardscrabble—an area of concentrated poor black residences on the northern outskirts of the city. There, in a matter of four or five hours, some forty or fifty white men, in the presence of a thousand interested (and presumably approving) spectators, destroyed every house in the settlement and then carried off the household goods. Despite the presence of police officers at the scene, no effort was made to halt the destruction—one watchman would later testify that he "considered he was doing his duty by going there and keeping as still as possible." Of the four whites charged in connection with the destruction, two were acquitted and the other two freed on a legal technicality after conviction. It seems clear that many Providence citizens agreed with the defense attorney's contention that Hardscrabble "was the resort of the most corrupt part of the black population, who supported their debaucheries and riots by carrying thither the plunder of their masters and pawning it for a participation in these disgusting scenes," and that "there was not a sober citizen in the town who could regret" its destruction.[16]

Providence's better known Snowtown Riot of September 1831 is also illustrative of racial antagonism in its purest form. By this date Snowtown (in the Smith Street–Olney Lane area of northern Providence) had replaced Hardscrabble as the major residential area for poor blacks, and there were similar complaints about its depravity. In addition to "the ordinary evils of houses of ill fame," a committee of the town observed, the respectable residents in the surrounding area had just cause to complain "of the midnight revels, the succession of severe and bloody affrays, and of the frequent, bold and open riots, carrying fear and alarm into numerous respectable families." The committee recorded its unanimous opinion that the area and its inhabitants "constituted a continuing nuisance of the most offensive character; and that justice to our fellow citizens requires that a prompt, speedy and effectual remedy should be provided."[17] Other less respected and respectable residents of the town obviously agreed that a "remedy should be provided," though it appears that darkness of skin was more offensive to them than the blackness of vice and corruption. On the night of September 21, 1831, an altercation between whites and Negroes at "some houses of ill fame on Olney's lane occupied by blacks" was followed by two successive forays by an increasing number of whites into Snowtown. On the second incursion (by a mob numbering about one hundred), after some warning shots had been fired, an unidentified Negro man—crying out, "Is this the way the blacks are to live, to be obliged to defend themselves from stones?"—shot and killed a white sailor. Within a half-hour a large and angry mob descended upon Snowtown and began the attacks on and destruction of black-occupied dwellings that would extend over a period of four days.

The police power of the town was utterly inadequate to quell the riot (though arrests were made), and the militia, when ordered out by the governor, initially proved to be almost equally ineffective. In the case of the Hardscrabble Riot, the mob action was as short as it was violent, but in this case the destruction continued night after night, and the town authorities became increasingly willing to employ any measures necessary to restore order. On the night of the twenty-fourth the riot was terminated abruptly when the harried militia fired a murderous volley into the mob, mortally wounding four men—a sailor and three artisans—and injuring fourteen others. At an overflowing town meeting the next day, the assembled citizens lamented both the riot and the loss of life incurred in quelling it, but resolved that the civil authorities were entirely justified in using such force (the sheriff had instructed the militia captain to fire), especially in view of "the open and lawless attack on private property." And it was doubtless the destruction of property and the defiance of authority that disturbed the town officials, not the assault upon the blacks (which the investigating committee implied was justifiable). It is worthy of note that the seventeen or eighteen houses destroyed or damaged in the riot were (insofar as is known) all owned by whites and that among these property owners were some of Providence's leading citizens, including the socially prominent Nicholas Brown, whose estate, two years later, was assessed for local taxation at more than half a million dollars.[18]

From all evidence, then, the Providence race riots appear to have been simple, uncomplicated expressions of racial antipathy. The attribution to the black population of vile habits and vicious practices—which was doubtless, in part, accurate—should be seen as symptomatic of these racial prejudices, not as a separate causative factor. It is likely that some considerable portion of the free persons of color were morally depraved—a condition at least in part related to the fact that almost the whole of the black population was economically deprived. But in this instance the Providence Negroes had reason to rejoice in their deprivation, for if they, rather than their white landlords, had owned their dwellings, Snowtown might well have been as thoroughly destroyed as was Hardscrabble seven years before.

The two cities yet to be discussed—Cincinnati and Philadelphia—were those most prone to racial violence. Between 1834 and 1842 there was a major race riot in one or the other of them in every year except 1837 (and, perhaps, 1840).[19] In none of the four major outbreaks in Cincinnati—in 1829, 1836, 1839, and 1841—does it appear that opposition to abolitionism or any other factor except racial antipathy played a significant role in the genesis of the riot, though that of 1839 was very narrowly focused on the activities of a single individual. In the City of Brotherly Love the proximate cause of the riot of 1838 was clearly antiabolitionism, but the mob actions of 1829, 1834, 1835, 1842, and 1849 seem to have been, from the beginning, unalloyed expressions of race hatred.

Little purpose would be served by detailed discussions of all these violent interludes. The Philadelphia riot of November 22, 1829, was short-lived and relatively mild, while the Cincinnati mob of September 27, 1839, contained fewer than fifty persons and contented itself with the destruction of a single building. The Philadelphia riot of October 9, 1849, though it lasted but a day and a night, was extremely violent, resulting in three deaths, many injuries, and the complete destruction of a tavern and a number of adjacent dwellings before disorder was finally suppressed by a strong force of militia.[20] These are notable only because the 1829 riot was the first significant anti-Negro outbreak in Philadelphia and because the other two mob actions were each directed against a single building—the black-operated California House in Philadelphia and the dwelling of "Negro doctor" John Woodward in Cincinnati.[21]

The first race riot in Cincinnati also occurred in 1829. As the city's black population increased fourfold between 1810 and 1820 and seemed destined to double again in the third decade of the century, many white Cincinnatians became disturbed. They pointed out that the restrictive statutes enacted in the first five years of Ohio's statehood were not being enforced and, in particular, that the acts of 1804 and 1807, requiring all Negroes to register and those arriving in Ohio after the enactment of the statute to post five-hundred-dollar bonds forfeitable for breach of peace or receipt of public poor relief, had become dead letters. As a result of these pressures (and a ward election contested on the issue), the township trustees announced their intention to enforce the discriminatory legislation. The Cincinnati blacks asked for a delay in the initiation of enforcement and pursued alternative courses of action—they petitioned the Ohio legislature for a repeal of the acts, and they investigated the possibility of immigration to Canada. Apparently impatient with the continued presence of the blacks and the failure of the authorities to act against them, on the night of August 22 about three hundred whites attacked the dwellings of a small number (30–40, perhaps) of free persons of color. Realizing that they could not expect city authorities to intervene, the blacks defended themselves with vigor, firing into the mob. At least one rioter was killed and others wounded, and the mob dispersed. The police quickly arrested ten Negroes and seven whites, but the mayor later discharged all of the blacks (noting that they had acted in self-defense), though he imposed relatively heavy fines upon the whites. There is no reason to believe that the black codes were, in fact, enforced in Cincinnati and little evidence to support the assertion that a large percentage of the city's blacks immigrated to Canada. In this instance, at least, the black community appears to have been totally victorious.[22]

Such Negro successes were not notable, however, for the remainder of the half-century. Despite limited black resistance, riot after riot raged through the black residential areas in both Cincinnati and Philadelphia. In the 1838 Pennsylvania Hall Riot, Philadelphia Negroes admittedly did not suffer greatly. The genesis of the outbreak was a series of interracial abolitionist meetings in the newly completed Pennsylvania Hall in mid-May, and that building remained the primary target of the mob. After the building's destruction by the rioters on the night of May 17, violent clashes between whites and blacks continued on the following night, when a black church was attacked and a black orphan asylum set ablaze. But in comparison with other riots of the period in these cities, both the physical assaults and the property destruction were limited. The destructive instincts of the greater portion of the mob were apparently satisfied by the initial burning of Pennsylvania Hall.[23]

The Philadelphia riot of July 13-14, 1835, and that in Cincinnati on April 11, 1836, might be characterized as moderately violent and destructive outbreaks. Each was sparked by an isolated incident not essentially racial in nature. In Cincinnati two boys—one white and one black—engaged in a street fight from which the black emerged victorious. In Philadelphia the event was more serious—a near-fatal assault with a hatchet upon Robert R. Stewart, former U.S. consul in Trinidad, by a "half-witted" young Cuban black whom Stewart had brought back with him from the Caribbean. In each city, mobs invaded the black residential areas, assaulted any Negroes they encountered, and set fire to a number of dwellings, compelling large numbers of the black residents (some hundreds in Philadelphia) to flee for their lives. The governor of the state moved with dispatch in Ohio, and a declaration of martial law and the threat of military force brought the disorder to a halt in Cincinnati after one night of violence and terror, but not before several blacks had died. After two days of somewhat less intense violence (there were apparently no deaths), the Philadelphia police were able to restore order without military intervention, perhaps assisted by the rumor (apparently accurate) that fifty to sixty armed and determined black men had barricaded themselves in a building behind the police lines. The fact that such isolated incidents could provoke violence of this nature speaks volumes about the depth and pervasiveness of the racial animosity that seethed beneath the surface of the cities.[24]

The Philadelphia riot of 1842 differed from these only in that it began with a general and unprovoked attack upon the free persons of color. On August 1 a number of Philadelphia blacks joined in a parade in commemoration of the end of slavery in the British West Indies. Though ostensibly a temperance assembly, the marchers left no doubt of their real purpose by the banners they carried. This procession was attacked by a large and hostile crowd, and two nights of assault and arson followed. Though it does not appear that any deaths resulted, there were numerous serious injuries resulting from vicious assaults by the mob on every black encountered and by periodic resistance by the intended victims. Both the Negro Presbyterian church and a nearly completed black-owned assembly hall were burned to their foundations, and many private dwellings also suffered extensive depredations. When the sheriff attempted to restore order, his posse was chased through the streets in a rout. The mob's control of that portion of the city (along the Philadelphia-Southwark boundary) was finally broken by the mayor's aggressive use of additional police and militia.[25]

Perhaps the most violent antiblack outbreaks in these two riotous cities were the 1834 Philadelphia riot and that of 1841 in Cincinnati. In late July and August of 1834 portions of the Philadelphia press had commented in understanding if not approving tones on the recent New York riot described earlier. These observations were interspersed with complaints about black incivility, and, additionally, minor assaults upon blacks occurred with increasing frequency. On the night of August 12 a white mob descended upon "a notorious spot in South street, near Eighth, where the illegal amusement of flying horses is carried on." It appears that the "flying horses" were ridden indiscriminately by blacks and whites, and that altercations arose over seating priorities. After wrecking this establishment, the mob turned to the purposeful assault upon blacks and the distruction of their property. Over the next three nights, two Negro churches and more than thirty houses occupied by free persons of color were destroyed or damaged and their contents broken up or carried away. White householders remained undisturbed even though their dwellings were adjacent to the buildings destroyed. Many blacks were beaten, a number seriously injured, and at least one—Stephen Jones—died of his wounds. Hundreds were forced to flee the area. A sheriff's posse, additional police with the mayor at their head, and local militia eventually restored order—a task made more difficult because the rioters were at work in that area of conflicting jurisdictions where the municipal boundaries of Philadelphia, Moyamensing, and Southwark converged—and a number of the participants were arrested. Initially the authorities appear to have stood aloof, but they eventually moved with a measure of determination, and Mayor John Swift on one occasion took about one hundred black males into protective custody to prevent their being attacked by a much larger mob. The actions of the mob, at least in the beginning, were to a degree orchestrated by recognized leaders. The careful selection of targets would alone be sufficient to create such a presumption, but, additionally, there is some evidence of periodic consultation. Nor can there be any doubt about the purposes of the mob and its leaders. "It is notorious," reported a committee charged with investigating the riot, "indeed, a fact not to be concealed or disputed, that the object of the most active among the rioters, was a destruction of the property, and injury to the persons, of the colored people, with the intent, as it would seem, to induce, or compel them to remove from this district." In this, at least, the mob failed. The blacks returned, restored their damaged dwellings, and began again, with painful slowness, to accumulate household goods and furnishings. The churches were rebuilt and the Negroes remained to be the target of later riots. Of the sixty rioters arrested, only ten were ever brought to trial, and none were either fined or imprisoned.[26]

Nothing in the disgraceful history of urban antiblack rioting in antebellum America perhaps quite matched the 1841 outbreak in Cincinnati. The hostility between the races had become extreme, and clashes on the last day of August and the first and second days of September heightened the tension. On Friday night, September 3, there began a reign of terror that was to last for two nights. Mobs numbering up to fifteen hundred, after destroying some Negro property in the business section, stormed into the black residential area at the east end of the city bent on destruction and assault. But the blacks, aware of the likelihood of such an attack, had armed themselves and were determined to protect themselves and their property. Firing repeatedly into the crowd, they forced the rioters out of the area. The mob soon returned to the attack, bringing with them a six-pound cannon, which they loaded with scrap metal and discharged again and again down Sixth Street. The firing continued until militia forces moved between the combatants at about 2 A.M.[27]

On Saturday morning a citizens' meeting was held at the courthouse. The situation was obviously extremely volatile and hazardous. It appeared that four people (two whites and two blacks) had been killed in the battle of the previous night and that some fifteen or twenty had been injured. Many of those in attendance at the meeting seem to have been at least as much disturbed by the Negroes' resistance as by the mob's attack. Their resolutions, it is true, condemned the riotous activity, requested parents and guardians of boys (who had apparently been much in evidence the previous night) to keep them off the streets, and called for "an efficient patrol to protect the persons and property of the blacks." But they also demanded that the blacks who had wounded two white boys on Thursday night be apprehended,[28] that the 1807 act (requiring free persons of color to post security bonds) be enforced "to the letter," and that the blacks be disarmed "of all offensive weapons." Additionally they resolved that "we view with abhorrence the proceedings of the Abolitionists in our city, and that we repudiate their doctrine."[29]

In the meantime, mobs continued to roam the city, driving all blacks that they encountered into the Negro district where the violence of the previous night had occurred. Every appearance suggested that the rioters anticipated making a murderous assault on the now-disarmed blacks on Saturday night, which would end in their expulsion or death. To prevent this, the city authorities took all the adult black males (some 250–300 of them) into protective custody and moved them, with considerable difficulty, to the jail, pledging that their families and property would be protected. This pledge was not honored, though the police, firemen, and militia were assisted by a body of eighty volunteer citizens. From dusk until almost dawn the rioters pillaged and destroyed, moving from point to point as the community's peacekeepers pursued them ineffectually. A number of additional injuries and much property damage resulted from the Saturday night activities. The riot came to an end on Sunday morning apparently more because the participants were exhausted than as a result of any action taken by the city, county, and state authorities. Some arrests did take place, but it is not clear that any of those taken into custody were ever convicted and punished. The Cincinnati press insisted that the mobs were led by Kentuckians from across the Ohio River and were composed of "the lowest and most violent order" (it is difficult to quarrel with the latter characterization, whatever the social standing of the participants). Kentuckians denied the charge and no hard evidence was ever presented, but, in any event, Cincinnati clearly had no shortage of violent bigots who wished to purge the urban population of its black component.[30]

From this dismal catalogue of mindless prejudice and conscienceless brutality a few patterns emerge. First, the outbreaks occurred only in the warmer months (never before April or after October), almost always in the summer, and were heavily concentrated in July and August. A number of explanations for this concentration quickly spring to mind. Rioting is not a pleasant activity when the nights are

cold and the winds are bitter, and few mobs—whatever their target—
either form or remain assembled very long when faced with adverse
weather conditions. But some reasons might also be suggested with a
more particular bearing on racial violence in this period. The urban
population was much more in the streets in summer than at other
seasons, and minor altercations were more likely to occur between
blacks and whites, because in most urban centers (especially in those
in the North) the streets and sidewalks were, with few exceptions, the
only unsegregated places in the city. Such incidents served to stimu-
late and aggravate the racial antagonisms that were always in plentiful
supply, and the result, all too often, was a mass assault designed (consciously or unconsciously) to rid the city of the offending (however
inoffensive) element of the population. Additionally, since these
warmer months were also the times when manual labor opportunities
were greatest, whites more often found themselves working with or in
close proximity to blacks or in competition with them, with woefully
predictable results. And finally, of course, the heat of July and August
might well be expected to produce shortness of temper that would
make participation in such riots more likely. On August 14, 1834, a
Philadelphia newspaper noted that "at no period for the last 40 years
have we experienced a succession of so many oppressively hot days as
we have had for the last two weeks," and described August 12—the
date of the outbreak of that city's most violent antiblack riot—as "the
hottest and most oppressive day we have had this summer."[31]

Climatic conditions, however, were clearly not all-important, for
other patterns were also present. The southern cities—which had the
longest periods of warm weather—were notably free from these disorders. Indeed, anything accurately describable as a racially motivated
riot was almost unknown in the major southern cities. The only real
exception was the 1835 Snow Riot in Washington. It is tempting to
argue that this freedom from racial disorder resulted from a pervasive
fear that any violent flouting of authority and the police power might
demonstrate the weakness of the institutions charged with keeping the
peace and thus encourage a slave uprising. This consideration was
doubtless operative, at least in part, in the Lower South, where there
were large numbers of slaves in the cities. New Orleans' police were
notoriously ineffectual in preventing crime or apprehending criminals
and vied with those of New York as the most venal and inept in the
country. But when a mob gathered in 1835 that gave evidence of an
intention to engage in some unspecified antiblack activities, the authorities moved swiftly and effectively to prevent any actual disorder.
But the cities of the Upper South had relatively few slaves, so that fear
of slave uprisings should not have been significant, yet they too,
although by no means free from mob activity of other sorts—indeed,

Baltimore had the reputation of being one of the most riotous cities of the antebellum era—had almost no race riots. It may be suggested that whites felt less threatened by blacks in the South because Negroes were more thoroughly suppressed; but black suppression was relatively thorough in all cities, and blacks competed far more extensively and effectively with whites for employment in the southern cities than in those farther north.[32] Certainly the absence of race riots cannot be explained as resulting from the fact that the number of free blacks in the southern cities was insignificant, for Baltimore had the largest free black population of any American city in 1850, and the number of free persons of color in New Orleans was also very large. Additionally, free blacks constituted a large proportion of the populations of the smaller cities of Charleston and Washington. It may be that Negroes in·the northern cities—conscious of residence in a nonslave area but experiencing little or no freedom, and having almost no "stake in society"—felt their condition more bitterly than their southern brothers, were more crushed by despair, and were quicker to take (and, hence, give) offense. Certainly the black resistance occasionally encountered by the white mobs in Providence, Philadelphia, and, more notably, Cincinnati would have been unthinkable in the South. Finally, the free black—despite his more extensive economic activity and greater numbers—presented a less visible target in the southern cities because in none of them was there anything remotely resembling a black residential area. In every real race riot from Cincinnati to Boston, the mob invaded the nineteenth-century equivalent of the black ghetto—a largely nonexistent entity south of Mason and Dixon's line.

Another observable pattern is that race riot activity was heavily concentrated in the 1830s. The reason for this concentration is not difficult to identify. That decade also saw the beginning of abolitionist agitation. Since abolitionism, of necessity, incorporated an assumption of human equality, it was perceived as a threat by those who not only shared the majority's belief in black inferiority but also lacked the self-confidence or the ingrained self image (based largely on economic success) of superiority to enable them to view equalitarianism with equanimity. The Cincinnati mob of 1841 occasionally turned aside from its pursuit of black victims to attack the house of an abolitionist or to destroy the press of an abolitionist journal, and the attacks on abolitionists in New York in 1834, in Washington in 1835, and in Philadelphia in 1838 spilled over into assaults upon the Negro population.[33] It is also possible that the arrival of the first large waves of immigrants in the 1830s provided the raw material for the anti-Negro mobs. Certainly a number of contemporary accounts mention the prevalence of the Irish among the rioters. But it must also be noted that New Orleans, St. Louis, Louisville, and Baltimore—all largely free of antiblack mob violence—had very large foreign-born populations and that the incidence of racial violence actually declined in the 1840s as the tide of immigration grew stronger.[34]

In all cities in America throughout the antebellum period, black residents were isolated by prejudice, suppressed, restricted, emotionally traumatized, and the object of casual insult and assault by any drunken, irritated, or arrogant white of however low degree. But in only a few, and for a limited period of time, did this smoldering cruelty flame into a white heat of mob violence. When it did, doubtless it seemed to many of those urban blacks directly affected but another, and more terrifying, chapter in an agonizing story that appeared to have no beginning and no end.

In all eras of recorded history cities have
been perceived as peculiarly subject to criminal and vicious activity.
The accumulation of wealth encouraged envy and covetousness and,
consequently, theft by stealth or by violence. Grinding poverty
seemed to make survival dependent upon petty larceny. And the concentration of population surely encouraged, if it did not make inevitable, a higher incidence of personal assaults. Moreover, the enactment
of legislation necessary for the health, safety, and convenience of the
dense population made a variety of acts or omissions criminal that, in
other environments, went unnoticed—allowing a dog to run at large;
casting shavings upon the ground; failing to clean a privy vault; or
permitting a chimney to go unswept.

The perception of the city as the seat of crime and vice was a view
widely held in antebellum America, and many observers asserted
that the most vicious and criminal components of the urban population were the recent immigrants and the blacks. In 1821 a committee
of the Massachusetts legislature complained that "the good order, and
tranquillity of this town [Boston], has of late years, been *often* and
much disturbed by violent riots at that part of the town, where persons
of colour are collected in great numbers."[1] The district to which the
committee alluded was "Nigger Hill"—an area on the north slope of
Beacon Hill whose center was Southac Street. Four years before the
legislative committee made its report, the Reverend James Davis had
described that thoroughfare in terms far less restrained and dis-
passionate than those of the committee. *"There* is the place where
Satan's seat is," he cried. *"There* awful impieties prevail; all conceivable
abominations are practiced; *there* the depravity of the human heart is
acted out; and from this sink of sin, the seeds of corruption are carried
into every part of town."[2]

Similar views prevailed in other cities. The New York Abolition
Society reported in 1806, "With regard to the moral improvement of
those of the blacks who reside in our city and its vicinity, we wish it
were in our power to give a more favorable account, but . . . it is to be
lamented, that the love of pleasure is most injuriously prevalent
among a considerable class, and that the idleness and vice which are its

concomitants, make them very often the subject of our penal laws."[3] And in 1848 George G. Foster—who had many praiseworthy things to say about Philadelphia's black community—lamented that while "with us [i.e., whites], not more than one-eighth are unmitigatedly vicious and depraved; with the colored people we fear we must say that not more than one-eighth are otherwise."[4]

It is likely that many of these blanket characterizations of the black population rested on nothing more substantial than selective perception, pervasive racial antipathies, and an almost complete lack of continuing contact with the black community. It is, nevertheless, true that blacks were disproportionately represented in the prisons, penitentiaries, jails, and workhouses of the nation's cities. It is also true that the extent to which they were overrepresented was sometimes exaggerated. In his reports of 1846 and 1848 Mayor W. W. Seaton of Washington asserted that one-half to three-quarters of the city's residents committed to the workhouse were free blacks, but the actual numbers suggest that the figure during the period from the late 1830s to 1850 was probably closer to two-fifths.[5] Additionally, in 1850 free blacks constituted roughly that same proportion (about forty percent) of those imprisoned for more serious crimes in the Washington jail and the District of Columbia penitentiary.[6] Even this lower figure, however, was slightly more than twice the proportion of the free persons of color in the whole population.

In other major American cities similar conditions prevailed in the antebellum era—blacks were convicted of criminal activity and imprisoned in numbers significantly greater than their proportion of the whole population would suggest to be normal. The only differences were those of degree. Throughout the 1830s and '40s Negroes constituted, on the average, just under thirty-two percent of the population of the Baltimore jail (the range was about 25%–34%), while the average free black component of Baltimore's population during the same period was slightly over sixteen percent. Thus, the black proportion in the jail population was slightly less than twice the free Negro percentage in the whole population—a figure marginally below that in Washington.[7] In New York City in the 1820s the proportion of blacks in the convict population of the Bridewell (the city jail) and the city penitentiary fluctuated widely between one-fifth and two-thirds, though only about one-twelfth of the whole city population was black. Twenty years later the proportion of Negroes in the prison population had dropped to between one-tenth and one-sixth, but these lower figures still ranged from 2½ to 4 times the black percentage in the whole population.[8] In Boston in the late 1830s and early '40s Negroes constituted about one-twelfth of the inmates of the house of correction—roughly four times the proportion of blacks in that city's population.[9] And despite Abigail Mott's assertion in 1839 that, in Philadelphia, "for crimes of magnitude, their [the free blacks'] proportion is very small; while in cases of petit larceny, they fall a little below the whites in the scale of virtue,"[10] it would appear that the situation there was hardly less dismal than in New York and Boston. Throughout the 1820s, '30s, and '40s, the free persons of color seem to have constituted between one-third and two-fifths of those accused and convicted of criminal acts in Philadelphia (occasionally, perhaps, as much as one-half), despite the fact that the black component of the population declined from about one-eighth to a little over one-twelfth.[11]

Similar conditions obviously prevailed in other major cities. In 1850 the federal census marshals recorded black convict populations that were more than six times as great as the Negro proportion of the whole population would justify in Boston, more than four times as great in Albany, and almost three times as great in Cincinnati. In New Orleans, the percentage of free Negroes in the parish jail was identical to the proportion of free persons of color in the whole population. Ten years earlier a local count in St. Louis found that free black convicts were five times as numerous as the number of free Negroes in the whole population would justify.[12]

It is both difficult and hazardous to generalize from data that is often partial and frequently derived from different sources. But it would appear that free blacks in the Lower South cities ran afoul of the law about as frequently as the rest of the free population, and in the Chesapeake cities were convicted of criminal activity in numbers about twice as great as their proportion of the whole population would justify. In the other major cities the percentage of free persons of color in the populations of the correctional institutions was probably 4–6 times as great as in the population as a whole.

There can be no real doubt that to a substantial degree these disparities resulted from the influence of pervasive racism and a callous disregard for the most redimentary concepts of equal justice. Police forces, which contained no Negroes, found minor infractions by persons of color, or, sometimes, their mere presence in the vicinity of a disturbance, cause for arrest. And juries, from which blacks were rigorously excluded, considered the arrest of Negroes to be, at the very least, prima facie evidence of guilt. At least in some measure, then, the deeply held belief that free blacks constituted a criminal class was, under these circumstances, a self-fulfilling prophecy.

Data separating the prison populations by both race and offense are much less common, but available evidence suggests that there were some differences in the kinds of criminal activity for which blacks and whites were imprisoned. It is hardly surprising that white prisoners were perhaps twice as likely as Negroes to have been convicted of such "literate" offenses as forgery, fraud, and passing counterfeit currency. Additionally, larger percentages of white prisoners were incarcerated for such violent crimes as murder (by a margin of about 5:3) and aggravated assault (by about 5:4). Roughly the same proportion of white and black prisoners were committed for rape and arson, but black prisoners were much more likely than whites (by a margin of 7:4) to have been convicted of various kinds of theft. Further, a larger percentage of black than white prisoners (by a ratio of more than 4:3) were jailed for violation of minor city ordinances. Finally, a substantial number of both black and white prisoners languished in jail because of an inability to post peace bonds or to pay fines and costs assessed for less serious infractions of the law.[13]

If blacks as a class were more likely than the rest of the urban population to be convicted of criminal activity, the discrepancy was even more pronounced among women. Blacks consistently constituted a much larger percentage of the female prison populations than of the male element. Data drawn primarily from New York, Philadelphia, and Baltimore suggest that in the 1820s and '30s the black women imprisoned in the city jails usually constituted a percentage of the female prisoners 2–3 times as large as the proportion of blacks among the male prisoners. In the next two decades this discrepancy became less pronounced. In the 1840s, for instance, the black percentages in the female prison populations were usually about twice (or less) that in the male element. In the penitentiaries, where those convicted of more serious crimes were confined, the relationship between the black male and female components was, in the earlier period, essentially the same as in the jails. By the 1840s, however, it had shifted dramatically, and blacks had come to comprise about twice as great a percentage of the male as of the female penitentiary inmates.[14] These patterns of black female incarceration doubtless resulted from a reluctance on the part of judges and juries to imprison white women, for there is some limited evidence that race-sex discrepancies of the magnitude revealed by the commitment statistics did not exist in the whole population of persons brought to trial before the courts.[15] It is possible that the startling reversal of this pattern in the penitentiary populations of the 1840s was produced by a greater willingness to incarcerate foreign-born women. Certainly the shift occurred at a time when the percentage of recent immigrants both in the whole population and among the inmates of correctional institutions was rising rapidly.

Black children, too, appear to have been confined to jails and prisons in numbers disproportionate to both the number of blacks and the number of minors to be found in the prison populations. In 1850, for instance, blacks constituted sixty percent of all persons incarcerated in the Maryland penitentiary at Baltimore who were under sixteen years of age at the time of commitment, and more than one-half of those under seventeen. In the same year almost one-half of the children under the age of fifteen in the Providence jail were black, as were all of the persons under sixteen in the District of Columbia penitentiary at Washington.[16] As early as 1829 the New York Society for the Reformation of Juvenile Delinquents had explicitly addressed this problem when the society began to plan for the construction of a house of refuge for black juveniles. In the absence of a separate building (and in the equally concrete absence of a willingness to integrate the existing facility), black juvenile offenders continued to be sent to other correctional institutions, intended for the incarceration of adult criminals. In 1829 alone, 145 Negro children were sent to the city penitentiary.[17] It is not clear that the opening of the House of Refuge for Colored Juveniles in New York in 1835 contributed very significantly to the amelioration of these conditions, for at no time during the first five years of its operation did the annual number of children admitted reach one-third of the number committed to the city penitentiary in 1829.[18]

Not only were blacks much more likely than whites to be charged with and convicted of criminal acts, but they also served longer terms in correctional institutions. A group of Philadelphia Quakers observed in 1849 that sentences imposed upon free blacks "for crimes of the same grade are much longer, and very few in comparison with the whites have been discharged by pardons. Up to the year 1846, out of 664 coloured prisoners 22 or 3.3 per cent. had been pardoned, while out of 1512 white prisoners, the pardons had been 217 or 14.22 per cent.!" And an analysis by the English divine, Robert Everest, of data from the same institution for the years 1849–51 confirmed these findings, showing the average time served to be thirteen percent greater for black prisoners than for whites.[19] Figures from other sources suggest that these observations would have been equally valid elsewhere. In New York in the 1820s, for example, blacks consistently constituted a larger proportion of the city prison population when the annual censuses were taken than they did of the entire number of persons committed throughout the year. Indeed, the annual census percentage was sometimes more than half again as great as the figure for all commitments. In the absence of evidence of a strong cyclical pattern of black imprisonment balanced by a countercyclical pattern for whites, there would appear to be no logical explanation for this discrepancy except a consistent significant difference in the lengths of sentences imposed on and served by blacks and whites.[20]

In certain cities—notably Baltimore and Washington—debtors who could not or would not discharge their obligations continued to be subject to imprisonment until well into or throughout the second quarter of the nineteenth century. It might be inferred that shopkeepers and others were less likely to extend appreciable credit to Negroes than to whites in this era and, consequently, that blacks would not constitute a significant portion of this component of the prison populations. But imprisonment for debt frequently followed upon the heels of very small obligations indeed—in some years roughly one-half of all those committed for nonpayment owed the complaining creditor less than ten dollars. Even so, in Washington the percentage of Negroes among imprisoned debtors appears to have been only slightly over one-half of the proportion of blacks in the entire population. But in Baltimore, where free blacks had significantly greater economic opportunities, larger numbers apparently had easier access to credit and suffered accordingly. From 1835 to 1850 the percentage of Negroes among the imprisoned debtors (though smaller than the percentage among convicted criminals) was almost always greater than the free black percentage of the whole city population, and usually about one-half again as large. The unpaid debts for which they were committed, however, were considerably smaller than those which prompted complaints against whites. It appears that over niety percent of the blacks (and about two-thirds of the whites) were imprisoned for obligations of less than ten dollars.[21]

Contemporary observers were also convinced that the black population of the cities was peculiarly given to gambling, drunkenness, and prostitution. In the late summer of 1840 a New York newspaper reported a police raid resulting in the arrest of forty-two individuals "in various low negro gambling houses and brothels in the 5th and 6th wards," and at the end of that decade George G. Foster asserted that in the Five Points area (in the sixth ward), "nearly every house and cellar is a groggery below and a brothel above." The prostitutes, he reported, were "of all colors, white, yellow, brown, and ebony black."[22] In New Orleans free women of color were repeatedly arrested and charged with engaging in prostitution, especially in locations along St. Peter's, Conti, and Burgundy streets, and "Aunt Henny" was a notorious black brothel keeper in St. Louis who maintained a biracial staff.[23]

Despite such reports, it is not easy to establish that the free black population was engaged in such activites to an unusual degree. For one thing, brothel keepers, prostitutes, and gamblers are not, as a rule, inclined to announce their vocations to census takers and directory compilers, though Mary Girard, perhaps an early convert to the gospel of advertising, is listed as a "madam" in a Philadelphia directory of 1820.[24] It is not possible, therefore, to place these activities in the context of larger employment patterns or to compare the incidence of whites and blacks engaged in them. Moreover, newspapers of the period notoriously gave exaggerated coverage to reports of incidents involving drunkenness, gambling, and illicit sexual activity and made them the objects of ribald humor, especially when they involved blacks or recently arrived immigrants. Additionally, courts frequently imposed fines as punishment for convictions of violating ordinances related to gambling and prostitution. Such offenses were, consequently, not reflected in the reports of the correctional institutions, and arrest statistics are much less readily available than commitment data. Finally, when sentenced to confinement, the offenders were frequently committed as vagrants, without any specification of the particular offense of which they were convicted.

There are some limited and partial data, however, that tend to support the contemporary observations regarding the prevalence of such activities among blacks. In 1850 more than a third of the Negro inmates of Boston's house of correction had been imprisoned for offenses related to illegal sexual activity and another quarter for drunkenness.[25] Between 1835 and 1850 blacks constituted almost a third of those incarcerated in the Baltimore jail for keeping a disorderly house and more than a third of those convicted of bastardy. These figures were roughly double the proportion of free blacks in the whole population. Negroes also made up almost one-half of those sentenced for gambling and almost a quarter of those committed for rioting (a term frequently equated with aggravated disorderly conduct and often associated with drunkenness).[26] These data would suggest that antebellum observers were not wholly in error in ascribing to the black population an above-average involvement in prostitution and gambling, but that they probably exaggerated the extent of black participation in public disorders.

It must also be remembered that, in several of the southern cities, Negroes could be arrested and imprisoned for actions which would not have been criminal if performed by a white person. Slaves might be committed by their masters "for safekeeping," and free blacks (usually children) were occasionally held in the same status for brief periods when it was believed that they were in danger of being kidnaped. Blacks who could not establish their claims to free status were frequently taken up and held as "runaways" (a condition that could also apply to an absconding white apprentice). To prevent the distortion of black "crime" statistics and to make them comparable with white statistics, prisoners classified under these headings have been wholly excluded from the data used in this chapter.[27] But it is not possible to remove from consideration many other cases of commitment for actions or activities that were offenses only when the individual involved was a black. Such convictions were frequently reported in a much broader category of cases under some such innocuous and unhelpful heading as "violations of various city ordinances." This discriminatory legislation is dealt with more fully elsehwere,[28] but in the present context it is important to note that free blacks might be imprisoned for such wildly diverse "criminal" activities as being abroad after curfew, marking a game of billiards, trafficking in farm produce, attending a religious service not authorized by the mayor, or strolling in certain prohibited areas of the city.

Free blacks in major antebellum American cities, then, were significantly more likely than whites to become inmates of the correctional institutions of the cities, counties, and states. This circumstance doubtless resulted, in part, from the economic conditions that prevailed among urban Negroes. It was hardly coincidental that the most economically deprived element of the cities' populations tended to commit a disproportionate number of crimes against property and that in each city the crime rates among free persons of color were roughly related, in an inverse fashion, to the levels of black occupational opportunity.

In one respect, at least, it cannot be said that this record resulted from the more scrupulous scrutiny of the black community by urban law enforcement personnel, for policing inside the concentrated black residential areas in the northern cities was sporadic and sometimes almost cursory. Hence, a large number of transgressions—especially those related to drunkenness, fighting, gambling, and illicit sexual activities—went undetected by a government and a community that were only minimally concerned with the preservation of peace and order or the enforcement of law within the ghetto. But outside of the black residential area, or when in contact with the urban authorities at any location, free blacks could expect to be more frequently arrested than whites in any given set of circumstances. Moreover, it was less likely that the charges against them would be dropped[29] and more likely that they would be found guilty. Once convicted, they would doubtless receive heavier sentences than whites guilty of the same offense and had very little chance of release before the completion of the sentence imposed.

When the laws themselves openly made it a crime to be black (by making otherwise inoffensive acts criminal when performed by Negroes), and when law enforcement personnel at every level acted covertly upon the same principle, it would hardly have been surprising if blacks had developed a certain calloused cynicism about the laws of the community and the peacekeeping forces of the community. For them, equal justice under law was not even a theoretical concept, let alone a practical reality.

8 The Poor You Have Always with You: Black Poverty and Urban Welfare

If the avenue to riches was an urban street—and to many nineteenth-century Americans this appeared to be true—it was, nevertheless, a road poorly marked and with many turnings. Unexpected hazards abounded; the pitfalls for the unwary (or even for the wary, for that matter) were both numerous and deep; and far more travelers, both black and white, lost their way than reached their anticipated destination. Nowhere else in antebellum America (if we except the individual plantation community of master and slave) did opulent wealth and utter destitution exist so extensively, so obviously, and in such close and continuing proximity. And while urban blacks shared, in some measure, the dream of riches, they also shared, in much greater measure, the reality of poverty.

Antebellum urban poverty was wholly unlike anything conveyed by the term "below the poverty level" in the last quarter of the twentieth century. It was significantly different from the genteel poverty of the family of young Charles Dickens in contemporary England or from the less than genteel poverty of the Bob Cratchit family. Antebellum urbanites would have made a distinction between the poor and the pauper. Very large percentages of the residents in the largest cities were poor. They lived in cramped and congested quarters, frequently rendered more crowded still by the presence of boarders (sometimes whole families) whose minute payments somewhat reduced the burden imposed by even the lowest rents. Their dwellings were stifling in summer and frigid in winter, when the cost of firewood became an intolerable additional expense. They had inadequate or no access to sanitary facilities. Their food was inferior in both quantity and quality and the facilities for its preparation and preservation were usually unsatisfactory at best. Their clothing rarely offered sufficient protection against the elements. The men usually followed such occupations as day laborers, stevedores, sailors, boatmen, whitewashers, woodsawyers, or, occasionally, the least rewarding artisan trades (e.g., cordwainers), while the women were frequently employed as servants, washers, or in sewing cheap garments. Children often sought employment at the age of ten or earlier. They had almost no financial resources, and a serious illness, an accident, or the loss of one or two weeks of employment by the principal breadwinner could well mean eviction, starvation, and utter destitution. This group lived on the knife-edge of existence and doubtless included most blacks in every city.

Pauperism was perceived as a condition of continuing and largely unrelieved dependence. The aged, the infirm, orphans, and widows with small children who had no relatives to assist them were seen as faultless, legitimate, and deserving paupers. The same could not be said of adult males and whole families unacquainted with steady employment (or efforts to obtain it), frugality, and ambition. Their plight was generally believed to result from physical, mental, or moral impairment and was usually declared to be associated with sloth, intemperance, and "vicious habits." But urban officials and guardians of the city's morals alike failed to recognize that a black with only marginally below average energy, determination, ambition, and ability could easily be reduced from the army of the poor to the ranks of the paupers by the unrelenting pressure of pervasive discrimination.

Thus, the leaders of urban society perceived poverty in general, and pauperism in particular, to be, in varying degrees, akin to both crime and disease. From either perspective it was apparent that the response should involve two sequential kinds of action—society must stop the crime and then reform the criminal, or, alternatively, relieve the symptoms and then effect a cure for the disorder.

Poverty was not new on the urban scene. American towns had found it necessary, almost from their foundations, to make provision for the care of the poor. The resources of both private charity and governmental activity had been marshaled to attack the problem. No one seriously believed that it would be wholly eliminated, for poor widows and orphans would always require assistance, and illness or economic crisis could at any time reduce normally self-sufficient workers and their families to a temporary condition of dependence. To aid such unfortunates was both a moral and a social responsibility. But urban leaders, sharing the "American Dream," continued to hope, however wistfully, that chronic pauperism might eventually be eliminated by a combination of controlled assistance, education, religious instruction, and, as a last resort, assisted emigration to agricultural regions.

As the urban populations grew in size and became increasingly heterogenous, the simpler relief structures of the eighteenth century proved both ineffective and subject to abuse by the knowledgeable among the chronic paupers. The early nineteenth century, consequently, was marked by various efforts to institutionalize poor relief

(both public and private) in order to ensure help for the truly unfortunate, deny assistance to the unworthy, and strengthen the re-
formatory impact of the relief process (and, incidentally, reduce the
cost of poor relief). One product of this movement was the establishment of almshouses in the major cities.

Since urban blacks were extensively restricted to low-opportunity
and other irregular occupations, had a very low incidence of property
ownership in most cities, and were universally described by contemporary observers as in large part poverty-stricken, it would seem likely
that large numbers of the free people of color would have qualified for
some form of poor relief. It is frequently exceptionally difficult to
determine whether they received such assistance and, if so, to what
extent.

Almshouse records, in part because of their centralized control and
full-time directors, are more readily available than those for other
varieties of relief, though for particular cities and for given periods
even almshouse data may be wholly unavailable or extremely partial.
Even when locatable, almshouse reports frequently did not show the
race of the inmates and are, consequently, without value in examining
the black community. It is at least likely that in some cities in which
the almshouse reports do now show Negro inmates—especially in the
Lower South—blacks were not admitted to the institutions. In other
such cases it is more probable (and sometimes certain) that blacks
were received into the almshouses, but data on their numbers are
either nonexistent or drawn from spotty, peripheral sources. Finally,
city almshouses were not established in a number of municipalities
(e.g., Pittsburgh, Cincinnati, Buffalo, New Orleans, and Louisville)
during the first half of the nineteenth century, and in other cities were
founded only very late in the period. In those towns the poor were
assisted by outdoor relief, sent (in small numbers) to county or sub-
sidized private institutions, or ignored.[1]

Even when almshouse figures showing the number of black inmates
are available, comparative analysis is made difficult because the responsible officials reported the data in different forms. The Baltimore
Trustees for the Poor, for instance, consistently published reports
showing the average monthly almshouse population, separated by
race, while almost all other reports stated the number of inmates
resident on a given date or the total number admitted during the year.
The Baltimore method is clearly superior for analytical purposes because it reflects, in some measure, any differences in the average
length of residence between blacks and whites. Additionally, it is
possible that the average period of residence was greater for all residents in the more northerly cities, where winters were both longer
and more severe, but the data available are inadequate to determine

the extent to which this might have been true. Given these difficulties, the best method of establishing the incidence of black residence in the urban welfare institutions is not to compare the number of black inmates with the size of the free black population, but rather to compare the percentage of blacks among the inmates (however stated) with the percentage of free blacks in the whole free population.[2]

Certainly these ratios appear to have differed considerably among the various cities and also to have varied (sometimes dramatically) over time. The Baltimore figures were rather more stable than those in other cities. Blacks in Baltimore constituted, on the average, just under one-fifth of the almshouse population during the late 1820s and '30s. This was only minutely—3–6 percent—greater than the proportion of Negroes in that city's free population. The 1840s saw an increase of roughly one percentage point in the relative size of the black almshouse population despite a more substantial decline in the percentage of Baltimore's free population that was black. Consequently, the black component in the Baltimore almshouse in the fifth decade of the nineteenth century was a quarter larger than the proportion of blacks in the whole free population. A more detailed examination of the annual data suggests that the economic panic of 1837 and its aftermath affected Baltimore's free blacks both more severely than the whites and over a more prolonged period of time. Before 1837 blacks almost never constituted as much as twenty-one percent of the almshouse population, but between 1838 and 1845 they never made up that small a percentage of the inmates, and in 1841 exceeded twenty-four percent, despite the fact that blacks then comprised a smaller proportion of the total free population than they had a decade earlier. Even in the last half of the 1840s the black component of the almshouse population was, on the average, almost one-fifth greater than the proportion of free persons of color in the city's free population.[3] It must be noted, however, that the increase in the size of the black component in the almshouse population did not necessarily reflect a deepening of black poverty in Baltimore, but may have resulted, rather, from increased ease of access for blacks to the institution.

Baltimore blacks, and probably those in other cities as well, tended to stay in the almshouse somewhat longer than their white counterparts. In 1831, for instance, over seventeen percent of all those admitted to the institution were blacks, but persons of color comprised more than nineteen percent of the average monthly number of inmates—more than a tenth greater.[4] The discrepancy between these two figures—admissions and inmates in residence—was much more pronounced elsewhere. In 1850 blacks comprised just over a tenth of those admitted to the Washington Asylum (that city's counterpart to the almshouse). But counts of asylum residents at two different times during the year showed the black proportion of the inmate population to be just under a sixth, in one case, and rather more than a fifth, in the other.[5] Though available data are sparse and spotty it would appear that urban blacks, who had slender or nonexistent financial resources and access to employment, and who were frequently the last hired and the first fired, were, conversely, the first to enter these institutions and the last to depart.

The variations over time were more dramatic in New York than in Baltimore. In the late 1810s and in 1820 the precentage of Negroes in the almshouse was about the same or slightly greater than their proportion in the city's free population. But the 1820s saw a relatively larger decline in black than in white inmates. Between 1821 and 1828 the black proportion of inmates was roughly two-thirds of the percentage of Negroes in the free population—significantly below the Baltimore figure. In the 1840s, however, the New York figure was the greater one. By 1843 the proportion of blacks in the New York almshouse was almost fifty percent larger than the Negro percentage of the city's population. Four years later, those blacks receiving institutional assistance from the city comprised a percentage of the inmate population more than three times as great as the Negro proportion of the general population. This dramatic increase between 1843 and 1847 was almost certainly the result of vastly improved access by blacks to the city's relief rolls. In the 1840s the Society for the Relief of Worthy Aged Paupers had established a "Colored Home" and by the mid-1840s was preparing to construct greatly enlarged facilities. In 1847, even before the new construction was begun, the New York Common Council voted to pay for the support of blacks in the society's establishment, "in consequence of their being no Alms House specially provided by the City authorities for colored paupers." The city officials were obviously much more willing to provide institutional relief for blacks now that they could be wholly separated from the white paupers, and in the late 1840s the number of inmates in the Colored Home more than doubled. By 1849 Negroes comprised about $17\frac{1}{2}$ percent of the city's institutionalized poor— more than six times the proportion of blacks in the whole population.[6]

In Philadelphia, too, the relative size of the black component in the almshouse population seems to have increased during the second quarter of the nineteenth century. In the late 1820s, the mid-1830s, and the late 1840s the proportion of blacks among the inmates was roughly the same—ranging from slightly more than one-seventh to a little below one-eighth. But during those two decades the percentage of blacks in the population of Philadelphia County (the area served by Blockly Alms House) declined dramatically. Consequently, the percentage of Negroes among the inmates was about two-thirds greater than the black proportion of the county population in 1827, more than three-quarters greater in 1834, and substantially more than two and one-half times as large in the late 1840s. By 1850–51, however (largely because of the enormous increase of foreign-born white inmates), the black component of the almshouse admissions fell dramatically to about one-fourteenth of the total—only a little over one-half greater than the black percentage of the county population.[7]

In the two northernmost cities, Albany and Boston, however, the trends would appear to have been the reverse of those in New York and Philadelphia, with the relative decline of the black inmate population being more pronounced in Boston than in Albany. At the beginning of the second quarter of the nineteenth century blacks comprised just under nine percent of Albany's almshouse population, almost double the proportion of blacks in that city's free population. But by the end of the half-century, though the number of almshouse residents had almost trebled, the number of black inmates had actually declined, and their percentage in the almshouse population was only a quarter greater than that in the whole population.[8] In Boston in 1813—a year in which that port city suffered acute commercial disruption—almost one-fifth of the persons admitted to the almshouse were blacks, a figure that was more than $4\frac{1}{2}$ times as great as the Negro proportion of the city's population. By 1833 the percentage of blacks in the inmate population had dropped to a level only $2\frac{1}{4}$ times as great as the black proportion of the whole population. And by the middle of the century the three blacks that the federal census enumerator found in the almshouse comprised well under one percent of the inmate population, a figure that was barely over three-fifths of the percentage of blacks among Boston residents. Thus, in relative terms, there were less than one-seventh as many black almshouse inmates in the Massachusetts metropolis in 1850 as there had been a little less than four decades earlier.[9] Since Boston in 1850 afforded its black residents the poorest occupational opportunities of any of these fifteen cities, and contained the smallest number of black real estate owners, the lowest value of black-owned real estate, and the third smallest percentage of black property owners,[10] it is almost certain that this enormous decline in Negro almshouse residents reflected an equally great reduction in access to that city's facilities for pauper care, rather than an improving economic position for free persons of color there.

In Washington, where blacks constituted about twenty-two percent of the free population, less than eight percent of those admitted to the alms house in 1845–46 were black, and the figure was only $10\frac{1}{3}$ percent in 1849–50, and still under eleven percent in 1850–51.

Hence, the level of black admissions ranged from rather more than a third to about one-half the Negro proportion of the free population. On the other hand, the precentage of blacks in the almshouse population reported by the federal census enumerator in 1850 (just over one-fifth) was substantially the same as the black proportion of the free population. And in Providence the federal census marshal in 1850 found an inmate population in the Dexter Asylum for Paupers that was roughly one-ninth black, although only about one in thirty of Providence's residents were Negroes.[11]

It is apparent that by the end of the fifth decade of the nineteenth century the relative proportion of blacks in the inmate populations of urban almshouses varied greatly from city to city. In Philadelphia and Providence the black inmate component was 2½–3 times as large as the percentage of blacks in the general population, and in New York about six times as large; in Albany and Baltimore the Negro percentages of the almshouse residents were from a fifth to a quarter greater than in the free populations; the proportion was substantially the same in Washington; while Boston's blacks were underrepresented (relatively) in the almshouse by a ratio of roughly 3:5.[12] These variations doubtless reflected both the extent of Negro poverty in the various towns and differentials in black access to the "humane institutions." There are no reliable indicators of the extent of either pauperism or temporary destitution among blacks, or any other portion of the urban populations, but the data on black occupational patterns and real estate ownership suggest that the relatively high proportion of Negroes in the almshouse populations of Philadelphia, New York, and Providence reflected similar levels of poverty in their black communities. At the other end of the scale, the relatively lower percentages of blacks in the Boston and Albany establishments almost certainly resulted from curtailed access. The Baltimore and Washington figures are more ambiguous but probably reflected both an economic deprivation somewhat less widespread than in more northerly urban centers and easier access to pauper institutions than in Boston and Albany.

In Providence's Dexter Asylum the inmates were not segregated by race, but it is likely (or, in some cases, certain) that officials in the other establishments physically separated blacks and whites with degrees of rigor depending only on the available facilities. In New York, the "city officials reserved the worst section of the house—a filthy, damp cellar," for occupancy by Negro residents. With the transfer of these inmates to the colored home in the 1840s, still greater separation was effected, and the city's regular humane facilities became "lily white." In 1850 the federal census marshal found only one black inmate—a lunatic in Bloomingdale Asylum—in all of the welfare institutions on Blackwell's Island (later Welfare Island), where such facilities had been concentrated in 1848. The commissioners of the Washington institution were insistent that white and black paupers not be allowed to "mingle together," and inmates and charitable and reform institutions were routinely segregated in Baltimore and Philadelphia.[13]

It would appear that the proportion of women among the Negro almshouse inmates was greater than their percentage in the general free black population, though the disparity was not very great. In Baltimore, for example, on the average, rather more than six-tenths of the adult blacks in the almshouse in the 1830s were women, and in the 1840s the figure was almost two-thirds. This was only marginally above the female proportion of the city's adult free black population in the 1830s but perhaps $\frac{1}{12}$–$\frac{1}{10}$ greater than that level in the 1840s. Among the white inmates the pattern was reversed—women were slightly overrepresented in the 1830s and substantially underrepresented in the 1840s. Among both blacks and whites women seem to have remained in the establishment longer than men, but the disproportion was much less pronounced among blacks.[14] The New York figures for 1816–26 show both white and black women to have been overrepresented, relative to their proportion in the city's population, in the adult population of the almshouse in the years before 1820. In the later years white females were underrepresented in the institutional population, while the precentage of black women among the inmates did not differ greatly from their proportion of the city's adult Negro population.[15]

It is difficult to determine with any acceptable degree of precision the relative size of the child population of the almshouses. To be sure, institutional reports sometimes specified the number of "children" in the house, but these reports did not state the age at which inmates were classified as adults. In the absence of such data it is not possible to relate these figures to a comparable component in the general population. A few suggestive figures may, however, be generated from the census data and the almshouse reports in Baltimore and New York. In Baltimore the percentage of children under fourteen appears to have been remarkably stable throughout the second quarter of the nineteenth century, constituting roughly one-third of the free persons of color and about three-eighths of the white population. At no time during these years did the "children's" proportion in the almshouse population comprise so large a component of either the white or the black inmates. Indeed, it was less than one-half that in the general population sixty percent of the time for whites and eighty-five percent of the time for blacks. Among whites, moreover, it was never less than one-third that of the general population, while for blacks it was less than one-third more than one-half of the time, occasionally dropping below one-sixth. In two-fifths of the years the percentage of "children" among black inmates was less than one-half of that among the whites. Among both racial groups, however, the trend over these years was the same—the proportion of "children" in the inmate population was much greater in the late 1820s and early 1830s than in the remainder of the half-century. In the first period the average annual proportion of "children" in the inmate population was something less than one-quarter for whites and about one-seventh for blacks; in the latter period these figures dropped to about one-seventh and one-thirteenth, respectively. By any measure, then, black children were not only much less likely to be received into the Baltimore almshouse than white minors, but this disparity became greater as the half-century wore on.[16] But the New York data reveal somewhat different patterns. Between 1816 and 1826 the proportion of "children" in the black almshouse population was, on the average, minutely greater than the percentage of free persons of color under fourteen years of age in the city (slightly over one-quarter)—a circumstance that indicates that this component of the population was much more extensively admitted to the New York establishment than to the Baltimore one. Nevertheless, white "children" formed a still larger percentage of the inmate population, averaging about 41½ percent during these years, as compared with roughly 36–38 percent of children under fourteen years in the white population of the whole city.[17]

In reality, spot checks suggest that these discrepancies in the percentages of children in the black and white inmate populations relative to comparable percentages in the whole populations were the product of three interrelated circumstances. First, though the incidence of child inmates per one thousand of the population under fourteen years of age was usually somewhat lower for blacks than for whites, this was probably largely a reflection of the fact that black children tended to seek employment—especially as live-in servants—at earlier ages than white children and, hence, did not accompany their indigent parents and younger siblings into the almshouses. Second, this pattern of early employment and the concomitant feeling that it was appropriate to Negroes probably moved white officials to bind out black children (especially as servants) at earlier ages than whites. Finally, and most importantly, the adult black almshouse population was frequently much greater than the white in proportion ot the size of the population fourteen years of age and older. In 1841, for example, the average of the monthly census in the Baltimore almshouse showed an incidence of black adult inmates of 9.3 per one thousand of the city's adult free persons of color, compared with 6.2 per thousand for adult white inmates. The comparable figure for "child" inmates was 1.4 per thousand for blacks and 1.7 for whites. This inflated incidence of black adult institutionalized paupers—half again as large as that for whites—greatly increased the relative size of the adult component of the black inmates and concomitantly reduced the relative size of the "child" component. This higher incidence of adult black inmates was, of course, primarily a reflection of their greater economic deprivation which produced, in turn, a higher proportion of persons forced to seek institutional assistance for reasons not connected with age or infirmity.[18]

As has been noted, urban poor relief was not confined to the assistance provided to almshouse inmates. Outdoor relief—that is, the distribution of food, fuel, and very limited amounts of money directly to individuals and families residing in their own dwellings—had long antedated the establishment of almshouses, and the commitment, however strong, to the moral and financial advantages of institutionalizing the city's pauper population could not wholly eliminate such direct assistance. Outdoor relief persisted in part because urban officials were repelled by the prospect of uprooting "decent" and "respectable" individuals—that is, orderly, clean, abstentious, church-going, native-born whites (especially widows)—from their homes and forcing them into close physical association with the drunken, filthy, criminal, and vicious persons who were presumed to make up the bulk of the pauper population. As the half-century wore on, a second consideration was also increasingly influential in preserving and extending the system of outdoor relief. Although the almshouse had originally been perceived as a means of reducing poor relief costs (as well as an instrument of moral reformation), as the urban populations burgeoned and came to include large numbers of indigent, and often unruly, immigrants, the financial burden of constructing and operating facilities to care for the expanding pauper population became politically insupportable. Though greatly enlarged establishments were constructed, these were always overcrowded, and city officials were compelled to rely heavily on noninstitutional assistance.

Unfortunately the reports of outdoor relief in the first half of the nineteenth century were even less revealing than the almshouse data. Sometimes only the total expenditures were reported, and when the number of recipients was stated separate figures for blacks and whites were often not given. It would appear that in a number of cities blacks were routinely excluded from the ranks of the "deserving" poor and, consequently, from the outdoor relief rolls. When the Scots clergyman, Robert Everest, visited Cincinnati in the early 1850s he noted that "no relief is given to the coloured poor. I learnt that by law the guardians have the option of relieving them, but on looking into the accounts, I observed that out of 3269 cases in which relief had been granted, only ten were of the coloured, and those ten were for expenses of interment."[19] Similar practices seem to have prevailed in New York well beyond the first third of the century, for in 1837 Mayor Aaron Clark complained to the Common Council that although food and fuel were distributed to whites—including ablebodied male immigrants—"sober colored widows, with small children, in extreme necessity" were denied such assistance.[20] It is probable that like conditions existed in other cities.

By the end of the first half of the nineteenth century, nevertheless, relief officials in some cities were distributing food, fuel, and money to indigent blacks. The New York guardians of the poor had opened the relief rolls to Negroes, and in 1850 their agents visited families containing almost one thousand blacks to determine their eligibility for money assistance, and twice that number lived in families visited to determine their eligibility for wood and coal. In that year almost four percent of the persons given outdoor monetary relief were persons of color, as were more than $7\frac{1}{2}$ percent of those receiving fuel. There was doubtless much overlap among these families, but these figures clearly establish that more than one-seventh (and if we include those in the Colored Home, almost one-fifth) of New York's Negroes were recognized as being potentially or actually qualified to receive some measure of public assistance. Over the next five years the number of blacks visited by relief agents almost doubled, and this in a period when no financial disordes troubled the nation's commercial metropolis.[21]

Philadelphia blacks clearly had access to ourdoor relief much earlier, though the available data are not always complete. Robert Purvis, an outstanding leader of the black community, asserted that in 1830 only twenty-two Negroes in the county were recipients of outdoor relief. That number constituted four percent of all persons receiving such assistance, but the figure may well have dealt with money relief, which was dispensed much more sparingly than fuel or food. A few years later Edward Abdy found that during the winter of 1831–32 wood had been distributed to more than four hundred Philadelphia blacks—about one-eighth of all persons receiving such assistance. Since Negroes comprised about one-twelfth of the population of Philadelphia County at this time, these data indicate that the proportion of Negroes on the outdoor relief rolls was roughly half again as great as their percentage in the general population. If, as one suspects, the reported number of recipients actually represents the number of families relieved, the figures suggest that $\frac{1}{10}$–$\frac{1}{8}$ of all black families were so assisted. This hypothesis is further supported by data (acknowledged to be incomplete) from the late 1840s showing that almost one-eighth of the Negro families in Philadelphia and Moyamensing—the areas of the county in which "the greatest destitution and wretchedness exist"—received some form of outdoor relief.[22]

The extent of this aid varied, but in most cases would seem to have been limited to a small supply of fuel in the winter months. Philadelphia blacks reported, regarding the aid granted in 1848–49, that "this relief consists in the greater number of cases of donations of wood; some receive a small supply of groceries in addition; some receive from a quarter to a half a ton of coal; and a few, fifty cents a week during sickness." And of the 286 families given wood, only 10 received more than a half a cord during the year.[23]

In Albany, during the year ending May 1, 1850, the overseer of the poor disbursed monetary relief to 1,830 persons, most of whom were heads of families. Of this number, 38 were black—a little over two percent of the relief recipients in a city whose population was about $1\frac{2}{3}$ percent Negro. Albany's free people of color fared still better in the distribution of free fuel, for about one-fourteenth (62) of the 804 families receiving wood or coal were black.[24]

It should be abundantly clear that the extent to which a given black community received public assistance—either institutionalized or outdoor—was an inadequate indicator of the level of poverty in that community. Some cities wholly excluded blacks from their relief rolls, and it is likely that in all of them it was easier for whites to obtain aid than blacks. Still, the available data do suggest that in large dynamic northern cities with substantial Negro populations—such as New York and Philadelphia—not less than $\frac{1}{5}$–$\frac{1}{7}$ of the black population could be classified as destitute in the mid-nineteenth century, and that the actual percentage was probably much larger. But the data also show that despite widespread and grinding poverty, public aid for urban blacks was rarely more than minimal.

The support of the indigent in the almshouses and the distribution of money and supplies to those in distress were designed for the general relief of paupers and were addressed directly to the condition of indigency. But cities provided public support for other institutions and functions that were designed, not to relieve poverty, but to provide the indigent with necessary services for which fees were usually charged, or to assist specific components of the indigent population that neither the almshouse nor outdoor relief seemed capable of serving adequately. In at least some cities blacks with mental illnesses were admitted to the public insane (or lunatic) asylums or whatever facilities the city provided. At the end of the first half of the nineteenth century blacks constituted almost a quarter of the "insane and idiotic" inmates of the Baltimore almshouse and a fourteenth of the insane patients in the Maryland Hospital, a state facility. In the late

1840s Negroes consistently comprised about five percent of the inmates at New York's public lunatic asylum on Blackwell's Island. As
in other humane institutions, their accommodations were both segregated and inferior to those provided for whites. Until 1842 insane
blacks in the Baltimore almshouse were confined in garret rooms.
With the completion of the new almshouse in that year, the black
female insane were moved into more satisfactory quarters in the old
building vacated by the transfer of white women patients to the new
facility. But there was no mention of better accommodations for black
males.[25]

In some cities free persons of color (and, in the southern urban
centers, slaves as well) were received into public hospitals. This was
not, to be sure, universally true. A physician who admitted a black to
the Massachusetts General Hospital in Boston in 1829, contrary to
policy, was reproved by the hospital authorities, and in the 1830s
blacks seeking admission were turned away. Even as late as 1850 the
federal census marshal found only one Negro among the 112 patients
in this establishment.[26] In New Orleans, however, not only had the
original donation of Don Andres Almonaster y Roxas, which formed
the basis for the development of the renowned Charity Hospital,
specified the admission (on a segregated basis) of free persons of
color, but by mid-century there was also a separate charity hospital for
free persons of color. And in Baltimore and New York census
enumerators reported something less than ten percent of the patients
in public hospitals to be black.[27] As is noted elsewhere (see p. 140)
free persons of color made up very large proportions of the patients in
the emergency smallpox hospitals established in various cities, as well
as substantial percentages of those inoculated by public vaccine physicians.

Private philanthropy. sometimes supplemented by public assistance, also supported institutions and organizations in a number of
cities which aided indigent Negroes. Concerned whites in New York
established not only the Colored Home, as has been noted, but also a
Colored Orphan Asylum, and Philadelphia's Union Benevolent Society, though dispensing limited outdoor relief to both whites and
blacks, apparently considered black indigents in the Moyamensing
area to be "a principal object of its care." New Orleans had an "institution for colored persons" in the 1830s, and in 1842 the Sisters of
the Holy Family, a recently founded Negro Catholic order,
established an Asylum for Elderly Colored Women and shortly expanded its area of activity to include black men as well. General private benevolent organizations, especially those dispensing noninstitutional assistance, doubtless gave some aid to black residents as well as

whites.[28] The Colored Home in New York well illustrates the inter-
mingling of private and public concerns. Though private donations
and bequests constituted the initial support for the Society for the
Relief of Worthy Aged Colored Persons, which operated this facility,
it was also given a grant of ten thousand dollars by the state in 1845
and after 1846 received a payment from the city for each inmate
admitted by order of the city officials.[29]

Black orphans were an object of particular concern to white
humanitarians. The plight of the orphan was generally recognized in
American (and Western) society, both rural and urban, as having the
strongest of claims on the humanitarian impulses of individuals and
governments alike. But those claims were by no means fully met in
relation to black children, for although public, church, societal, and
generally philanthropic orphan asylums were established early and
shortly proliferated in most cities, they almost universally denied admission to children with any discernable trace of Negro ancestry. In
the 1830s, for example, black children were not admitted to the three
private orphanages in New York nor to the city facility known as the
Long Island Farms.[30]

It was this circumstance that moved two New York women, Anna
H. Shotwell and Mary Murray, to initiate efforts in 1833 to form the
Association for the Benefit of Colored Orphans, which was
established in 1836. It appeared initially that the formation of the
association would be an exercise in futility, for "so violent was the
prejudice against the colored race, that three long months were spent
in a fruitless search for a suitable building. Property-owners could be
induced, on no conditions, to lease an empty dwelling for such use."
The association was eventually compelled to purchase an inadequate
structure of Twelfth Street, where they received their first charges.
Thereafter the path was easier. In 1842 the city granted the association twenty lots on Fifth Avenue and added twenty more after a
substantial building was erected there in 1843. Continuing support
came from the state, private donations and bequests, the Manumission
Society, and payments by the city for orphans sent by city officials.
Though some black leaders originally opposed the creation of a segregated facility, by the 1850s black churches, associations, and individuals joined in supporting the asylum. The number of children in residence grew from 29 in 1837, to between 60 and 80 in the early 1840s,
and to 209 by the end of the half-century. These children, who were
between the ages of two and ten when admitted, were fed, clothed,
housed, and educated (four schools were in operation by 1850), and,
after they reached twelve years of age, apprenticed, usually to farmers.[31] Thus did a variety of charitable impulses—public and private,

black and white, institutional and individual—combine to provide protection and assistance to "a most helpless class of persons, against whom the doors of the ordinary charities of the city were shut."[32]

The decision to establish a Negro orphanage in New York may well have been inspired by a similar movement in Philadelphia a decade earlier. There a group of women members of the Society of Friends succeeded, after eight years of intermittent efforts, in founding the Shelter for Colored Orphans in 1822. The support obtained by this institution—entirely private and mostly from Quakers, blacks, and members of the Abolition Society—was both limited and irregular, and the total annual expenditures apparently never amounted to as much as three thousand dollars for more than a quarter of a century after its founding. In the first decade and a half of its existence the institution occupied a variety of rented buildings (usually inadequate) before a more substantial facility was erected on a donated lot in the late 1830s. The inmates—whose number rarely exceeded fifty in the first half of the nineteenth century—were admitted, supported, educated, and apprenticed on substantially the same terms as those that prevailed in the New York establishment. Though its activities were necessarily modest, the shelter, one contemporary observed, "rescued many little ones from the abodes of wretchedness and vice which abound in some neighborhoods . . . of our city."[33]

In the last dozen years of the half-century benevolent residents of Cincinnati and Providence launched rather more limited efforts to provide facilities to care for Negro orphans. In Cincinnati the Orphan Asylum for Negro Youth was organized in 1844 by cooperative endeavors of blacks and whites and was incorporated the following year. Its house on Ninth Street was large enough to accommodate 60–70 residents but its capacity was never strained for "the children being put out to various employments, as soon as they become capable of usefulness; there are . . . rarely more than twelve or fifteen inmates dwelling at one time in this asylum." And, indeed, those operating the orphanage would appear to have been easily convinced of black children's readiness for employment, for in 1850 the census marshal reported only nine children in residence—seven between five and seven years of age and two ten-year-olds.[34]

The Providence facility was largely the work of Anna A. Jenkins and other benevolent white women. In 1838 they organized the Providence Association for the Benefit of Colored Children and shortly established a shelter on Wickenden Street. The incorporation of the association in 1845 made it possible to acquire property and administer bequests, and Mrs. Jenkins almost immediately donated a plot of ground on Olive Street. At least one substantial gift and a successful subscription drive enabled the association to erect a new building there in 1849. At neither of the facilities, however, did the inmates number as many as thirty, which, considering the size of the Providence black community (1,499 in 1850), is hardly surprising.[35]

Given the relatively high death rates among urban free blacks, it is likely that there were far more Negro orphans than were accommodated, for however short a time, in these institutions. It would seem that most of them were cared for by black families, while older children were probably bound out by such city officials as the guardians of the poor, either directly or through the instrumentality of the orphans' courts.

Although it is not possible to state with any degree of precision the extent of black urban poverty—either absolutely or comparatively—in the first half of the nineteenth century, such data as are available strongly support the contemporary perception that they constituted the most deprived and destitute element in the urban population.[36] But it would appear to be equally certain that in no city were aged, orphaned, widowed, ill, and indigent blacks afforded access to public or private relief commensurate with the extent of their deprivation. Increasingly restricted on the lowest rungs of the economic ladder, urban blacks found that the prejudice and discrimination that inhibited their advancement operated with almost equal strength, when they were reduced to complete dependency, to deny (or at least limit) the assistance necessary to survive. Perhaps nothing else in urban life demonstrated more starkly the belief of all but a handful of benevolent whites that the Negro's "place" was "somewhere else."

9 Black Is for Mourning:
Urban Negro Mortality

On occasion men have hoped to find in the city a temporary refuge from an imminent threat of death—a threat posed by invading armies in ancient Greece or by summer fevers in antebellum South Carolina. But with rare exceptions urban centers have been perceived rather as nurseries of disease, vice, and violence, lacking the advantages associated with rural living—fresh air, pure water, wholesome diet, invigorating exercise, and plenty of rest.

Antebellum Americans had no doubt that in daylight or darkness death stalked the streets of every large city in as many guises as Pandora's box had troubles. At the worst of times—as when epidemics struck—people fled to the countryside, and at all times they lived, in some measure, with fear. It was not a pleasant thing, but it was a price to be paid in order that one might enjoy the benefits of urban life— paid by the wealthy because the rewards were great and, in any event, the burden in most years fell much more heavily on the poor, and paid by the poor because they felt fatalistically that they had no alternative. And generally speaking, urban blacks were the poorest of the poor.

There was a considerable measure of truth in this dismal view of the nineteenth century American city. Certainly where people were packed densely into cramped dwellings in narrow streets and alleys, into rotten hovels and fetid cellars, communicable diseases of all varieties flourished, and epidemics could decimate whole populations before the city fathers—jealous of the reputation of their metropolis— could be brought to acknowledge their existence.

Though comparable mortality figures for urban and rural areas are rare because of the absence or partial nature of the rural data, it would appear that urban mortality rates were, in fact, significantly higher than those in the countryside. By the middle of the nineteenth century the reporting of deaths, under the Massachusetts registry law, seems to have been relatively complete in all sections of the Bay State. In 1850 Suffolk County (almost ninety-five percent of the population of which was by that date within the boundaries of the city of Boston) reported 3,800 deaths out of 16,476 in the entire state. Thus, the mortality rate in Suffolk County was more than 26 per 1,000, as compared with less than 15 per 1,000 in the rest of the state—almost seventy-five percent higher than in the less urbanized counties.[1]

Not only were urban areas assumed to be less healthful than the rest of the country, but it was also routinely asserted that, in the cities, the black mortality rate was significantly greater than that for whites. Dr. Josiah Curtis, in 1855, declared "on the authority of the City Register," that the death rate among Boston's blacks was "greater than that of the whole city," despite the fact that more than one-half of them lived in one of the most healthy wards. But he gave no figures to support his statement and Boston's published mortality tables (like those of Massachusetts previously cited) were not separated by race in the first half of the nineteenth century. Philadelphia's renowned medical statistician, Dr. Gouverneur Emerson, noted that the virulent 1818 fever epidemic was "almost exclusively confined to the blacks inhabiting the narrow streets, courts, and alleys of the southwestern parts of the city and suburbs," and New York's "Banker-street Fever" of 1818 is also supposed to have wreaked havoc among that city's black cellar-dwellers.[2] But such comments were frequently impressionistic.

The only mortality data covering all fifteen cities for the same period of time and collected under a single authority are those reported by the United States Census Office in 1850 (see appendix D). These figures are highly unreliable and bear little resemblance to those contained in the reports of city authorities. Unfortunately, local data are not uniformly available, for a number of cities began to collect the information on deaths very late in the period, and some never did it very effectively. Others did not separate the data by race for all or a part of the half-century. It is not consequently possible to calculate reliable mortality tables for these fifteen cities for the first half of the nineteenth century or, indeed, for any year within that period. Table 9-1 does, however, give average annual mortality rates by decades for four cities—Baltimore, Charleston, New York, and Philadelphia— and may be viewed as at least suggestive of conditions within the largest cities in the United States during the period.

These locally collected figures show black mortality rates higher than those for whites in nine of the eleven sets of data. Nor were these differences marginal in size. In Philadelphia in the 1820s the black mortality rate was nearly double that of the whites, and the disporportion of Negro deaths was almost as great in New York in the same decade. In eight of the nine cases (Baltimore in the 1820s is the sole exception), the black mortality rate was at least twenty-five percent higher than that for whites. Only in Charleston in the third and fourth decades of the century do the figures in table 9-1 indicate a lower

Table 9-1   Average Annual Mortality Rates for Four Cities[3] (deaths per 1000 population)

		1821–30	1831–40	1841–50
Baltimore[a]	Black	29.1	33.9	30.6
	White	24.4	25.6	23.2
	Aggregate	25.5	27.4ᐧ	24.5
Charleston[b]	Black	28.4[c]	25.6	25.4[d]
	White	32.0[c]	26.0	17.2[d]
	Aggregate	29.8[c]	25.8	21.4[d]
New York[a]	Black	50.8[c]	40.7[e]	39.1
	White	26.3[c]	28.9[e]	30.5
	Aggregate	28.2[c]	29.7[e]	30.8
Philadelphia[b]	Black	45.8	32.5	
	White	23.6	24.1	
	Aggregate	25.6	24.8	

(a) Includes stillborn. (b) Excludes stillborn. (c) Based on data for nine years. (d) Based on data for eight years. (e) Based on data for seven years.

mortality rate among blacks than whites. But the difference in the 1830s was miniscule, and in any event one suspects that both figures result from a gross underreporting of slave deaths—especially those of young children—an element that made up about one-half of the city's population and almost ninety percent of its blacks.

There were, of course, some very great variations among the annual figures. The Negro mortality rate (including stillbirths) rose to over 60 per 1,000 population in Baltimore in the cholera year of 1832, was less than a third of that in 1840, and was below 30 deaths per 1,000 half of the time. In New York, the black mortality rate (including stillbirths) peaked at over 70 per 1,000 in 1825 and was less than 30 per 1,000 in only two of the twenty-six years included in the table. The figures in Charleston and Philadelphia are proportionately lower because they do not include stillbirths, which usually accounted for 5–10 percent of the total deaths. In the City of Brotherly Love black mortality rose to over 61 per 1,000 (in 1823) as compared with Charleston's 51 per 1,000 (in 1836). In Philadelphia, however, the death rate among Negroes was below 30 per 1,000 in only three of the twenty years, while in Charleston it was under 30 per 1,000 more than two-thirds of the time and occasionally dipped below 20 per 1,000.[4]

Since the local figures were compiled by different individuals and under different circumstances, precise comparisons are impossible. Some tentative conclusions about urban black mortality in general might, however, be drawn from the available data. It appears almost certain that the death rate among urban blacks, contrary to the implications of the 1850 census data (see appendix D), was, with rare exceptions, higher than for whites. This conclusion, which is clearly indicated by the figures in table 9-1, is also strongly supported by less comprehensive sets of data from other cities. In 1840 the Negro mortality rate in Boston was more than sixty percent higher than that for whites (32.4 and 20.2 per 1,000, respectively), and in the late 1850s averaged almost twenty-five percent higher than for whites. A sampling of Providence statistics in the 1840s shows death rates to have been, on the average, more than sixty-five percent higher for blacks than for whites (41.7 and 25.0 per 1,000). And late in the same decade Washington's blacks had an average annual mortality rate of 25.9 per 1,000 compared with 19.8 for whites—a differential of more than thirty percent. New Orleans was a notable exception to this pattern. There in 1849—a year of cholera and yellow fever epidemics— the death rate among whites (92.2 per 1,000) was almost forty percent higher than among blacks (66.3 per 1,000), as the city's white population was almost literally decimated.[5]

This peculiarity of New Orleans illustrates another conclusion that can be drawn—tentatively, at least—from these data. The discrepancy between black and white mortality rates tends to be greatest in the northern cities, less in the Upper South, and in the Lower South tends to disappear entirely or, indeed, to be transformed into a pattern of Negro death rates lower than those for whites. Certainly in New Orleans this may be a result of extraordinarily high white death rates, for the black mortality rates, though lower than those for whites, are still up to twice as great as those for Negroes in some northern urban centers. But in other southern cities the black mortality rate was frequently absolutely less than in northern population centers. This may have been, in part, a product of poor reporting (especially of slave deaths) by officers charged with this responsibility, but there is no hard evidence to support such a hypothesis.[6] It is possible, of course, that such discrepancies simply reflected the superior economic position of free blacks in southern cities (see chapter 2, above), better housing, and a much smaller proportion of unacclimated black in-migrants in the cities of the slave area (see pp. 5–6, 249).

A third conclusion suggested by these data is that the black mortality rate tended to decline in the later years of the half-century. Of the four cities examined in table 9-1, only Baltimore appears to be an exception to this trend, and that is largely because of the abnormally high number of deaths in the cholera year of 1832 and in 1849, when typhus struck the black population. In 1832, for instance, the number of Negro deaths was more than eighty percent greater than the average for the other nine years of that decade. This decline (which was not observable in the white mortality rates) was doubtless in part the result of improved public health practices, which naturally had greater direct impact on the less affluent elements in the urban populations.

Well-to-do and middle class whites had already fled the low-lying sections of the cities before those areas were ordered drained by health officials and had already had their families vaccinated against smallpox before municipal authorities moved to make such protection universal. It was probably natural that blacks—who made up a little over one-quarter of Washington's population—should constitute more than half of those immunized by the vaccine physicians, and that roughly forty percent of those so inoculated in Baltimore in 1829 and 1831 should come from the less than a quarter of the population that was black. The poor (and especially the blacks, in cities where they were numerous) were practically the only persons who availed themselves of the services offered by the special hospitals established in time of epidemic. In 1845 Negroes—mostly free—made up over two-thirds of the patients treated in Baltimore's smallpox hospital.[7] Thus, as public health measures became more effective, the astronomical urban black mortality rates (apparently *averaging* more than 65 per 1,000 in eighteenth-century Boston) declined, though they remained higher—usually 25–40 percent higher—than those for whites.[8]

The elevated black mortality rate was primarily the product of the poor and crowded housing conditions and limited access to nonemergency medical care. There were few black physicians and fewer still who were adequately trained, and although white practitioners treated blacks, it seems unlikely that they established a "family physician relationship" with them (or with poor whites either, for that matter). Some private hospitals, at least, admitted blacks, but it appears likely that cost and other factors discouraged their use of these institutions. Nor do they appear to have been welcome or comfortable in public hospitals. In New Orleans—where blacks had unusually good access to a wide variety of facilities—in the 1840s Negroes made up considerably less that one percent of the patients at Charity Hospital, though they constituted almost a quarter of the population.[9]

Urban black housing is examined elsewhere in this study and need not be discussed in detail here. It is sufficient to note that health officers and other observers alike often identified housing conditions as a major factor contributing to high black mortality rates, especially during epidemics. They made repeated reference to cellars and "hovels," and such adjectives as "wretched," "crowded," "miserable," and "lothsome" recur frequently.[10]

It is, of course, possible that blacks were physiologically more susceptible to some diseases than were whites, but it is patently impossible, on the basis of the data available in the antebellum era, to separate effectively physiological susceptibility and environmental conditions. It remains true, however, that some disorders produced higher mortality rates among blacks than among whites, while the reverse was true of others.

Certainly contemporary observers insisted—either by overt statement or by implication—that certain diseases were more prevalent among, and more frequently fatal to, blacks. Perceived as particularly deadly to Negroes were cholera and smallpox among the epidemic diseases, and consumption (tuberculosis), pneumonia, and cholera infantum among the chronic complaints. During the 1832 cholera pandemic it was repeatedly noted that the scourge was more fatal to blacks than to whites. A report from Philadelphia concluded with the comment that the deaths in one of the suburbs all "were of very intemperate and wretched colored persons," and a Baltimore health officer was careful to point out that almost one-half of the newly reported cholera victims were black. In the summer of 1850 the Washington Board of Health noted the persistence of smallpox throughout the past year, but observed that the disease was confined "almost entirely to the negroes, and those in the humbler sphere of life," and added that "few cases occcurred . . . among the better class of citizens."[11] As to cholera infantum—a summer intestinal disorder of young children—Gouverneur Emerson stated that it and similar complaints were, in Philadelphia, "generally confined to the offspring of the poor, and especially prevail among the blacks." Adult Negroes were believed to be particularly susceptible to respiratory complaints, and the author of the Washington Board of Health report in 1850 was more specific still, asserting the "mulattoes . . . , particulary the females" were "particularly liable" to consumption.[12]

It is not easy to test these contemporary hypotheses as vigorously as one might like. Many cities (as has been noted) did not separate death statistics by race. And a number of those that did disaggregate the gross deaths by race did not extend this division to the lower levels of data encompassing such matters as age, sex, and cause of death. Usable information is available for a handful of years in a few cities, however. The Charleston "cause of death" figures were consistently separated by race, and the Washington Board of Health followed the same practice when it began to make reports in the late 1840s. Additionally, the New York City Inspector also published the statistics in this fashion for a time in the 1830s and early '40s. By examining the first three Washington reports, a sample of five New York annual listings, and the Charleston 1822–48 data it is possible to reach some tentative conclusions.[13]

These data suggest that the contemporary observations were not in every case valid. Cholera and smallpox, indeed, killed a disproportionate number of blacks in these cities. In Charleston, for instance, almost eighty percent of all cholera victims were blacks, though Negro deaths from all causes comprised less than four-sevenths of the total in the general mortality list. The smallpox statistics were similar; blacks accounted for seventy-five percent of the deaths. In Washington the figure was seventy percent—more than double the proportion of Negro deaths (30.1%) in the general list. In New York, though black smallpox victims comprised a much smaller 10.4 percent of the total, that figure was still almost half again as great as the proportion of Negroes in the total number of deaths (7.0%).

But if contemporaries were correct in their assessment of black susceptibility to cholera and smallpox, they erred in other particulars. Though it would appear that respiratory complaints were slightly more deadly to blacks than to whites, only in New York (of these three cities) was the proportion of Negroes among either pneumonia victims or those succumbing to consumption as much as ten percent greater than the black components in the general mortality lists; blacks made up 9.6 percent and 10.3 percent, respectively, of the deaths attributed to pneumonia and consumption—1/3–1/2 greater than in the total deaths. And the proportion of Negro children who died of cholera infantum was actually 1/4–2/3 lower than the percentage of blacks in the general death lists in Washington and New York and only minutely above that level in Charleston. A number of cholera infantum deaths might well have been reported under the heads of diarrhea and dysentery, but the proportion of Negro deaths in these categories was from more than a fifth to almost two-thirds less than in the total deaths in all three cities.

A careful examination of these urban mortality figures also makes it possible to identify other complaints that were unusually dangerous to Negroes. In all three cities Negro deaths attributed to dropsy (a generalized edema) were disproportionately great, ranging 30–50 percent above the black percentage of total deaths. In Washington and New York apoplexy (stroke) also killed blacks in unusual numbers—Negroes constituted 44.7 percent and 8.4 percent, respectively of such deaths—though this was not true in Charleston. Unusually large numbers of Negro deaths were attributed to intemperance and delirium tremens in the same two cities—43.1 percent and 10.2 percent, respectively, of all deaths from these causes—but in Charleston the percentage of such victims who were black constituted only about one-half of the Negro proportion in the general mortality lists. On the other hand, ninety-five percent of all tetanus victims were black in Charleston, the only one of these cities in which this disease was of any significance, as were more than two-thirds of the "teething" deaths. Among other childhood complaints, black mortality was unusually high from whooping cough in Washington and Charleston (where 42.9 percent and 72.2 percent, respectively, of the victims were black) and remarkably low from scarlet fever, with the black proportion of such deaths ranging 35–50 percent below the Negro percentage of the total mortality in these three cities. Finally, in Washington and Charleston blacks made up ⅖–⅔ of those whose deaths were attributed to unknown—or, at least, unrecorded—causes.[14]

Obviously it would be desirable to determine the extent to which the pattern of black mortality in the cities differed from that in the rural areas, if, in fact, it did so. As has been noted, the 1850 census mortality statistics are of doubtful reliability. There is no reason to belive, however, that the data are more inaccurate for any one cause of death than another. Hence, if one deals only with the percentage of Negro deaths reported under each "cause of death" heading in relationship to the black percentage of all deaths, a considerable amount of the distortion may well be eliminated.

Some differences between urban and rural areas do, in fact, appear to have existed. The national figures (doubtless heavily nonurban in nature) showed average or low proportions of blacks dying of cholera and smallpox, and the same is true of apoplexy. Influenza, on the other hand, appears to have been much more of a threat to nonurban than to urban blacks. The same is true of "teething," where the census figures show the proportion of Negro deaths to have been seventy-five percent greater than the black percentage in the general mortality list; of the cities analyzed above, only Charleston showed a high Negro death rate from "teething," and in that case the difference was barely over one-fifth. Negro deaths from dropsy, however, were only 26.5 percent higher than in the general list, while in the cities the figure ranges 30–50 percent above that level. Among the major respiratory diseases, the census figures show a very low black mortality from consumption nationwide, but the proportion of blacks succumbing to pneumonia is higher (forty percent above that in the total mortality figures) than in any of the cities examined. The black mortality rate from tetanus and whooping cough was high in the nation, as it was in the cities. In short, it would appear that urban blacks suffered more from apoplexy, cholera, dropsy, and smallpox than did those in smaller towns and rural areas.[15]

It is extremely difficult to reach any conclusions about the extent of child mortality among urban blacks. The deaths of children under ten usually accounted for 40–50 percent of the total mortality for the whole population. But the mortality tables by age were almost never disaggregated by race. Very limited data are available for Charleston and New York, and these suggest that child mortality was disproportionately high in Charleston as compared with both black mortality in general and child mortality of the whole population. During the period 1822–48, children under ten years of age comprised roughly twenty-six percent of the white and about twenty-eight percent of the black population; for the same period, deaths in this age group comprised 23.4 percent of all white deaths and 39.6 percent of all Negro deaths, and this despite the fact that the reported mortality rate for blacks was slightly lower than that for whites in Charleston. In New York, on the other hand, the death rate among black children appears to have been rather lower than might have been expected, given the very high mortality among both blacks and children. The bills of mortality for 1838, 1842, and 1844 show children under ten constituting 38.6 percent of all Negro deaths and 51.6 percent of those of whites. The 1840 census showed this age group constituting twenty percent of the black and twenty-six percent of the white population.[16]

The data on the relationship between black male and female mortality are almost as scarce as those dealing with children. Officials compiling mortality lists rarely separated the male and female deaths by race. Such data as are available, however, consistently indicate the same relationships. In Charleston in the period 1822–48 and in New York in the late 1830s and early '40s even the figures are almost identical. In each city something over fifty-six percent of the black population was female, and in each city black female deaths averaged something less than fifty-one percent of all Negro deaths. In Washington (1848–51) the discrepancy is even more pronounced. There black female deaths, on the average, made up less than half of the total black mortality, despite the fact that almost sixty percent of the Negro population was female. In New Orleans (1849), too, females constituted almost three-fifths of the black population, but their deaths made up less than two-fifths of the Negro mortality totals.[17]

A lower mortality rate among females was, of course, usual in the antebellum era. The 1850 census figures showed the black population to have been 50.2 percent female, but persons of that sex comprised only 48.1 percent of the total Negro deaths. A similar relationship existed in the white population, where females made up only 46.15 percent of the mortality lists while comprising 48.72 percent of the total white population.[18] What is remarkable, therefore, is not that the female mortality figures were lower than their proportion of the population, but the magnitude of that difference. The census figures reveal a difference of about two percentage points between the female proportions of the population and the total deaths, but in the cities the difference between these two figures was frequently three times as great. There were similar, though slightly smaller, differences in the white urban and national figures as well. These data (though derived from a relatively small number of sources) suggest, then, that the elevated black male mortality rate (relative to that of the females) was largely an urban phenomenon, though the slight differences between urban black and urban white figures further suggest that race (or the black environment) may have been an intensifying factor.[19]

One of the most obvious anomalies in table D-1 is the wide variation in the reported death rates for slaves. Unfortunately, urban slave mortality is one of the most difficult of all mortality figures to determine. Baltimore alone, among the nation's fifteen largest cities, appears to have maintained separate death data on slaves and free blacks, but not until the end of the first quarter of the nineteenth century. For most of the officials (white) who compiled the statistics, race doubtless seemed much more significant than condition. But the figures in table 9-2 suggest that their view may well have been erroneous. The Baltimore reports showed an increase in the slave mortality rate between 1824 and 1850 so pronounced as to produce an actual increase in the average number of slave deaths from 78.7 per year in the 1820s to 180 per year in the 1840s, despite the fact that the slave population declined by about one-third in those years. During those same years the white mortality rate remained essentially stable and that for free blacks declined by more than a quarter. By the 1840s the mortality rate for free persons of color exceeded that for whites by only 3½ deaths per 1,000, but the rate for slaves was more than double that for the rest of the population.

Table 9-2   Average Annual Mortality Rates in Baltimore[20] (deaths per 1,000 population)

	FPC	Slave
1824–30	36.5	18.8
1831–40	34.6	33.9
1841–50	26.7	58.8

The annual figures show the same trend in a pronounced fashion within the decades. Before 1836 the free black mortality rate dropped below 30 per 1,000 population five times (and in two of those years the rate was 29.5 and 29.9 per 1,000) and rose as high as 64.7 per 1,000 in the cholera year of 1832. In the same period the mortality rate for slaves exceeded 30 per 1,000 in only two years, peaking at 41.7 per 1,000 in 1832, and was actually below 20 per 1,000 in three of the first four years for which data are available. In the last fifteen years of the half-century these trends were dramatically reversed. The death rate for Baltimore's free blacks during this decade and a half exceeded 30 per 1,000 only four times (only once after 1838) and reached 35 per 1,000 only in 1836. The slave mortality rate in the same period, however, dropped below 30 per 1,000 only in 1836, was greater than 40 per 1,000 two-thirds of the time, and averaged 89.4 deaths per 1,000 and in the last three years of the period, exceeding 90 per 1,000 in 1848.[21]

It is possible, of course, that these remarkable shifts reflected nothing more than increasingly accurate reporting of deaths among this particular portion of the population. Certainly the census marshals in Baltimore were informed of only slightly over one-fifth of the number of slave deaths recorded by the board of health. But there is no evidence to support this hypothesis and little reason to believe that such dramatic improvements in the efficiency of the reporting officers should have been confined to a single group of people comprising (in 1850) less than two percent of the population. It may well be that the escalation in the slave mortality rate was accurately reported and reflected significant changes in the work and residence patterns of urban slaves in Baltimore. As early as the beginning of the second quarter of the nineteenth century Hezikiah Niles noted, "Many that are slaves go pretty much at large, and are regarded as free." There can be little doubt that the proportion of urban slaves permitted to "hire their own time," and, concomitantly, charged with providing their own food, clothing, and housing, increased in the latter portion of the half-century. These people had few or no financial resources, and, consequently, as David Bailie Warden earlier observed in relation to Washington's slaves, their "place of repose is generally a cellar, the dampness of which is favorable to the propagation of contagion." These circumstances may well have produced a genuine increase in Baltimore's slave mortality rate.[22] In any event, if the Baltimore figures are representative, urban slaves had a much higher mortality rate than·did either the free persons of color or the whites.

Thus, although urban blacks fell victim to the diseases and complaints of the city in disproportionately large numbers, the urban condition may well have had a less deleterious effect upon blacks than upon whites. The differential between black and white death rates—as well as the black mortality rate itself—decreased as the half-century wore on and cities expanded their public facilities for dealing with such epidemic diseases as cholera and smallpox—both major killers of blacks. But it appears likely that the mortality rate became greater for slaves, and that for free blacks it was larger in northern than in southern cities. But of whatever condition and wherever located, the urban Negro lived intimately with the respiratory complaints of the winter and the intestinal disorders of the summer; with the choking despair of epidemics at all seasons; and with death as a constant companion—because he was urban, because he was poor, and because he was black.

10 The Substance of Things Hoped For: Urban Black Education

One of the more persistent axioms in American society has been that education is essential to personal happiness, the key to moral improvement, the surest avenue to economic success, and the foundation of community progress. Combining as it does the major (and sometimes apparently contradictory) themes of individualism, democracy, communitarianism, optimism, the search for order, ambition, the work ethic, self-improvement, and the belief in the inevitability of progress, it draws strength from a variety of diverse, and often antipathetic, elements in American society. Those who thought man inherently evil saw schools as instruments to encourage conformity and to sanction the imposition of restraints, while the supporters of the concept of man's innate goodness viewed the educational process as a severing of bonds and removal of constraints, enabling invidiuals to realize their potential. The conservative valued the educational experience because it preserved and transmitted the community's heritage and the progressive because it fostered change. The "intellectuals" applauded educational institutions because they, more than any other element in the community, strove to develop an appreciation for art, letters, philosophy, abstract thought, and the search for ultimate truth, while successful entrepreneurs extended equally strong support on the grounds that a mind strengthened by study and honed by discipline had a competitive edge in the pursuit of profit.

Educational development in the cities was consistently in advance of that in the less urbanized areas, in part because the diversity and complexity of urban life seemed to demand more intellectual development; in part because the cities always had large numbers of inmigrants whose children needed to be acculturated to the urban environment; and in part simply because the concentration of population produced a more extensive and spatially concentrated market for education and training. To this demand both the community and individual entrepreneurs responded in diverse ways. Black Americans held these views no less firmly than whites and perceived with equal clarity that their individual and communal advancement—especially in a nonagricultural society—required the literacy, intellectual development, and acquisition of nonmanual skills that appeared to be obtainable only through an organized educational process. Indeed, it is possible that blacks, because they largely lacked such other instruments of advancement as family influence, access to capital, relative freedom from class restraints, and community acceptance of their aggressiveness and ambition, placed greater faith in the liberating qualities of education than did the whites and, hence, sought its presumed benefits more earnestly. Theirs was a hope born of despair; an agonizing need to believe that at least one path to improvement was not barred to them.

But communities committed in varying degress to the necessity for ensuring the education of their citizenry did not always perceive the need to include blacks in the process. For it appeared to many of those influential in developing educational structures that Negroes would be forever prevented by their race from participating in the major areas of activity for which the academic experience was designed to prepare students—nonmanual labor, intellectual pursuits, and the political process. Hence, as urban centers in the first half of the nineteenth century developed more and more complex and comprehensive public-funded and community-directed school systems, blacks were excluded entirely from their benefits, or, if admitted, their access was narrowly circumscribed and their level of achievement severely limited. Throughout the period under consideration, free persons of color were prohibited from attending public schools in the six southern cities examined and in Cincinnati as well. In the other urban centers, their admission to public educational facilities was on a limited and segregated basis.

Publicly funded schools, therefore, played a less significant role in the black urban educational experience than they did for whites. But though Negro efforts to obtain instruction were fragmented, they were not wholly individualized, for action by groups and organizations played crucial roles in the establishment and maintenance of schools which, though not publicly supported, were still community institutions. These approaches were common to both the black and the white segments of the urban populations in the early years of the century—before the establishment and development of the public schools—but for the reasons noted above they persisted much longer in the Negro community.

Most black nonpublic schools fell into one of three categories—entrepreneurial, institutional, or philanthropic. The entrepreneurial schools were those in which instructional and all other costs were defrayed by tuition paid by parents or guardians on a per-pupil basis. In the case of institutional schools, churches or other organizations provided quarters for the school and sometimes guaranteed the salary of the instructor, though tuition was usually charged and was frequently expected to cover all costs except housing. Philanthropic schools were organized and at least partially funded by persons or groups outside the black community and, though sometimes charging fees to those able to pay, usually admitted students without reference to their ability or willingness to meet tuition charges.

The process of establishing a school in antebellum America was an extremely simple one. Accreditation and certification were unknown (though the eighteenth-century Boston town government licensed schoolmasters)[1] and unmissed. Education—even public education— partook heavily of the entrepreneurial spirit and it was assumed that good teachers would flourish at the expense of those who were inferior—a kind of academic Gresham's Law. A teacher (self-announced) and a room became a primary school if students could be persuaded to enroll, and schools with fewer than a dozen pupils were by no means uncommon. This circumstance makes it very difficult to trace the beginnings of black education in American cities, for any individual, black or white—moved by ambition, concern, philanthropy, or any other worthy or base motive—could bring into existence an educational institution whose life span might be measured in months rather than years. Because of this enormous flexibility these one-teacher schools, usually entrepreneurial in nature, played an important role in the education of both black and white urbanites well into the nineteenth century.

As early as 1704 in New York and 1732 in Philadelphia white teachers offered instruction to blacks (in one case, gratuitously), and the New York school, taught by Elias Neau, appears to have survived for a decade or more. A century later, in 1818, what was apparently the earliest educational opportunity offered to the blacks of Pittsburgh resulted from a similar act of individual philanthropy by a concerned white teacher. Black education in Philadelphia was given a firmer institutional base when the Quakers, in 1770, undertook such instruction as a continuing commitment, which would extend well into the nineteenth century. This work was supplemented by the establishment in 1789 of a society which supported evening schools for adults and another in 1792 devoted to the education of Negro women. Though not officially connected with the Philadelphia Meeting, the influence of the Friends was strong in both of these organizations. Meanwhile, after earlier efforts by the Bray Associates in New York collapsed during the Revolutionary era, the New York Manumission Society provided a substantial base for Negro instruction when it founded, in 1786, the first of a series of schools from which the black public educational system would eventually rise.[2]

Before the end of the eighteenth century free persons of color in several of the cities with large black populations had already begun to make communal efforts to obtain educational facilities for their children. Philadelphia blacks used their newly established independent churches as instruments and in the 1790s opened schools associated with both the St. Thomas's Episcopal and the Bethel Methodist churches. One of several concerns that impelled some Charleston free persons of color to form the Brown Fellowship Society in 1790 was the desire to create an institutional base to support a school for Negro children. And some cooperative effort almost certainly preceded Joseph Townsend's advertisement of 1797 for a teacher to conduct the "Baltimore African Academy now ready to begin."[3]

It is worth noting that in the eighteenth and early nineteenth centuries there were a few chinks in the wall of educational segregation. Although the public schools in Boston and Providence (and apparently in Philadelphia, as well) were not initially segregated by law or policy, the harassment of black students was so extensive and so intense as to produce a near-total exclusion of free persons of color. But private teachers did, in a few cases, accept black students in predominantly white schools. Such practices were apparently not rare in Washington in the first decade of the nineteenth century and seem to have persisted in some measure in New Orleans as late as the 1830s. Though much less common than in Washington, integrated classrooms were not unknown in Baltimore either, but the practice seemingly did not survive the first decade of the century. Farther to the north, however, there is little evidence that private teachers either wished or dared to admit blacks, though "light" Negro children are supposed to have been enrolled in some private schools in Cincinnati as late as 1835. In Providence, "it was considered a disgraceful employment to be a teacher of colored children and still more disgraceful to have colored children in white schools." Nevertheless, at least one respected schoolmaster—John Lawton—admitted a few Negro children if their parents could pay his high fees. But Bronson Alcott found Boston less liberal on such matters, and the admission of a black girl to his classroom was quickly followed by an exodus of white students and the speedy demise of the school. By 1820 racial segregation would appear to have been virtually universal in the private as well as the public schools in all the major cities, with the possible exception of New Orleans.[4]

William B. Hesseltine has identified the "trustee tradition" as one of the persisting themes which heavily influenced the structuring of American soceity.[5] Hesseltine emphasizes that this tradition was manifest in the desire to use political instrumentalities to induce or compel Americans to behave in a "moral" fashion. But it also impelled men and women of wealth and standing—individually or in association—to assist those less fortunate than themselves. These philanthropic impulses took various forms and made themselves felt in many areas of American life. The deep deprivation and near-universal social rejection of the Negro population made it an obvious object for philanthropic activity. And philanthropists were perhaps even more strongly committed than Americans in general to a belief in the benefits conferred by education.

Philanthropic support for black education was particularly notable in the northern section of the country, and some evidence of this impulse was manifest in almost all of the northern cities examined. In some instances zealous whites undertook the education of free persons of color without the promise or anticipation of significant financial reward. In 1818 Robert Smith opened a free school for black children in Pittsburgh, and though he was later paid a small stipend by the overseers of the poor, the remuneration was inconsequential. A year or two later Eliza Gano, the daughter of a white Baptist minister, opened a short-lived school for blacks on the Lancastrian monitorial plan in Providence; and in 1845–46 the Reverend Augustin Paris, a Catholic priest, instructed a hundred or so black girls in St. Louis, until public pressure forced the closing of the school in conformity with the newly enacted (1847) state statute prohibiting the instruction of blacks. In Cincinnati, despite strong local disapprobation, a number of Lane Seminary students undertook the instruction of 100–300 Negro children in the 1830s in at least four schools, and taught 40–50 adults at night. Cincinnati was also the location of one of the most ambitious examples of individual philanthropy in the field of black education—the Gilmore High School for Negroes. Established in 1844 by Hiram S. Gilmore, a wealthy British clergyman, this institution's five teachers, under Gilmore's direction, taught up to three hundred black scholars Latin, Greek, drawing, and music, as well as "the branches usual to a full English course of study." Though fees were collected from those able to pay, others were not turned away, and school funds were expended for clothing as well as books for poorer pupils, and parents were even occasionally paid for the income lost by the withdrawal of a child from the labor market. Income—even including the proceeds of fund-raising trips by student groups in Ohio, New York, and Canada—apparently never equaled the expenditures, and it is likely that Gilmore (who turned the school over to one of his teachers in 1848) received financial support from other interested parties.[6]

Aside from that of Gilmore, most individual philanthropic efforts were both small-scale and short-lived. Of greater importance were the activities of organizations, whose sponsorship, in most cases, promised both greater and more dependable financial support. Such promises could, of course, prove illusory. In 1817 Charlotte Ludlow took the lead in forming an "African Society" in Cincinnati, but the school established under its auspices appears not to have long survived its founding. In New Orleans the Ursuline nuns, who had opened a school for Negro children in 1831, found themselves financially unable to continue to staff both black and white schools and transferred their Negro pupils to the care of the Carmelites in 1838. Both orders charged high tuition fees but some nonpaying or reduced fee students were apparently admitted. The support of established white humanitarian societies was more substantial. In Providence the Rhode Island Abolition Society furnished some of the funding for a night school for blacks in 1806, and the Boston Society for the Religious and Moral Instruction of the Poor maintained both a school for Negro girls and another for adults in the 1820s.[7]

It was in Philadelphia and New York, however, that the efforts of white associations to provide black educational opportunities were most extensive and had the greatest impact. In the City of Brotherly Love the Quakers were early in the field, with the Monthly Meeting establishing a school for blacks in 1770, supported by the voluntary contributions of Friends. The support of this institution was made still more firm when Anthony Benezet, who had served on the school committee and for a time as master, left a substantial sum for its support on his death in 1784. In that same year a separate school for girls was established under the same auspices. These schools continued to operate, first in Willing's Alley and after 1845 in newly constructed quarters in Raspberry Street, throughout the antebellum era. Though fees were collected from those able to pay, support came primarily from the bequests of Benezet and other Friends, with the deficiency being supplied by the Philadelphia Monthly Meeting. Quakers were also active in other educational efforts. In 1808 the Philadelphia Association of Friends for the Instruction of Poor Children established the Adelphi School for whites, and in 1822, after the public school system came into existence, devoted all of their resources to the education of Negro children. These three schools, in 1849, enrolled about one-half as many black pupils as the public schools, making a significant contribution to Negro education. Additionally, the Association of Friends for Improving the Condition of the Free People of Colour conducted a night school for older girls which enrolled eighty pupils in 1848, while more than four hundred men and women were instructed at night in the Raspberry Street facility.[8]

Other philanthropic organizations also provided educational opportunities for Philadelphia's free persons of color. The Philadelphia trustees of the Bray Associates continued active at least through the

1830s, operating schools for up to sixty black scholars or, when the number declined, supporting them in other private schools. In addition, for several years in the second decade of the century the Union Society for the Support of Schools and Domestic Manufactures, for the Benefit of the African Race, conducted a school for forty or so boys. In the 1820s and '30s, as the infant school movement gained strength, this form of educational experience was also made available to Negroes. The Infant School Society maintained one or more schools for black children 2–5 years of age from 1827 throughout the remainder of the first half of the nineteenth century.[9]

Because of the substantial commitment by the Quakers and by various charitable associations, the Pennsylvania Society for Promoting the Abolition of Slavery did not play nearly so active a role in black education in Philadelphia as its counterpart did in New York. Nevertheless, the society established a school as early as 1794 and at the turn of the century was giving limited assistance to two private black schools. In 1809 it erected a building for educational purposes where it conducted classes for 100–300 boys and girls for more than thirty years. It also established an infant school in the early 1840s.[10]

In New York the Manumission Society played the major role in black education in the first quarter of the nineteenth century. In 1787, two years after the organization's foundation, it established the African Free School in a house in Clift Street. This institution, which was subsequently divided into boys' and girls' departments, enrolled roughly a hundred pupils annually in the early years of the century. Because of the substantial increase in enrollment after 1809, when instruction on the Lancastrian monitorial plan was inaugurated, a second school was opened in 1820 and four more in 1831–32. This rapid expansion was possible because the society had become the recipient of state public educational funds. Enrollments of 600–800 were common in the 1820s and roughly double those figures in the early 1830s. To the usual elementary subjects were added needlework for the girls and navigation and astronomy for the boys, but few pupils qualified for the advanced classes, and average daily attendance was frequently about one-half of the number enrolled. In 1834 the African Free Schools were transferred to the control of the New York Public School Society, the major local recipient of state funds. Even before this date they had, for practical purposes, ceased to be philanthropic undertakings and had become public schools.[11]

Despite the elementary nature of the subjects offered to most black students, these schools were intellectual nurseries for a number of Negro leaders. Among the students in the African Free Schools in this era were the abolitionist leaders Samuel Ringgold Ward and

Henry Highland Garnet; the internationally renowned Shakespearean actor Ira Aldrich; Alexander Crummell, who would earn a B.A. degree at Cambridge University; and James McCune Smith, who later took B.A., M.A., and M.D. degrees from the University of Glasgow.[12]

The Manumission Society also maintained evening schools for black adults at least in the 1790s, and Arthur Tappen gave some assistance to the short-lived educational efforts of the Phoenix Society; otherwise there was remarkably little interest in black education displayed by individual white philanthropists or by white humanitarian institutions. It must be acknowledged that this apparent lethargy was in part the product of the general satisfaction with the activities of the Manumission Society, coupled with the availability of state educational funds for the African Free Schools.[13]

Black men and women did not, however, passively await an outpouring of white benevolence to educate their children. Rather, they sought opportunities for instruction avidly when available and zealously used such social instruments as they possessed to institutionalize their joint efforts. And if existing organizations proved ineffective or insufficient, they established new associations—formally or informally—for the purpose.

As is noted elsewhere (pp. 193–94), the black religious congregations were active in the educational field, for reasons both theological and social. Before the century was a decade old, for example, there were black schools associated with the Bethel African Methodist Church and St. Thomas's African Episcopal Church in Philadelphia, and the African Baptist Church in Boston. Congregations in other cities followed suit, and in 1844 the national African Methodist Episcopal Church directed (futilely, as it turned out) specific ministers to establish secondary schools in Baltimore and Philadelphia.[14]

Perhaps in no city was the involvement of black churches in the educational process more extensive than in Baltimore. Before the nineteenth century was a decade old both the Sharp Street Methodist and the Bethel African Methodist Episcopal churches had established schools. Both persisted throughout the antebellum era, the former being transformed into Union Academy—with a rather more advanced curriculum—in 1828 by its new master, William Lively, a respected and experienced black educator. Both schools employed multiple instructors. Other church-connected schools were maintained by the Asbury AME Church (intermittently, ater 1831), the Presbyterians (from the 1810s), the Episcopalians (established in 1823), and the Baptists (from at least the 1820s). The St. Francis Academy for girls was established in 1829 by the Colored Women's Society in connection with the black Oblate Sisters of Providence, whose chapel had come to be viewed as a parish church by many of Baltimore's Negro Catholics. It not only had a substantial local patronage but also attracted boarding students from Washington, Philadelphia, and elsewhere. Very spottty evidence suggests that each of these schools usually enrolled 50–100 pupils.[15]

In a less formalized setting the black churches made additional contributions to the education of urban Negroes through their Sunday schools. These organizations should not be thought of simply as extensions of the religious exercises of the congregations. "Their brief sessions," as James M. Wright noted, "were divided between inculcating religious and moral precepts and teaching the elementary studies of the common schools; the line distinguishing them from the day schools was not, therefore, to be strictly drawn."[16]

Many Sabbath schools, especially in the earlier years of the nineteenth century, were established and maintained by white individuals, churches, and associations. For example, black Sunday schools were opened by a Mrs. Upfold in Albany in 1816, by two white women in Cincinnati in 1817, by the Reverend John Mason Peck in St. Louis in 1818, by "certain pious young gentlemen and ladies" in Albany in 1820, and by a Miss Wescott in Providence in 1821. White churches were particularly active in such activities in Washington, Baltimore, St. Louis, and Charleston. Schools were supported by Boston's Society for the Religious and Moral Instruction of the Poor in the 1820s and by the Pittsburgh Sunday School Association a little earlier.[17]

The second quarter of the nineteenth century saw the Sunday schools for blacks come more and more under the control of the black congregations. This would doubtless have been a natural development in any event, but it was further encouraged by a partial withdrawal of white churches from the field in some Upper South cities in the aftermath of the Nat Turner uprising.[18] The rise in importance of the independent black Sunday school was accompanied by an increase in the number of black teachers, though white Sabbath school instructors were not rare at any time during the first half of the nineteenth century and beyond. By the end of the antebellum era Sabbath schools connected with black churches were to be found almost everywhere that such congregations existed, from the Methodist chapels of New Orleans to the First African Baptist Church in Albany. These schools were perhaps most extensive in Baltimore, Philadelphia, and Washington, which were also notable centers of independent black congregational development. The black Sunday school differed from its white counterpart not only in its greater emphasis on developing literacy but also in servirtg a large number of adult pupils. Blacks as old as ninety, for instance, attended Albany's First African Baptist Sunday School in the 1820s. They were, consequently, more nearly community institutions than the white Sabbath schools, and enrollment and attendance were often substantial. By the mid-1820s Albany's three black Sunday schools enrolled 200–250 students, and almost a sixth (more than 200) of all the Sabbath school children participating in the 1824 Cincinnati Independence Day parade were black. By the end of the antebellum era about 800 Negro children attended Sunday schools in Washington, over 1,600 in Philadelphia, and almost 2,700 in Baltimore.[19]

In their search for educational opportunities the urban free persons of color did not rely solely on existing institutions, but also organized themselves—both formally and informally—into associative groups to establish and maintain schools. It seems likely that some cooperative effort preceded the establishment of a school in the home of Primus Hall in Boston in 1798 as well as the opening of the Baltimore African Academy in 1797. And Charleston's Coming Street School, taught by the white schoolmaster W. W. Wilburn, was managed by a black board of trustees. Though not involved in the conduct of the school, the Woolman Benevolent Society, a Negro beneficial association, was a major financial contributor to the support of the first black school in Brooklyn.[20]

Other black organizations, more formal in nature, existed wholly or in part to support black educational institutions. One of the basic purposes of Charleston's Brown Fellowship Society (1790) was "to maintain schools for Negro children," and its Minors Moralist Society was founded in 1803 primarily to provide education for black indigent and orphan children. An association of free persons of color was conducting a school in Carter's Alley in Philadelphia as early as 1804, and in 1818 the Augustine Education Society was formed under the leadership of prominent blacks, with the ambitious design of establishing a seminary for more advanced studies. New York Negroes were also early in the field, forming an educational society in 1812, and in the late 1830s the Phoenix Society maintained a secondary school for blacks for about two years, thanks largely to white financial support. The Society for the Promotion of Education among Colored Children, which was established in 1847, was a more notable effort of the whole black community, and within two years its school had an enrollment of well over three hundred pupils. Separate black educational associations were less common elsewhere, but the Resolute Beneficial Society operated a school in Washington from 1818 to 1822, and the Pittsburgh African Educational Society conducted a short-lived school in the early 1830s.[21]

Given the affluence of a number of free blacks in New Orleans, it was not surprising that it should be the site of one of the most substantial and financially secure private institutional educational undertakings. In the 1840s an association of Catholic free men of color founded the École des Orphelins Indigents (also known as the Institution Catholique des Orphelins Indigents). The basic funding was provided by a bequest from Madame Bernard Couvent, a free woman of color, subsequently supplemented by substantial donations from two other wealthy free Negroes, Aristide Mary and Thomy Lafon. Bilingual instruction was provided to both orphans and pay pupils by a staff of eight teachers educated in Santo Domingo and France. Less extensive was Baltimore's Wells School, whose foundation was a bequest of William Wells, a well-to-do free black. The trustees of the Wells bequest operated the school continuously from 1835 until well after the Civil War.[22]

Perhaps the most ambitious effort of blacks to provide for the education of their children in an institutional fashion occurred in Ohio. In 1835 delegates from a number of black communities met in Columbus to "devise some way of increasing the means to educate their people." To this end they formed the School Fund Society, under whose auspices black schools were established in Cincinnati and several other Ohio towns. The society and its schools eked out a precarious existence for two years before the movement collapsed in the panic year of 1837.[23]

Entrepreneurial schools not only embodied much of the spirit of antebellum American society but also appeared to be well adapted to responding to (though not necessarily satisfying) the educational needs of the urban free black communities. The size of the black populations in the major towns created a substantial and concentrated market for the specialized services of potential educators. The individual entrepreneurial teacher possessed the ultimate flexibility for meeting the demands of this black educational marketplace by shifting the location of the school, changing the curriculum, or modifying the level of expectation for pupil performance. The support of an entrepreneurial school required no institutionalization of the community's desire for educational opportunities and no advance or long-term commitment of scarce financial resources. Nor was any significant monetary investment necessary on the part of the schoolmaster before the pupils (and, with luck, the tuition payments) arrived. It was, therefore, to be expected that entrepreneurial schools should play a major role in educating the urban black population, especially in those cities in which neither philanthropic nor public action and support provided continuing and substantial educational opportunities for free persons of color.

There were doubtless entrepreneurial schools for Negroes in all of the cities throughout most of the half-century, but all record of perhaps most of them has long since perished, and many others are known only from a reference to the name of a teacher or a location. In general, their most extensive development would appear to have been in the cities in the slave area (with the exception of St. Louis, where free blacks seem to have had few educational opportunities other than those provided by the churches) and in the northern cities of Cincinnati (where they were wholly excluded from the public schools), Philadelphia, and New York. In New York the African Free Schools were, at least until the late 1820s, clearly inadequate to serve the large and increasing black population, which found educational alternatives in private schools. In 1812 there were at least three in operation, and by the end of the third decade of the century there were no fewer than a half-dozen, three of which were said to be "excellent."[24]

In Philadelphia, where public support for black education was rather more limited, entrepreneurial schools played a still more prominent role over a longer period of time. At least a half-a-dozen existed by 1813, and they enrolled about 270 pupils. A quarter of a century later the number of establishments had more than doubled, and though their enrollment had not increased proportionately they still provided instruction for almost a quarter of the Negro children attending school. By the end of the first half of the nineteenth century the number had grown to at least nineteen, though it appears that they provided instruction for a smaller percentage of the black pupils than they had a decade earlier. These educational establishments were small, having, almost without exception, a single teacher and enrolling fewer than fifty (more commonly 20 or 30) pupils. Most of these provided their students with only such educational rudiments as reading, writing, spelling, and basic mathematics—the equivalent, presumably, of the public primary school curriculum. In 1849, however, John Ross was teaching "the higher branches and the languages," and Sarah M. Douglass, who was for years Philadelphia's leading black schoolmistress, not only taught "the higher branches," but was also reported to possess "a good cabinet and philosophical apparatus." The curriculum in these two schools was perhaps equivalent to that in the public grammar schools, and that of Douglass's establishment may have been more advanced. The only other private school in the first half of the nineteenth century to attempt to provide Philadelphia's blacks with anything other than a primary education was the short-lived Clarkson High School in the late 1830s. It is doubtful that its program ever justified its name or equaled that provided by Sarah Douglass.[25]

Antebellum Cincinnati gave every indication of being a promising field for black teachers. It had a substantial free Negro population which was, despite an 1849 state statute to the contrary, wholly excluded from the public schools before 1852. Moreover, philanthropic effort (aside from that of Hiram S. Gilmore) was individualized, spasmodic, and inadequate, and the educational efforts of the black churches were hardly more than minimal. Nevertheless, black teachers who essayed to open schools found the necessary support lacking during the first third of the century; though schools were established as early as 1820 and a number of efforts were made, none survived long. Educational opportunities for blacks would appear to have been available only irregularly before 1834, "teachers being few and patronage slack." In that year Owen T. B. Nickens, a black educator from Virginia, established a school that would survive until he abandoned it in 1852 to take charge of the public school of the eastern district. Perhaps encouraged by Nickens's success, other teachers ventured into the field, and several schools (some enrolling over two hundred pupils) were established.[26]

In the southern cities, except for the very substantial efforts of Baltimore's Negro churches, blacks relied heavily on private pay schools for the education of their children. These were often taught by ministers and met in church buildings, but apparently without church or other institutional support. In the 1830s Baltimore's blacks had access to a number of entrepreneurial schools, some half-dozen of which were taught by free women of color who had been educated at St. Francis Academy. Perhaps the most notable of these independent Negro schoolmasters was William Watkins, whose five sons would follow him into the teaching profession. Black educational efforts were apparently extremely sporadic in Louisville throughout the first four decades of the nineteenth century, but in the 1840s a number of free Negro teachers (at least two of them women) opened schools that quickly attracted a substantial number of both free and slave students, the latter being received only with the written consent of the owner. Henry Adams, a Baptist minister, was first in the field in 1841, and he was quickly followed by Robert M. Lane, the Reverend Peter Booth, William H. Gibson, and others. Adams's school grew so large that it eventually required a staff of five.[27]

Probably no urban black community in the country supported more private tuition schools than that in the nation's capital. From an early date Washington free blacks appear to have been determined to secure the advantages of education for their children at whatever cost. In the early years, to be sure, they benefited from the willingness of a number of whites to teach Negroes and a casual acceptance by the local population, but most of the financial burden throughout the half-century—and almost all of the institutional responsibilities as well, in the second quarter of the century—were born by the free blacks themselves. From the time that a small group of determined, illiterate, slave-born blacks, led by George Bell, erected the Bell School House on Capitol Hill in 1807, there was a constant expansion of the number of schools, though a slight pause occurred following the "Snow Storm" of 1835. At least thirty-four locations are known within the city of Washington where schools for blacks were operated between 1807 and 1850, and the actual number of schools may well have approached fifty. While many of these were short-lived, others lasted for decades. Anne Maria Hall taught schools at various locations for a quarter of a century, and James Enoch Ambush for more than a decade longer; in 1834 the Reverend John F. Cook took over a school founded a decade earlier at Fourteenth and H streets, NW, and he and his sons operated it for twenty-five years; and Martha and Louise Parke Costin, David Brown, and Matilda and Alexander Hays all operated schools for more than fifteen years. From the 1820s on, there were always multiple schools available to the free person of color in the nation's capital—in the late 1840s there were three operating simultaneously between Twenty-second and I and Twenty-third and K streets, NW. This availability was a tribute to the determination and sacrifice of the free black community. M. B. Goodwin spoke no more than the truth when he wrote in 1871, "The colored people of the District have shown themselves capable, to a wonderful degree, of supporting and educating themselves, while at the same time contributing by taxation to the support of white schools, from which they were debarred, and that, too, when in numerous cases they had previously bought themselves and their families from slavery at very great expense."[28]

Much less is known about the entrepreneurial schools for free persons of color in New Orleans, though they were apparently fairly numerous. One G. Dorfeuille opened a school for blacks in 1813, and by 1822 there was one school for both boys and girls taught on the Lancastrian plan, as well as several "common schools" for free blacks. There is no reason to believe that such establishments became less numerous over the next three decades—the 1850 census marshals reported nine free black male teachers—but they increasingly did not advertise their existence to the white community, and were usually held in private houses without any outward indication of their presence. Most would not accept slaves as pupils (though there were a few exceptions), and some admitted only children with "light" skins. A number of these schools apparently closed their doors in the 1850s. The private schools of Charleston seem to have been even more numerous in relation to the size of the free Negro population. There are references to at least sixteen black schools (four of them taught by whites) in the antebellum era. The most notable black schoolmaster of the city was Thomas S. Bonneau, who conducted a school for a quarter of a century before his death in the late 1820s. Bonneau's school was so large that he required two assistants. Generally speaking, these schools were open only to free persons of color, though an occasional slave child was admitted. After the early 1830s prohibitory legislation forced black teachers to teach clandestinely, though white instructors of black pupils continued to operate openly. Hence, the accessibility of education to Charleston's free persons of color may well have been significantly reduced during the 1840s.[29]

The antebellum era saw the establishment and development of public school systems in all of the cities examined in this study. Before 1850, however, blacks were denied access to publicly funded educational facilities in all the southern cities and in Cincinnati as well, though the state of Louisiana appropriated small amounts of money to assist private schools for black children as early as 1848.[30] In both Washington and Baltimore free persons of color made an effort to obtain some small portion of the public school funding, but without success. In the 1840s Baltimore free blacks petitioned for the assignment of public school money to provide partial support for two black pauper schools already in being. The city authorities refused this request, ostensibly because they feared that the state would withhold all public school funds from the city if blacks should share in any way in their distribution. An 1849 plea to the Washington authorities for a grant of public funds to support schools for the free people of color had no greater success, but, rather surprisingly, the matter became an issue in the following mayoral election. City Councilman Jesse E. Dow had favored granting the request. When, as a candidate for the mayoralty in 1850, he was attacked for these views, he reiterated and defended them. Dow was overwhelmingly defeated by his Whig opponent, Walter Lenox.[31] But it was not only in southern cities that authorities were reluctant to grant blacks a share of the public educational funds. In 1787 Prince Hall and other Boston Negroes requested of the Massachusetts legislature that "some provision may be made for the education of our dear children," noting that they then derived "no benefit from the free schools in the town of Boston, which we think is a great grievance, as by woful [*sic*] experience we now feel the want of a common education." Their prayer was not granted, however, and a quarter of a century would elapse before public funds would be committed to the education of the black children of Boston. A similar petition in Providence in 1806 was equally unavailing.[32]

In none of the nine northern cities, however, was there more determined opposition to educating blacks at public expense than in Cincinnati. The phraseology of the original Ohio statute (1825) authorizing the levying of school taxes and the establishment of public schools would appear not to have excluded blacks from attending. By the time Cincinnati established its public educational system, in 1829, however, the state legislature had remedied this "defect" in the law by supplementary legislation that specifically barred Negroes from the public schools and relieved the blacks from the obligation to pay the tax levied for school support. Blacks in Cincinnati's first ward—where almost forty percent of the city's black residents lived—immediately (1830) petitioned school authorities to establish a school "for the benefit of their children," but the 1829 act enabled the board to ignore their plea. An 1844 Ohio Supreme Court decision that children who were more than half white were "entitled to the benefit of the common schools" would appear to have had no practical effect. But in 1849, as a result of a complicated political situation, the state legislature passed an act requiring the establishment of separate black schools managed by directors elected by black taxpayers. The Cincinnati authorities still resisted, declaring the act to be unconstitutional, and withheld funds until the state's highest court upheld the law's validity. Even then, the city officials declared themselves not authorized to erect school buildings for blacks; the squabble continued through two additional changes in the law, and it was not until 1858 that Cincinnati's first black public schoolhouse was erected.[33]

In Albany and Buffalo the public school systems remained embryonic until 1844 and 1839, respectively. Blacks appear not to have been accommodated by these earlier systems in any way, but Buffalo had a public "African School" a year after the reorganization of the system. The Albany school officials established Wilberforce School in the basement of the "African Church in Hamilton street" as a part of an involved transaction by which the city lent five hundred dollars to the trustees of the church, taking a mortgage on the lot, and agreed that the loan would never be called as long as the trustees permitted the school to be held in the basement. This peculiar arrangement had the interesting effect of discouraging black demands for better quarters. Though assistants were usual in the Albany public schools and not rare in those of Buffalo, the Negro school in each city was placed in charge of a single teacher.[34] In Brooklyn, a school supported largely by the Woolman Benevolent Society continued to receive small amounts of public school money, most of which went to support the white schools more fully. When the school district plan was implemented in Brooklyn this institution became a district school, and a second black school was established during the 1830s. This arrangement continued under the reorganized board of education after 1843. These two schools enrolled 123 children in 1843 and 556 in 1850.[35]

Though Providence had supported a number of public schools from the first year of the nineteenth century, blacks had not been welcomed and had later been specifically excluded. When the state statute of 1828 provided for the use of state funds, however, Providence free persons of color immediately petitioned for the establishment of a separate school for their children. This request was granted in the same year, and a second school was quickly added as the Providence system came to embody two types of elementary schools—the primary and the "writing." By the 1840s it would appear that one of these schools had been elevated to the position of a grammar school. The Negro children's instructors were paid ¼–⅜ less than their counterparts in the white schools. Pittsburgh was somewhat more laggardly. There the public educational system was not initiated until 1835, and blacks were initially excluded. In 1837, in response to a petition from the free people of color, two separate black schools were established. The number quickly dropped to one, however, under the tutelage of John N. Templeton, an able free Negro instructor. And even that school was badly housed and underfunded throughout the 1840s.[36]

As has been noted, Philadelphia's free people of color had unusually extensive access to educational facilities in the second decade of the nineteenth century, thanks to the philanthropic activities of various groups, the active efforts of black churches, and the presence of a sizable number of entrepreneurial schools. During this period public education in the City of Brotherly Love was in its embryonic stages, consisting of the use of public funds to pay the tuition of pauper pupils in private schools. It appears, however, that such assistance was available only to white children. When a Pennsylvania statute of 1818 provided for the establishment of public schools in the city and county of Philadelphia, the change did not initially benefit blacks, for all of the original schools were for white children. In 1820, however, the Abolition Society petitioned the directors of the public schools to provide instruction for the city's Negro children. After two years of platitudinous support for this course, coupled with shoddy evasion of action, the directors suddenly realized that the declining white enrollment (a reduction of almost forty-five percent between 1821 and 1822) might drive the per-pupil cost of the public schools' Lancastrian instruction above acceptable levels. They then secured a room in a former church in Mary Street and, in the fall of 1822, opened the first black public school in Philadelphia, with an initial enrollment of just under two hundred boys and girls. Four years later the girls were transferred to another school in Gaskill Street, with the original facility in Mary Street being retained for the boys. In this separation of the sexes the Negro schools conformed to the pattern of the other public schools, but (except for the common use of the Lancastrian system of instruction) they cannot be said to have conformed in any other way. The makeshift quarters were decidedly inferior to the newly constructed schoolhouses occupied by the whites, and the level of instruction would seem to have been equally substandard—in 1826–27, only about one-eighth of those enrolled had begun to learn to write, while the remainder pursued less advanced studies.[37]

In the 1820s and later, Philadelphia's free people of color protested discriminatory practices and fought to secure equal access to education for their children. Their bitter complaints in 1827 secured the abandonment of the existing facilities and the transfer of the black pupils to the Lombard Street School in 1828, when that school's white students were moved to a newly constructed building. After graded schools were established (and Lombard Street was the last school to abandon the Lancastrian tutorial system in which a single teacher might be responsible for the instruction of two hundred or more students at all educational levels), an effort to close the only black grammar school and provide only primary education (i.e., grades 1–3) for Negro children was defeated by vigorous protest from the black community in 1840.[38]

To the Lombard Street School was added a primary school in Northern Liberties in 1836, another on Gaskill Street in the early 1840s, and a third in West Philadelphia later in the decade. Hence, by the end of the first half of the nineteenth century there were five public schools: two grammar (the Lombard Street facility housing both a boys' and a girls' school); one "secondary," or advanced primary, in Northern Liberties; and two primary. Black children were not admitted to the high school, established in 1837. Black school enrollments remained relatively low—500–600 in all public schools in the 1830s and just over nine hundred by the late 1840s. It would appear that, throughout the three decades after the establishment of the public schools, the black public school students never amounted to so much as one-half of all Negro children attending school or so much as one-third of all Negro children of school age. Average attendance figures were, moreover, much lower in black than in white schools. In 1844–45, in only four public schools in the city and four more in the remainder of the county (out of 137 schools for which data are available) was the average daily attendance less than eighty percent of the enrollment, but every black public school then in existence (three in the city and one in Northern Liberties) was to be found in that list. Black public education in the City of Brotherly Love can hardly be said to have been a smashing success.[39]

The transfer of the African Free Schools from the Manumission Society to the Public School Society in 1834 made little difference in the financing of black education in New York City, for the Manumission Society had been receiving state educational funds for a number of years. The transfer was, however, unpopular in the black community, which had considerably less confidence in the leadership of the heretofore all-white Public School Society than in its long-time friends and benefactors in the Manumission Society. There was also probably some considerable discontent when, in integrating the Negro schools into the two-tier system of the Public School Society, six of the seven schools transferred were designated as public primary schools and only one—that in Mulberry Street—as a "public school" (i.e., roughly comparable to the later elementary school in New York or the grammar school in Philadelphia). These factors, coupled with the anti-Negro violence of the mid-1830s, greatly reduced the attendance in these schools. The Public School Society moved to arrest and reverse this decline by converting one of the primary schools to a public school and erecting a new building on Laurens Street to house it. A Negro instructor, Ransom F. Wake, was named as principal of the new school and the white principal of School Number One (Mulberry Street) was replaced by another black, John Peterson. Additonally, the society organized public meetings in the black community to explain the new course of studies and appointed a Negro agent, Prince Leveridge, to visit black families and encourage their support of the schools. This reorganization placed the black schools of the society on the footing that they would continue to occupy throughout the 1830s and '40s—two public schools and five public primaries. Enrollment increased during these years, though it appears not to have reached the level of the early 1830s. In the mid-1840s another public educational component emerged in New York—the ward school. These schools were publicly supported but controlled by local boards rather than the Public School Society. Two ward schools for Negro children were established in the more rural areas of northern Manhattan—in Yorkville and Harlem—before 1850. Thus, by the middle of the nieteenth century there were ten public schools for blacks, heavily staffed by black teachers. Four of these lay north of Fifteenth Street—three of them north of Fortieth Street—at a time when Fourteenth Street marked the northern edge of the built-up area.[40]

The origins of black public education in antebellum Boston somewhat resembled those in Philadelphia and New York, but Boston was unique among the major cities in experiencing a serious and substantial attack upon racial school segregation. The black school established in Primus Hall's house in 1798 was taken over a few years later by a group of philanthropic whites and later (1808) was sustained by the African Baptist Church. In 1812 the town of Boston began its support of Negro education by appropriating two hundred dollars a year to this school, and it was also made the recipient of the five-thousand-dollar bequest of Abel Smith in 1815 "for the free instruction of colored children in reading, writing, and arithmetic." In 1835 the city completed the construction of a new building for it, and it was named Smith School, in honor of its benefactor.[41]

Meanwhile, the Boston public school system had gradually evolved into a three-tiered structure of a Latin School, three reading schools, and three writing schools by 1800. No students were admitted to the lowest level of this system (the reading schools) unless they were at least seven years of age and had "previously received the instruction usual at women's schools" so as to be able "to read the English language by spelling the same." But as the Boston population became more heterogeneous, fewer children could meet these requirements. Consequently, in 1818, the town decided to establish a system of primary schools for children aged four to seven. Blacks almost immediately petitioned for a primary school for their children, and one was opened in 1820. Though one other black public school existed for a short time (1831–35) before being closed for lack of patronage, and another primary school appears to have existed briefly in the 1820s, these two schools—one grammar and one primary—essentially constituted the black component of Boston's public school system throughout the remainder of the antebellum era. Blacks were not admitted to either the Latin School or the English High School, established in 1821. Between 1830 and 1845 the enrollment of Smith School varied from less than 100 to more than 250, but seems usually to have been under 200. It would appear that fewer than 100 black primary students were usually enrolled. The year 1845 was probably a fairly typical one for Smith School. Its enrollment of 180 was the lowest of any grammar school except one restricted to boys that had just opened in that year, and its average attendance constituted a smaller percentage of its enrollment (61.11%) than was true for any other school in the system—indeed, the average for all of the white grammar schools was more than sixteen percentage points higher.[42]

Boston blacks had long been somewhat more assertive about the public education available to their children than had free persons of color in some other cities. In 1819, for instance, they had sought and obtained the right to visit Smith School and listen to the recitations. As early as 1840 a few Negroes and some whites, led by black writer William C. Nell, lodged a petition with the school committee asking for a total desegregation of Boston's public schools. Both this and similar petitions in 1844, 1845, and 1846 were rejected, the last rejection being accompanied by a statement alleging that it had been found to be nearly impossible to get black children to enroll in any save segregated schools and asserting that separate schools were legal, just, and desirable. Segregation was brought under renewed attack in 1849 when efforts were made to induce blacks to boycott Smith School, to develop a private, integrated, alternative school, and to secure a court ruling that segregated schools were unconstitutional. The Negro community was deeply divided on the issue at this time because of the existence of a concurrent effort to place Smith School under the direction of a black principal. Smith School survived, the alternative school collapsed, and the Massachusetts Supreme Court upheld the legality of segregated education in *Sarah C. Roberts* v. *City of Boston* in 1849. But the white master of Smith School was removed and replaced by Thomas Paul, Jr., a free man of color. Not until 1855 would legal segregation of Boston's schools disappear, in conformity with a state statute enacted in that year.[43]

The educational experiences of antebellum urban free blacks were, thus, diverse, A few generalizations are certainly possible, and a few common assumptions can be examined. It is possible that a majority of the Negro children in schools attended public schools in Boston, Providence, Albany, Buffalo, Brooklyn, and Pittsburgh, though it is difficult to be certain in any case. It is almost certain that fewer than one-half of the black pupils in New York and Philadelphia were enrolled in public schools. Black education in the southern cities was heavily dependent on entrepreneurial schools, though black churches played a significant role in Baltimore. In the first third of the nineteenth century the support of white philanthropic organizations was of great importance in fostering black education in New York and Philadelphia. The role of the Sunday school, while almost impossible to assess with precision, certainly cannot be ignored in any of the cities.

In all of the cities the level of instruction available to blacks was, with rare exceptions, elementary in nature. The grammar schools theoretically offered the equivalent of an eighth grade education, but it is clear that at least some of the black grammar schools did not remotely approach this level of achievement. With the exception of Gilmore's high school in Cincinnati, no institution of secondary education for blacks existed in the major cities in 1850, earlier efforts in Philadelphia, New York, and Baltimore having collapsed. This void would be partially filled in the early 1850s by the establishment of the Institute for Colored Youth in Philadelphia, William Crane's educational center for blacks in downtown Baltimore, and Charles Avery's Allegheny Institute, across the river from Pittsburgh.[44] But in 1850 probably the most advanced black educational institutions (aside from Gilmore's) were Sarah M. Douglass's school in Philadelphia and John F. Cook's in Washington.

Whites intimately involved with the instruction of blacks frequently stated or implied that Negroes were more zealous in seeking education opportunities than were whites.[45] And there was much demonstrable truth in this assertion, for the sacrifices made by free persons of color to establish and maintain schools can be characterized only as remarkable. Nevertheless, these same people, as they sought support for black education, emphasized the large number of Negro children who attended no schools, and every public school enrollment or attendance list revealed black children to be less likely than whites to enter the schools and more prone to absenteeism when enrolled. Reliable comparable black and white data encompassing all kinds of schools in these cities are impossible to obtain. The closest approximation is to be found in the data collected by the 1850 census marshals by questioning heads of households regarding the number of children who had attended school at any time during the past year. These data are obviously partial in a number of respects, especially as they relate to black children. In Charleston, for instance, it would appear that much of the instruction of Negro children in 1850 was carried on by free black teachers, clandestinely and in violation of state law. Under these circumstances it is likely that free persons of color would deny that their children had attended such schools. Indeed, the proportion of black children reported as attending school was lower in Charleston than in any other of the fifteen cities, but it is also worth noting that only forty-five adult free black males were reported as illiterate in the Charleston District. Table 10-1 displays the comparable figures for the proportion of white and black children attending school during the 1849–50 school year. The figures are for the county, parish, or district (with one exception) because the data are not reported for the cities, except in the case of Washington.

Obviously, low school attendance may reflect many things other than lack of zeal for education. It should be remembered that there were fewer and smaller black schools; those schools were not always well distributed in relation to the black population pattern; most schools required the payment of some fees, which, however small, were burdensome to the economically deprived free people of color; economic deprivation usually mandated withdrawal of children from school at an earlier age and after fewer years of attendance in order to obtain employment; and the schools available to black children usually did not provide so many years of programed instruction as did those for whites. Perhaps the most significant observation to be made about these figures is that with very few exceptions (notably Albany and Charleston), cities with relatively high white school enrollment also had relatively high black school enrollment, and vice versa, with the

Table 10-1   Percentage of Children attending School during the 1849–50 School Year[46]

	White Percentage[a]	Rank Order	FPC Percentage[a]	Rank Order
(Albany) Albany Country	83.48	4	46.44	8
(Baltimore) Baltimore County	59.36	14	22.31	12
(Boston) Suffolk County[b]	90.01	3	78.65	1
(Brooklyn) Kings County	73.21	4	59.16	5
(Buffalo) Erie County	98.07	1	69.17	3
(Charleston) Charleston District	70.65	10	5.44	15
(Cincinnati) Hamilton County	71.98	9	37.60	11
(Louisville) Jefferson County	68.99	11	43.52	9
(New Orleans) Orleans Parish[b]	68.60	12	43.30	10
(New York) New York County[b]	76.56	5	59.28	4
(Philadelphia) Philadelphia County	73.58	6	57.75	6
(Pittsburgh) Allegheny County	72.96	8	47.20	7
(Providence) Providence County	90.16	2	76.24	2
(St. Louis) St. Louis County	45.74	15	13.11	14
(Washington) Washington City	63.82	13	21.42	13

(a) Number attending school as a percentage of children between the ages of five and fourteen. (b) City and county identical or essentially coterminous.

six southern cities occupying the lowest six positions for white enrollment and six of the lowest seven for blacks.

The teachers in black schools—even when white—did not occupy the same position in the white-dominated society as did teachers in the white schools. In the public systems they almost always received lower salaries, and it would appear that their qualifications were less carefully scrutinized. As some New York Negroes observed in 1827, "We are so skeptical, that we cannot believe, that almost *anyone* is qualified to keep a school for our children. Enemies may declaim upon their dulness and stupidity; but we would respectfully inquire, have they not had dull and stupid instructors; who if placed in any other than a colored school, would hardly be considered as earning *their salt*."[47]

The attitude of the free people of color toward white instructors in their schools changed considerably throughout the first half of the nineteenth century. This shift was the result in part of greater self-consciousness and self-confidence in the black communities, and in part of other changes that had taken place both inside and outside of those communities. The nature of the average white instructor in a black school changed dramatically over a period of years. Early in the nineteenth century such teachers were usually well-qualified individuals inspired primarily by philanthropic motives to aid in lifting up a population which American society considered inferior by nature and attempted to make inferior by suppression. They may have been paternalistic and patronizing, but they were usually capable and concerned. After the first third of the nineteenth century—after slavery had disappeared in the North and the hope for its voluntary elimination in the South had died, after the rise of the colonization movement, the Nat Turner episode, and the emergence of abolitionist agitation—fewer whites appeared willing to devote their energies to such undertakings. Additionally, qualified black instructors were more available, while the white instructors hired to teach in black public schools by white board members tended to be poorly prepared or desperate for employment, or both.

By 1850 much instruction in Negro schools was in the hands of black teachers. The instructors in entrepreneurial black schools were almost wholly black, except for a few individuals in Charleston and St. Louis. The schools conducted by black churches had long been taught primarily by Negro instructors, as had the few opened by other black organizations. The much-diminished number of schools under the control of white philanthropic organizations—a few remained in New York and Philadelphia—apparently employed a considerably larger proportion of black instructors than they had three or four decades earlier, but white teachers were not uncommon. In the black public schools the number of Negro instructors had increased dramatically in the 1830s and '40s. Although in Providence, Albany, and Buffalo these schools would appear to have been staffed wholly by whites, in New York they had been largely in the hands of black teachers from the 1830s on. Many of these black teachers were women; the number of black male teachers may have remained stable or actually declined during the second quarter of the century, but hard evidence is difficult to obtain. The census enumerators reported only forty-eight black male teachers in all fifteen cities in 1850, though some others might, of course, have been listed as following other occupations—certainly a number of clergymen also conducted schools. There are none listed in four cities, and more than two in only six cities. More than five-eighths of all those listed resided in Baltimore (13), New Orleans (9), and New York (9). A check of all free black occupations recorded in fifty-seven city directories extending over a span of four decades has unearthed only one (Philadelphia in 1820) in which the number of black male teachers listed was greater than the number reported by the 1850 census marshals.[48] It seems almost certain that by 1850 well over a majority of black students were being taught by black teachers.

Black education in these cities in the antebellum era attempted to confront two great realities—the nature of the urban environment and the nature of the free black population. To win material rewards in the increasingly complex urban society demanded greater sophistication and better intellectual training. The depersonalization of societal relationships required a greater reliance on written documents to define responsibilities and rights, to transmit information, and to organize activities. The institutionalization of much activity in the cities meant that the relationships between cause and effect and between the existence of a need and its satisfaction were almost always indirect, usually complex, frequently obscure, and sometimes irrational. Only those who fully comprehended the institutional approach and understood the labyrinthine patterns of functional relationships could hope to survive, let alone prosper, in such an environment, and more and better educational opportunities appeared the quickest and surest way to achieve this competence.

But to secure these educational opportunities was, in most cities, more difficult for free persons of color than for other population elements. For this was a people identified by most white Americans as permanent occupants of the lowest strata of society. Many would have asserted that they should be grateful that American—and, especially, urban American—society was so generally affluent, so mobile, and so successful that they were in better circumstances and more secure in their persons and property than their counterparts elsewhere in the world. They should be content with "their place," which was destined by God. In a highly competitive and individualistic society it was expected that free persons of color should be neither aggressive nor assertive. Hence, many urbanites saw no reason for Negroes to have access to more than the most rudimentary educational opportunities. The population that had to overcome this substantial resistance had, in 1800 (with a few exceptions), recently emerged from slavery, with all of the conditioning that that status embodied. Their financial resources were minute; of their own people, only a few were qualified to act as instructors; and their community institutions were weak and new. One of the remarkable accomplishments in American history is the degree to which they marshaled their slender financial and human resources, the rapidity with which they strengthened their institutions, and the effectiveness with which they developed educational opportunities adapted to their needs. In this they were aided, of course, by the trustee tradition deeply embedded in American culture and by American legal and philosophical principles that did not permit equal protection of the laws and equal access to public institutions to be everywhere and always (only most places and usually) totally denied, though such protection and access were, even at best, substantially restricted.

One barrier, however, seemed never to fall. Except for a handful of individuals—notably ministers, teachers, physicians, and editors—access to employment appeared not to be favorably affected by educational advancement. In 1848 a distraught father in Charleston wrote that his son had received the best education available and had been tutored by a graduate of the College of Charleston. He had then gone to Philadelphia, doubtless anticipating wider opportunities, but was still without "any steady calling." The purpose of the letter was to solicit for his son a position with the American Colonization Society—an organization dedicated to the removal of just such people from the American scene. Almost two decades earlier Charles C. Andrews, then approaching the end of a long and distinguished career as principal of New York's African Free School in Mulberry Street, narrated the experiences of one of his students "with a respectable education and an irreproachable character," who had been unable, because of his race, to complete an apprenticeship as a blacksmith in either New York or Philadelphia, and had "resolved to leave the country and go to the Colony of Liberia." Andrews noted that "a few" of his pupils had "obtained trades of the following descriptions; viz. Sail Makers, Shoe Makers, Tin Workers, Tailors, Carpenters, Blacksmiths, &c.," in spite of great difficulties. "Many of our best lads," he added, "go to sea as stewards, cooks, sailors, &c. Those who cannot procure trades, and do not like to go to sea, become waiters, coachmen, barbers, servants, laborers, &c." The Negro boy, he commented somewhat bitterly, after five or six years in school, left "with every avenue closed against him, which is open to the white boy, for honorable and respectable rank in society, doomed to encounter as much prejudice and contempt as if he were not only destitute of that education which distinguishes the civilized from the savage, but as if he were *incapable* of receiving it." "It is a plausible argument," he admitted, "which the ignorant are cunning enough to use, that they can do as well, in all stations filled by those whom we educate, and get as much wages as they can, and are as well off without education as with it."[49] If one who had given his life to black education could speak thus, was it any wonder that many students and many parents saw no reason for continuing longer in school than was necessary to acquire a precarious literacy?

Whatever else they did or did not accomplish, the Negro schools contributed significantly to the building of black communities. In them its leaders were trained. In some measure the community was gratified by the successes of their schools and suffered for their deprivations. The mere existence of the schools gave blacks a legitimate claim to consideration from the city's leadership in an area where it was embarrassing for those officials to refuse a plea so eminently justifiable on moral and ethical grounds. The struggles for the establishment of black public schools, for the appointment of black instructors, and for the upgrading of instruction made the school a focus of community feeling, and that pulling together of concerns strengthened the bonds of the black community and heightened its self-consciousness.

Openly—and probably privately as well—black leaders and doubtless a large majority in the Negro communities never lost faith in the individual and community values of education, however justifiable such pessimism might have been. They believed because they had the will to believe, because they had the need to believe, and because the act of not believing extinguished hope. And black urban Americans desperately needed and wanted to believe that somewhere in the walls that hemmed them in there was a breach, that in some manner they could set their feet or their children's feet upon a path that would lead them out of the welter of discriminations and the morass of restraints that structured their lives. They hoped that education would bring them some measure of economic success, would make them demonstrably meritorious, would for a moment and on however small a stage make the color of their skin irrelevant.

11 Unity through Separation: The Negro Church in the City

Because of the concentration of population and because of the psychological need for establishing communities of belonging in the amorphous mass, church organizations have long prospered in the cities. For blacks and immigrants, in particular, the social, communitarian role of the church has been of great importance. But unlike the immigrant church, which was brought with its adherents and established coincidently with their arrival, the black church was native to these shores and rooted in the white American culture. Hence, far from being enabled to use the church from the beginning to foster community development and give worth to identification with the community, American blacks had first to perceive the existence of their ethnic community and then establish and foster the black church as an instrument of further community development. In this involved and complicated process, urban blacks took the leading role.

There appear to have been no separate black congregations in the English colonies before the outbreak of the American Revolutionary War, and, indeed, with the exception of four Baptist congregations in three of the smaller southern towns—Williamsburg in Virginia and Augusta and Savannah (2) in Georgia—none seems to have emerged before the last decade of the eighteenth century.[1] It is entirely likely, of course, that Negro members of biracial congregations frequently met separately in the church buildings or elsewhere well before the first recognized black congregations appeared. And it is certain that black churchmen in increasing numbers began to preceive advantages in racially separated church organizations during the same period that white churchmen, in even greater numbers, became increasingly uncomfortable with biracial congregations that forced them to confront weekly the conflict between their religious professions and their individual prejudices.[2] Nevertheless, black religious leaders did not rush to sever their ties with the white-controlled churches and denominations, for they had a lively appreciation of the difficulties—especially the financial difficulties—inherent in establishing separate organizations. Survival, let alone success, depended upon the adherence of enough communicants to create viable units for worship and monetary support; and that, in turn, depended upon the emergence of events that would unify black church members in opposition to some congregational policy or practice that their white coreligionists would not relinquish. In short, the emergence of a sense of black community must, in some measure, precede the emergence of the black church.[3]

Blacks and whites in some congregations groped uncomfortably and hesitantly, but without recrimination, toward a solution to a dimly perceived problem and eventually separated to the relief and satisfaction of both elements with evidence of considerable goodwill and a modicum of mutual respect. But in a number of instances a sufficient sense of community to support separation was the product of the psychological trauma of discriminatory practices within the biracial churches. These distinctions among communicants were, of course, by no means new. But in both the northern and the Upper South cities increasing numbers of the Negro church members were free, not slave, and, thus, unwilling placidly to accept discriminations which they had seen as inevitable concomitants of their servile status, but which they now perceived with greater clarity as springing from distinctions based on race, not condition. Additionally, free persons of color were able to exercise a degree of choice not permitted to the slave, and an increase in the number of black communicants who could make a choice proportionately increased both the possibility and the likelihood of the establishment and maintenance of black congregations.

The experiences of a group of Philadelphia blacks in the period 1780–1820 illustrates both the factors impelling initial separation and the hesitancy (even reluctance, perhaps) of Negro churchmen to sever the last remaining ties with the white religious organizations. In Philadelphia, as elsewhere, blacks had been attracted to Methodism by its early and open opposition to slavery, by the emotionalism of its services, and by the physical integration (initially) of blacks into the "classes" into which Methodists were divided. From the beginning, racial segregation seems to have been the rule in meetings, however, and only a handful of blacks appear to have played any role in the church save that of auditor. As the number of Negro communicants increased at St. George's Church in Philadelphia, so, too, did the discomfiture of the white members. When the congregation outgrew the seating capacity of the church, it was the black members who stood throughout the service, surrendering the seats they had previously occupied at the rear of the sanctuary to the whites while a gallery was planned and constructed to increase the capacity of the meeting house. It was at this time (early 1786) that Richard Allen, a slave-born unordained black itinerant Methodist preacher, returned permanently to his native Philadelphia. Six years previously Pennsylvania had adopted a plan of gradual emancipation, and for perhaps a slightly shorter period of time Allen had been a free man, having purchased his freedom from his master, a Delaware planter. Less than three years earlier the English had acknowledged the independence of the United States, and a little over a year before, American Methodism had established its independent status in a conference at Baltimore. Allen's ministry had been largely confined to blacks (who by that date comprised roughly one-sixteenth of the membership), and it was to serve this body of the population that the elder in charge of St. George's had invited him to return to Philadelphia. Apparently already convinced of the desirability of establishing separate black congregations, Allen quickly gathered a "class" of some forty-two persons, which he intended should form the nucleus of a separate black church, subject to the discipline and government of the Methodist Episcopal Church. He gained the support of only three other black members for this proposal, however, and the white leadership opposed the scheme even more vigorously.[4]

The views of at least some of the black communicants underwent considerable modification as a result of certain events in April 1787. When the congregation again occupied the renovated sanctuary, Negro members were directed to take certain seats in the gallery. Either there was some misunderstanding regarding the seats specified, or else a handful of the black members sought a public confrontation,[5] for Allen, Absalom Jones, and a few other Negroes took seats elsewhere. After efforts had been made by the white trustees physically to remove them, the group "all went out of the church in a body and they were no more plagued with us." They were subsequently joined in their secession by some, but not all, of the remaining Negro communicants.[6]

For the next two years these men and other blacks held religious services under the general auspices of the Free African Society—a preexisting beneficial association in the organization of which Allen had played a major role. Then in 1789 Richard Allen and his supporters left the society. Ostensibly their departure resulted from their devotion to Methodism coupled with their awareness that the majority of the society's members, doubtless in part because of their resentment of their treatment at St. George's, were turning toward other faiths. Allen also objected to the delay in organizing a separate black church (though steps were taken in 1790) and may well have feared that any congregation finally emerging from the society would not be sufficiently independent of white control. His apprehensions were confirmed when, in 1794, a majority of the members still left in the society, under the leadership of Absalom Jones, voted to seek affiliation with the Episcopal Church, and, upon petition, were accepted and constituted the African Church of St. Thomas. They were, however, specifically prohibited from participating in Pennsylvania Episcopal conventions—a prohibition that was not rescinded until the Civil War.[7]

Allen, meanwhile, continued to conduct services for Philadelphia's black Methodists, who, in 1794, purchased a lot at Sixth and Lombard streets, moved to it a frame building, and organized the Bethel African Methodist Episcopal Church. From the beginning this congregation viewed itself and was considered as an integral part of American Methodism. Bishop Francis Asbury preached the dedicatory sermon, and its services were held under the general direction of the white elder in charge at Philadelphia. But in 1796 the congregation was separately incorporated in order to secure its independence in managing its own affairs. The act of incorporation provided for the Philadelphia elder to nominate the preacher and to administer the church ordinances to the members, but his power in the management of the congregation's temporal affairs was more limited. The separateness of the body was further emphasized by the requirement that only "Africans and descendents of the African race" be admitted to membership and that all trustees and class leaders, as well as exhorters and local preachers, were to be Negroes. Nevertheless, Bethel Church, the incorporation papers stated, would "continue forever in union with the Methodist Episcopal Church of Philadelphia, subject to the government of the present Bishops and their successors in all their ecclesiastical affairs and transactions, except in the temporal rights and property of the aforesaid Bethel Church." What the black Methodists sought, and what they thought they had achieved, was temporal congregational independence coupled with ecclesiastical connection with a denomination that they valued for its theology, order of worship, early opposition to slavery, and religious concern for Negroes.[8]

What the Bethel congregation did not know was that despite an earlier refusal of Allen to deed the church property to the conference (which, as a matter of denominational policy, held title to the property of all churches under its jurisdiction), the white minister who drafted the articles of association had incorporated a rather tortuously phrased statement that in 1805 was interpreted as depriving the congregation of full control of its property. This discovery (sparked by a demand from the elder in charge of St. George's) initiated a decade of increasing division between black and white Methodists in the City of Brotherly Love. Doubtless the blacks were disturbed by the rapid erosion of the church's stance against slavery in the first decade of the nineteenth century; certainly the whites were affronted when the Bethelites, in 1807, amended their articles of association in such a manner as to deny almost all power to the elder and secured the state's approval of the change without informing any of the white leaders. In

1813 and 1815 the black communicants prevented white elders from preaching at Bethel, and when the elder in charge brought suit to enforce his ecclesiastical authority, the Pennsylvania Supreme Court refused his request for a writ of mandamus and, in essence, declared Bethel to be independent.[9]

In Baltimore a number of black Methodists had withdrawn from the Lovely Lane and Strawberry Alley churches a few years before the Philadelphia split occurred and for essentially the same reasons—racial discrimination in seating and exclusion of blacks from any control of the church. They clung to a precarious existence throughout the 1790s and began to gain strength and stability under the leadership of Daniel Coker in the early nineteenth century. After a long struggle to maintain a connection with Baltimore Methodists, they secured the incorporation in 1816 of an independent Negro Methodist church—Bethel. It was primarily the union of these two churches (though representatives of three other small congregations were also present) that, in April of 1816, formed the African Methodist Episcopal Church—the first independent black denomination in the United States—with Richard Allen as its first bishop.[10]

The activities of Philadelphia's black Methodists in these three decades (1786–1816) vividly illustrate the complex interaction of pressures, discrimination, loyalties, resentments, and fears that moved many black churchmen along the path of independency. Initially rejecting the idea of separate meetings, some Negro Methodists were molded into a community by arrant discrimination and seceded from St. George's. But still they sought to preserve a connection with white Christians, and a majority of the seceders found the establishment of a separate church wholly within another denomination the most satisfactory compromise, despite the fact that they were excluded from that denomination's councils. Allen and his followers insisted that Methodism was better adapted to the religious need of blacks than Episcopalianism and tried to preserve that connection. But they demanded a greater degree of independence than was accorded other congregations. After a period of uneasy alliance, independence of control proved more important than the religious connection and complete separation followed. The movement was capped by the organization of a wholly black national denomination. Thus, a combination of leadership and events awakened among some Negroes a sense of community sufficient to sustain a separate church; and such churches would, in their turn, nourish the further development of the black community.

A major factor contributing to the establishment of wholly black Methodist organizations was the degree of congregational subordination to higher authority that prevailed in the early years of that denomination's development. This consideration was influential not only in the founding of the AME Church but also in the emergence of another black Methodist denomination—the African Methodist Episcopal Zion Church—which originated in New York. In that city's John Street Church, as in Philadelphia's St. George's, increasing black membership in the late eighteenth century contributed to seating problems. As early as 1796 Bishop Francis Asbury permitted Negro members to meet in the "interval of the regular preaching hours of our white brethren," but this arrangement was by no means satisfactory, and the Negro communicants continued to seek a more manageable solution in the form of a separate black congregation. Accordingly, Zion Church was organized in 1800 and incorporated in 1801 with the concurrence of the General Conference of the Methodist Episcopal Church. The articles of agreement required that only "Africans or their descendents...be chosen as Trustees," but also specified that Zion should "continue forever in union with the Methodist Episcopal Church in the City of New York," and that the elder presiding in that city should appoint ministers to serve the church. This compromise appeared to work fairly satisfactorily, and in 1818 what was probably the major difficulty was removed when Zion and Asbury (in part an offshoot of Zion) were constituted a separate "charge," which meant that they would be entitled to a full-time minister. At that time these two congregations appear to have enrolled more than fifteen-sixteenths of all black Methodists in the city. The separation of the Zion-Asbury charge from the New York Methodists occurred in 1820 when its white minister, William M. Stillwell, joined his uncle, Samuel Stillwell, and some three hundred other members in the "Stillwell Secession" from the Methodist Church—a movement involving disputes over lay influence and financial organization. The Zion and Asbury congregations apparently joined the movement because they feared they might lose control of their property. Once separated, however, the Negro Methodists were unwilling to assume again the subservient position they had occupied, and when the effort to establish a black conference within the Methodist Episcopal Church failed in 1821, they began to move in the direction of an independent organization. Refusing to affiliate with the newly established AME denomination, Zion and Asbury joined with Wesley Church in Philadelphia, a congregation on Long Island, and two other smaller bodies to form the African Methodist Episcopal Zion Church in 1822.[11]

The AME and AME Zion churches competed vigorously for members throughout the antebellum era, with the AME body growing more rapidly than the Zionites. A third group of independent Negro Methodists—the African Union Church, which sprang from the Ezion congregation in Wilmington, Delaware—grew even more slowly and remained the smallest of the three separate black denominations.[12] One reason for the rapid early growth of the AME membership was the adherence of some fourteen hundred Charleston Negroes (many of them doubtless slaves) who had apparently already separated physically from the white Methodists of that city under the leadership of Morris Brown and Charles M. Corr. This branch of the AME Church was wholly destroyed in the aftermath of the Denmark Vesey affair in 1822, but its communicants then constituted roughly one-fifth of the national AME membership.[13]

Not all Negro Methodists joined congregations affiliated with the independent denominations. In Philadelphia in the early 1820s, for example, there were three black Methodist congregations—Bethel (AME), Wesley (AME Zion), and Zoar (a black mission of St. George's M.E. Church). Membership figures are difficult to obtain and unreliable when found, but it would appear that early in the third decade of the nineteenth century something over ninety-six hundred blacks were communicants of the AME Church (before its suppression in Charleston), perhaps fourteen hundred belonged to the AME Zion congregations, and roughly 45,000–50,000 were affiliated with regular Methodist Episcopal churches.[14] The AME and AME Zion churches were, however, heavily urban—more than six-sevenths of the members claimed for the AME Zion denomination at the time of its organization were affiliated with churches in New York and Philadelphia, and over ninety-two percent of the initial AME membership was to be found in New York, Philadelphia, Baltimore, and Charleston.[15] Additionally, the black communicants of the regular Methodist Episcopal Church were much more numerous in the South. Of the sixteen conferences in the United States reported by that church in 1828, eight lay north of Mason and Dixon's line. But only 9,697 of the denomination's 59,043 Negro communicants were to be found in those conferences, and 8,354 of these were in the Philadelphia conference.[16]

Methodism, whether regular, AME, or AME Zion, continued to attract blacks in considerable numbers, though it must be acknowledged that in the African denominations the growth in congregations was more notable than the increase in membership. Twenty-five years after the foundation of the AME Church the total membership was only about double the original number, while the number of Negro regular Methodists had roughly trebled.[17] But northern urban Negroes obviously found regular Methodism less attractive, for although the more than 4,500 black regular Methodists in Baltimore outnumbered AME members by roughly three to two, the annual conference reported only 11 black regular Methodists in Brooklyn, 34 in New York, and 231 in Philadelphia and its suburbs.[18]

As had been previously noted, blacks comprised very large proportions of Methodist communicants in the urban centers. In Baltimore in 1800, for instance, three of every eight members of the "classes" were blacks; in Brooklyn at the same time almost two-fifths of the members were Negro; and the figure was more than one-fifth in New York in 1802. In Louisville in 1820 almost one-third of the Methodists were black and by 1835 their proportion was well over one-half. Negroes constituted roughly three-tenths of the membership in Washington in 1806 and over a third in 1825, and in Charleston are supposed to have made up more than eighty percent of the Methodist membership throughout the antebellum era.[19]

Under these circumstances—and given the nature of the relations between black and white in the United States—the separation of the membership along racial lines was almost inevitable. Aside from the independent and semiindependent bodies already mentioned, separate, but subordinate, black Methodist congregations were established in many cities. Meetings of blacks in the Sharp Street Church in Baltimore began in 1792; St. George's in Philadelphia in 1796 opened a black chapel that would eventually be Zoar Church; the Cincinnati Methodists organized Deer Creek Chapel in 1815; and at least as early as 1820 the Negro members of Washington's Ebenezer Church had formed a separate congregation.[20]

The practices both of forming separate black regular Methodist congregations and of establishing wholly independent Methodist churches spread rapidly in the second quarter of the nineteenth century. By 1850 only Charleston among these fifteen cities had no separate Negro Methodist congregation (though there were many black Methodists there and separate meetings were doubtless held). Buffalo had a single AME church established in the late 1820s, but each of the other thirteen urban centers had two or more Negro Methodist congregations and in almost every case two or more different national organizations were represented. Albany, Boston, Cincinnati, New Orleans, Providence, and St. Louis each had two or three such congregations, and in Brooklyn, Louisville, Pittsburgh, and Washington the number ranged between four and six. New York, Philadelphia, and Baltimore—with seven, nine, and ten, respectively—had the largest number of separate black Methodist churches and also the greatest variety. Baltimore's congregations, for instance, included five regular Methodist, three AME, one AME Zion, and one Methodist Protestant, while AME, AME Zion, regular Methodist, and African Union congregations were to be found in Philadelphia. The wholly independent denominations claimed many adherents, with the AME Church being represented in all fourteen urban centers, though the Zionites, except for a single congregation in Pittsburgh, were to be found only in the eastern seaboard cities of Boston, Providence,

Brooklyn, New York, Philadelphia, Baltimore, and Washington. Nevertheless, a large number of Negroes preserved a connection with the white-controlled Methodist Episcopal bodies. Congregations of this nature were to be found in Albany, Baltimore (where they constituted one-half of all black Methodist churches), Boston, Cincinnati, Louisville (where three of the four black Methodist congregations were connected with local white churches), New Orleans, Philadelphia, St. Louis, and Washington. Despite these conservative tendencies, the independent AME and AME Zion denominations gathered classes or congregations in most of these urban centers during or before the 1820s and had footholds in all but New Orleans and St. Louis before the end of the 1830s. Of the sixty or more black Methodist churches in these cities at the middle of the nineteenth century, over two-thirds were affiliated with one or the other of the black-controlled denominations.[21]

The reasons impelling black separation from white-controlled congregations are not far to seek. Racial discrimination was almost as prevalent in the churches as elsewhere in American society—which is to say it was universal—and such practices were not peculiar to or more stringent among Methodists than other Christians. Though large numbers of congregations admitted Negro members, segregated seating had become almost universal by the end of the first third of the nineteenth century. A Providence free black recalled that in the second decade of the century many Negroes "attended no church at all, because they said they were opposed to going to churches and sitting in pigeon holes, as all the churches at that time had some obscure place for the colored people to sit in."[22] Almost identical terms were used by a Boston Negro two decades later, and at about the same period the Cambridge don Edward Abdy, after commenting on the universality of such accommodations, observed that "at Albany, there is one where a curtain is placed in front to conceal the occupants, when there are any; for those for whom they are destined, seldom enter them, and speak of them with the contempt they deserve, as 'martin-holes,' and 'human menageries.'"[23] Even in churches where pews were sold or rented the restrictions still held. When, in 1830, Frederick Brinsley, a free man of color, came into possession of a pew in Boston's Park Street Meeting House by virtue of the owners' default on a debt, he was prohibited by the church officers from occupying his property, or any other pew on the main floor, and a constable was stationed at the door of the pew to protect the ethnic purity of the congregation.[24] Nor did the existence of a black majority in a congregation lead to a relaxation of these discriminatory practices—in Louisville's Fourth Street Methodist Episcopal Church, Negroes were still confined to the gallery despite the fact that they made up roughly five-sixths of the membership. In every section of the country and in every religious body such segregation was almost universal.[25]

Galleries, or other forms of assigned seating, were, of course, unmistakable symbols that white churchmen, though unwilling openly to exclude believers, did not welcome Negroes to the religious community. Blacks were not slow to recognize this fact, and when an Albany Methodist congregation resolved to rent its pews or a Washington Baptist church erected a gallery, a mass exodus of Negro members followed. And the persistence of this discrimination eventually drove many blacks who accepted it temporarily into membership in separate congregations and discouraged still more from attending such "biracial" churches.[26]

In addition to enduring the "routine" indignity of segregated seating, black communicants were made to feel their inferior status even more painfully at the communion table. In New York's Scotch Presbyterian Church late in the eighteenth century racial prejudice was so pronounced that the pastor found it necessary personally to escort a black parishioner of well-established piety and devotion when she came forward to take communion. Both in that city and in New England in the 1840s the English traveler Charles Lyell, when attending Episcopal churches, "saw all the white communicants first come forward, and again retire to their pews, before any of the colored people advanced." Such practices were, of course, common in the Methodist church, and the final separation of black Methodists in Cincinnati was sparked by the removal of two black preachers from the communion table after a general invitation had been extended to all ministers present. Week after week and year after year Negro Protestants were made to realize that though God might be no respecter of persons, His church in America clearly was.[27]

On occasion, as might be expected, specific incidents crystallized black resentments and produced an exodus from a white-controlled church. Washington's Wesley AME Zion Church was founded in 1833 by Methodists who left Ebenezer Church when a slaveholder was named as its minister—an appointment that would have been unthinkable forty years earlier when John Wesley's antislavery spirit was still strong in the church. Members of Brooklyn's separate black Methodist congregation in 1818 were so offended by the proslavery views of the pastor of Sands Street Church—the "mother church" which they had recently left—that they severed all ties with the regular Methodists and affiliated with the newly established AME denomination. Five years before the secession that led to the establishment of Wesley AME Zion Church in Washington, some members had left the Ebenezer congregation because of the refusal of the white ministers to take black infants in their arms when administering the sacrament of baptism. And in 1815 Cincinnati's Negro Methodists—who were by that date not only confined to the gallery but were also "compelled to suppress their inclinations to leap and shout"—were moved to establish a separate congregation when "one of the colored brethren, feeling an almost irresistible impulse to shout aloud and thus give vent to the feeling which filled his breast, thrust his handkerchief into his mouth to prevent the outbreak" and burst a blood vessel.[28] It is doubtful that even these (and similar) isolated events would have produced racial separation had they not occurred against a backdrop of pervasive prejudice and discrimination in the churches accompanied, in many cases, by white encouragement of the formation of black congregations.

Since these distinctions and discriminations were present in almost all churches, black congregations of many persuasions were formed, though separate denominational structures emerged only among the Methodists and (to a much more limited degree) the Baptists.[29] Methodism was doubtless attractive to Negroes because of its simplicity of preaching, emotional services, and early antipathy to slavery. But Baptists also valued "plain" preaching and emotionally participatory services, and had, in the seventeenth century, expressed reservations about the moral acceptability of slavery. In addition, Baptists offered a less complex church government, congregational independence, and an ordination process that could produce as many ministers as were needed. Consequently, in areas where Baptists were strong, blacks were attracted to this denomination in considerable numbers.

Separate congregations of Negro Baptists had emerged in several smaller southern towns before 1800, but their development in the major cities dates from the first decade of the nineteenth century, when black Baptists established separate churches in Boston (1805), New York (1807), and Philadelphia (1810). Initially the congregations were very small, none of them exceeding twenty in number. In 1820 a church was founded in Albany, and the previous year had seen the establishment in Providence of a Negro union congregation with strong Baptist predilections, which would eventually constitute the Meeting Street Baptist Church. A few years later black Baptist churches were formed in New Orleans (1826) and St. Louis (1827). The 1830s was a period of greater growth for black Baptists in the urban centers and saw the first appearance of separate congregations in Cincinnati, Washington, Louisville, Baltimore, and Buffalo, as well as the formation of additional churches in New York, Philadelphia, and Providence. Churches were established in Brooklyn and Pittsburgh in the next decade, and by 1850 some twenty-five congregations of black Baptists were distributed among fourteen of these fifteen cities—only in the Deep South city of Charleston was there no acknowledged congregation. Most of these churches appear to have been connected with the regular, white-controlled regional associations and, in at least some instances, sent Negro delegates to associational meetings.[30]

Because of the nature of the organization of the Baptist Church, few black churchmen in that denomination were known beyond the confines of a single city, but there were occasional exceptions. The Paul family was particularly notable in the Northeast. Thomas Paul founded both the African Baptist Church in Boston in 1805 and the Abyssinian Baptist Church in New York in 1809, though he was identified throughout his ministry primarily with the Boston body. The Abyssinian congregation was later served by Benjamin Paul, and Nathaniel Paul was the first pastor of Albany's First African Baptist Church.[31] The Reverend Henry Adams occupied a similar position in the West. Born in South Carolina, he established a Baptist church in Louisiana before coming to Louisville in 1839 as the first minister of the black Fifth Street Baptist Church. He also served, for a short time, the Baker Street Baptist Church in Cincinnati.[32] And still later in the antebellum era Sampson White served successively as pastor of churches in New York, Brooklyn, and Washington.[33]

The numerical growth of the black Baptists was spotty. The denomination appeared not to thrive in the stony soil of New England—by the mid-1840s the larger of Providence's two congregations contained only about 60 communicants and the other roughly half that number. By the same period, however, there were approximately 900 Negro Baptists in New York, about equally divided between the Abyssinian and Zion congregations—only the Methodists attracted a greater number of free persons of color. In Philadelphia the Baptist Church appears initially to have attracted fewer blacks. After all, both the black Methodists and the black Episcopalians had formed their churches before 1800, and until after the first third of the nineteenth century membership in the black congregations of these denominations, and the Presbyterians as well, seems to have run well ahead of that of the black Baptist bodies. By the late 1830s, however, the Baptist predilections of in-migrants from the slave area probably moved that denomination into second place among Philadelphia's Negro churches—ahead of the Presbyterians and Episcopalians, but still behind the Methodists. In the late 1840s it was asserted that, in all of the Negro Baptist churches in the City of Brotherly Love, "perhaps there is not one hundred of the whole number of members, over twenty-five years old, who are not direct from the South." But in the southern cities the Baptist faith appears not to have been overwhelmingly dominant among blacks. Certainly the number of black Baptists remained small in both Charleston and New Orleans, and neither of the Negro congregations in Baltimore had so many as 100 members in the 1850s (though there were, at the same time, three black Methodist churches with more than 1,000 members each). Negroes in the border state cities west of the Appalachians, on the other hand, seem to have been attracted to the Baptist Church in greater numbers. In the late 1840s the Reverend John Berry Meachum claimed over 500 members for his African Baptist Church in St. Louis, and his was probably the largest black church in that city. Larger still was Louisville's Fifth Street Baptist Church, with 650 communicants in 1848; even there, however, Negro Methodist congregations doubtless had more members—by a ratio of perhaps 4:3—than did the Baptist churches.[34]

Aside from the Methodist and Baptist churches, no Protestant denomination was more active in working with Negroes or more successful in attracting blacks in the antebellum era than the Presbyterians. As with other denominations, blacks were members of many biracial Presbyterian congregations. But, as with the other denominations, Negro Presbyterians occupied subordinate positions, and where there were sufficient numbers of black communicants, separate congregations were sometimes formed. In areas where the Congregational Church was strong, Presbyterianism was, in general, slower to develop (largely because of doctrinal similarities) and Negro Presbyterianism slower still. Hence, no black Presbyterian congregations emerged in either Boston or Providence before the middle of the nineteenth century. But in ten of the other thirteen cities (all except Albany, New Orleans, and St. Louis) black Presbyterian congregations existed at some time before 1850. Philadelphia saw both the earliest emergence of separate Negro congregations and the fullest development of black Presbyterianism in the antebellum era. In 1806 Archibald Alexander, pastor of the Third Presbyterian Church, took steps looking to the establishment of a separate black church. In the following year John Gloucester, a slave who had been for several years studying for the ministry under the direction of Union Presbytery in Tennessee, was brought to Philadelphia to pursue this work. A separate congregation—the First African Presbyterian Church—was founded in 1807 and taken under the care of the presbytery in 1811. Gloucester, who had been licensed to preach by the Union Presbytery in 1810, continued to serve the church until his death in 1822. A conflict over the choice of his successor produced a split and the establishment of the Second African Presbyterian Church, with Jeremiah Gloucester (John Gloucester's son) as pastor. The third of Philadelphia's Negro Presbyterian churches—Central—was formed in 1844 by a group that left the Second Church as a result of a disagreement over the choice of a minister. This congregation selected as its pastor Stephen Gloucester (another son of John Gloucester). During the half-century the number of Philadelphia's black Presbyterians in separate congregations grew from 22 in 1807, to 123 in 1811, to 324 in 1838, to over 500 in the 1850s.[35]

Aside from Philadelphia's First African Church, no other separate black Presbyterian congregation was formed in these cities until the third decade of the century. In 1822 the Colored Presbyterian Church (later Prince Street, and still later Shiloh) was organized in New York. Its minister, Samuel E. Cornish, had been at work among the city's free blacks for over a year prior to the church's formation, and most of the original twenty-five members came from biracial Presbyterian congregations. This church experienced a steady and substantial growth over the next two decades and by the mid-1840s enrolled over four hundred members.[36]

In the other major cities, the development of separate black Presbyterian churches was a phenomenon of the 1840s. That decade saw the formation of congregations in Baltimore, Brooklyn, Buffalo (founded by James Gloucester, another son of John Gloucester), Cincinnati, Louisville, Pittsburgh, and Washington, as well as the organization of a second church (Emmanuel) in New York and a third (Central) in Philadelphia. Additionally, Charleston's Second Presbyterian Church gathered a subordinate black congregation and constructed the city's largest church building to house it. Within a decade, attendance at the services of this body was greater than that of any other Charleston congregation.[37]

Given the educational requirements for ordination in the Presbyterian church, black ministers were in short supply, and a short-lived black-operated academy in Philadelphia in the early nineteenth century did little to alleviate the situation. At the end of the first quarter of the century there are supposed to have been only three qualified Negro Presbyterian ministers in the United States. Doubtless this circumstance inhibited the formation of separate churches, and certainly it necessitated a resort to various expedients. In a number of cases, white ministers served Negro churches, at least temporarily. Stephen Gloucester acted as Central's minister in Philadelphia despite the fact that he had only been licensed as an evangelist and not ordained, and Charles Gardner, a Methodist, supplied the First African Presbyterian Church in the same city for three years and later apparently accepted the Presbyterian discipline and was installed as the church's pastor. John F. Cook, the first pastor of Washington's Fifteenth Street Presbyterian Church, had been licensed to preach by the AME Church, but helped to form the Presbyterian congregation and was ordained after he became the church's minister. And since the Charleston church was not truly independent it is not surprising that a white minister—John L. Girardeau—occupied its pulpit.[38]

Despite these and other drawbacks, more than a dozen Presbyterian churches served the blacks in two-thirds of these cities in the 1840s. There were, in the 1850s, probably 300–600 black Presbyterians affiliated with separately organized congregations in each of the cities of New York, Philadelphia, and Charleston. In at least some areas black Presbyterian ministers participated in meetings of the presbytery, for Theodore S. Wright was elected moderator of New York City's Third Presbytery in 1845. Early in the next decade J. W. C. Pennington occupied that some position, and A. N. Freeman held the comparable office in the Brooklyn Presbytery.[39]

Ranking probably fourth among the denominations in attractiveness to urban blacks, despite its early start, was Episcopalianism. As has been previously noted, the first denominational religious congregation to grow out of the Free African Society in Philadelphia was St. Thomas's African Episcopal Church in 1794, with Absalom Jones as its minister. A year later Jones, who had been born a slave in Delaware almost a half-century before, was ordained a deacon. Raised to the priesthood in 1804, he served St. Thomas's Church until his death in 1818. The membership of the infant congregation numbered 246, a majority of the Free African Society having decided upon the denominational affiliation. Many of these, including Jones, had, of course, originally been communicants of St. George's Methodist Church, and their decision to form an Episcopal (rather than a Methodist) church was doubtless more the result of resentment than theological conviction. Hence, George F. Bragg, a historian of black Episcopalianism, was at least partially correct when he referred to this body as "really a congregation of colored Methodists conforming to the Episcopal Church."[40]

The rise of black Methodism in Philadelphia probably produced a considerable erosion in St. Thomas's membership. Although Jones claimed more than five hundred members in 1803, there is some reason to believe that that figure actually represented the cumulative total of all names entered on the church roll since its foundation. In 1806 the membership was estimated at one hundred fifty. Jones's death was followed by more than a decade during which St. Thomas's was served by white ministers (or no ministers at all), assisted by black lay readers. This circumstance can hardly have contributed to the vitality of the church or the size of its membership. But the advent of the Reverend William Douglass as rector in 1834 apparently sparked a recovery, for by the 1850s the membership was over three hundred, and the annual average number of confirmations in the early 1840s was fifty percent higher than at the beginning of the century. Additionally, a second black Episcopal congregation (the Church of the Crucifixion) was formed in 1847.[41]

Fifteen years after the formation of St. Thomas's, New York's Negro Episcopalians began to meet separately. Carefully nurtured by Trinity Church, this body matured as St. Philip's Church. Though not recognized by the diocese as a separate church until its first building was erected in 1819, its congregational life antedated that event by a decade. Peter Williams, the congregation's minister until his death in 1840, was appointed a lay reader in 1812, ordained a deacon in 1819, and raised to the priesthood in 1826. By the mid-1840s the membership exceeded three hundred.[42] In the meantime, another New York black congregation (St. Matthew's) had been gathered by Isaiah G. DeGrasse in 1840. Following DeGrasse's departure in 1842, the membership declined precipitously to no more than twenty parishioners in 1844. But in 1845 young Alexander Crummell revived the congregation as the Church of the Messiah, and its membership quickly rose above one hundred.[43]

New York and Philadelphia were the only cities in which more than a single black Episcopalian congregation was formed in the first half of the nineteenth century. But in three other of the urban centers separate black churches were established. St. James's Church in Baltimore was formed in 1827 as a result of three years of missionary activity by William Livingston, a free man of color who had been ordained a deacon in St. Thomas's Church in 1824. Christ Church in Providence was incorporated in 1842, but black Episcopalians had first met separately in that city three years earlier. The embryonic congregation was briefly served in 1840 by Isaiah DeGrass (who in the same year gathered St. Matthew's congregation in New York) and he was followed (as later in New York) by Alexander Crummell, who was then a student at Boston Theological Seminary. The third of these churches was St. James's in Brooklyn which was separated from St. Mark's in 1846, though remaining in some respects a mission of that congregation. None of these was a strong congregation. The Baltimore church never had as many as one hundred communicants; Christ Church apparently eked out a precarious existence for less than two decades before it expired; and the Brooklyn congregation is not even mentioned by the earliest historian of Negro Episcopalians, George F. Bragg.[44] Additionally, in 1849 Charleston Episcopalians established a separate, but subordinate, church (Calvary) for black communicants, and in the mid-1850s a group of New Orleans Negro Episcopalians were authorized to hold separate services weekly. Only Christ Church (Providence), of these seven regularly organized congregations, appears to have been permitted to participate in diocesan affairs.[45]

The number of Negro Episcopalian ministers was, as might be expected, limited. The Pennsylvania diocese waived the required knowledge of Latin and Greek to permit the ordination of Absalom

Jones, and other dioceses may have made similar concessions, officially or unofficially. Almost all black congregations, at one time or another, were served by white priests.[46]

In addition to these Methodist, Baptist, Presbyterian, and Episcopalian churches, there were several other separate black religious congregations—many of them short-lived—in some of the northern cities. Between 1826 and 1828 Mark Jordon, a black preacher licensed for the purpose, attempted to gather a Dutch Reformed congregation in New York, but with little success. A Lutheran church existed in Philadelphia in the late 1830s, with a Negro pastor, the Reverend John Jones, and for a short time in the early 1840s there seems also to have been a black Unitarian society. Charles B. Ray, a black Congregational minister, was successful in forming a congregation in New York in 1845, and shortly thereafter a black Disciples of Christ church came into existence in Cincinnati with Aaron Wallace as its pastor.[47] Separate congregations of black Catholics were almost unheard of in the United States before the Civil War, but the short-lived Chapel of the Nativity was established in Pittsburgh in 1844, served by a white priest, for Negro communicants, and St. Francis's Chapel of Baltimore's Convent of the Oblate Sisters of Providence (an order of black sisters established in 1829) attracted many black Catholics, although it was primarily intended to serve the members of the order.[48]

Thus, by 1850 there were well over one hundred separate black religious congregations in these fifteen cities. In almost every case the separation had been mutually desired by both white and Negro communicants, though the Philadelphia Methodists attempted to forestall the development of the first black congregation in that city. Moved by religious zeal, a spirit of philanthropy, paternalism, or, perhaps, a subconscious guilt because of the relief inspired by the departure of black members, whites frequently lent assistance to black churches. When Richard Allen and Absalom Jones went to the white community for financial assistance, Allen reported that they "met with great success. We had no reason to complain of the liberality of the citizens." And the St. Thomas's parsonage was the bequest of a white resident, William Bradford. The ground upon which St. James's Episcopal Church was built in Baltimore was the gift of James Bosley, and other whites contributed to the construction of the church. Similar, if less extensive, white assistance marked the erection of St. Phillip's Church in New York. Nor were the Episcopalians alone in this activity. Moses Brown purchased the lot on which the Providence African Union Church and Schoolhouse was built. White Baptists contributed heavily to the construction of the First African Baptist Church in Boston, and William Crane was largely responsible for bringing both Moses C. Clayton and Noah Davis—early black Baptist preachers—to Baltimore. Baltimore mayor Elisha Tyson was of repeated assistance to a number of Negro congregations, especially that of the Bethel AME Church. A white slaveowner donated the land on which the first black Baptist church in Louisville was built, and white men served as clerks of the first two Negro Baptist congregations established in that city.[49]

White assistance was, however, sporadic and usually available only in the initiatory stages of church development. The black church in urban America was overwhelmingly the vision of the black spirit, organized by black minds, built by black hands, and the solace of black souls. As a black institution, it shared the material poverty of the urban Negro. Its ministers were frequently poorly paid. John Gloucester was never officially installed as pastor of Philadelphia's First African Presbyterian Church, possibly because the congregation was unable to provide adequate financial support. Richard Allen made many financial contributions to Bethel congregation, but received from the church a total of eighty dollars. At the end of the first quarter of the nineteenth century the pastor of Bethel AME Church in Baltimore—one of the largest in the denomination—was paid less than two hundred dollars annually. And the Reverend George Wells, the first pastor of Louisville's Green Street Baptist Church, received no money from the congregation and supported himself by working in brickyards in the summer and pork packinghouses in the winter.[50]

Black church buildings, too, tended to be smaller and less valuable than those of white congregations. The discrepancy was doubtless less pronounced in property values than in salaries paid, because communicants sometimes donated their labor to aid in the construction of black church buildings. There were, as might be expected, some differences both among denominations and among cities. In 1826 New York's St. Phillip's congregation worshiped in the third smallest Episcopal church in the city, which was roughly one-half the median size of buildings occupied by white congregations, while the black Presbyterians likewise occupied the third smallest church of that denomination—about two-thirds of the median size of the white church buildings. The Abyssinian Baptist Church, however, was almost exactly the median size of that denomination's religious structures, while black Methodists worshiped in the fifth largest and two of the three smallest Methodist churches. Elsewhere, the value of the black Methodist church in Washington in 1830 was twenty-five percent higher than the average value of white Methodist churches, but in 1846 in Brooklyn only the most valuable of three Negro Methodist churches was worth as much as the least valuable of those occupied by whites. In Philadelphia in 1838 the value of black-owned church property per member ranged from $6.00 for Baptists, to $17.76 for Methodists, to $61.85 for Presbyterians, and to $360.00 for Episcopalians.[51]

It is readily apparent that the value or size of these black religious structures reflected not only the relative poverty of their communicants, but also differentials among the denominations generally. Consequently, although Negro Episcopalian and Presbyterian churches tended to rank low in value or size among all churches in the denomination, they tended to rank high among black churches. The suggested "high status" position of these congregations within the black communities is further supported by analyses of the occupations followed by the officers of various black churches. These rather diverse and decidedly spotty sets of data generally show the highest proportion of common laborers and other unskilled workers among the Methodist church officers and the largest proportion of high-opportunity occupations among Presbyterians and Episcopalians, with Baptist officers falling between these two extremes. Such data are heavily influenced by different occupational patterns in the various urban centers, but the conclusion is almost inescapable that, though all black churches occupied "low-status" position in the whole urban social spectrum, within the black communities the Episcopalian and Presbyterian congregations were accorded "high status," while the Methodists and the Baptists—especially the former—occupied lower positions on the social scale.[52]

These church structures, as might be expected, were usually located in the areas of densest black settlement in those cities where such residential concentrations existed (see chapter 4). In mid-nineteenth-century Philadelphia, for example, eight of the nine black churches in the city (and three of five in the suburbs) were found within two blocks of the Philadelphia-Moyamensing boundary, between Fifth and Twelfth streets. Similar circumstances prevailed elsewhere. All of Boston's black churches were in the "Nigger Hill" area, and all of Brooklyn's in, or adjacent to, the area of most heavily concentrated black residence in the fourth and fifth wards. In New York, eight of the ten black churches south of Fourteenth Street were located in, or around the perimeter of, the black residential concentration in the fifth and eighth wards, and similar (though somewhat less pronounced) patterns existed in Cincinnati and Providence.[53]

In separating from the white churches the urban Negroes did not create an environment for worship free from discrimination and harassment, for these were conditions endemic to the society in which the black churches existed. In the southern cities black religious meetings were regulated, as were all gatherings of Negroes. And in all cities the black church and its congregation—a visible symbol of the black community—were inviting targets for concentrated attack in periods of mob violence.[54]

But the process of separation did eliminate racial discrimination during the worship proceedings and also created an institution that could serve blacks in other ways. The Negro churches, for example, conducted Sunday schools which, in the early nineteenth century, combined religious instruction with education designed to produce literacy. Within two years after the establishment of Albany's African Baptist Church, its Sunday school was in operation, and by the mid-1820s enrolled almost 200 scholars. In Baltimore in the early 1840s Sunday schools in the two AME churches enrolled almost 300 students, and within three years after the organization of Noah Davis's Baptist Church 50 were enrolled in its classes. Such activities were, throughout the half-century, increasingly a part of the church programs. By the mid-1850s nineteen black churches in Philadelphia and its vicinity—Baptist, Episcopalian, Methodist, and Presbyterian—enrolled almost 1,900 pupils in Sabbath schools taught by more than 180 teachers.[55] In many instances, these and other independent Sunday schools were taught by white instructors (sometimes in the face of considerable opposition); in Charleston in the late 1850s George Daughaday was "beaten by a mob and then held under a pump" for conducting a black Sunday school. But more commonly white instruction was viewed by the religious community as a commendable enterprise.[56] By the middle of the nineteenth century, however, such instruction was heavily in the hands of Negroes and associated with black churches.

Black churches also provided burial sites for Negroes. Nearly all private and church cemeteries were closed to blacks, and almost the only resting place for their bodies was the local potter's field (where they were still segregated). Black churches (as well as private burial societies) acted to provide their members and other Negroes as well with graves that were better maintained, frequently more conveniently located, and certainly less depressing and degrading than the potter's field.[57]

Less directly connected with religious activities than either Sabbath schools or cemeteries were the day schools devoted to secular education that were connected with many black churches. As is elsewhere noted, educational opportunities for Negro children were few, and those that existed, especially in the earlier years of the nineteenth century, were, with the exception of a few philanthropic efforts, largely initiated and supported by the blacks themselves. The Negro church buildings often housed day schools, not only because these structures were well adapted to the educational practice of the day, but also because their congregations both perceived this as an obligation to the larger black community and, in some cases, served as the organizing units to provide financial support for the schools. Some church buildings—the African Baptist Church in Boston and St. James's Episcopal Church in Baltimore, for example—were deliberately constructed so as to include facilities for a school. Philadelphia's Bethel Church was operating a day school as early as 1794,

St. Thomas's African Episcopal Church by 1804, and their example was followed by later churches of all denominations. In part, to be sure, this practice can be seen as related to the connection between Protestantism and biblical study (which demands literacy). But to a greater degree it would appear to have been a response to a deeply felt need in the black community.[58]

Black congregations—especially the Methodists and Baptists—also served as instruments of social control for their membership and, consequently, helped to shape the congregation as a social model for the larger black community. Churches expelled or otherwise punished members for adultery, frequenting "dame houses," slander, theft, excessive drinking, and profane swearing, as might be expected. But also subjected to church discipline were a variety of other offenders—a man who, without his wife's knowledge, sold household goods to pay rent; a woman who would not submit to her husband "as a dutiful wife"; a married couple who engaged in a heated quarrel; a businessman who did not properly divide the receipts of a partnership; and persons engaged in street brawls.[59]

No aspect of the Negro church was more important than its interrelationship with the black community. As has been noted, a sense of community among some blacks—even if nothing more solid than a community of resentment—had, in some measure, to be called into existence before the separate black church could be brought into being. But once formed, the Negro congregations were dynamic instruments for developing community consciousness and for strengthening community bonds. It has been estimated that the proportion of urban blacks attending religious services in Providence doubled after the formation of separate congregations, and white churchmen in Baltimore found, to their surprise, that free blacks were twice as likely to be "professors of religion" as whites. And in 1836 a survey of Boston's black families showed well over a quarter of the adult males and more than two-fifths of the adult females to be "connected with churches."[60] Doubtless many Negros became church members because they found, for the first time, a religious service in which they could participate without being branded as inferior and a form of worship better attuned to their emotional needs. But at least equally compelling was the fact that in these congregations they linked hands with others who shared the anxiety, the pain, the resentment, the despair, the fear, and, withal, the desperate need to be confirmed in the conviction of their worth as human beings and their hope of a better day—who, in short, shared all those things wholly experienced and understood only by those who were bound together by blackness. In a world where every lever of power was held by a white hand and every symbol of authority was white, the separated church stood as a towering monument to the zeal, strength, and determination of the American Negro—a black rock casting a cooling shadow in a harsh desert of whiteness.

This institution gathered other institutions around it—Sunday school classes, social organization, schools—and became, to an even greater degree, both the cement and the symbol of the black community. Black ministers, protected in some measure by their profession and sharing, to however small a degree, a fellowship with other men of similar calling, spoke out with greater frankness on matters of importance to all black people, and the church stood more clearly as the center and the soul of the black community. It was no accident that antislavery groups met in black churches, or that more than one-half of those blacks listed by one writer as abolitionist leaders in New York were ministers, or that more than one-half of those persons classified by another as "distinguished Negroes" in the period before 1831 were church leaders.[61] For the black church was both the most certain avenue of advancement for ambitious and able Negroes aspiring to positions of leadership, and the single rostrum from which black voices consistently spoke to black concerns—almost the only window between the black and the white communities.

Thus, the black church came to serve blacks in ways that biracial churches never could in the antebellum era. These different ways were not so much religious in nature, for although Negro churches changed the form of their services to some degree, they continued in most respects to share a theology and a church order that were essentially white creations. The real differences related to the role of the church in the community. No concern for human betterment, however sensitive, could ever have made the biracial churches the single-minded instruments of black community development or the unadulterated voices of black concerns that the Negro churches became instantly and inevitably. It was the irony and the tragedy of antebellum America that only through separation could the black church fulfill its destiny as a developer of unity.

12 Fruits of Discrimination— Seeds of Community: Associational Activities of Urban Blacks

Americans have been characterized as a nation of "joiners." This tendency to band together for mutual protection or advantage, for the achievement of mutually agreed upon goals, or simply for the establishment of mutuality was intensified in the cities, at least in part because other American traits and conditions were more strongly evident in urban settings. The urban populations always contained disproportionate numbers of the "uprooted," those individuals and families, whether native or foreign-born, who had left the place and society of their birth and early nurture. Furthermore, group migration (with its attendant transference of preexisting social relationships) to the cities was rare. Moreover, urban populations, at any given point in time, appear to have been more transient than those of small towns and rural areas, with both recent arrivals and natives changing their places of residence, or leaving the city entirely, with unusual frequency. In the cities, too, the relatively unstructured society and the relatively open economy were more in evidence, and both societal and governmental units displayed less personalized concern for the well-being (or, at least, survival) of individual residents. Beset by uncertainties, adrift in an amorphous mass of humanity, and perhaps to some degree disoriented, urbanites sought a measure of economic, social, and psychological security by creating or joining societies of smaller scale.

Near-unanimous prejudice and discrimination herded urban blacks into smaller subcommunities and (in the northern cities) largely restricted their place of residence to relatively concentrated Negro districts. But in other respects they shared the uncertainties, anomie, and disorientation of other urbanites. Additionally, the restrictions they endured in such matters as access to public relief and public education encouraged them to play a still more active role in the formation and support of organizations designed to alleviate their distress, share their burdens, and facilitate individual and group advancement.

The struggle to survive was the strongest impulse to cooperative action. Largely restricted to the least rewarding occupations, many of which, by their nature, afforded only irregular or seasonal employment, urban free persons of color were rarely able to acquire property or to accumulate any financial resources upon which to draw when unemployed or ill or to guarantee any measure of security to their families in the event of the death of the principal breadwinner. Additionally, public and private relief appears to have been available to blacks only on a limited basis.[1] Under these pressures it is not suprising that blacks early established associations to provide assistance in times of distress and that such societies greatly outnumbered all other black associational bodies. It is not possible to state with absolute accuracy the time of establishment of many of these organizations or, except in rare instances, the number in existence at any given date, for most were never incorporated, and only a few have left any record of their activities beyond a passing reference in some ephemeral or peripheral source.

These aid societies were of two types. A few organizations existed that could be classified as benevolent societies—that is, their purpose was to secure donations from the more affluent Negroes and to dispense such funds to assist some specific less-favored group in the black community (e.g., widows and orphans). But a much larger number of the aid associations were beneficial societies, whose purpose was to organize the limited resources of the poor and provide for the mutual support of their members. They routinely collected very small weekly dues and dispensed equally minute payments in the event of unemployment, illness, or death of their members.

Several of these beneficial societies existed before the end of the eighteenth century. The Free African Society, which was organized by Richard Allen and Absalom Jones in Philadelphia in 1778, appears to have been the first established in the major cities. Though better known as the agency which organized the religious activities of the black seceders from St. George's Methodist Church, this association clearly was conceived, at least in part, as a beneficial society and operated as such. But its energies apparently exhausted by serving as an instrument for the creation of separate black churches, its mutual aid functions seem to have been taken over by two societies associated with the newly established black Episcopal Church—the Female Benevolent Society of St. Thomas (1793) and the male African Friendly Society of St. Thomas (1795). At least one additional benevolent society—the Benevolent Daughters (1796)—existed in the City of Brotherly Love before the turn of the century, and there may well have been others.[2] By 1790 mutual aid societies existed in the Deep South urban centers as well. Free persons of color in New Orleans organized the Perseverance Benevolence and Mutual Aid Association in 1783, only five years after the founding of Philadelphia's Free African Society, and two Charleston organizations—the Brown Fellowship Society (1790) and the Free Dark Men of Color (1791)—were founded within the next ten years. The Brown Fellowship Society, in addition to providing benefits for distressed members, apparently also served as an early credit union, for members were authorized to borrow money from the treasury. At least two other societies—the Boston African Society (1796) and a New York association that in 1797 possessed a burial plot and a church site—also antedated the end of the century. The basic operating principles of these societies were simple and would be common to similar bodies formed later. Once admitted to fellowship, members paid small weekly dues (usually twenty-five cents). Benefits were dispensed by committees and consisted of payments to members who were ill, the burial of any member whose estate was insufficient to provide for interment, and the support of widows and the training of orphans of members.[3]

The movement to establish mutual aid societies spread rapidly to black communities in other cities in the nineteenth century. In 1818 the Woolman Benevolent Society was formed in Brooklyn, and a similar association existed in Baltimore at least as early as 1821. By the late 1820s at least two beneficial societies—the Young Men's Union Friendly Association and the Mutual Relief Society, composed of older men—were at work in Providence. The fourth decade of the century saw the establishment of the Female Lundy Society in Albany and a similar organization for black women in Cincinnati, and by the 1850s (and probably well before that time) various beneficial societies were established by the free persons of color in the nation's capital. It is highly likely that such organizations were formed by blacks in the other cities (where other types of black societies certainly existed) as well, but specific evidence has not been located.[4]

Naturally, the number of mutual aid societies increased—in some cases, where there were large numbers of free persons of color, dramatically—in the various cities throughout the first half of the nineteenth century. For example, the New York African Society for Mutual Relief was established in 1808 and incorporated two years later. This association was perhaps the most prosperous and prestigious of the antebellum black societies. Despite the loss of its entire treasury to an absconding officer in 1812, the organization quickly built a substantial surplus, which was invested in rental property. By the early 1850s the annual rental income was more than ten times as great as the membership dues collected. This remarkable financial feat was apparently accomplished largely by restricting the membership to a relatively few (about sixty-five) carefully selected blacks who seem to have made few or no claims upon the society's resources. This circumstance leads one to suspect that its true purposes were more social than beneficial—a conclusion bolstered by its "inordinate influence in the Negro community."[5]

The black communities of Philadelphia, Charleston, and, to a much lesser degree, New York appear to have been particularly active in forming mutual aid societies in the first two decades of the nineteenth century. New York's African Society assisted in organizing the Wilberforce Philanthropic Society in 1818, and Charleston's free persons of color established such societies as the Humane and Friendly in 1802, the Minors Moralist in 1803, and the Friendly Union in 1813. In the City of Brotherly Love the Negro community created such associations as the Whitesonian (1818), the Angola Beneficial (1808), the Male African Benevolent (1811), the Rush Benevolent (1805), the Wilberforce (1810), the Angolian (1808), the Sons of Africa (1810), the Benezet Philanthropic (1812), the Female Benezet (1818), the Daughters of Aaron (1819), and the American Female Bond Benevolent Society of Bethel (1817).[6]

But it was the decades of the 1820s, 1830s, and 1840s that saw the most substantial growth in the numbers of beneficial associations. Between 1820 and 1835 alone over forty were formed in Philadelphia and almost as many in Baltimore. No fewer than three additional societies were established by the free black community of Charleston before 1850, and at least that many in each of the cities of New Orleans, Boston, Cincinnati, and Providence. Several were formed in New York, and at least one more each in Brooklyn and Albany.[7]

Many of these societies were organized by blacks who were already associated together, either formally or informally, for other purposes. A large number, for example, brought together members of various black religious congregations. In Philadelphia, the African Friendly Society of St. Thomas, the Sons of St. Thomas, and the Daughters of St. Thomas were obviously Episcopal in origin; while the names of the United Sons of Allen, the African Female Bond Benevolent Society of Bethel Church, the Daughters of Zion Angolian Ethiopian Society, the Female Methodist Assistance Society, and Union Benevolent Sons of Bethel, the Female Beneficial Philanthropic Society of Zoar, and perhaps a dozen others indicate Methodist connections; and the religious orientation of the Female Baptist Assistance Society is equally clear. In Baltimore, too, the Female Wesleyan Association and the Daughters Bethel Association obviously emerged from church memberships, as did the New York Benevolent Branch of Bethel; and Charleston's Brown Society appears to have had Episcopal origins. The Abyssinian Benevolent Daughters of Esther in New York was probably the creation of members of the Abyssinian Baptist Church, and doubtless a number of other societies in various cities were at least initially related to religious bodies, though the connection is less obvious.[8]

Blacks following the same occupations—and, consequently, already sharing many of the same concerns—frequently formed beneficial societies. By the late 1830s Negro coachmen, porters, and "mechanics" had founded societies in Philadelphia and Baltimore, and in the latter city Negro barbers, brickmakers, and caulkers had also established beneficial associations. Seamen pursued an occupation both hazardous and irregular, and it is hardly surprising that black sailors formed a mutual aid society in New York as early as 1810 and that before the end of the first half of the century a second such organization existed in the nation's largest city as well as a similar association in Providence. The ships' cooks and stewards sailing from New York, doubtless for like reasons, founded an association in 1839. Other skilled artisans probably established aid societies in these and other cities but no record of their activities remains. People following occupations at the bottom of the economic ladder were, naturally, less likely to organize occupationally oriented beneficial societies because they lacked the resources and the sense of identification with their jobs. But New York's American League of Colored Laborers may have served, in part, as a beneficial society.[9]

It is likely that some mutual aid associations had neighborhood affinities, with all or most of their members living within a very small geographic area. Others, such as the New York African Society and Charleston's Brown Fellowship Society obviously drew from a narrow socioeconomic stratum throughout the whole city. But for very many such organizations, bearing such imaginative and diverse, but unrevealing, names as the Rising Perseverance Free Sons of Thompson, the Humane and Friendly Society, and United Brethren, the Daughters of Isaiah, the United Daughters of Hester, and the Friendly Daughters of Nehemiah, there is no evidence that the membership was united by anything save their deprivation, their foresight, and their blackness.[10]

As the names of many of these societies indicate, black women were active in the organization and support of mutual aid associations. This was a natural result of the relatively large number of free women of color who were employed—usually as servants, laundresses, stewardesses, and cooks—and their inadequate access to public relief facilities. With rare exceptions, it is not possible to state with any degree of accuracy the extent of female employment, black or white, in American cities before 1860. Until that date the census enumerators did not record women's occupations, and the city directories, in general, grossly understated such employment because they usually reported only householders and heads of families. An examination of fifty-nine directories in these fifteen cities, for instance, shows only sixteen free women of color employed in such commonly followed occupations as servants, chambermaids, house cleaners, or "days work," and many of these listings do not record the employment of any black women included in the directory. The extent to which the directory listings, in general, inaccurately reflected the actual occupational patterns of free women of color is partially indicated by the fact that those five directories that reported women's occupations most extensively showed them constituting ¼–⅓ of all employed free blacks; additionally, the Charleston census of 1848 reported females as comprising more than fifty-four percent of all free persons of color for whom occupations were recorded.[11]

It is not, therefore, surprising that black women, whose labors produced a significant portion (often, doubtless, the whole) of their families' incomes, should have availed themselves of the protection of mutual aid societies. Indeed, the very limited evidence available suggests that they may have joined such organizations more frequently than males. Three lists of black beneficial societies in the 1830s show the female associations to have constituted well over one-half of all the organizations reported by name in Philadelphia and an equal proportion of all Baltimore societies whose names reveal the sex of their members. This is true even of compilations that include the artisan mutual aid associations (which were restricted to males by the existing occupational patterns). The Philadelphia list of 1838 further indicates that women made up more than three-fifths of the membership of all Negro beneficial societies, and their organizations dispensed almost one-half of the total assistance in 1837. Male societies, however, were usually more prosperous—all four of the Philadelphia associations whose annual subscriptions for 1837 were as great as five dollars per member were male, as were five of the six with fund balances of five hundred dollars or more. An occasional society (e.g., the Union Bond Society of New Orleans) enrolled both men and women, but such organizations were rare.[12]

It is not possible to compile anything resembling a complete list of black beneficial societies in the nation's major cities in the first half of the nineteenth century. Many associations survived only briefly, and some that existed for longer periods of time may never have been mentioned by contemporary compilers (mostly white) of community records. Most, of course, were not incorporated and, hence, found no place in the official records. The extent of Negro participation in mutual aid societies and the scope of their assistance are even more difficult to assess, for membership and expenditure figures are rarely available. In some cases, however, individuals or organizations did compile occasional lists of, or make passing references to, these associations. The data for Philadelphia and Baltimore are fuller than for other urban centers, but even for these cities the information is doubtless incomplete.

Philadelphia is supposed to have had 11 black beneficial societies in 1811, 43 (plus "several . . . that have not made their returns") in 1831, more than 50 in 1832, 119 in 1838, and 106 in 1849. Seventy-nine of these societies reported a membership of 7,372 in 1838, and 76 associations claimed 5,187 members in 1849. Some blacks apparently belonged to more than one organization, however, for in 1849 only 4,904 (about one-half of the adult Negro population) reported that they belonged to such societies. In 1831 the 43 associations listed by name were reported to have paid out a little over $5,800 for relief during the previous year, while eight years later 79 organizations reported expenditures of more than $14,000 in the panic year of 1837. And in 1849 Philadelphia's black beneficial societies are supposed to have assisted 681 black families.[13]

In Baltimore in 1835 *Niles' Weekly Register* reported that blacks had established 35–40 mutual aid societies, and this assertion is further substantiated by the publication of a list in 1838 which contained the names of thirty-one black beneficial associations as well as an acknowledgment that there were "a few more smaller societies whose names cannot be ascertained here." Membership is less certain, but it was asserted that the various organizations enrolled 35–150 members. If the average number of members was 75, then the total membership for such societies in Baltimore in the late 1830s would have been between 2,600 and 3,000—much lower than in Philadelphia, but quite substantial.[14] Other and less detailed statements suggest that in the late 1830s and early 1840s there were probably more than thirty black beneficial societies in New York, five or more each in Providence, Charleston, and New Orleans, and at least two in Cincinnati.[15]

All of these figures are doubtless, in some measure, incomplete. Very roughly, it might be possible to say that by about 1840 there were probably well over two hundred black mutual aid societies in the nation's major cities and that their total membership was probably not less than 13,000–15,000. Since many urban blacks joined more than one beneficial society, it may be safe to suggest that as many as ten thousand blacks in these cities were affiliated with mutual aid organizations, and the figure may have been much larger.

A number of the organizations that have been characterized as beneficial societies may well have devoted some portion of their resources to assisting needy blacks who were not members. To the extent that this was true, their function could have been denominated as benevolent, rather than beneficial. Certainly some are known to have played a dual role. For example, the Woolman Benevolent Society gave timely and continuing support to the establishment and maintenance of a school for black children in Brooklyn. Moreover, Charleston's Brown Fellowship Society interested itself in the development of black educational opportunities from its inception, and though the children of its members were doubtless the prime beneficiaries of its activity, others do not appear to have been excluded from the schools encouraged by the society. More clearly benevolent was the work of the Minors Moralist Society, also in Charleston. For almost forty-five years after its foundation in 1803, it considered the education of indigent and orphaned free black children to be one of its primary purposes. In addition, the Resolute Beneficial Society sponsored a school in Washington in the late 1810s and early '20s, and New York's Phoenix Society maintained a black high school for a few years in the mid-1830s.[16]

Other Negro associations were more clearly designed to assist nonmembers. Their activities, like the subordinate undertakings of the beneficial and literary societies noted above, were primarily directed toward the support of black education. A Philadelphia society, in 1804, and the New York Society for the Promotion of Education among Colored Children, in 1847, both established schools, and a Negro society was formed in New York in 1812 to maintain a school for black orphans. The African Dorcas societies of New York and Philadelphia, it is true, had the broader purpose of distributing clothing to infirm and indigent persons of color, but a significant portion of their activities appears to have been directed to encouraging school attendance by providing clothing for destitute students. More clearly benevolent in nature was the Philanthropic Society of Pittsburgh, which Martin R. Delany helped to organize in 1834, and whose sole announced purpose (initially) appears to have been to relieve black indigents.[17]

Though not readily observable in their external functioning, the intention of encouraging moral and ethical behavior was deeply embedded in the structure of black mutual aid societies. At the time of its foundation in 1846 New Orleans' Colored Female Benevolent Society of Louisiana declared its purposes to include the "suppression of vice and inculcation of virtue among the colored class," as well as "to relieve the sick and bury the dead." The Boston African Society not only provided in its 1796 rules—as did many later organizations—that any member "bringing on himself any sickness, or disorder, by intemperance" should forfeit any claim to benefits, but further declared "that we take no one into the Society, who shall commit any injustice or outrage against the laws of the country," and also obligated its members to "watch over each other in their Spiritual concerns." The pervasiveness of these views was accurately assessed by a group of Philadelphia blacks in 1832, when they observed, of the more than fifty Negro beneficial associations then existing in that city, "The members of these societies are bound by rules and regulations, which tend to promote industry and morality among them. For any disregard or violation of these rules,—for intemperance or immorality of any kind, the members are liable to be suspended or expelled."[18]

Some Negro organizations addressed themselves primarily to the moral uplift of urban blacks. As early as 1809 a Society for Suppression of Vice and Immorality was founded in Philadelphia, and the Bible societies formed in New York and Baltimore (and probably elsewhere) doubtless considered themselves to be engaged in this work as well. More numerous still were the temperance societies. By the late 1830s and the early '40s there were associations in Providence and Cincinnati with more than 200 each, an organization in Pittsburgh with 170 enrolled, another in Buffalo with over 300 members, and one in Philadelphia which claimed 800 adherents. In addition roughly 1,500 Negroes had joined three temperance societies in Baltimore. Urban blacks also formed temperance organizations in Washington, Boston, Albany, Brooklyn, and at least five in New York in the 1830s. These organizations were often closely associated with black churches and were probably more numerous than surviving references suggest.[19]

Aside from the beneficial societies, probably no type of black association was more numerous than those organizations that may be generally characterized as literary societies. Among these were found library associations, debating societies, lyceums, and organizations devoted to declamation, prose writing, poetry, and the study of literature. Free persons of color appear to have organized only a few literary societies in the first third of the nineteenth century, when urban blacks tended to concentrate their earliest associative efforts on the foundation of religious and beneficial organizations, and to direct their initial activities in the field of intellectual advancement toward securing basic educational facilities for their children. A small number of such organizations are known to have existed even then, however. There was a debating society with twenty members in Boston in 1825, and in the next year a black group in Brooklyn was busily engaged in collecting books to establish a library. The next half-dozen years saw the formation of many societies in various of the major cities around the country. There is reference to a reading room society in Philadelphia dating from 1828, and in 1831 a group of Negro women organized the Female Literary Society. In 1830 Charleston's free men of color established the Bonneau Library Society, named for that city's most respected black schoolmaster, and the same year saw the formation of the New York Philomathean Society; both of these organizations were long-lived and influential in their respective communities. By the late 1830s the latter had a circulating library of six hundred volumes and was presenting lectures twice weekly. The year 1831 also saw the establishment of the Theban Society in Pittsburgh and the Boston Minors Exhibition Society, which were followed in 1832 by the Afric-American Female Intelligence Society of Boston. The Minors Exhibition Society was unusual (probably unique) in both restricting its membership to young people and enrolling persons of both sexes.[20]

The year 1833 almost appears to constitute a milestone in the organization of black literary societies. Of the associations existing before that date, only a couple seem to have survived for any considerable period of time or to have exerted much influence in the black communities. But from 1833 onward urban blacks formed greater numbers of associations, some of which undertook more ambitious programs and achieved positions of community prominence. It was in 1833, for example, that a number of young black men (and a few whites) formed the Phoenix Society in New York. Among its officers were such prominent members of the Negro community as Peter Williams, David Ruggles, Charles B. Ray, Samuel E. Cornish, and Christopher Rush. Not only did this association quickly establish a library, reading rooms, reading and discussion groups, and a course of lectures, but it also formed subordinate ward societies charged with performing some of the same functions in their smaller communities and with visiting all black families in their wards and urging upon them the benefits of education and intellectual development. Some of the scientific lectures sponsored by the association attracted up to five hundred auditors, and for a brief time it sponsored a high school for Negro children. It was an institution of such obvious promise that in the year of its foundation the members of the Third Annual Convention for the Improvement of the Free People of Colour urged their state vice presidents and secretaries "to use their exertions to form Phoenix Societies, similar to those in the City of New York." That same year saw the establishment of a literary society in Providence and the Philadelphia Library Company of Colored Persons. This latter association had the backing of such respected Philadelphia blacks as Robert Purvis, Robert Douglass, Jr., and Robert C. Gordon, Jr., and within five years secured papers of incorporation, enrolled 150 members, collected a library of six hundred volumes, and established a debating department.[21]

During a period of five years in the mid-1830s (ending with the panic year of 1837), urban blacks in the nation's major cities founded well over a score of literary and intellectual development associations. In addition to the Phoenix Society, free persons of color in New York organized the Ladies Literary Society, the Garrison Literary Association, and the Female Literary Society, and four others were formed either in 1837 or very shortly thereafter. The Garrison Association was entirely for young blacks, enrolling persons between the ages of four and twenty. Its meetings—which attracted over 150 persons—were held in the public school on Laurens Street until one of the school trustees objected to the use of Garrison's name. The organization, however, preferred to surrender its meeting place rather than abandon its name—a decision that was supported by the prestigious Philomathean Society, which offered the Garrisonians the use of their hall.[22]

Philadelphia blacks were almost as energetic in forming literary associations as were their compatriots in New York. In the mid-1830s Negro women founded the Minerva Literary Society and the Edgeworth Society to foster reading, recitation, and the writing of poetry and essays. The male segment of the black population was equally active, organizing the Banneker Society, the Rush Library Company and Debating Society, and the Demosthenian Institute. Both of these latter associations quickly collected small libraries, and the Demosthenian established a lecture series and, in 1841, a weekly newspaper—the *Demosthenian Shield*—with more than one thousand subscribers.[23]

The free black communities in other major cities shared the zeal for cultural and intellectual advancement that marked the middle years of the 1830s. Boston Negroes founded the Thompson Literary and Debating Society before 1835, and in 1836, the Boston Philomathean Society (which was apparently modeled on the New York Philomathean) and the Adelphic Union for the Promotion of Literature and Science. This latter society was extremely active, presenting to large audiences extensive courses of scientific and cultural lectures by prominent black and white leaders, and sometimes allowing women to speak. In addition the Young Men's Debating Society was established, probably in 1837 or early 1838. And in Providence members of the black community formed both a literary association and a debating society during these years.[24] Urban Negroes also organized debating and literary societies in Buffalo and Pittsburgh, and a lyceum in Cincinnati, whose semiweekly lectures were attended by audiences of 150–300 people. By the middle of the decade both the Young Men's Mental Improvement Society and the Phoenix Society were at work in Baltimore, and within a couple of years blacks in the nation's capital had established a debating society and a literary association.[25]

The frequency of formation of new literary societies diminished after the panic of 1837, doubtless both because of economic conditions and because the number of societies already in operation by that date made it less likely that new associations could attract many members. Nevertheless, these years saw the foundation of two new societies in Albany, one in Cincinnati, the Gilbert Lyceum in Philadelphia, and new literary associations in Boston and Pittsburgh. The Gilbert Lyceum was unique not only in enrolling both men and women as members but also in numbering both males and females (including Philadelphia's leading black schoolmistress, Sarah M. Douglass) among its founders.[26]

As in the case of beneficial societies, it is impossible to speak with confidence about the extent of black participation in the formation and support of literary associations. Certainly well over two score existed in the major cities of the United States at one time or another during the second quarter of the nineteenth century. The actual number may well have been half again as great—James Forten noted the existence of "many literary societies" in the Philadelphia black community in 1837, and rather more than a decade later George G. Foster commented on the "numerous debating societies among the colored people, where questions of the greatest interest are discussed, and that too with quite as much dignity and ability as frequently characterize our own [i.e., white] legislative bodies."[27]

To gauge the number of free persons of color enrolled in these societies is more difficult still. The Philadelphia Library Company of Colored Persons claimed 150 members in 1838, and a few years earlier New York's Garrison Literary Association is supposed to have enrolled an equal number of young people. But membership figures of this magnitude would appear to have been highly unusual. Reports to the National Convention of Colored Citizens in 1843 show 40 persons affiliated with a Cincinnati society and an equal number of members divided between two Albany societies. In Philadelphia the Rush Library Company and Debating Society is supposed to have enrolled 22 persons in 1837, 41 in 1838, and 30 in 1841, while the Minerva Literary Society reported 20 members in 1838 and 30 in 1840. The membership of four other Philadelphia associations in the late 1830s and early '40s ranged between 20 and 42.[28] These figures would suggest that it was a rare black literary organization that enrolled more than 50 persons and that many associational membership rolls did not show half that number. Overlapping memberships were not unknown but would appear to have been far less common than in beneficial societies. The influence exerted by these organizations was, however, much greater than their enrollment indicates, for audiences of up to 500 persons sometimes attended their lectures and debates. Clearly literary societies were far less common among urban blacks than mutual aid associations and directly involved many fewer persons—a circumstance that was hardly surprising, given their level of economic deprivation.

Though intended as instruments of moral and intellectual cultivation, the black literary societies doubtless occasionally served other purposes as well. Since their ranks included many of the most accomplished and concerned persons in the black community it is likely that protests and petitions were framed in their meeting places and circulated among their members. Since such bodies (and, to a lesser degree, the beneficial societies as well) constituted recognizable centers of black community consciousness it likely that many personal, as well as general, appeals were addressed to them. The multiple areas of their concern were, perhaps, well illustrated by the objects found by the Washington police in the possession of a group of two dozen black men apprehended for assembling contrary to the ordinances of the city governing free persons of color—a Bible, a copy of Seneca's *Morals,* a volume entitled *Life in Earnest,* the constitution of a society whose purpose was "to relieve the sick, and bury the dead," and a subscription paper circulated for the purpose of raising $650 "to purchase the freedom of Eliza Howard," whose owner had agreed to sell her for that amount.[29]

Fraternal societies partook, in some measure, of the characteristics of both the beneficial and the literary associations. That is, their functions included the assistance of infirm members of their order and their families, widows, and orphans, as well as the moral and mental uplift of their adherents. The Masonic order was the oldest and strongest black fraternal organization in the antebellum era, having its inception in Boston on the eve of the Revolution. Prince Hall, the founder of black freemasonry in America, was born in Barbados in 1748, the son of an Englishman and a free mulatto woman of French ancestry. Arriving in Boston at the age of seventeen, he engaged in soapmaking (and probably in harnessmaking) and within eight years had acquired sufficient real estate to qualify as a voter. He early joined the Methodist church and shortly became a minister. In 1775 he and fourteen other Negroes were initiated in a British army lodge and authorized to meet under dispensation until they received a charter. The Provincial Grand Master for Massachusetts, however, refused Hall's application for a charter, and after the conclusion of hostilities (during which Hall served for six years in the Revolutionary forces), a warrant was issued by the Grand Lodge of England in 1784 for the establishment of the African Lodge in Boston. This body was made a Grand Lodge in 1791, with Hall as Provincial Grand Master—a post he held until his death in 1807.[30]

In the late 1790s the African Grand Lodge of Massachusetts (redesignated the Prince Hall Grand Lodge shortly after Hall's death) authorized the founding of Masonic lodges in Providence and Philadelphia. The Providence lodge seems to have been established because residents who were members of the Boston lodge found it difficult to attend meetings. Perhaps the membership was too limited to support the lodge, however, for it appears not to have survived very long after the turn of the century. Philadelphia, on the other hand, quickly emerged as the strongest center of black freemasonry in the country. To the initial African Lodge of 1797 (Number 459) was quickly added another (Number 544) founded in 1798 by a group of black seamen under a charter from a Grand Lodge in Germany. During the first decade and a half of the nineteenth century the Prince Hall Grand Lodge issued charters for the founding of three more lodges in Philadelphia, and the German lodge apparently authorized the organization of another. Some of these bodies appear to have been short-lived, for not more than four lodges seem to have participated in the organization of the First Independent African Grand Lodge in 1815, at which time Philadelphia Masons terminated their relationship with the Prince Hall Grand Lodge. The unity of the order in the City of Brotherly Love was, however, quickly destroyed by internal dissension, which led to the creation of another Grand Lodge (Hiram) in 1818. The Hiram Grand Lodge participated (together with three other Grand Lodges) in the formation of the National Grand Lodge in 1848, but resumed an independent status less than two years later. All in all, it appears that ten or more subordinate lodges may have been founded in Philadelphia between 1797 and 1850, but probably not more than half that number survived the first half of the nineteenth century.[31]

In the first quarter of the century freemasonry was introduced in the black communities of the other eastern seaboard cities of New York, Washington, and Baltimore. The Prince Hall Grand Lodge issued a warrant in 1812 under which the first lodge (Boyer) was established in New York and also chartered three others in 1826. The Boyer Grand Lodge of Free and Accepted Masons of the State of New York—the fourth in the United States—was formed in 1845. It also appears that at least one lodge existed in Brooklyn in the late 1840s. The First Independent African Grand Lodge of Pennsylvania issued the warrants under which were established the Social Lodge in Washington in 1822 and the Friendship Lodge in Baltimore in 1825. Two others followed rather quickly in Baltimore, and Hiram Grand Lodge chartered the Universal Lodge in Alexandria and the Felix Lodge in Washington in 1845 and '46. Grand Lodges were formed for Maryland in 1845 and the District of Columbia in 1848.[32]

The spread of black freemasonry to the urban centers beyond the Appalachians was largely the work of one man—Richard H. Gleaves of Philadelphia, who was made Deputy Grand Master of the Independent Grand Lodge in 1846 and immediately embarked on a western missionary tour spectacular in its success. In 1846 he established the St. Cyprien Lodge in Pittsburgh, and in 1847 he secured the denunciation of a "bogus" lodge in Cincinnati and organized there the Corinthian Lodge and the True American Lodge (composed of the members of the old "bogus" lodge). The next year saw the establishment of St. John's Lodge in the Ohio metropolis, and in 1849 these three Cincinnati bodies formed the Ohio African Grand Lodge, with Gleaves as Grand Master. The next year he organized the Mt. Moriah Lodge, which was composed of Louisville residents, though it met in New Albany, Indiana, for about three years. And in the early 1850s he was successful in forming lodges in New Orleans and St. Louis.[33]

The so-called "higher degrees" of freemasonry were also established among antebellum urban blacks. After an abortive effort in 1776, Royal Arch masonry was introduced in Philadelphia in 1820, in which year the first black commandery of Knights Templar was also founded. For almost three decades these were the only black units of these orders, but in 1849 and 1850 more than a half-dozen new bodies were created. These years saw the establishment of Royal Arch chapters in Baltimore, Cincinnati, Washington, and New York; the organization of commanderies of Knights Templar in Baltimore and Cincinnati; and the formation of Scottish Rite councils in Philadelphia and Cincinnati. In addition, a council of the Order of Memphis (later to be absorbed into the Scottish Rite) was established in New York in 1850 by Richard Cowes who, after being initiated in Milan, Italy, in 1837, had been active in this work in the West Indies.[34]

Perhaps more than any other black organization, Prince Hall masonry consciously sought to attract members notable for their economic success, intellectual development, and social prominence. Consequently, unusually large numbers of early leaders of the urban black communities were Masons. Prince Hall, the founder, was active in both religious and educational activity and among other adherents were such notable figures as Richard Allen, Absalom Jones, and James Forten of Philadelphia; John W. Prout, William Wormley, George Bell, and William C. Costin of Washington; Martin R. Delany of Pittsburgh; and William H. Gibson of Louisville.[35]

The Order of Odd Fellows was apparently the only other national or international fraternal order with urban black chapters in the first half of the nineteenth century. Of more recent origin than the Masons and much more heavily oriented toward mutual assistance, the Odd Fellows had attracted large numbers of adherents in England by the end of the first third of the nineteenth century and soon gained a foothold in the United States. In 1842 two black literary societies—the Philomathean Society of New York and the Philadelphia Library Company of Colored Persons—sought admission to the order but were refused by local authorities for reasons of race. Peter Ogden, a free man of color who had been admitted to an Odd Fellows lodge in Liverpool, then obtained a charter from the Grand United Order of Odd Fellows of England, under which the Philomathean Lodge of New York was established in the spring of 1843. By the end of 1844 this initial black Odd Fellows body had been joined by a second in New York and one each in Philadelphia and Albany.[36]

The order sustained a rapid growth in the years immediately following its establishment in the United States. Lodges were formed in Boston and Washington in 1846 and in Baltimore in 1848, and in a number of smaller cities as well before the end of the decade. By 1850 there were no fewer than nineteen active lodges (including those in the British West Indies), probably two-thirds of which were located in the nation's largest cities. There were apparently no lodges west of Pennsylvania before 1850. Like the Masons, the Odd Fellows labored to ensure that their membership would include only persons of undoubted probity, and in pursuance of this goal the order in 1846 prohibited the admission of any person "known to be (directly or indirectly) a gambler in lotteries or policy playing."[37]

It appears that the Odd Fellows were less elitist than the Masons in recruiting members—an early historian of the order emphasized its difference from freemasonry by noting that the Odd Fellows accepted "men of every rank and station." Nevertheless, important black leaders were to be found among its adherents, including George T. Downing, Patrick H. Reason, and James McCune Smith in New York and James McCrummill in Philadelphia.[38]

Both the Masons and the Odd Fellow—particularly the latter—were actively employed in mutual aid activities—especially in burying deceased members and in assisting their widows and orphans. Because the Masonic membership tended to be drawn from the more affluent element in the black communities this function was, both theoretically and practically, of less importance to members of that order. Both orders restricted their membership to men of good moral character, thus serving as "reform" or "uplift" bodies, and membership in each, in some measure, probably both recognized and encouraged intellectual development as well—certainly the Masonic lodges seem to have included a number of persons prominently identified with the educational advancement of the Negroes. Though much less numerous than beneficial or literary organizations—their secrecy made them particularly suspect in the southern cities—fraternal associations appear to have grown rapidly in the 1840s. It is likely that 25–30 black Masonic lodges and perhaps a third as many associations of Odd Fellows were established in the nation's major cities before the early

1850s. All of the Odd Fellows lodges and possibly as many as one-half of the Masonic bodies were founded after 1840.

The fraternal societies, many of the literary associations, and some of the beneficial and benevolent organizations obviously served a social function as well. The regular meetings—sometimes weekly, but usually less frequent—provided opportunities for informal conversation and discussion as well as dispatch of business and presentation of the official program. The ritual of the fraternal assocaitions was as attractive to blacks as to whites and was sometimes copied by other societies, which devised uniforms and symbols and elaborated procedures. Some organizations held banquets or special meetings which were more purely social in nature on such occasions as the anniversary of the founding of the society. And a few associations, such as the St. Cecilia Society and the Société des Amis Réunis of New York, appear to have existed solely for social purposes.[39]

All societies, for whatever purpose they were formed, created subcommunities within the larger community and doubtless gave their members a deeper sense of belonging—a more personal sense of identification. This is a function integrally related to all associative activities of all people in all eras. But because blacks comprised a subcommunity of people rejected, suppressed, restricted, and constrained by the larger society, these associations appear also to have played an opposite role within that racial subcommunity—that of fostering a sense of community among all blacks. When black Freemasons participated in the ceremonial laying of cornerstones for black churches or meeting halls; when members of Negro fraternal and other societies marched through the streets in full regalia on a festive occasion; when free men of color in solemn array and precise order followed the corpse of a departed brother; when black men and women of obvious intellectual attainments read poetry, or delivered declamations, or debated fine points of law, philosophy, or aesthetics, it would appear that black auditors and observers who were not members of these societies nevertheless took pride in these activities and were gratified to be a part of a black community that could produce such people and support such organizations.[40]

It is notable that organizations clearly devoted to fostering the largest sense of community among blacks continually and strongly recommended the formation of smaller societies. In the early 1830s a series of national conventions of free blacks took place in Philadelphia and New York. These meetings and the establishment of the national organization were sparked by the 1829 attempt to force Negroes to leave Cincinnati, and in the 1830s drew delegates—almost entirely from urban areas—from the states along the eastern seaboard from Massachusetts to Maryland and the District of Columbia.[41] Resolutions were passed urging the creation of independent conventional societies, moral reform organizations, and literary associations. The conventional societies were envisaged as constituent members of the American Society, and a few were apparently formed, though they seem not to have survived very long. The convention of 1834 recommended the formation of local moral reform associations, and that of 1835 created an American Moral Reform Society, which held annual meetings well into the 1840s. Local bodies were certainly established in Philadelphia and Pittsburgh, but apparently not farther to the north. Both the conventional societies and the moral reform associations were perceived as instruments for building community identification among blacks and for mounting a broad-gauge attack on social, economic, political, and legal problems that plagued the Negro communities. At an earlier date New York's Phoenix Society had operated in a somewhat similar fashion, and that circumstance was doubtless influential in causing the national convention of 1833 to advocate the formation of Phoenix societies in other cities.[42]

Occasionally other local organizations were founded specifically for purposes of general community development. Among these were the New York Association for the Political Elevation and Improvement of People of Color in 1838 and Washington's Civil and Statistical Association (1850), which was devoted to the "educational, moral, and financial advancement" of the black population of the nation's capital.[43]

Thus, a handful of black urban associations were specifically designed to have community-wide impact. Additionally, the connection of the moral reform associations and the conventional societies with national bodies extended their function of developing community self-awareness beyond the boundaries of a single city, and the same could be said of the fraternal orders and the black religious denominations.

But almost every black society played at least five overlapping roles. First, the association enabled its members to do in concert—well or badly—those things which they could not accomplish satisfactorily as individuals: to protect themselves and their families from the worst effects of illness, unemployment, and death; to develop their intellectual or literary abilities; to satisfy their desire for ceremony, ritual, and color to enliven an otherwise drab existence. Second, and coincidentally, participation in the day-to-day operations of the societies gave their members a measure of experience in institutional management and made them more familiar with, and, hence, more comfortable in dealing with, institutions—their own and those of the white society. Third, these organizations provided opportunities for social intercourse that were particularly important to a people whose participation in the larger society was narrowly circumscribed and whose access to public entertainments was severely limited by their own poverty, the prejudices of white society, and, occasionally, by law. Fourth, affiliation with one or the other of these societies gave the individual a recognized place in a smaller and more personal sub-community and in some measure counteracted the anomie and disorientation fostered by the fluidity, rootlessness, and apparent ephemerality of urban life. It created a sense of belonging, heightened self-awareness, and seemed to reduce at least some portion of urban existence to potentially manageable dimensions. And, finally, the knowledge of the existence of black organizations and their public activities fostered, however modestly, the sense of community among all Negroes in the metropolis. This is not to say that competition for membership, support, and preeminence was unknown (or even uncommon) among black societies or that there did not exist strongly held differences of opinion. But even the presentation of the claims of rival organizations or the public airing of divergent views increased the consciousness of a black community to which the appeals were made and about the elevation of which the opponents contended. On the national level a well-known example of such a clash was the split between the Philadelphia and New York (or "reformer" and "practical") interests that brought about the collapse of the Negro Convention Movement in the mid-1830s. But (aside from personal ambitions) the reason for the division was strong disagreement about what course of action would most benefit American Negroes, and it is difficult to believe that black community consciousness was not increased, rather than diminished, by the controversy.[44]

Although the extent of urban black associative activity would appear to have been, at least in part, a function of the size of the Negro community, it is nevertheless notable (insofar as the uneven and sketchy data will permit generalization) that black societies were much less common in the Lower South and perhaps in some Upper South cities as well. This was, of course, largely the result of white fear and distrust of black assemblies in a slave society and consequent legislation prohibiting such gatherings. But additional considerations may well have been the superior economic position of free persons of color in the southern cities (which reduced the need for beneficial societies) and the relatively small number of black in-migrants, who might be expected to be most affected by a sense of rootlessness.

Forced out of the "whole society" by prejudice and discrimination, urban blacks early found that they could wholly rely only on themselves and could wholly trust only themselves. Theirs was, initially, a society of exclusion. But the process of forced separation did not automatically unite the excluded population. As they sought the solace of religion, a measure of protection from want, moral betterment, intellectual growth, social intercourse, and individual realization, they created structures around which coalesced meaningful subsocieties and from which radiated filaments of social consciousness which eventually formed themselves into a tenuous, fragile web of community. And if, in large part, this community had grown without conscious direction—like a plant blindly adapting to the harshest of environments, driven solely by an instinct to survive—the final product was, nevertheless, a sentient organism. In the rotting fruit of discriminatory separation were found the fertile seeds of community.

13 Am I Not a Man? Black Participation and Protest

However much they were repressed, segregated, and restricted, urban blacks were, nevertheless, undeniably *there*—they existed as a part of an urban population, as components of an urban organism, and as occupants of urban space at a particular point in time. They could not, thus, be wholly excluded (nor could they, even had they wished to do so, wholly exclude themselves) from participation on the stage of urban life. Many types of participation were almost automatic and only minimally volitional since they were related to survival in the urban environment. Blacks worked for such wages as they could obtain and so participated in the production of goods, the delivery of services, and the establishment of price levels. They rented dwellings, bought property, and paid taxes, enriching those who despised them and supporting governments that suppressed them. They moved about the city as unobtrusively as possible, from home to work to market to shop, purchasing the necessities of survival and such small luxuries as they could afford, adding their mites to the commercial activity of the city. They were married, gave birth, and reared their children, sickened, recovered, lived, and died, adding to and subtracting from the sum of human life in the city with statistical anonymity. Year by year their activities of a more communal and volitional nature took place in ever more complete isolation from the larger community as they attended black schools, organized black associations, and worshiped in black churches.

Certain small segments of black actions and activities, however, were public in nature—a part of or addressed to the whole, white-dominated society. Some of these actions constituted participation in activities that were routinely considered to be almost entirely white concerns; others took the form of public protests against an activity, a condition, or an institution of the white society considered detrimental to black interests.

Perhaps no sphere of activity was more universally thought of as a white preserve than that of politics. But although there appear to have been no black candidates for public office in the major antebellum American cities, blacks either had or were believed to have the right to vote in two-thirds of these fifteen cities at one time or another

216

during the first half of the nineteenth century. In only one, how-ever—Boston—did blacks have access to the polls (legally, if not actu-ally) on the same terms as whites throughout the half-century.

Suffrage was, of course, controlled (with rare exceptions) by con-stitutional or legal provisions applying equally to entire state popula-tions. The state of Massachusetts never restricted suffrage by race, and, consequently, Boston's free black males who were otherwise qualified were legally entitled to vote. Moreover, they appear to have exercised this right from an early date. In the fall of 1800 a Boston newspaper, analyzing the recent election in an effort to account for the increase in the Federalist vote, identified a bloc of "forty men of color in Boston" (presumably all those who voted) as a contributing factor. And in 1813 the Republicans accused the Federalist Washington Be-nevolent Society of bribing an influential black leader named Prince (who was a Republican) to persuade Negro voters to support the Federalist candidates. The black vote could hardly have been viewed as crucial, however, for except in 1800 and 1801 (when Elbridge Gerry was able to secure the support of a small majority of the Boston voters) the Boston electorate returned substantial Federalist majorities throughout the late eighteenth and early nineteenth cen-turies.[1]

With the substitution of a taxpaying for a property qualification in 1821 and the introduction of printed ballots in 1830 black participa-tion appears to have increased. The number of ballots cast by blacks rose to 117 in 1830, to 249 in 1838, and to 357 in 1845. It is likely that most Boston Negro voters were Whigs, and given the Whig dominance throughout this period the black vote was clearly not cru-cial. The level of black voting was relatively high, however, for the 1838 black votes constituted just over three percent of all ballots cast at a time when blacks made up about $2\frac{1}{3}$ percent of the city's popula-tion. And in 1845 blacks, who then constituted about $1\frac{2}{5}$ percent of Boston's population, cast $3\frac{1}{2}$ percent of the votes.[2] These figures are even more remarkable in light of the fact that almost fifty-five percent of Boston's adult blacks were females and, hence, wholly excluded from political activity.[3]

The black voters in New York are supposed to have played a more crucial role. Here, as elsewhere, the blacks were almost universally Federalists (and later Whigs), and until 1821 their access to the ballot box was regulated by the same laws that governed white voting. The impact of the Negro vote in New York City was potentially increased by its geographic concentration, and was believed to have been de-terminative in the 1813 Federalist victory in the state. "The votes of three hundred Negroes in the city of New York," one observer later asserted, "decided the election in favor of the Federal party, and also decided the political character of the legislature of this state."[4] The black vote is also supposed to have provided the margin of Whig victory in the fifth and eighth wards in the 1830s. Such claims are, however, poorly documented and of doubtful validity. The reference to 300 black Federalist voters in 1813 is from a speech by a Republican delegate to the 1821 state constitutional convention, in which the speaker was advocating placing restraints on Negro voting—hardly an impeccable source. Other delegates to this convention placed the black vote in the nation's largest city at 100 in 1819 and 123 two years later. It would seem that only gross fraud could have produced 300 black votes in New York City during the second decade of the nineteenth century, given the electoral qualifications then in existence. After 1821 free blacks in the state could vote only if (in addition to other qualifications) they owned property valued at $250—a requirement not applicable to whites. The state census of 1825 showed only 16 qualified black voters in Manhattan, and it appears unlikely that the number much exceeded (if it ever reached) 100 during the remaining years of the half-century. The fifth ward usually produced Whig majorities of 100–250 in the 1830s, and although the eighth ward was more narrowly divided, only in 1838 did the Whig margin drop below fifty votes. The 1835 state census, however, reported only 68 qualified black voters in the entire city and only 3 each in the fifth and eighth wards. Black leaders repeatedly insisted that much larger numbers of the city's free men of color could have satisfied the property qualification (the numbers mentioned ranged perhaps 200–1,000) but did not choose to establish their eligibility. There were, however, only 152 black taxpayers in the city in 1835.[5]

For whatever reason, it would appear that black voter participation was much lower in New York than in Boston, and that, clearly, was what the city's whites wanted. Metropolitan voters consistently supported the racially restrictive property requirement much more heavily than those in the rest of the state. An 1846 proposal to remove the discriminatory clause from the constitution was approved by fewer than fifteen percent of the city electorate though almost twice as large a percentage of the voters in the rest of the state were favorably disposed. By 1860 the disparity was even greater, and a similar proposal was supported by fewer than a seventh of the voters in Manhattan as compared with two-fifths of those in the rest of the state.[6]

In the other major cities in New York black political participation was even lower. In 1835 there were only thirty qualified black voters in Brooklyn, seven in Albany, and four in Buffalo, and ten years later the figures were fifty-three, twenty, and twenty-one, respectively.[7]

Like the free Negroes in New York and Massachusetts, those of Rhode Island had been entitled to vote under the original constitution of the state; the Rhode Island blacks, however, were subsequently excluded. By the colonial charter that served Rhode Island as its first state constitution, "freemen" were entitled to vote, and it is probable—James T. Adams says certain—that there were some Negro "freemen" in the state. But it is unlikely that any significant number of blacks either qualified as electors or exercised the franchise while that charter was in effect. An 1822 statute provided that only whites could thereafter be admitted as "freemen," but left unresolved the status of any blacks who might have been admitted earlier. But the 1836 suffrage law was unmistakably clear—voting was restricted to white males.[8] When, in 1842, as a byproduct of the bitter conflict over expanded suffrage and legislative reapportionment known as the "Dorr War," Rhode Island blacks regained access to the ballot box at the same time that suffrage qualifications were drastically reduced, the Providence Negroes quickly took an active role in the political process. The blacks were prepared to plunge immediately into the political melee at least in part because they had been well organized and actively engaged in 1841 in the fight for equal suffrage. As dependable supporters of the Law and Order party, which had been responsible for the elimination of the racial restrictions on voting, the black voters of Providence were much sought after, because there was some measure of uncertainty regarding the outcome of the political flux in the city and the state. So strong was the loyalty of Providence blacks to their party (and, after 1847, to the Whig party, to which most Law and Order partisans gravitated) that neither the presence of a slaveholder at the head of the national ticket nor the obvious attraction of a Free Soil candidate could force or lure them from their allegiance. They numbered perhaps as many as 150, and the Law and Order (and later Whig) leaders considered them important enough to their success to devote money, time, and energy to their cultivation and to enlist the assistance of respected black spokesmen. Among these were William J. Brown, a successful shoemaker who was active in black social organizations; James Hazard, a clothing store proprietor and one of Providence's wealthiest blacks; and Episcopal minister Alexander Crummell, who had been prominent in the struggle for equal suffrage.[9]

The eighteenth-century constitutions of Pennsylvania did not restrict voting to whites, though the state courts held in 1836 (*Fogg* v. *Hobbs*) that Negroes were not "freemen" within the meaning of the constitution and were, consequently, not qualified to vote. It would appear that some blacks had voted in the intervening decades, but not, it was asserted, in the urban centers. Even so respected an individual as James Forten apparently believed that Negroes had more to lose than to gain from direct participation in elections, for although he marched his fifteen white employees to the polls in September 1822 to vote for the Federalist candidate for the U.S. House of Representatives, Samuel Breck, he did not bring his black employees, nor did he, himself, offer to vote. Nevertheless, Cyrus Bustil, a member of a prominent Philadelphia free black family, clearly took an active role in a meeting of the Democratic Society of that city in summer 1800, for he was singled out for personal abuse by the Federalist *Gazette of the United States*. Though the court's decision in *Fogg* v. *Hobbs* was severely criticized, it harmonized with majority sentiment in the state, and the constitution of 1838 specifically restricted the suffrage to whites.[10]

In the adjoining state of Maryland, however, the right of free men of color to vote was not in question. True, the state constitution of 1776 had, in a manner similar to that of Pennsylvania, extended the suffrage to all "freemen" who satisfied property and residence qualifications, but Marylanders, unlike their northern neighbors, seem clearly to have understood "freemen" to have included blacks. Not only did blacks exercise the franchise (though doubtless in very small numbers) in the late eighteenth and early nineteenth centuries, but many whites apparently viewed the practice as a natural concomitant of the democratic process. In 1794 a joint communication was issued by several committees appointed by the inhabitants of various districts adjoining the town of Baltimore and "by the mechanical, Republican, and carpenters' societies of Baltimore Town" to examine and report on the proposed charter under which the city of Baltimore would be established. The committees declared the document to be "defective and dangerous" in the following respect: "In making the body corporate to consist *only* of the free white inhabitants of said town, whereby free negroes and the people of color are excluded from any direct share in the making and administration of those laws by which themselves are to be governed, contrary to reason and good policy, to the spirit of equal liberty and our free constitution." The proposed legislation was not passed—doubtless in part because of this and twenty-three other criticisms by the committees—and the 1796 charter incorporating the city provided that electors should "have the same qualifications as voters for delegates to the General Assembly."[11]

Nevertheless, with the growth of the free Negro population in the state from an insignificant figure in 1776 to over 8,000 in 1790 and more than 19,500 in 1800, Marylanders became increasingly uncomfortable with the future implications of equal suffrage. The first retrograde movement came in the form of a legislative statute of 1783 that denied suffrage to slaves freed after that date and to their descendents. Though this act guaranteed that the number of black voters in the state would remain forever inconsequential, it did not blunt the thrust for more radical action. In 1809 legislation was passed that restricted voting to whites, and this restriction was incorporated into the constitution by amendment in 1810. So quietly and quickly did the legislature act that black voters received the first intimation of their disfranchisement when their ballots were rejected by election officials.[12]

Technically, free blacks were entitled to vote in Lousville between 1792 and 1799, but since the census marshals found only a single free Negro in 1800 the entitlement was clearly irrelevant, even if it could have been exercised. Ohio, Missouri, South Carolina, Louisiana, and the city of Washington consistently barred voting by blacks, though it was alleged that desperate politicians voted free Negroes in close races in Louisiana (though apparently not in New Orleans) in the second quarter of the nineteenth century.[13] In any event, it was only in Boston and Providence that there was significant political participation by free blacks, and only in the latter city was the black vote sufficiently important to achieve recognition by white leaders.

However few individuals may have been directly affected and however slight their collective political impact, the black communities of Providence, New York, and Philadelphia did not accept the elimination or restriction of Negro suffrage with placid resignation. They accurately perceived that the absence or diminution of black political influence was less important than the creation of yet another official caste mark denoting Negro inferiority. The strongest and most immediate protest came from Philadelphia, where, in the spring of 1838, a number of free men of color met in Stephen Gloucester's Presbyterian church to organize a response to the constitutional proscription of the previous year. This gathering included such respected black leaders as Gloucester, Bishop Charles Brown, Robert Douglass, James J. G. Bias, and four members of the renowned Forten clan—James, Sr., James, Jr., Robert, and Robert Purvis, who had married a daughter of the elder Forten. The body directed the preparation of a public statement, which was issued later in the same year as the *Appeal of Forty Thousand Citizens, Threatened with Disfranchisement, to the People of Pennsylvania*. Purvis, who was largely responsible for the document, produced no humble plea for the granting of a boon to a subject population. His was an angry demand for justice and a stinging condemnation of the arrant racism that underlay the exclusion of blacks from the electoral process. After destroying the legal sophistry on which *Fogg* v. *Hobbs* rested and defending the worth and reputation of the black population he scathingly noted: "We ask a voice in the disposition of those public resources which we ourselves have helped to earn; we claim a right to be heard, according to our numbers, in regard to all those great public measures which involve out lives and fortunes, as well as those of our fellow citizens; we assert our right to

vote at the polls as a shield against that strange species of benevolence
which seeks legislative aid to banish us—and we are told that our
white fellow citizens cannot submit to an *intermixture of the races!*"
Purvis went on:

> Are we to be disfranchised lest the purity of the *white* blood should
> be sullied by an intermixture with ours? It seems to us that our
> white brethren might well enough reserve their fear, till we seek
> such alliance with them. We ask no social favors. We would not
> willingly darken the doors of those to whom the complexion and
> features which our Maker has given us, are disagreeable. The ter-
> ritories of the commonwealth are sufficiently ample to afford us a
> home without doing violence to the delicate nerves of our white
> brethren, for centuries to come. Besides, we are not intruders here,
> nor were our ancestors. Surely you ought to bear as unrepiningly
> the evil consequences of your fathers' guilt, as we those of our
> fathers' misfortune.... Give us that fair and honorable ground
> which self-respect requires to stand on, and the dreaded amalgama-
> tion, if it take place at all, shall be by your own fault, as indeed, it has
> always been.

Nor did the Philadelphia blacks ask any political favors, according to
Purvis. "We would have the right of suffrage," he asserted, "only as
the reward of industry and worth. We care not how high the qualification be placed. All we ask is, that no man shall be excluded on account
of his *color,* that the same rule shall be applied to all."[14]

If New York's black community could boast no precise counterpart
to Purvis's slashing attack on bigotry and political exclusion, continuing black protests nevertheless emanated from the nation's largest city
regarding the dual suffrage criteria established in 1821. Associated
with the addresses and petitions were such men as Thomas Jennings,
Henry Sipkins, Charles L. Reason, Philip A. Bell, and Charles B. Ray.
It is obvious that they spoke for a large number of the city's black
residents—in 1837 a petition for equal suffrage was signed by 620
Negro men (apparently it was not thought proper that women should
petition for a constitutional change that would not affect them). In the
1830s and '40s various black associations were active in this fight, with
the Political Improvement Association of New York and the Political
Association of New York (both of which were founded in 1838 and
later merged) committing themselves almost solely to the elimination
of discriminatory suffrage and the encouragement of black political
participation. Even earlier in the field was the Phoenix Society which,
though active in other areas as well, was later accurately characterized
as "completely devoted to the task of equalizing the Negroes' political
and civil rights with those of whites." But their efforts, like those of

their counterparts in Philadelphia, were unavailing, for in 1846 (and again in 1860) the electorate overwhelmingly rejected equal suffrage amendments to the state's constitution. In 1846 only 27.59 percent of the voters supported the amendment, and of the counties containing the state's four largest cities only Erie (Buffalo) recorded a larger proportion of favorable votes (28.25%).[15]

Only in Rhode Island were efforts to restore equal suffrage successful. There the Providence blacks ventured to hope that they might force restoration by appealing to the honored axiom of "no taxation without representation," for their property was taxed by the city. In pursuit of this goal a meeting was convened in 1840 which, after hearing the remarks of a number of interested parties, including Edward Barnes, Providence's largest black property holder, appointed a committee to present their case to the legislature. That body acknowledged the legitimacy of the complaint but was adamantly opposed to restoring voting rights to Negroes. One choleric Newport representative stated the case plainly, if inelegantly, when he demanded, "Shall a Nigger be allowed to go to the polls and tie my vote? No, Mr. Speaker, it can't be. The taxes don't amount to more than forty or fifty dollars; let them be taken off." Consequently, by an act of 1841 the legislature provided that black-owned property "shall not be liable to any town or state taxes in any manner whatsoever."[16]

Within less than two years, however, Providence blacks would be constitutionally recognized as voters. Though Rhode Island Negroes—and particularly those of Providence—were active in pressing their case, the turnabout was actually the by-product of an abrasive controversy over suffrage and representation among the state's whites. Since the 1830s a number of Rhode Island leaders had struggled to expand the suffrage (which was anachronistically restricted) and reapportion legislative seats. Balked by the intransigence of the legislature, the Suffragist party in 1841 issued a call for the election of delegates to a constitutional convention. Rejecting the existing suffrage requirements, the organizing committee directed the acceptance of the ballots of "all male American citizens, (natives and foreigners, and without distinction of color)." But it quickly became apparent that many Suffragists were unprepared to follow their doctrine to the point of black reenfranchisement. In Providence (a hotbed of Suffragist activity) the fifth ward clerk resigned rather than accept the ballot of a black, though he had found no difficulty in receiving the votes of whites who did not meet existing suffrage qualifications. A committee of Providence blacks, led by Episcopal minister Alexander Crummell, urged the members of the Suffragist convention to adhere to their creed and provide for equal suffrage and warned: "It is the warrant of history . . . that thus striking off from us the . . . precious birthright of free men, ... the poisoned chalice may be returned to the lips of those who departed from their principles." The appeal was to no avail, and the Suffragist constitution—like that of the competing Landowner (later Law and Order) party—restricted voting to whites, though it provided for a later referendum on black suffrage. In the "Dorr War" which followed, the Providence blacks (apparently wholly disillusioned with the Suffragists) generally supported the Landowner faction and assisted in patrolling the streets of the town when the white troops left to attack the Suffragist stronghold at Chepachet. Late in 1842, after the "rebellion" had collapsed, a third constitution was submitted to the electorate by the Law and Order convention. It differed from that submitted a few months earlier in only a few details, but one of those details was all important to the black community—the word "white" did not appear in the section enumerating the qualifications for voters. Still fearful of public reaction, the convention provided for a separate vote on black suffrage. By a three-to-one margin the electorate approved equal suffrage, and Rhode Island became the only state during the first six decades of the nineteenth century to extend voting rights to previously disfranchised blacks.[17]

No aspect of Negro existence in the United States—neither disfranchisement, nor deprivation, nor discrimination—provoked more deep and continuing concern and commitment from urban free blacks than slavery. The free people of color in northern (and some southern) cities stood ready at almost all times to condemn the institution that still held in bondage millions of their fellow blacks. Although blacks had not been welcome in the early abolitionist societies—Robert Purvis was the only nonwhite admitted to the Pennsylvania Society for Promoting the Abolition of Slavery between 1775 and 1856—they took an active role in the antislavery organizations that emerged after 1830. Six Negroes, including Robert Purvis and James McCrummill of Philadelphia, James G. Barbados of Boston, John B. Vashon of Pittsburgh, and Peter Williams of New York, were on the original board of managers of the American Anti-Slavery Society in 1833. These men were also active in local organizations, as were Samuel Snowden of Boston, David Ruggles, Samuel E. Cornish, Theodore S. Wright, Christopher Rush, Thomas Van Rensselaer, J. W. C. Pennington, and James McCune Smith, all of New York, and James Forten, John C. Bowers, and Charles W. Gardner of Philadelphia. Black women, too, were prominent in the antislavery movement. Sarah M. Douglass and the three Forten sisters—Harriet Forten Purvis, Sarah Forten, and Margaretta Forten—were among those organizing the Female Anti-Slavery Society of Philadelphia in 1833, and Susan Paul was one of five counsellors of the Boston Female Anti-Slavery Society, established in the same year. In addition, Susan Paul,

Sarah Forten, Sarah M. Douglass, and Grace Douglass (Sarah's mother) played active roles in the three Anti-Slavery Conventions of American Women, held in 1837, 1838, and 1839. Yet even at abolitionist meetings blacks sometimes encountered prejudice and discrimination. A few days after Charlotte Colemen had, in February 1841, taken a seat in the white section of the hall in which the Boston Female Anti-Slavery Society met, she received a remonstrance from one of the white members—Mrs. Elisha Blanchard—who insisted that "traditions must not be violated." Nevertheless, "colored people" were, Mrs. Blanchard assured Mrs. Coleman, "very well in their place."[18]

Urban blacks also maintained separate antislavery organizations. Boston Negroes had established the General Colored Association of Massachusetts in 1826 and later added a number of others, including the African Abolition Free-Hold Society and the African Female Anti-Slavery Society. In the 1830s New York blacks founded the Roger Williams Anti-Slavery Society and the Female Wesleyan Anti-Slavery Society, and the same decade saw the establishment of Philadelphia's Leavitt Anti-Slavery Society, a black antislavery society in Providence, and Negro juvenile antislavery societies in Pittsburgh, Providence, and elsewhere. The next decade recorded the foundation of the Young Men's Anti-Slavery and Literary Society in Pittsburgh, and New Orleans blacks organized the Dieu Nous Protège, which, though not espousing abolition (for obvious reasons), existed for the purpose of assisting individual slaves to obtain their freedom.[19]

Additionally, numerous vigorous condemnations of slavery emanated from urban black meetings and from individual Negro residents of the nation's major cities, growing ever harsher throughout the half-century. In 1808 the Reverend Peter Williams, Jr., delivered an oration in New York's Zion Church celebrating the statutory prohibition of the foreign slave trade (and, inferentially, praising the spread of emancipation in the North and condemning the continued existence of slavery in the South). "Oh God!" he proclaimed, "we thank thee, that thou didst condescend to listen to the cries of Africa's wretched sons; and that thou didst interfere in their behalf . . . ; and when the bleeding African, lifting his fetters, exclaimed, 'am I not a man and a brother,' then with redoubled efforts, the angel of humanity strove to restore to the African race, the inherent rights of man."[20] A member of Boston's African Society, in an essay published by that body in the same year, spoke more directly to the issue. "Slavery," he asserted,

hath ever had a tendency to spread ignorance and darkness, poverty and distress in the world. Although it hath advanced a few, yet many have been the sufferers; it was first invented by men of the most malicious dispositions, and has been carried on by men of similar character. . . .

Freedom is desirable; if not would men sacrifice their time, their property, and finally lose their lives in the pursuit of it? If it was not a thing that was truly valuable, should we see whole nations engaged in hostility, to procure it for their country, wives and children? Yea, I say there is something so dreadful in slavery that some had rather die than experience it.[21]

And more than a quarter of a century later—a quarter-century that had seen a doubling of the slave population—James Forten spoke with equal force and greater urgency in addressing the newly founded Ladies Anti-Slavery Society in Philadelphia. Defending the commitment to immediate emancipation; castigating the racism inherent in northern opposition to abolitionism; and condemning the "dangerous doctrine of gradualism," he asked, "Who can look upon slavery and not shudder at its inhuman barbarities?" "It is," he asserted scathingly, "a withering blight to the country in which it exists—a deadly poison to the soil on which it is suffered to breath—and to satiate the cravings of its appetite, it feeds, like a vulture, upon the vitals of its victims."[22]

During the same period, black-authored antislavery pamphlets emanating from the cities became increasingly militant in tone. To such stinging denunciations of slavery as those embodied in the Boston African Society's 1808 essay and Daniel Coker's 1810 *Dialogue between a Virginian and an African Minister* were added dire warnings (and implicit threats) to slaveholders. In 1829 New York's Robert Alexander Young published a pamphlet predicting not only the destruction of the institution, but of slaveowners as well, if they refused to accept the inevitability of universal freedom, and in the same year David Walker, a black Boston used clothing dealer, published his designedly inflammatory *Appeal . . . to the Colored Citizens of the World*. Arguing from religious principles, political theory, philosophy, and history—illuminated by the white heat of passionate indignation and resentment—Walker sounded what was doubtless the most militant note yet heard from a black in the swelling chorus of protest against human slavery. He castigated his fellow Negroes for their meekness and patient endurance—"a grovelling servile and abject submission," Walker called it—under the oppressions of slavery and discrimination, and urged them to take such physical action as might be necessary to secure their freedom.[23] "Never make an attempt" to secure freedom "until you see your way clear," he counseled, but

If you commence, make sure work—do not trifle, for they will not trifle with you—they want us for their slaves, and think nothing of

murdering us in order to subject us to that wretched condition—
therefore, if there is an *attempt* made by us, kill or be killed. Now, I
ask you, had not you rather be killed than to be a slave to a tyrant,
who takes the life of your mother, wife and dear little children?
Look upon your mother, wife and children, and answer God
Almighty! and believe this, that it is no more harm for you to kill a
man, who is trying to kill you, than it is for you to take a drink of
water when thirsty; in fact, the man who will stand still and let
another murder him, is worse than an infidel, and, if he has common
sense, ought not to be pitied.[24]

"Are we MEN!!" Walker cried, "I ask you, O my brethren! are we
MEN? Did our Creator make us to be slaves to dust and ashes like
ourselves?"[25]

The publication of Walker's book, coming at a time when rumors of
slave uprisings were widespread, and shortly followed by the Nat
Turner affair, sent a tidal wave of terror and rage surging across the
South. Well before the Northampton outbreak, southern legislatures
had responded with statutes prohibiting teaching slaves to read and
write, quarantining ships with black crew members, further restricting
the activities of free people of color, and punishing the circulation of
"seditious" publications intended to incite slave revolt with great se-
verity, including the death penalty. Some of the more extreme demands of agitated southerners included—with scant concern for legal
forms, constitutional provisions, or states' rights dogma—the extradi-
tion of Walker and the printer to a southern state for trial and the
passage of federal legislation prohibiting the publication of such
tracts.[26] Boston Mayor Harrison Gray Otis responded to this furor,
and to a direct communication from the mayor of Savannah, by assur-
ing southerners that Boston officials "regard it [the *Appeal*] with deep
disapprobation and abhorrence"; that Boston's citizenry "hold in
. . . absolute detestation, the sentiments of the writer"; and that he
believed "that the book is disapproved of by the decent portion even
of the free colored population of this place." Otis's examination of
Walker's *Appeal* convinced him that "notwithstanding the extremely
bad and inflammatory tendency of the publication, he does not seem
to have violated any . . . laws." "You may rest assured, sir," he wrote to
the mayor of Savannah, "that a disposition would not be wanting on
the part of the city authorities here, to avail themselves of any lawful
means, for preventing this attempt to throw fire-brands into your
country." Otis added that Boston officials would "publish a general
caution to captains and others, against exposing themselves to the
consequences of transporting incendiary writings into your and the
other southern states."[27]

Fourteen years later a graduate of New York's African Free School, Henry Highland Garnet (then a Presbyterian minister in Troy) presented an equally militant "Address to the Slaves of the United States" to the 1843 National Convention of Colored Citizens in Buffalo and proposed its adoption by the convention. Arguing that submission to slavery was sinful and resistance a moral obligation, he eulogized Denmark Vesey, Nat Turner, Joseph Cinque of the *Armistad,* and Madison Washington of the *Creole.* "Brethren," he declared, "the time has come when you must act for yourselves. It is an old and true saying that 'if hereditary bondmen would be free, they must themselves strike the blow.' " "However much you and all of us may desire it," he added, "there is not much hope of redemption without the shedding of blood." Garnet concluded his "Address to the Slaves" with a fervid summons to action:

> Let your motto be resistance! *resistance!* RESISTANCE! No oppressed people ever secured their liberty without resistance. What kind of resistance you had better make, you must decide by the circumstances that surround you, and according to the suggestion of expediency. Brethren, adieu! Trust in the living God. Labor for the peace of the human race, and remember that you are FOUR MILLIONS.[28]

After extensive debate dominated by the opponents of the meaure, in which A. M. Sumner of Cincinnati asserted "that the adoption of that address by the Convention would be fatal to the safety of the free people of color of the slave States, but especially so to those who lived on the borders of the free States," the 1843 convention declined to adopt the "Address" by a vote of eighteen to nineteen, and, when reconsidered, defeated it by a larger margin. Consequently, there was little reaction to Garnet's call for resistance; it was not published until five years later and even then its circulation appears to have been small and confined largely to the northern states. (Walker, on the other hand, had made strenuous efforts to distribute his *Appeal* in the slave area.)[29]

It should be noted that delegates from the larger cities objected strongly to Garnet's radical statement. Frederick Douglass from Boston, Charles B. Ray from New York, and A. M. Sumner from Cincinnati were the most vocal opponents of the measure, and of the fourteen delegates from Albany, Boston, Buffalo, Cincinnati, and New York only the two from Albany (J. H. Townsend and William P. McIntire) consistently supported the adoption of the "Address."[30] This opposition doubtless sprang from a lively appreciation of the adverse effect that the promulgation of such an inflammatory statement would have on the position of the free blacks in the South and the blood bath that would ensue if the slaves should, in fact, resort to physical force. Certainly it cannot be taken as an indication that urban blacks were lukewarm in their opposition to the institution of slavery or insensitive to the sufferings of their enslaved brothers and sisters, for, as has been noted, they—especially Ray and Douglass—were active in the abolitionist cause.

Since fugitive slaves often sought concealment in the cities, urban free blacks were frequently energetically engaged in hiding, protecting, purchasing, and, sometimes, forcibly liberating runaways. The panic-stricken flight to Canada by dozens of black urbanites when President Fillmore signed the new Fugitive Slave Act in 1850 gives some indication of the numbers of escaped slaves that the northern cities harbored. Forty members of a single black church in Boston departed for the British dominions, as did an estimated 150–200 Negroes from the vicinity of Pittsburgh. In Buffalo some 130 members of a black Baptist church left, and it was thought that a similar migration took place among Methodists. Not all of those who fled were runaways, of course. Many were doubtless family members, friends, or free persons of color who feared that the provisions of the act would be used to cloak extensive kidnaping of free blacks. But a sizable number were probably absconding slaves.[31]

Although free black resistance to the seizure of alleged fugitives was more visible and perhaps more extensive in the 1850s, several urban Negro communities had earlier developed formal or informal structures to protect free persons of color and to assist runaways. In Baltimore, where a rapidly growing free black community offered the priceless boon of anonymity to fleeing bondsmen—and where, consequently, rural slaveowners or their agents looked first for their lost property—the potential for false identification and fraudulent seizure was doubtless great. The trepidation engendered by this peril moved blacks to establish in 1819 a relief society to aid persons threatened with enslavement by such practices, and eight years later to found the Baltimore Society for the Protection of Free People of Color. The vigilance committees, established in New York in November 1835, in Philadelphia in August 1837, and in Boston in September 1846, were much more openly designed than were the Baltimore societies to shelter, defend, and facilitate the movement of fugitive slaves. Some of the most prominent members of the black communities were active in these committees—Robert Purvis, Alexander Crummell, Stephen D. Gloucester, Robert B. Forten, Charles W. Gardner, and James C. McCrummell in Philadelphia, and David Ruggles, Theodore S. Wright, Thomas Van Rensselaer, and Samuel E. Cornish in

New York. Within only a little over a year after its founding the New York vigilance committee numbered 100 members and proudly announced that it had "protected from slavery" (an ambiguous term) a total of 335 persons. The Philadelphia body must have grown with similar rapidity, for over a period of seven years 35 different persons are known to have been actively involved in the functioning of the committee, and a female vigilance committee had been established. A Pittsburgh society of earlier origin—the Philanthropic Society—assumed similar responsibilities.[32]

Elsewhere, less institutionalized structures served similar purposes. In Boston, both before and after the organization of a vigilance committee, an informal network of blacks and concerned whites operated in the 1840s out of the West End homes and shops of such activist blacks as Peter Howard, John J. Smith, and Lewis Hayden. Their chief activities would appear to have been concealing fugitives and expediting the passage of those who wished to push farther north. The black associates apparently took almost all of the risks and bore most of the burdens. Looser still were the processes by which the black communities raised money in an emergency (or, sometimes, on a less urgent basis) to purchase the freedom of slaves, especially recaptured runaways. In the fall of 1850 a mass meeting in New York's Zion Church quickly collected the necessary funds to secure the return of a slave who had been arrested and taken back to Baltimore, and a few months later John B. Vashon and other Pittsburgh blacks acted with even greater alacrity and procured money to obtain the release of a reclaimed fugitive before he was even carried out of the city.[33]

In some instances, however, urban blacks responded to efforts to reclaim fugitives in a more aggressive manner. The legal code might view such payments as legitimate, and the slaveowner might regard them as inadequate remuneration for property rights he surrendered, but to the black community they doubtless appeared to bear a more striking resemblance to ransom paid to kidnapers or tribute to warlords. It is hardly surprising, therefore, that from time to time their frustration and their fear generated a determination to seize freedom as a right rather than buy it as a commodity. As early as September 1824, some one hundred fifty Philadelphia Negroes "armed with bludgeons" attempted to effect the rescue of a fugitive as the sheriff's officers were conveying him from the court to the jail. The officers, with their prisoner, fell back before the incensed blacks until the "magistrates, constables, and all the officers of the mayor's court (which was compelled to adjourn)" came to their assistance. The mob was then dispersed and seven ringleaders arrested.[34]

In 1836 a number of Boston's black residents forcibly liberated fugitives Eliza Small and Polly Ann Bates, and six years later, after failing to free George Latimer from his captors, that city's free people of color both contributed to the fund used to purchase his freedom and participated in the circulation of a petition to the legislature that was influential in securing the passage of the Massachusetts Personal Liberty Act of 1843. And twice in the winter and spring of 1847 fugitives apprehended in Pittsburgh by their masters were forcibly liberated by blacks and expeditiously dispatched to Canada. Indeed, by that date it did not require the seizure of a runaway to rouse the Negroes of Pittsburgh to action; the mere presence of an enslaved African was sufficient. In the late 1840s and early '50s Pittsburgh's free blacks enticed or assisted to freedom the slaves of several masters passing through the city. These "rescues" were, of course, effected by stealth rather than violence.[35]

The passage of the Fugitive Slave Act of 1850 ignited both fear and anger in the northern urban black communities. Many black residents, as has been noted, fled to Canada, and others girded themselves to resist the anticipated onslaught of slave catchers. And the Shadrack rescue in Boston in early 1851—when the fugitive was physically wrested from federal officers by "two huge negroes"—certainly suggested that the black communities in the larger northern cities might play a major and effective role in efforts to thwart the operation of the 1850 act. And as they secreted runaways and assisted them in their flight they assuredly did so. But though blacks gathered mobs to protest one other seizure in Boston (that of Thomas Sims in 1851) and one in Cincinnati (in 1853), and were actively involved in rescues in smaller towns, they did not again confront the federal judicial officers in the major cities. Only two of twenty-two recorded rescues occurred in these urban centers (both in Boston), despite the fact that almost a quarter of the actions brought under the 1850 statute were lodged in eleven of these fifteen cities (no proceedings were initiated in Charleston, Louisville, New Orleans, or Providence). There is no entirely satisfactory explanation for this absence of physical confrontation; certainly blacks in the larger cities appear to have been better organized and sometimes more assertive than those in smaller communities. It is possible that, in the major urban centers, a large number of those Negroes most inclined to employ physical force to free apprehended runaways were themselves fugitives and that their departure for Canada in 1851 stripped these cities of a major portion of their most aggressive blacks. The nature of local white attitudes may also have been influential, for it would appear that the white residents of the larger cities of the North were generally more hostile to blacks than those in smaller communities and less supportive of the antislavery movement.[36]

Free persons of color further demonstrated their continuing commitment to the universal abolition of African slavery by celebrating the anniversaries of various acts of emancipation. On July 14 of each year Boston blacks observed the anniversary of the end of slavery in Massachusetts. In New York, Albany, and probably in other New York cities, the final elimination of Negro servitude in that state was celebrated by processions and other festivities—not, however, on the actual anniversary date of July 4, which the blacks apparently considered inappropriate in view of the incomplete nature of their freedom and the persistence of slavery elsewhere in the nation, but on July 5 or 6 instead. Free blacks in Baltimore and some other border state cities observed the anniversary of Haitian independence, while those in Philadelphia, Pittsburgh, and Providence celebrated the emancipation of the slaves in the British West Indies each August 1.[37]

Aside from the continued existence of Negro slavery, perhaps nothing so provoked the wrath of the urban free black communities as the white-sponsored proposals to "return" the blacks to Africa. Obviously this reaction did not arise from satisfaction with the lot of free people of color in the United States or a belief that conditions might not be better elsewhere in the world. Emigration to Canada was certainly viewed favorably, and the efforts of the Haitian government to attract black immigrants from northern and border state cities in the mid-1820s not only were moderately successful but were actually assisted in New York by black spokesmen. In that city the leadership of the Haitian Emigration Society included respected members of the black community who, in the next decade, strongly condemned the activities of the American Colonization Society—e.g., Peter Williams, Samuel E. Cornish, and Samuel Ennalls.[38]

But free people of color perceived a great and iniquitous difference between the movement (or flight) of individual blacks to settled and developed areas outside of the United States in search of freedom and opportunity and the American Colonization Society's proposed massive resettlement of an entire population in an uninhabited area on another continent. Though colonization spokesmen might present their scheme as an encouragement (indeed, a necessary precondition) to the abolition of slavery, and though some whites in the Lower South suspected that the organization was tainted by abolitionist ideas, the Negro communities (with clearer vision) saw it as a racist program for the elimination of the free black presence in the United States. Border state whites sometimes spoke more honestly on this matter than either their northern or their southern compatriots. Early in 1828 Hezekiah Niles, after applauding the practice of freeing slaves on the condition that they go to Liberia, added candidly, "But for ourselves, we are more anxious that colored persons, *already free,* should be encouraged to seek a home in the land of their ancestors" (italics added). At almost the same time that Niles was penning these sentiments, a Washington grand jury expressed the hope that slavery might at some future date be abolished, but for the present asserted that "the great object . . . , indeed the sole object, to be accomplished, is not the abolition of slavery, but the removal of a difficulty in the way of abolition which makes abolition unwise, if not impossible, by opening a way for the removal of the colored population, *now free,* or hereafter to be manumitted" (italics added). But perhaps the most incontrovertible evidence of the purpose of colonization was incorporated in the Maryland Act of 1831 which imposed a tax to support the transportation of Negroes to Liberia. The levy was apportioned among the counties, not on the basis of their slave population, but in proportion to the number of free persons of color within their boundaries.[39]

It was, moreover, clear from the first that the founders of the American Colonization Society considered the free people of color to be the most immediate (and probably the most important) objects of the society's "benevolence." At the initial meeting in Washington on December 21, 1817, looking to the formation of that organization, the presiding officer, Henry Clay, in his opening remarks, characterized free blacks as "useless and pernicious, if not dangerous," and asserted that it was desirable "to drain them off." Elias Caldwell, who would serve as the society's first secretary, viewed these conditions as the product of a discriminatory society, but he too saw no acceptable alternative to emigration. "The more you improve the condition of these people," he declared, "the more you cultivate their minds, the more miserable you make them."[40]

Consequently, the intensity of black opposition to colonization varied directly with the activity of whites in promoting such projects. The establishment of the American Colonization Society in early 1817 was quickly followed by the organization of local auxiliary bodies along the eastern seaboard, in Baltimore, New York, and Philadelphia in 1817, and in Charleston and Providence in 1819. In January, 1817—within days after the first steps were taken to create the society—Philadelphia blacks met at Bethel AME Church to voice their protest. Denouncing Clay's remarks as "an unmerited stigma attempted to be cast upon the reputation of the free people of color," they reprobated colonization proposals as "not only . . . cruel, but in direct violation of those principles, which have been the boast of this republic." In the summer of the same year the Negroes of Philadelphia followed up their assault by adopting a more extensive statement condemning colonization as a barrier, rather than an aid, to emancipation, which must be productive of misery to both those transported and those left behind, and two years later resolved that "the people of color of Philadelphia now enter and proclaim their most solemn protest against the proposition to send their people to Africa, and against every measure which may have a tendency to convey the idea that they give the project a single particle of countenance or encouragement."[41]

There were few other immediate protests, however, for the threat of colonization appeared to diminish as financial contributions to the society declined precipitously in the wake of the 1819 panic, as colonizing efforts in Africa suffered repeated reverses, and as the auxiliaries "sank into quiescence." But when the colonization society assumed a more expansive and aggressive posture in the late 1820s and early '30s under the leadership of Ralph R. Gurley—resuscitating feeble auxiliaries and establishing new ones, increasing its income, thrusting out into the Old Northwest, and publishing the *African Repository*—black voices were again raised in protest. In Baltimore, which by the beginning of the second quarter of the nineteenth century had probably the largest free black population among the major cities, the society attracted considerable support and, concomitantly, provoked strong black opposition. In 1826 a free black named Jacob Greener harassed a colonizationist speaker with sharp questions and suggested that the society should make the education of Negro children its first object of concern, and three years later William Watkins, perhaps the most prominent of Baltimore's black schoolmasters, published a powerful attack upon colonization in Benjamin Lundy's *Genius of Universal Emancipation.* "We had rather die in Maryland under the pressure of unrighteous and cruel laws," Watkins asserted, "than be driven, like cattle, to the pestilential clime of Liberia, where grievous privation, inevitable disease, and premature death, await us in all their horrors." A year earlier the Reverend Hosea Easton had voiced similar sentiments in an address to Providence's free black community, and in an Independence Day sermon in 1830 Peter Williams, the rector of New York's St. Philip's Episcopal Church, both denounced the purposes and castigated the methods of the colonizationists. "It is very certain, that very few free people of color *wish* to go to that *land.* The Colonization Society *know* this, and yet they do certainly calculate, that in time they will have us all removed there," declared Williams, who only a few years before had worked actively to assist voluntary emigration to Haiti. "How can this be effected," he asked, "but by making our situation worse here, and closing every other door against us?"[42]

The most voluminous outpouring of black condemnation came in 1831 and appears to have been stimulated by rising antislavery activity, by the increasingly vehement denunciation of African colonization by abolitionists, and especially, by the passionate speeches and writ-

ings of William Lloyd Garrison. Clearly, however, these activities did
not create or, to any significant degree, structure the nature of Negro
opposition to colonization. Rather, they merely incited a more extensive expression of those sentiments to which the free people of color
were already deeply committed. In most matters of substance, the
statements of the early 1830s mirrored those of the previous decade,
though the rhetoric of the latter period was less restrained and showed
greater willingness to condemn the motives of the colonizationists. A
New York meeting declared the address of the state colonization
society to be "unjust, illiberal and unfounded," and added, "we claim
this country, the place of our birth, and not Africa, as our mother country, and all attempts to send us to Africa we consider gratuitous and
uncalled for." A mass meeting of Boston Negroes asked, "How can a
man be born in two countries at the same time?" and characterized the
American Colonization Society as a "clamourous, abusive and peace-
disturbing combination." Baltimore's free people of color resolved
that "we consider the land in which we were born, and in which we
have been bred, our only *'true and appropriate home'*—and that when *we*
desire to remove, we will apprise the public of the same, in due season."
The free blacks of Washington announced that they "view[ed]
with distrust the efforts made by the Colonization Society," and
those of Brooklyn declared that the "false sympathies and friendships"
of the colonizationists "are as foreign to us as the coast of Africa!" "We
will not leave our homes, nor the graves of our fathers," resolved the
blacks of Providence, and in a similar vein those of Pittsburgh proclaimed, "Here we were born—here we will live by the help of the
Almighty—and here we will die, and let our bones lie with our
fathers." The resolutions of Pittsburgh's free people of color were, in
fact, the most outspoken of the 1831 addresses. After condemning the
purposes, assumptions, and motives of the colonizationists, the Pittsburgh Negroes, under the leadership of John B. Vashon, declared that
"we do consider every colored man who allows himself to be col-
onized in Africa, or elsewhere, a traitor to our cause," and added
sarcastically, "We now inform the Colonization Society, that should
our reason forsake us, then we may desire to remove. We will apprise
them of this change in due season."[43]

Rather naturally, the views of the urban black communities were
influential—indeed, determinative—in shaping the position of the
Convention for the Improvement of the Free People of Colour. Especially in the 1830s, it was largely controlled by its urban delegates.
From its inception this national body reprobated African colonization
proposals and castigated the American Colonization Society. At its
organizational meeting and at every subsequent convention held during the 1830s the membership adopted condemnatory statements,

charging colonizationists with slandering the black population and undercutting their efforts at advancement. The official resolutions of these bodies usually carefully avoided condemnation of the membership and leadership of the American Colonization Society, denouncing only its purposes and methods, but sometimes such distinctions were difficult to perceive or maintain. "This society had most grossly vilified our character as a people," charged the members of the third annual convention in 1833; "it has taken much pains to make us abhorrent to the public ...; and the hypocrisy that has marked its movements deserves our universal censure." Perhaps the single most impassioned assault upon the colonization society in these meetings was contained in New Yorker William Hamilton's opening address to the 1834 assembly. "However pure the motives of some of the members of that society may be," he declared,

> yet the master spirits there are evil minded towards us. They have put on the garb of angels of light. Fold back their covering, and you have in full array those of darkness. . . .
>
> This society is the great Dagon of the land, before whom the people bow and cry, Great Jehovah, and to whom they would sacrifice the free people of color. That society has spread itself over this whole land; it is artful, it suits itself to all places. It is one thing at the south, and another at the north; it blows hot and cold; it sends forth bitter and sweet; it sometimes represents us as the most corrupt, vicious, and abandoned of any class of men in the community. Then again we are kind, meek, and gentle. Here we are ignorant, idle, a nuisance, and a drawback on the resources of the country. But as abandoned as we are, in Africa we shall civilize and christianize all that heathen country. . . .
>
> They have resorted to every artifice to effect their purposes, by exciting in the minds of the white community, the fears of insurrection and amalgamation; by petitioning State legislatures to grant us no favors; by petitioning Congress to aid in sending us away; by using their influence to prevent the establishment of seminaries for our instruction in the higher branches of education.

If for no other purpose, said Hamilton, the need to condemn the American Colonization Society and its schemes would alone justify the annual meetings of the convention.[44]

So determined was the black resistance to the efforts of whites to "return" them to their "natural home," and so vehement was their repudiation of the arguments by which the colonizationists attempted to justify and sustain their program, that some urban Negroes became inordinately sensitive to the use of any terminology that might suggest, however slightly, that the free people of color considered themselves more African than American. In spring 1838 the teachers in New York's black public schools successfully petitioned the board of trustees of the Public School Society to change the designation of these schools from "African" to "Colored." And a decade later the author of a pamphlet with the carefully constructed title of *A Call Upon the Church for Progressive Action, to Elevate the Colored American People* urged the elimination of the word "African" from the names of all religious organizations. The use of this term, the writer asserted, constituted "an available excuse for a powerful enemy, the American Colonization Society, to use with extraordinary effect and bitter zeal as a weapon of our own make, to expel ourselves from our beloved country."[45]

Whether participating in the political process, protesting discriminatory restrictions, condemning slavery, assisting fugitives, or denouncing white efforts to deport him to Africa, the urban black might appear to be playing an unaccustomed role. But a more careful consideration would suggest that assertiveness was a quality that was neither rare nor unappreciated in the black communities. Without black initiative there would have been no black churches or associations; the educational facilities available to Negro children would have been much less extensive; and the occupational opportunities, property ownership, and access to adequate housing of free people of color would have been even more limited than was the dismal case. There were, however, some significant differences between the sorts of activities that were aimed at individual betterment and the development of institutions useful within the black communities, and those associated with voting and protests against disfranchisement, slavery, and colonization. For one thing, the latter kinds of actions took place on a much more public stage, and it would have been surprising if they had not been accompanied by a measure of trepidation. After all, one of the advantages that the urban environment offered to the free black was the cloak of anonymity that, by rendering the individual black less conspicuous, might enable him to avoid some forms of harassment and unobtrusively to make some small material gains. It must have taken an unusual combination of courage, strength of will, and commitment to abandon the relative safety of facelessness and namelessness and place one's self or, by inference, the black community in a position of public prominence that might well, if experience was a reliable guide, make the individual and the community a target for abuse, further discrimination, or even physical assault—not a few blacks believed that David Walker had been poisoned because of his publication of the *Appeal*. It is not to be wondered at that few free persons of color or black institutions in the southern cities—and none in those of the Lower South—felt able to meet such a challenge.

It should be remembered, too, that while efforts at personal advancement and institutional development represented an acceptance of the existing social and economic systems and attempts to achieve some measure of success within their frameworks, the fight for equal suffrage, the moral arraignment of slavery, the attempts to prevent the rendition of fugitives, and the denunciation of colonization and colonizationists embodied assaults upon and challenges to these systems. If visibility alone was hazardous, how much more likely to provoke retaliation was such condemnation of the white society and its mores.

Yet in many free black communities a number of people were to be found who were willing to venture themselves in the service of causes they perceived as inextricably interwoven with the elevation of free people of color in the American society. In the process of voicing, in the name of all free people of color, their protests against the continuation of slavery and the racially denigrative program of African colonization, these men and women were not only forcefully opposing elements in American life that were, in the highest degree, detrimental to both the well-being and the image of the Negro in the United States, but also were raising a standard to which their fellow blacks could repair. By providing another focus of interest for concerns shared by all black Americans, they thus contributed appreciably to the deepening of the sense of community among urban blacks. These protests, striking, as they did, at the root assumption of racial inferiority from which the structures of slavery and colonization sprang, probably more than any other kind of black activity caused more and more free blacks to ask, and more and more whites to hear, perhaps the most troublesome question in American life—"Am I not a man?"

Conclusion

From farms, from towns and villages, and from the smaller cities they came, seeking the city and what they hoped to find there. Huddled in rotten shacks crammed into narrow alleys or on the backs of lots; employed, if at all, in only the most menial occupations; excluded from much of the city's life and activity; harassed and assaulted; mired in perpetual poverty and often unrelieved want; even the poorest stayed, clinging to what little the city grudgingly gave, and daring, against all experience, to hope for a better tomorrow. Many, of course, wrested more—of both material and social value—from the recalcitrant city. They sought and clung to the city to the extent that by the 1840s more than a fifth of the nation's free blacks resided in these cities, as compared with something over one-eighth at the beginning of the century—hoping always doubtless for much more than they found but, even at worst, finding something.

Perhaps the greatest gift of the city to its black residents was anonymity. For the fugitive slave it was a boon without price, for by submerging himself in the heterogeneous and fluid urban population he could become a pebble on a beach, identifiable and reclaimable, except in rare instances, only by accident. He was thus enabled not only to seize freedom for himself but also to bequeath it to his children. But even for the free black there were advantages to being unrecognized and unrecognizable, for though prejudice, suppression, and subordination were no less prevalent and pervasive in the city than in the countryside, it was, nevertheless, possible for the individual free person of color to minimize, at least to some degree, their impact upon him. At the very least, personal hostilities generated by an act, an attitude, or insufficient servility would not follow him hour after hour and day after day, calling down upon his head the wrath of others. It is a measure of the degraded and subject status assigned to the Negro in antebellum America that such depersonalization and loss of visible identity were perceived as desirable.

The city, of course, potentially promised other things to its black residents. Not the least of these was economic opportunity. For many free people of color the promise was illusory, but other thousands found, or continued to believe they would find, some advantage not offered by other environments. Certainly there was greater and more concentrated demand for unskilled labor, artisan employment, and entrepreneurial activity in the cities than elsewhere, and to the degree that blacks could, in the face of the extensive societal restraints that often existed, avail themselves of these opportunities, their economic condition would be likely to improve. The substantial number of black artisans in the Lower South cities constituted a clear example of such success. But even in the least favorable urban conditions blacks made marginal gains. In the northern and Upper South cities they were strongly entrenched in barbering, meeting a demand largely created by the urban environment, and the same could be said of black carters, clothes dealers, hucksters, woodsawyers, and operators of oyster cellars.

It was in the cities, too, that blacks found or created the most extensive opportunities for educational and intellectual advancement. The size of the black urban populations alone made possible some opportunities by providing a visible market for the services of entrepreneurial teachers and by stimulating the concern (as smaller numbers of Negroes might not have done) of various philanthropic individuals and organizations. Additionally, black organizations (e.g., churches and associations), whose existence was made possible by the size and density of the urban populations, supported educational activities. And the associations themselves sponsored libraries, debates, lectures, and musical performances for free black residents, who were commonly barred from attending or participating in similar activities presented by or under the auspices of white groups or organizations.

Much black immigration to the cities in the first half of the nineteenth century probably did not result from decisions made after a careful weighing of pros and cons and a calculated consideration of available alternatives, and in like fashion most of the native black urbanites who remained in the city doubtless were more influenced by inertial factors and unexamined perceptions that by a meticulous analysis of the advantages and disadvantages of continued residence in a given metropolis. It is likely that the presence of a larger population of the urban Negro's "own kind"—together with the social and psychological advantages that potentially accrue from such a circumstance—was perceived as a desirable condition to be attained and one to be surrendered with reluctance, and, hence, swayed the decisions of a very large number of free people of color.

Increasingly, as the half-century wore on, the relatively large urban free black populations offered more than a simple aggregation of a larger number of the free Negro's "own kind." There gradually emerged not only a variety of subcommunities but also a very real sense of a larger black community within the city—a perception of being a part of a discernible whole bound together by common concerns not shared by those outside the group.

Various factors doubtless contributed to the development of the urban black communities. Certainly the size of the Negro population was of some importance, for there is probably some demographic equivalent of a "critical mass" that is necessary to generate the social and psychological implosion and fusion which can produce a sense of community and sustain the interactions required to foster its maturation. But this process was accelerated by the density of black residences in certain sections of the larger northern cities in particular, compacting free people of color into a discernible spatial cluster even as the sense of communal identity became stronger. Thus, the antebellum equivalent of the racial ghetto contributed to the nurturing of the black community.

It would appear that the perception of the larger black community was also fostered by the establishment of black organizations and associations, despite the fact that such bodies created smaller subcommunities of their members. For the public activities of fraternal orders, literary associations, and debating societies stimulated black pride, and the organizations themselves often addressed concerns shared by the whole black population. Black churches in particular, though dividing free people of color into groupings that sometimes evinced a measure of hostility toward each other, were, nevertheless, potent instruments for building black community identification, as they increasingly separated themselves from their white coreligionists, as they provided forums for the discussion of black problems, and as their ministers took more and more active leadership roles in areas of secular concern to Negroes. Schools, too—whether public or private—became centers of black interest and raised black hopes for the betterment of the race.

The suppression, harassment, and assaults encountered by free people of color in all segments of urban life certainly must have strongly stimulated community identification. When so many burdens were borne, so many indignities endured, and so many pains suffered because they were black, it was inevitable that their blackness should become the central and overriding consideration in their lives. The impersonality of racial discrimination and exclusion, the impersonality of racial insults and attacks, and, above all, the impersonality of the assaults by white mobs invading the Negro districts were impossible to deal with (or perhaps even endure) psychologically as an isolated individual. Nothing—not the fact that one was an American, or a Philadelphian, or a property holder, or a father, or a barber, or a Methodist, or a voter, or a Mason—was one-third so significant as the fact that one was black in a society that legally, socially, and politically viewed Negroes as innately inferior and undesirable as occupiers of urban space. Surely few things in the life of the urban black were more self-evident than the existence of this community of exclusion, suppression, and, withal, resentment.

But the fuller flowering of the urban black communities may be said to have been the product of more assertive and less inward-looking activities. The plight of their brethren held in slavery stirred black hearts and united black wills as did few other considerations. When a slave pursuing freedom sought aid and shelter or when efforts were made to return a fugitive to bondage, there quickly emerged within the black urban populations—often without the necessity of providing an organized structure—a zealous and determined spirit of community that facilitated the raising of money to ransom those threatened with reenslavement; concealed and succored the persons and nourished hope in the souls of runaways; expedited the flight of fugitives, passing them from domicile to domicile and from city to city; and, as a last resort, mustered a committed cadre to attempt a forcible rescue of some reclaimed fugitive from state or federal authorities. Surely many urban blacks must have viewed such bold and venturesome individuals as agents of the black community, carrying with them the hopes, fears, frustrations, and desperation of all, as they interposed themselves, in the name of their common blackness, between imperiled Negroes and the white society and law. Surely the opposition to the continuation of slavery came as close as any other consideration to uniting into a single body all black residents of the city.

The opposition to slavery—like the sporadic black resistance to white mobs—was, in large measure, defensive in nature. Perhaps the most affirmative demonstrations of black community solidarity were associated with the demands for Negro rights and some measure of black equality. Free black spokesmen—many of them leaders in the Negro subcommunities formed by churches and associations, or teachers in black schools—attacked the white community's exclusion of blacks from many of the services and facilities available to the city's whites and from important governmental functions limited to Caucasian residents. They demanded access to public schools; they fought for suffrage; they struggled for service on city-licensed transportation vehicles; some even went as far as to attack segregation in public facilities; and with each blow struck for a black cause the components of the black community were riveted more firmly together. In the onslaughts against discriminatory practices, and the the slashing assaults upon colonization as well, the leaders of the increasingly self-conscious black communities condemned the mores of the white society that supported, and, indeed, made almost inevitable, such practices and programs. Implicitly or explicitly they censured that society's racism (hardly an arguable point), reproved its exclusivism, reprobated its suppression, reproached its discrimination, rebuked its selfishness, execrated its brutality, and denounced its inhumanity; and underlying these judgments lay their bitter condemnation of the society's duplicity, hypocrisy, mendacity, and faithlessness to the elements and implications of its own vaunted creed.

For the "American Dream" was a creation of the white society and a codification of its aspirations, to which free people of color had in some measure come to give their allegiance and to incorporate into their vision of the future. It was a bitter irony of American life that the result was a conflict—always abrasive and frequently violent—between dreamers of the same dream. That urban blacks fell short in their attempt to make the dream their own was much more the result of white intransigence than of any ineptitude, incapacity, or lack of concern on the part of the free people of color. By unremitting efforts, by sacrifice, and by sustained pressure—both individual and communal—urban free Negroes assaulted the wall of prejudice that separated black and white Americans. The wall was occasionally breached—sometimes at important points—and often (morally, at least) undermined, but in antebellum America even the urban blacks, who were frequently in the vanguard of the fight, were able to grasp but the shadow of the dream.

Table A-1

Cities	1800	1810
Albany	680	n.a.
Baltimore	5,614	7,686
Boston	1,174	1,464
Brooklyn	641	n.a.
Buffalo	n.a.	n.a.
Charleston	10,004	13,143
Cincinnati	20[a]	82
Louisville	77	495
New Orleans	3,000[a]	10,911
New York	6,367	9,823
Philadelphia	4,265	6,354
Pittsburgh	102	185
Providence	656	871
St. Louis	371[b]	n.a.
Washington	746[c]	2,304

Appendix A:
Urban Black Population

Growth in the Black Population in Fifteen Cities, 1800–1850 (Slave and Free)

1820	1830	1840	1850	Increase, 1800–1850	
				Number	Percent
754	1,050	886	860	180	26.47
14,683	18,910	21,166	28,388	22,774	405.66
1,687	1,875	2,427[e]	1,999	825	70.27
847	973	1,775	2,424	1,783	278.16
32	219	503	675		
14,127	17,461	16,231	22,973	12,969	129.64
433	1,090	2,240	3,237	3,217	>10,000.00[g]
1,124	2,638	4,049	6,970	6,893	8,951.95
13,592	26,038	33,280[f]	26,916	23,916	797.20
10,886	13,977	16,358	13,815	7,448	116.98
7,582	9,806	10,507	10,736	6,471	151.72
286	473	710	1,959	1,857	1,820.59
979	1,213	1,302	1,499	843	128.51
n.a.	1,232[d]	2,062	4,054	3,683	992.72
3,641	5,459	6,521	10,271	9,525	1,276.81

Source: See note 1.
(a) Estimated. (b) Viles, "Population of Missouri before 1804," p. 208. (c) Bryan, *National Capital* 2:136n. (d) Scharf, *St. Louis* 2:1015 (figure for 1828). (e) This is the census figure, which is almost certainly erroneous (see p. 6). A more accurate figure would probably be 1,977. (f) In this and the subsequent tables, the 1840 census data for New Orleans have been purged of the entries for Fauxbourg Tierne and McDonough-town. (g) Resulting from a very small number of blacks in 1800.

Table A-2   Percentage of Blacks in the Populations of Fifteen Cities, 1800–1850

Cities	1800	1810	1820	1830	1840	1850
Albany	12.86	n.a.	5.97	4.34	2.63	1.69
Baltimore	21.17	21.60	23.40	23.46	20.69	16.79
Boston	4.71	4.40	3.97	3.05	2.60[e]	1.46
Brooklyn	26.96	n.a.	11.80	7.84	4.90	2.50
Buffalo	n.a.	n.a.	1.53	2.53	2.76	1.60
Charleston	53.14	53.19	57.01	57.65	55.47	53.44
Cincinnati	2.67[a]	3.23	4.49	4.39	4.83	2.80
Louisville	21.45	36.48	28.02	25.51	19.09	16.14
New Orleans	35.29[a]	63.28	50.01	56.50	39.63	23.13
New York	10.53	10.19	8.80	6.90	5.23	2.68
Philadelphia	10.33	11.83	11.90	12.19	11.22	8.85
Pittsburgh	6.59	3.88	3.95	3.76	3.36	4.20
Providence	8.62	8.65	8.32	7.21	5.62	3.61
St. Louis	35.67[b]	n.a.	n.a.	24.64[d]	12.52	5.21
Washington	23.24[c]	28.07	27.49	29.00	27.91	25.68

Source: See note 1.
(a) Estimated. (b) Viles, "Population of Missouri before 1804," p. 208. (c) Bryan, *National Capital* 2:136n. (d) Scharf, *St. Louis* 2:1015 (figure for 1828). (e) This figure is computed from the census data, which are almost certainly erroneous (see p. 6). A more accurate estimate would probably be 2.13%.

Table A-3   Index of Change in Black Percentages in the Populations of Fifteen Cities, 1800–1850 (1.0000 = 1850)

Cities	1800	1810	1820	1830	1840	1850
Albany	7.6095	n.a.	3.5325	2.5680	1.5562	1.0000
Baltimore	1.2609	1.2865	1.3937	1.3973	1.2323	1.0000
Boston	3.2260	3.0137	2.7192	2.0890	1.7808[e]	1.0000
Brooklyn	10.7840	n.a.	4.7200	3.1360	1.9600	1.0000
Buffalo	n.a.	n.a.	.9563	1.5813	1.7250	1.0000
Charleston	.9944	.9953	1.0668	1.0788	1.0380	1.0000
Cincinnati	.9536[a]	1.1536	1.6036	1.5679	1.7250	1.0000
Louisville	1.3290	2.2602	1.7361	1.5805	1.1828	1.0000
New Orleans	1.5257[a]	2.7358	2.1621	2.4427	1.7134	1.0000
New York	3.9291	3.8022	3.2836	2.5746	1.9478	1.0000
Philadelphia	1.1672	1.3367	1.3446	1.3774	1.2678	1.0000
Pittsburgh	1.5690	.9238	.9405	.8952	.8000	1.0000
Providence	2.3878	2.3961	2.3047	1.9972	1.5568	1.0000
St. Louis	6.8464[b]	n.a.	n.a.	4.7294[d]	2.4031	1.0000
Washington	.9050[c]	1.0931	1.0705	1.1293	1.0868	1.0000

Source: See note 1.
(a) Estimated. (b) Viles, "Population of Missouri before 1804," p. 208. (c) Bryan, *National Capital* 2:136n. (d) Scharf, *St. Louis* 2:1015 (figure for 1828). (e) This figure is computed from the census data, which are almost certainly erroneous (see p. 6). A more accurate estimate would probably be 1.4589.

Table A-4   Changes in the Slave Population in Fifteen Cities, 1800–1850

| Cities | Total Slave Population | | | | | | Changes, 1800–1850 | |
	1800	1810	1820	1830	1840	1850	Number	Percent
Albany	542	n.a.	109	0	0	0	−542	−100.00
Baltimore	2,843	3,713	4,357	4,120	3,199	2,946	+103	+3.62
Boston	0	0	0	0	0	0		
Brooklyn	445	n.a.	190	0	3	0	−445	−100.00
Buffalo	n.a.	n.a.	8	0	0	0		
Charleston	9,053	11,671	12,652	15,354	14,673	19,532	+10,479	+115.75
Cincinnati	0	0	0	0	0	0		
Louisville	76	484	1,031	2,406	3,430	5,432	+5,356	+7,047.37
New Orleans	2,200[a]	5,961	7,355	14,476	18,208	17,011	+14,811	+673.23
New York	2,868	1,686	518	17	0	0	−2,868	−100.00
Philadelphia	55	2	3	11	0	0	−55	−100.00
Pittsburgh	10	0	1	0	0	0	−10	−100.00
Providence	0	6	4	0	1	0		
St. Louis	301[b]	n.a.	n.a.	n.a.	1,531	2,656	+2,355	+782.39
Washington	623[c]	1,437	1,945	2,330	1,713	2,113	+1,490	+239.17

Source: See note 1.
(a) Estimated. (b) Viles, "Population of Missouri before 1804," p. 208. (c) Bryan, *National Capital* 2:136n.

Table A-5   Percentage of Slaves in the Populations of Fifteen Cities, 1800–1850

Cities	1800	1810	1820	1830	1840	1850
Albany	9.91	n.a.	0.86	0.00	0.00	0.00
Baltimore	10.72	10.43	6.94	5.11	3.13	1.74
Boston	0.00	0.00	0.00	0.00	0.00	0.00
Brooklyn	18.71	n.a.	2.65	0.00	0.01	0.00
Buffalo	n.a.	n.a.	0.38	0.00	0.00	0.00
Charleston	48.09	47.23	51.06	50.69	50.15	45.44
Cincinnati	0.00	0.00	0.00	0.00	0.00	0.00
Louisville	21.17	35.67	25.70	23.27	16.17	12.58
New Orleans	25.88[a]	34.57	27.06	31.41	21.68	14.62
New York	4.74	1.75	0.42	0.01	0.00	0.00
Philadelphia	0.13	0.00	0.00	0.01	0.00	0.00
Pittsburgh	0.65	0.00	0.01	0.00	0.00	0.00
Providence	0.00	0.06	0.03	0.00	0.00	0.00
St. Louis	28.94[b]	n.a.	ñ.a.	n.a.	9.30	3.41
Washington	19.41[c]	17.51	14.68	12.38	7.33	5.28

Source: See note 1.

(a) Estimated. (b) Viles, "Population of Missouri before 1804," p. 208. (c) Bryan, *National Capital* 2:136n.

Table A-6 Nativities of Adult Free Persons of Color in Fifteen Cities in 1850 (by percentages)

Cities	State of Residence	Other States			Foreign Countries			Unknown etc.
		Slave	Free	Total	Carib'n	Other	Total	
Albany	82.80	7.53	9.14	16.67	0.00	0.54	0.54	0.00
Baltimore	94.58	3.19	1.27	4.46	0.34	0.33	0.67	0.28
Boston	32.59	21.37	22.59	43.96	1.94	7.48[a]	9.42	14.03
Brooklyn	58.10	22.42	16.27	38.69	1.74	1.20	2.95	0.27
Buffalo	19.90	57.96	10.70	70.90[b]	0.25	5.47[c]	5.72	3.48
Charleston	96.74	0.42	0.05	0.47	2.36	0.42	2.78	0.00
Cincinnati	14.99	71.89	11.11	83.00	0.15	0.74	0.88	1.13
Louisville	62.84	32.16	4.51	36.67	0.20	0.29	0.49	0.69
New Orleans	74.67	9.78	1.21	10.90	11.01	2.71	13.72	0.70
New York	49.51	19.54	25.00	44.59[d]	2.18	1.85	4.04	1.86
Philadelphia	39.26	49.39	8.36	57.75	1.48	0.45	1.93	1.00
Pittsburgh	44.27	50.68	3.59	54.27	0.09	1.20	1.28	0.17
Providence	56.68	20.58	20.06	40.64	0.51	1.75	2.26	0.62
St. Louis	30.14	54.22	13.14	68.40[e]	0.10	1.25	1.36	0.14
Washington	37.18	61.45	0.76	62.21	0.02	0.15	0.17	0.43

Source: See note 2. For the purposes of this study, analyses have been made of the places of birth of all free persons of color over the age of sixteen in the cities examined. The results are stated as percentages of the total number of such persons recorded by the census enumerators. The figures are more accurately indicative of black migration to the cities than nativity studies of the whole free black population, because the younger population elements, naturally, include large numbers of children of recent in-migrants. Nativities of persons born within the United States were recorded only by state, and it is not, consequently, possible to determine the extent of rural-urban migration within individual states.
(a) Includes 4.82% born in British North America. (b) Includes 2.24% "American." (c) Includes 3.98% born in British North American. (d) Includes 0.04% "U.S." (e) Includes 1.04% "American" and "U.S."

Table A-7   Changes in the Free Black Population in Fifteen Cities, 1800–1850

Cities	Total Free Persons of Color						Increase, 1800–1850	
	1800	1810	1820	1830	1840	1850	Number	Percent
Albany	156	n.a.	645	1,050	886	860	704	451.28
Baltimore	2,771	3,973	10,326	14,790	17,967	25,442	22,671	818.15
Boston	1,174	1,464	1,687	1,875	2,427[d]	1,999	825	70.27
Brooklyn	196	n.a.	657	973	1,772	2,424	2,228	1,136.73
Buffalo	n.a.	n.a.	24	219	503	675		
Charleston	951	1,472	1,475	2,107	1,558	3,441	2,490	261.83
Cincinnati	20[a]	82	433	1,090	2,240	3,237	3,217	>10,000.00[e]
Louisville	1	11	93	232	619	1,538	1,537	>10,000.00[e]
New Orleans	800[a]	4,950	6,237	11,562	15,072	9,905	9,105	1,138.13
New York	3,499	8,137	10,368	13,960	16,358	13,815	10,316	294.83
Philadelphia	4,210	6,352	7,579	9,795	10,507	10,736	6,526	155.01
Pittsburgh	92	185	285	473	710	1,959	1,867	2,029.35
Providence	656	865	975	1,206	1,301	1,499	843	128.51
St. Louis	70[b]	n.a.	n.a.	n.a.	531	1,398	1,328	1,897.14
Washington	123[c]	867	1,696	3,129	4,808	8,158	8,035	6,532.52

Source: See note 1.

(a) Estimated. (b) Viles, "Population of Missouri before 1804," p. 208. (c) Bryan, *National Capital* 2:136n. (d) This is the census figure, which is almost certainly erroneous (see p. 6). A more accurate estimate would probably be 1,977. (e) Resulting from very small numbers of free blacks in 1800.

Table A-8   Percentage of Free Blacks in the Populations of Fifteen Cities, 1800–1850

Cities	1800	1810	1820	1830	1840	1850
Albany	2.95	n.a.	5.11	4.34	2.63	1.69
Baltimore	10.45	11.17	16.46	18.35	17.56	15.05
Boston	4.71	4.40	3.97	3.05	2.60[d]	1.46
Brooklyn	8.24	n.a.	9.16	7.84	4.89	2.50
Buffalo	n.a.	n.a.	1.15	2.53	2.76	1.60
Charleston	5.05	5.96	5.95	6.96	5.32	8.01
Cincinnati	2.67[a]	3.23	4.49	4.39	4.83	2.80
Louisville	0.28	0.81	2.32	2.24	2.92	3.56
New Orleans	9.41[a]	28.71	22.95	25.09	17.95	8.51
New York	5.78	8.44	8.38	6.89	5.23	2.68
Philadelphia	10.20	11.82	11.90	12.17	11.22	8.85
Pittsburgh	5.95	3.88	3.93	3.76	3.36	4.20
Providence	8.62	8.59	8.29	7.16	5.61	3.61
St. Louis	6.73[b]	n.a.	n.a.	n.a.	3.22	1.80
Washington	3.83[c]	10.56	12.80	16.62	20.58	20.39

Source: See note 1.
(a) Estimated. (b) Viles, "Population of Missouri before 1804," p. 208. (c) Bryan, *National Capital* 2:136n. (d) This figure is computed from the census data, which are almost certainly erroneous (see p. 6). A more accurate estimate would probably be 2.13%.

Table A-9 Ratio of Females to Each Male in the Populations of Six Southern Cities, 1820–50

Cities	1820		1830		1840		1850	
	White	Slave	White	Slave	White	Slave	White	Slave
Baltimore	1.0088	1.2139	1.0553	1.4849	1.0892	1.7365	.9848	2.1109
Charleston	1.0013	1.2216	1.0278	1.2656	.9086	1.3165	.9547	1.2630
Louisville	.5822	1.0828	.5905	1.1198	.8508	1.4801	.8607	1.2539
New Orleans	.6434	1.7150	.6756	1.5167	.6854	1.3570	.7273	1.4950
St. Louis	n.a.	n.a.	n.a.		.6316	1.1997	.7419	1.0979
Washington	1.0071	1.2102	1.0318	1.2821	1.0550	1.6394	1.0467	1.8827

Source: See note 3.

Table A-10   Ratio of Females to Each Male in the Populations of Fifteen Cities, 1820–50

Cities	1820 White	1820 FPC	1830 White	1830 FPC	1840 White	1840 FPC	1850 White	1850 FPC
Albany	1.0810	1.3455	1.0077	1.5060	1.0816	1.3133	1.0632	1.2051
Baltimore	1.0088	1.3667	1.0553	1.3990	1.0892	1.4745	.9848	1.3488
Boston	1.0908	1.2315	1.1127	1.1676	.9011	.7348[a]	1.0797	1.1752
Brooklyn	.9009	1.2347	1.0890	1.4949	1.0627	1.1985	1.0819	1.1779
Buffalo	.8273	1.4000[b]	.7155	.8099	.8909	.8699	.9741	1.0455
Charleston	1.0013	1.3676	1.0278	1.5885	.9086	1.6724	.9547	1.5395
Cincinnati	.8721	.9772	.9016	1.0644	.8964	1.2289	.8918	1.0723
Louisville	.5822	.8600[b]	.5905	.9829	.8508	1.0633	.8607	1.2034
New Orleans	.6434	1.5646	.6756	1.4485	.6854	1.2709	.7273	1.4769
New York	1.0397	1.4721	1.0569	1.3343	1.0763	1.3628	1.0230	1.2655
Philadelphia	1.1381	1.4015	1.1389	1.4323	1.2278	1.6360	1.1760	1.4646
Pittsburgh	.9920	1.1269	.9367	1.3416	1.0338	1.1006	.9748	1.1599
Providence	1.0942	1.5194	1.0582	1.6332	1.0786	1.4272	1.0768	1.2508
St. Louis	n.a.	n.a.	n.a.	n.a.	.6316	.9888	.7419	.8841
Washington	1.0071	1.2613	1.0318	1.3316	1.0550	1.4669	1.0467	1.4008

Source: See note 1. The census returns before 1820 did not divide either slaves or free blacks by age or sex. FPC denotes free persons of color.
(a) This figure is computed from the census data, which are almost certainly erroneous (see p. 6). A more accurate figure would probably be 1.0832.
(b) Based on fewer than one hundred persons.

Table A-11   Ratio of Female Children to Each Male Child in the U.S. Population,
1820–50

	1820	1830	1840	1850
White	.9519	.9531	.9544	.9689
Slave	.9433[a]	.9835	.9973	1.0140
FPC	.9630[a]	.9723	.9783	1.0105

Source: See note 4.
(a) Under 14 years of age; others under 10 years of age.

Table A-12   Ratio of Females to Each Male in National and Urban Populations,
1820–50

	1820	1830	1840	1850
White, national	.9679	.9656	.9565	.9502
White, urban average[a]	.9485	.9570	.9647	.9772
FPC, national	1.0715	1.0827	1.0715	1.0817
FPC, urban average[a]	1.2949	1.3239	1.2539[b]	1.2447
Slave, national	.9518	.9836	.9955	.9995
Slave, urban average[c]	1.2887	1.3338	1.4549	1.5172

Source: See note 5.
(a) Average of data for individual cities in table A-10. (b) This figure is computed from
the census data, which are almost certainly erroneous in the case of Boston (see p. 6).
A more accurate figure would probably be 1.2771. (c) Average of data for individual
cities in table A-9.

Table A-13   Ratio of Free Black Females to Each Male in Twelve Cities and Counties
in 1850

Cities (Counties)	City	County
Albany (Albany County)	1.2051	1.1749
Baltimore (Baltimore County)	1.3488	1.3015
Brooklyn (Kings County)	1.1779	1.0761
Buffalo (Erie County)	1.0455	.9550
Charleston (Charleston District)	1.5395	1.4376
Cincinnati (Hamilton County)	1.0723	1.0797
Louisville (Jefferson County)	1.2034	1.1740
Philadelphia (Philadelphia County)	1.4646	1.3427
Pittsburgh (Allegheny County)	1.1599	1.0781
Providence (Providence County)	1.2508	1.2171
St. Louis (St. Louis County)	.8841	.8846
Washington (District of Columbia)	1.4008	1.3679

Source: See note 6.

Table A-14 Percentage of Children in the Populations of Six Southern Cities, 1820–50

Cities	1820[a]		1830[b]		1840[b]		1850[b]	
	White[c]	Slave	White	Slave	White	Slave	White	Slave
Baltimore	37.97	36.19	26.40	21.84	26.73	20.16	26.06	18.33
Charleston	35.20	32.71	25.23	28.89	23.68	27.14	22.93	17.61
Louisville	30.87	40.25	22.63	23.69	26.97	25.80	26.07	22.13
New Orleans	28.69	25.85	24.29	22.78	24.80	21.18	21.43[d]	18.94[d]
St. Louis	n.a.	n.a.	n.a.	n.a.	19.59	24.36	22.17	18.98
Washington	37.75	40.67	29.32	26.57	26.72	24.81	26.30	22.24

Source: See note 7.
(a) Under 14 years. (b) Under 10 years. (c) Estimated. (d) Includes suburbs.

Table A-15   Percentage of Children in the Populations of Fifteen Cities, 1820–50

Cities	1820[a]		1830[b]		1840[b]		1850[b]	
	White[c]	FPC	White	FPC	White	FPC	White	FPC
Albany	39.65	29.30	26.81	19.81	28.22	22.91	26.21	21.28
Baltimore	37.97	33.80	26.40	24.48	26.73	24.62	26.06	24.02
Boston	34.70	24.18	23.09	19.84	21.97	17.14[d]	22.02	20.01
Brooklyn	36.06	37.60	29.56	24.36	28.07	22.97	n.a.	n.a.
Buffalo	40.52	33.33[e]	26.82	22.37	27.37	24.25	n.a.	n.a.
Charleston	35.20	38.10	25.23	38.25	23.68	32.35	22.93	26.50
Cincinnati	39.67	35.33	27.96	24.77	24.89	21.52	25.52	22.86
Louisville	30.87	30.11[e]	22.63	25.00	26.97	26.33	26.07	22.43
New Orleans	28.69	45.07	24.29	30.69	24.80	31.81	21.43[f]	23.96[f]
New York	37.36	26.74	25.46	19.87	26.01	20.06	23.59	18.76
Philadelphia	35.29	29.34	23.38	20.49	23.50	19.64	24.99[f]	21.06[f]
Pittsburgh	40.91	43.86	27.41	21.35	27.89	20.85	26.98	23.79
Providence	34.24	25.13	24.16	15.84	24.27	20.83	22.89	22.55
St. Louis	n.a.		n.a.		19.59	21.66	22.17	18.03
Washington	37.75	37.38	29.32	26.53	26.72	28.10	26.30	25.82

Source: See note 1 and DeBow, *Statistical View*, pp. 395–98.

(a) Under 14 years of age. (b) Under 10 years of age. (c) Estimated. (d) This figure computed from the census data, which are almost certainly erroneous (see p. 6). A more accurate estimate would probably be 21.04. (e) Based on fewer than one hundred persons. (f) Includes suburbs.

Table A-16   Percentage of Children in National and Urban Populations

	1820[a]		1830		1840		1850	
	Nat'l.	Urban[b]	Nat'l.	Urban[b]	Nat'l.	Urban[b]	Nat'l.	Urban[b]
Slave	43.44[c]	35.13	34.90	24.75	33.93	23.91	31.82	19.71
White	43.73[c]	36.35[c]	32.53	25.89	31.60	25.38	28.64	24.40
FPC	39.28	33.52	30.04	23.83	28.82	23.67[d]	27.36	22.39

Source: See note 8.

(a) Under 14 years of age; others under 10 years of age. (b) Average of city figures in table A-14 for slaves and table A-15 for whites and free persons of color. (c) Estimated. (d) This figure is computed from the census data, which are almost certainly erroneous in the case of Boston (see p. 6). A more accurate estimate would probably be 23.93.

Appendix B: Urban Free Black Occupational Patterns

The Federal Census and Free Black Occupations

In 1850 the census marshals were directed, for the first time, to record the specific occupations of all males over sixteen years of age. Since, by this date, the name and "color" of each free individual were also entered, a comprehensive picture of free black male employment was presented. Unfortunately, the census office prepared aggregated tables based on this information for only two cities—New Orleans and New York—and both of these aggregations (especially that for New York) contained substantial errors.[1] It is, consequently, necessary to extract and aggregate the data from the manuscript census returns for each of the fifteen cities investigated. This has been done, and the resultant data form the basis for the tables in this appendix and the generalizations in the text.[2]

The total data on free black occupations were extracted from all of the records cited in note 2. No sampling was employed. The more than three hundred fifty occupations listed were divided into eight categories: unskilled (e.g., laborer, mariner, woodsawyer); semiskilled (e.g., sexton, gardener, well digger); personal service (e.g., servant, barber, waiter); transportation (e.g., carter, drayman, porter); food service (e.g., cook, baker, pastry cook); artisan (e.g., carpenter, tailor, blacksmith); entrepreneurial and mercantile (e.g., fruit dealer, boardinghouse keeper, peddlar); and professional managerial, artistic, clerical, scientific, etc. (e.g., minister, teacher, musician). In addition, twenty blacks followed seventeen occupations that were listed as unclassifiable (e.g., bone player, planet reader, magnetiseur). These categories were grouped into three blocks of occupations roughly corresponding to low, medium, and high occupational achievement and economic opportunity. Group A (low) included the unskilled, semiskilled, and personal service categories; group B (medium) contained the transportation and food service categories; and group C (high) consisted of the artisan, entrepreneurial, and professional, etc., categories. Unless otherwise specified, the occupational percentage figures are the percentages of all free black males for whom occupations were recorded. The census returns for the fifteen cities contain the names of 19,748 free men of color for whom occupations were recorded, with the numbers ranging from less than 200 in Buffalo to more than 6,200 in Baltimore. Census marshals did not list women's occupations.

The two best indicators of black occupational achievement and opportunity for economic success are the proportion of the total employed black males following group A (low opportunity) occupations and the proportion employed as artisans. Obviously, the greater the percentage of black males engaged in group A occupations in a city or a group of cities, the less likely it is that that particular population block will advance economically. Conversely, where a larger segment consists of artisans the chances of economic success are proportionately greater. Table B-1 shows the percent of free black males engaged in group A occupations in 1850 in each of the fifteen cities examined, and table B-2 shows the percent following artisan trades. In each table the cities are arranged in descending order of black occupational opportunity as indicated by that particular measurement (i.e., increasing percentage of group A employment and decreasing percentage of artisan employment).

It is also possible to combine these two indicators into a single simple index of black occupational opportunity (I.O.O.). The formula for the construction of this index is:

$$\text{I.O.O.} = \frac{\%\ \text{Artisan} - \%\ \text{Group A} + 100}{200}$$

If all blacks in a given city were artisans, the index figure would be 1.00; if all were employed in group A occupations, the index figure would be 0.00. Hence, the higher the index figure, the greater the degree of occupational achievement and opportunity. If this index were being constructed for white males, it would be desirable to substitute all group C occupations for the artisan category used here. But the mercantile and professional category occupations did not, for reasons discussed elsewhere (see pp. 22–25), represent the same level of achievement or offer the same opportunity for economic advancement for blacks that they did for whites. This index is more accurately indicative of the economic position of blacks in the various cities than the data provided in either of the other two tables, for it also takes cognizance of that segment of the black population that followed occupations other than those in the most favorable and least favorable groups. Table B-3 shows the index of occupational opportunity for black males in each of the fifteen cities under consideration.

In exploring regional differences, I have used the same methods of analysis discussed above. The regional groupings employed are the following: Lower South—Charleston and New Orleans; Upper South—Baltimore, Louisville, St. Louis, and Washington; Lower North—Cincinnati, Philadelphia, and Pittsburgh; New York—Albany, Brooklyn, Buffalo, and New York; New England—Boston and Providence. It should be emphasized that the figures that follow are not the average of the individual city percentages for each subregion, but a recalculation using as the analytical universes the combined listings of employed free black males in all of the cities in each subregion.

Table B-1   Percentage of All Employed Free Black Males Following Group A Occupations in 1850 in Fifteen Cities

New Orleans	17.65
Charleston	21.24
Louisville	58.50
Buffalo	58.79
Baltimore	60.21
Philadelphia	65.74
Cincinnati	67.41
St. Louis	69.70
Brooklyn	70.83
Albany	73.17
New York	73.77
Providence	75.23
Washington	75.72
Pittsburgh	76.61
Boston	77.34

Table B-2   Percentage of All Employed Free Black Males Employed as Artisans in 1850 in Fifteen Cities

New Orleans	63.97
Charleston	62.52
Baltimore	17.55
Louisville	13.25
Washington	11.83
Brooklyn	8.36
Philadelphia	8.35
Cincinnati	8.26
Albany	6.34
Boston	5.77
Providence	5.50
New York	5.44
Buffalo	4.95
Pittsburgh	3.93
St. Louis	3.25

Table B-3   Index of Occupational Opportunity for Free Black Males in 1850 in Fifteen Cities

New Orleans	.7316
Charleston	.7064
Baltimore	.2867
Louisville	.2738
Buffalo	.2308
Philadelphia	.2131
Cincinnati	.2043
Brooklyn	.1877
Washington	.1806
St. Louis	.1678
Albany	.1659
New York	.1584
Providence	.1514
Boston	.1421
Pittsburgh	.1366

Table B-4   Percentage of All Employed Free Black Males Following Group A Occupations in 1850 in Cities in Five Subregions

Lower South	18.54
Upper South	62.82
Lower North	67.50
New York	72.75
New England	76.51

Table B-5   Percentage of All Employed Free Black Males Employed as Artisans in 1850 in Cities in Five Subregions

Lower South	63.61
Upper South	15.74
Lower North	7.77
New York	5.85
New England	5.66

Table B-6   Index of Occupational Opportunity for Free Black Males in 1850 in Cities in Five Subregions

Lower South	.7254
Upper South	.2646
Lower North	.2014
New York	.1655
New England	.1458

City Directories and Free Black Occupations

The use of directory data to investigate free black male occupational patterns is complicated by a number of considerations. In many cases the compilers included no (or very few) blacks in the listings, and in the 1840s and '50s an increasing number of directory publishers dropped the racial designations that had prevailed earlier. Additionally, directory compilations were less complete than census enumerations, and one suspects that their accuracy in reflecting the condition of the whole free black male population might be in some measure affected by the unscientific manner in which the sample available for analysis was created. There is nothing that the investigator can do reclaim the unrecorded or undesignated urban blacks, but there are two ways to deal with the questions raised about the reliability of the directory listings as samples. First, an investigation can be conducted wholly separate from the census data and confined entirely to the analysis across time of the directory materials, thus dealing with a more nearly constant data base. Second, the effort can be made to establish the degree of correlation between the census enumerations and the directory listings. Both methods have been used in the preparation of this study, but it must be emphasized that these approaches must be employed with caution. It is especially important not to exaggerate the significance of minor shifts in the reported occupational patterns.

In many northern cities the directory compilers included none or few of the black residents in their listings in the first third of the nineteenth century and thereafter ceased to identify any blacks that were included. Spot checks suggest that most directory compilers in these cities continued to ignore blacks after they dropped the free-person-of-color designations from their listings. In the early directories of some southern cities, free Negroes were also much under-represented. By the 1840s and '50s, many of the directories still identifying blacks contained an unscientific sample of ¼–⅓ of the employed free black males, though the figure was closer to ten percent in New Orleans, nearer one-half in some Charleston and Boston directories, and perhaps exceeded two-thirds in Providence. For nine of the fifteen cities (Baltimore, Boston, Brooklyn, Charleston, New Orleans, New York, Providence, St. Louis, and Washington) there are directories with sufficiently large black components in the listings and extending late enough into the half-century to make it possible to reach some suggestive conclusions about the shifting patterns of free black employment during the antebellum era. In a few cities there is directory data as early as the 1820s, but in most towns the earliest usable compilations date from the 1830s and, in some cases, the early 1840s.

Boston and Providence compilers abandoned racial designations in the mid-1840s, but in the other seven cities black directory entries were identifiable into the 1850s.[3]

Table B-7 does not include data from all of the directories employed. In preparation for this analysis, dozens of directories were examined. Data on black occupations were gathered from fifty-seven directories for these fifteen cities and full analytics were prepared for forty-nine. All data on free black occupations were extracted from each directory and, as was true in the analysis of the census data, no sampling was employed. A number of these listings were then tentatively excluded because they contained fewer than one hundred free black males for whom occupations were recorded, and a few others were removed because there were fuller listings available within a short space of time. The excluded group was then reexamined, and a few directory listings which contained one-eighth or more of the estimated number of free black males over sixteen years of age (even though the total number of entries was between 50 and 100) were returned to the group intended for analysis. In addition, one of the listings containing slightly over one hundred entries was excluded because it represented only about 2½ percent of the estimated number of free black males above sixteen years of age. The resulting twenty-six directory listings were then analyzed in the same manner as the 1850 manuscript census data (see pp. 258–59). The figures in parentheses indicate the number of free black males in each directory for whom occupations were listed.

Comparison of Census and Directory Data on Free Black Male Occupational Patterns

For six of the fifteen cities (Baltimore, Brooklyn, Louisville, New Orleans, New York, and Washington) it has been possible to obtain relatively full directory listings removed by no more than three years from the date of the 1850 census enumeration.[4] When the entries are arranged by the eight occupational categories previously discussed, the coefficients of correlation (r) between the census data and the directory data range from .8604 for Louisville to .9880 for Brooklyn, with an average of .9440. When further aggregated into the three occupational groupings, the coefficients of correlation naturally rise, ranging from .9786 for Baltimore to .999997 for Louisville, with an average of .9926. However, the percentage figures for each of the categories do not, in every case, conform to the same figures as computed from the census data nearly as closely as the coefficients of correlation would suggest.[5] The most meaningful way in which to display the relationship between the occupational patterns derived

Table B-7   Index of Occupational Opportunity for Free Black Males in Nine Cities Based on Directory Listings

Cities	1818–22	1830–32	1835–36	1838	1840–43	1844–46	1850–54	1859
Baltimore	.2259 (912)	.2877 (1274)			.2686 (1767)		.2668 (2767)	
Boston	.1467 (75)		.1590 (151)		.1629 (199)	.1635 (244)		
Brooklyn				.1265 (87)	.1652 (109)		.2096 (198)	
Charleston			.7351 (117)					
New Orleans				.7417 (180)			.7768 (112)	.7039 (287)
New York					.2651 (613)	.2598 (847)	.2377 (1050)	
Providence		.0348 (115)	.0726 (130)		.1059 (170)	.1178 (242)		
St. Louis					.2800 (50)		.2708 (168)	
Washington	.3241 (54)						.2330 (337)	

from the analysis of these two sets of data would appear to be that used in table B-8.

Table B-8   Index of Occupational Opportunity for Free Black Males Derived from Census and Directory Data in Six Cities

City	Census	Directory
Baltimore	.2867	.2668 (1851)
Brooklyn	.1877	.2096 (1851)
Louisville	.2738	.2500 (1851)
New Orleans	.7316	.7768 (1852)
New York	.1584	.2377 (1852)
Washington	.1806	.2330 (1853)

Comparison of Free Black and White Male Occupational Patterns

In each of the six compilations used (see note 6), individual occupations (and the number so employed) are listed and these have been aggregated and analyzed as previously described (see pp. 258–59). Dawson and De Saussure give separate tables for free blacks and whites, so it is possible to compare data collected at the same time by precisely similar processes. The other compilations do not separate the employment statistics by race, and, consequently, it is necessary to compare the data from these sources with the free black male occupational data taken from the 1850 manuscript census. It is unlikely, however, that any dramatic changes in occupational distribution occurred within a period of five years, and population growth would have little impact on the analysis, since all comparisons are of percentages, not raw numbers. Since the data do not permit (except in Charleston) a black/white comparison, the free black male data is compared with the total free male figures on occupations (i.e., slaves have not been included in the Charleston figures). In Charleston, Boston, and New York, women are listed separately and can easily be excluded. The Providence, Cincinnati, and Louisville listings do not distinguish entries by sex. Five hundred twenty individuals following strongly sex-linked occupations (e.g., midwife, seamstress, and milliner) have been excluded from the Louisville compilation, and 800 such persons have been removed from the Providence listing. There are probably a few female entries remaining in the Providence, Louisville, and Cincinnati data, but I believe the number to be small and to have no significant impact on the comparisons here presented.

For reasons previously discussed, the black index of occupational opportunity is not a device that should be used for comparing employment patterns of black male and total free male populations. Tables B-9 and B-10, however, present a comparison of some relevant data elements.

Table B-9   Percentage of Employed Males Following Specified Occupations in Six Cities, 1845–55[6]

	Total Free	Free Black
Charleston	(3,716)	(273)
Group A	15.71	23.07
Artisan	16.30	50.18
Group C	79.36	57.51
Louisville	(14,654)	(400)
Group A	19.34	58.50
Artisan	42.50	13.25
Group C	73.68	21.00
Cincinnati	(35,461)	(896)
Group A	28.52	67.41
Artisan	46.00	8.26
Group C	66.49	15.18
New York	(176,419)	(3,550)
Group A	21.00	73.77
Artisan	41.00	5.44
Group C	69.85	10.37
Boston	(24,917)	(503)
Group A	27.34	77.34
Artisan	39.58	5.77
Group C	69.70	16.11
Providence	(14,853)	(417)
Group A	31.49	75.23
Artisan	45.21	5.50
Group C	65.08	12.84

Note: The figures in parentheses indicate the total number of employed males reported in each category in each compilation.

Table B-10   The Charleston Labor Force of 1848 Analyzed by Race and Condition[7]

	Percent White	Percent Free Black	Percent Slave	(N)
Employed males	48.06%	3.76%	48.17%	(7,257)
Laborers	18.30	1.81	79.89	(1,049)
Unskilled workers	33.21	1.54	65.25	(1,364)
Group A	15.57	1.86	82.58	(3,392)
Artisans	43.19	12.43	44.37	(1,102)
Group C	81.40	4.52	14.08	(3,474)

Appendix C: Urban Free
Black Property Ownership

Real Estate Ownership

In 1850 the United States census enumerators were instructed to ascertain the actual value of any real estate owned by each person enumerated and to enter the figure in the appropriate column on the forms furnished by the Census Office. Thus, the manuscript census returns should provide data for both accurate and comprehensive analysis of real estate ownership by urban blacks, since actual value, rather than the assessed value, was to be recorded and the information was collected by persons who were not agents of any governmental entity that levied a tax on real estate. Unfortunately, the reality falls far short of the expectation. It is by no means certain that the individuals questioned were informed that the figures requested would not be used for tax purposes or that they credited such assurance if it was, in fact, given. Additional uncertainties arise from the fact that not all of the census marshals, unhappily, appear to have been equally thorough in collecting and recording data on real estate holdings. In the case of Providence the returns do not show a single real estate owner—black or white—in the entire city![1] And finally, the value of

Table C-1   Free Black Real Estate Ownership in Fourteen Cities in 1850[2]

Cities	Value of Real Estate	Number of Owners	Average Value of Holding
New Orleans	$2,354,640	650	$3,623
Philadelphia	327,000	77	4,248
Cincinnati	317,780	118	2,693
Charleston	200,600	47	4,268
Brooklyn	145,785	98	1,488
Baltimore	137,488	101	1,361
New York	110,010	71	1,549
Washington	108,816	178	611
Louisville	95,650	63	1,518
Pittsburgh	74,200	38	1,953
Buffalo	57,610	41	1,405
St. Louis	49,650	16	3,103
Albany	44,400	32	1,388
Boston	41,900	13	3,223

Table C-2   Percentage of Real Estate Owners in the Free Black Population in Fourteen Cities in 1850[3]

New Orleans	6.56
Buffalo	6.07
Louisville	4.10
Brooklyn	4.04
Albany	3.72
Cincinnati	3.65
Washington	2.18
Pittsburgh	1.94
Charleston	1.37
St. Louis	1.14
Philadelphia	0.72
Boston	0.65
New York	0.51
Baltimore	0.40

comparable pieces of real estate varied enormously from city to city, with property values being much higher in larger cities than in smaller metropolitan areas and greater in rapidly growing towns than in relatively stagnant urban centers.

Table C-3   Percentage of Real Estate Owners in the Populations of Four New York Cities[4]

Cities	Whole Population (1855)	Black Population (1850)	Ratio of % (Whole:Black)
Albany	4.83	3.72	1.3:1
Brooklyn	5.30	4.04	1.3:1
Buffalo	8.29	6.07	1.4:1
New York	2.35	0.51	4.6:1

In several cities local data on free black real estate ownership conform closely to those reported by the federal census marshals in 1850s. The Boston tax list of 1845, for instance, includes only 3 of the 345 identified as persons of color in the city directory of that year.[5] But these figures are by no means incompatible with those derived from the census data, which show only 3 blacks holding real estate of sufficient value to ensure their inclusion on this tax list.[6] Robert C. Reinders, on the basis of his examination of incomplete tax returns of the 1850s, estimated free black property holdings in New Orleans at $2,000,000–$2,500,000, which correlates closely with the census figures.[7] The findings of an 1847 inquiry into the conditions of Philadelphia's black population closely approximated the census figures on the value of black-owned real estate, but reported a significantly larger number of landowners—enough to increase the percentage of black real estate owners by about six-tenths of a percentage point. The wording of the 1847 study, however, suggests the possibility of some confusion in identifying owners of real estate.[8] Nor is the reported holding of $209,000 worth of real estate by Cincinnati's blacks in 1840 in any way incompatible with the 1850 census figure.[9] At first glance the appearance on the Baltimore tax list of 1852–53 of 338 blacks holding $289,492 worth of property suggests a gross underreporting by the 1850 census enumerators. But the 1852 figure includes personal as well as real property. Not only did more blacks hold personal property than real estate, but Philadelphia figures for 1847 suggest that real estate constituted only about forty-five percent of all black-owned property in this era. Given these considerations, the tax list data appear to conform moderately closely to the census findings.[10]

Table C-4   Free Black Female Real Estate Ownership in Fourteen Cities in 1850[11]

Cities	Whole Population			Real Estate Owners		
	# FPC	# FWC	% FWC	# FPC	# FWC	% FWC
New Orleans	9,905	5,906	59.63	650	302	46.46
Louisville	1,538	840	54.62	63	20	31.17
Washington	8,158	4,760	57.24	178	35	19.66
Philadelphia	10,736	6,380	59.34	77	15	19.48
Charleston	3,441	2,086	60.62	47	8	17.02
Cincinnati	3,237	1,675	51.75	118	20	16.95
St. Louis	1,398	656	46.92	16	2	12.50
New York	13,815	7,717	55.86	71	8	11.27
Pittsburgh	1,959	1,052	53.70	38	4	10.53
Baltimore	25,442	14,610	57.42	101	10	9.90
Buffalo	675	345	51.11	41	4	9.76
Albany	860	470	54.65	32	2	9.38
Brooklyn	2,424	1,311	54.08	98	8	8.16
Boston	1,999	1,080	54.03	13	0	0.00

Slave Ownership

The 1830 census, which Carter G. Woodson and his associates analyzed in 1924, did not, in fact, identify individual slaveholders or the number of slaves that individuals owned. Instead, the census forms contained long lines, extending across two pages, on which the marshals recorded the name of the head of the household and indicated by entering numerals in various columns the sex and age block (e.g., 10–24, 24–36, 26–55, 55–100) of each member of the "family" under three categories—whites, slaves and free persons of color. Woodson and his associates had no alternative except to record the slaves so listed as a single holding owned by the head of the household. Such was not necessarily the case. It may well be that the slaves listed in a single "family" were held by more than one of the free members of the "family"—a circumstance that would increase the number of slaveowners while decreasing the average size of holding. It is also possible that some or all of the slaves residing in a free black "family" were held by white owners but were being allowed to "hire their own time" and, since they were permitted to make their own living arrangements, boarded with free Negro families. To the extent that this practice was common the absolute number of slaves held by free blacks would be diminished, the number of free Negro slaveowners would almost certainly be reduced, and the size of individual and average holdings would be variously affected. It would seem impossible to deal with the census data in any way other than that chosen by Woodson and his associates, but the potential for error (perhaps of considerably magnitude) should be noted.

Table C-5   Free Black Slaveholding in Five Cities in 1830[12]

Cities	# FPC Slaveholders	% of FPC Holding Slaves	# Slaves Held by FPC	Average FPC Slaveholding
New Orleans	753	6.51	2,363	3.14
Charleston	262	12.43	1,324	5.05
Baltimore	98	0.63	163	1.66
Washington	83	2.65	167	2.01
Louisville	5	2.16	8	1.60

Table C-6   Free Black Slaveholding Families in Five Cities in 1830[13]

Cities	# FPC Families	# FPC Slaveholders	% FPC Families Holding Slaves
Charleston	337	262	77.74
New Orleans	1,645	753	45.78
Washington	608	83	13.65
Louisville	54	5	9.26
Baltimore	2,423	98	4.04

Table C-7   Size of Free Black Slaveholdings in Five Cities in 1830[14]

Cities	1–4	5–9	10–19	20–29	30–39	40–49	Total
New Orleans	602	126	24	0	1	0	753
Charleston	167	64	28	2	0	1	262
Baltimore	86	12	0	0	0	0	98
Washington	75	8	0	0	0	0	83
Louisville	5	0	0	0	0	0	5

Table C-8   Free Black Women Slaveholders in Five Cities in 1830[15]

Cities	Total FPC Population	All FPC Slaveholders	Percentage of Women in Various Groups FPC Slaveholders, by Size of Holding				
			5–9	10–19	20–29	30–39	40–49
Baltimore	58.32	22.45	0.00	*	*	*	*
Charleston	61.37	67.94	62.50	67.86	0.00	*	100.00
Louisville	49.57	40.00	*	*	*	*	*
New Orleans	59.16	49.80	49.21	62.50	*	100.0	*
Washington	57.11	42.17	37.50	*	*	*	*

*No FPC holdings of this size.

Appendix D: Urban Black Mortality Rates

The United States Census Office made a strenuous effort to compile mortality data for the entire population in 1850, but the results can best be characterized as spotty. Because many jurisdictions did not maintain either death or interment records, the census marshals secured the information by questioning each head-of-household. The census figures show a higher mortality rate in the fifteen largest cities than in the country as a whole, but the difference was not great—18.4 deaths per thousand in the cities as compared with 16.1 in the national black population. But the reported Negro death rate varied enormously from city to city, with Boston's 26.5 per thousand figure being almost five times as great as that for Charleston (5.7 per thousand).[1]

In only forty percent of these cities—Baltimore, Brooklyn, Louisville, Philadelphia, Pittsburgh, and Washington—was the reported black mortality rate higher than that for the whites. In none of these six cities, moreover, was the differential as much as five deaths per thousand of population, and in three case the difference was less than 1½ deaths per thousand. These census data further suggest that urban residence affected black mortality rates less than those for whites. In the country as a whole the reported mortality rate was 13.5 deaths per thousand for whites and 16.1 per thousand for blacks. In the aggregated population of the nation's fifteen largest cities these figures rose by more than eleven full percentage points—to 24.6—for whites, and by only two points—to 18.4—for blacks. Thus, in this aggregated urban population the white mortality rate was reported to be one-third higher than that for blacks, though the black mortality rate considerably exceeded that for whites in the nation as a whole.

Figures collected by city inspectors, boards of health, or other local officers ar agencies do not, however, correspond to those reported by the Census Office. The Baltimore Health Office, for instance, recorded 4,625 deaths in 1850 while Baltimore residents reported almost one thousand fewer (3,655) to the census marshals. Based on the 1850 population, these local figures indicate mortality rates of 26.5 per thousand for whites, 31.7 per thousand for blacks, and 27.4 per thousand for the aggregate population, as compared with 20.9, 25.1,

Table D-1   Mortality Figures for Fifteen Cities as Reported in the U.S. Census of 1850 (deaths per 1,000 population)[2]

	Whites	Slaves	FPC	Blacks[e]	Aggregate
Albany	23.7		16.3[d]	16.3[d]	23.6
Baltimore	20.9	18.0[c]	25.9	25.1	21.6
Boston	35.9		26.5[c]	26.5[c]	35.8
Brooklyn	21.2		25.6[c]	25.6[c]	21.3
Buffalo	28.0		23.7[d]	23.7[d]	27.9
Charleston	16.0	5.2	8.1[d]	5.7	10.5
Cincinnati	42.4		23.5[c]	23.5[c]	41.9
Louisville	22.9	29.1	5.2[d]	23.8	23.1
New Orleans[a]	33.4	20.6	14.3	18.6	29.8
New York	23.2		18.4	18.4	23.0
Philadelphia[b]	17.0		18.1	18.1	17.1
Pittsburgh	17.0		18.4[d]	18.4[d]	17.1
Providence	21.7		16.7[d]	16.7[d]	21.5
St. Louis	50.5	14.3[d]	49.4[c]	26.4	49.2
Washington	14.4	19.4[d]	16.5	17.1	15.0

(a) Includes Orleans and Jefferson parishes. (b) Includes Philadelphia County. (c) Based on fewer than one hundred deaths. (d) Based on fewer than fifty deaths. (e) Includes both slaves and free persons of color.

and 21.6, respectively, according to the census figures. Similar conditions prevailed in New York, where the city inspector's records showed more than forty percent more deaths than the Census Office reported (16,978 to 11,883) and, unlike the census data, showed substantially identical mortality rates for blacks and whites (39.2 per thousand for whites and 32.5 for blacks).[3]

Note on Sources

The most cursory examination of the documentation of this study will indicate the impossibility of preparing a bibliographical statement conforming to any of the usual formats. A full bibliography would be so lengthy as to be both unmanageable and prohibitively expensive, while the wildly diverse nature of the sources makes it futile to attempt to prepare a useful bibliographical essay. It would appear that the only viable alternative is to make a few statements about various types of materials and to refer the interested reader to the notes for more specific citations. Immediately following this note is an index of initial citations, which will enable readers to locate full citations of all sources easily.

Two more general studies of the free black in antebellum American should be mentioned: Ira Berlin, *Slaves without Masters: The Free Negro in the Antebellum South* (New York: Random House, 1974), and Leon F. Litwack, *North of Slavery: The Negro in the Free States, 1790–1860* (Chicago: University of Chicago Press, 1961). Neither of these authors specifically addresses the urban black experience, and, consequently, their works were not directly contributory to the preparation of this study, but both are excellent and perceptive treatments of the broader aspects of free black life.

There are several examinations of free persons of color or of blacks in general in the states in which these cities are located. Perhaps the most satisfactory is Herbert E. Sterkx's *The Free Negro in Ante-Bellum Louisiana* (Rutherford, N.J.: Fairleigh Dickinson University Press, 1972). Also valuable, though now badly dated, are Edward R. Turner, *The Negro in Pennsylvania: Slavery—Servitude—Freedom, 1639–1861* (Washington: American Historical Association, 1911), and James M. Wright, *The Free Negro in Maryuland, 1634–1860* (New York: Columbia University Press, 1921). Less useful, but still worth consulting, are Irving H. Bartlett, *From Slave to Citizen: The Story of the Negro in Rhode Island* (Providence: Urban League of Greater Providence, 1954); Donnie D. Bellamy, "Free Blacks in Antebellum Missouri, 1820–1860," *Missouri Historical Review* 67 (January 1973): 198–226; Jeffrey R. Brackett, *The Negro in Maryland* (Baltimore: Johns Hopkins University, 1889); Alice

Dunbar-Nelson, "People of Color in. Louisiana—Part II," *Journal of Negro History* 2 (January 1917): 51–78; Charles T. Hickok, *The Negro in Ohio, 1802–1870* (Cleveland: Western Reserve University, 1896); and Frank U. Quillin, *The Color Line in Ohio* (Ann Arbor: George Wahr, 1913). None of these works focuses on—and most hardly mention—the free black urban experience.

There are a few studies of free blacks in some of these fifteen cities. Two valuable treatments are Rhoda G. Freeman's wide-ranging "The Free Negro in New York City in the Era before the Civil War" (Ph.D. dissertation, Columbia University, 1966), and James O. Horton's more restricted "Black Activism in Boston, 1830–1860" (Ph.D. Dissertation, Brandeis University, 1973). Less satisfactory, but containing much useful material, are Donald M. Jacobs, "A History of the Boston Negro from the Revolution to the Civil War" (Ph.D. dissertation, Boston University, 1968), and Leonard P. Stavisky, "The Negro Artisan in the South Atlantic States, 1800–1860: A Study of Status and Economic Opportunity with Special Reference to Charleston" (Ph.D. dissertation, Columbia University, 1958). Two explorations of the Cincinnati free black community based heavily on newspaper sources are Richard C. Wade's "The Negro in Cincinnati, 1800–1830," *Journal of Negro History* 39 (January 1954): 43–57, and Carter G. Woodson's "The Negroes of Cincinnati Prior to the Civil War," *Journal of Negro History* 1 (January 1916): 1–22. Helpful in exploring the history of Charleston's free people of color are two articles by E. Horace Fitchett: "The Origins and Growth of the Free Negro in Charleston, South Carolina," *Journal of Negro History* 26 (October 1941): 421–37, and "The Traditions of the Free Negro in Charleston, South Carolina," *Journal of Negro History* 25 (April 1940): 139–52. Also useful to lesser and varying degrees are Herman D. Block, *The Circle of Discrimination: An Economic and Social Study of the Black Man in New York* (New York: New York University Press, 1969); John Daniels, *In Freedom's Birthplace: A Study of the Boston Negroes* (Boston: Houghton Mifflin, 1914); W. E. B. DuBois, *The Philadelphia Negro: A Social Study* (Philadelphia: University of Pennsylvania, 1899); Leo H. Hirsch, Jr., "The Negro in New York, 1783–1865," *Journal of Negro History* 16 (October 1931): 382–473; and Julian Rammelkamp, "The Providence Negro Community, 1820–1842," *Rhode Island History* 7 (January 1948): 20–33.

It must be acknowledged that very few of the studies cited in the preceding paragraphs have made any significant contribution, either individually or collectively, to this book. But they do contribute to a general understanding of the urban free blacks in antebellum America and occasionally (e.g., Freeman's dissertation) contain useful specific information.

And it is upon the collection, aggregation, analysis, and interpretation of vast amounts of specific data that this study rests, rather than on a synthesis of other scholars' syntheses or the testing of previously advanced theses or interpretations. The truly contributory sources, therefore, are multitudinous, and, at the same time, the individual importance of each such source is usually minute. It is possible, however, to speak in general terms about some of the more useful *varieties* of sources. In a number of cases I will make reference to specific notes in which representative samples of such materials are cited.

Several contemporary explorations—usually heavily statistical—of separate urban black communities have been helpful in a variety of contexts. Three Philadelphia compilations are unusually extensive: Benjamin C. Bacon, *Statistics of the Colored People of Philadelphia* (Philadelphia: Board of Education of the Pennsylvania Society for the Abolition of Slavery, 1859); Pennsylvania Society for Promoting the Abolition of Slavery, *The Present State and Condition of the Free People of Color, of the City of Philadelphia and Adjoining Districts* (Philadelphia: By the Society, 1838); and *A Statistical Inquiry into the Condition of the People of Colour, of the City and Districts of Philadelphia* (Philadelphia: Kite and Walton, 1849). Three other items—none as valuable as the Philadelphia compilations—are: "The Condition of the Colored Population of the City of Baltimore," *Baltimore Literary and Religious Magazine* 4 (April 1838): 168–76; Ohio Anti-Slavery Society, *Condition of the People of Color in the State of Ohio* (Boston: Isaac Knapp, 1839); and R. Spaulding, "Coloured People of Boston," *African Repository* 13 (March 1837): 88–91. A more general statement—highly argumentative, but containing some useful data (most drawn from the 1850 federal census)—is James F. Clarke's *The Present Condition of the Free Colored People of the United States* (New York: American Anti-slavery Society, 1859).

Three contemporary periodicals that contain much contributory material are: the *African Repository* (1825–1851); *DeBow's Review* (1846–1850); and *Niles' Weekly Register* (1811–1849; titled *Niles' National Register* after September 1, 1837). The *African Repository* was an official publication of the American Colonization Society and, consequently, must be employed with particular caution.

Useful in a number of contexts, especially in demographic matters, are the published returns of the federal censuses. The 1850 report is by far the most extensive, and mention must also be made of the extremely valuable compilation prepared by the superintendent of that census: J. B. D. DeBow, *Statistical View of the United States* (Washington: A. O. P. Nicholson, 1954). Also helpful, when available, are state and city censuses; see appendix B, note 6 for a listing of several of these compilations.

Essential in providing data on free black employment, nativity, and property ownership are the manuscript returns of the 1850 federal census (see chapter 2, note 8). City directories constitute the only generally available resource for exploring free black residential patterns and for the analysis of free black occupational patterns before 1850. Additionally, they provide much material on free black institutions and organizations. A representative sample of those employed can be found in appendix B, note 3.

Without access to a variety of reports and other publications of urban governmental and quasi-governmental bodies (often buried in more inclusive compilations), many areas of free black urban life simply could not have been adequately explored. By their very nature such sources are manifold, and the complete calendaring of those used is utterly impractical. Illustrative entries, however, will be found in various footnotes: e.g., ordinances (chapter 5, note 21; chapter 7, note 7); mortality (chapter 9, notes 3, 5); education (chapter 10, note 39); welfare (chapter 8, notes 3, 11, 25); property ownership (chapter 3, notes 6, 7; appendix C, note 5). Data on many of these same aspects of the urban black experience can be culled from the minutes of the American Convention of Abolition Societies (see chapter 10, notes 10, 11), and the proceedings of the so-called National Negro Conventions (see chapter 2, note 42; chapter 13, note 44).

Contemporary personal statements by antebellum blacks are not numerous, but some exist. Most extensive, of course, are slave narratives. A large number of these have been consulted, but few are even slightly germane to this study. Other black memoirs are harder to find and are usually not very helpful when located. Only one can be cited as making a substantial contribution to understanding an urban free black community—William J. Brown, *The Life of William J. Brown, of Providence, R.I.* (Freeport, N.Y.: Books for Libraries Press, 1971; orig. pub. 1883).

Dozens of travel accounts have been examined, perhaps the most useful of which are: Edward S. Abdy, *Journal of a Residence and Tour in the United States of North America, from April, 1833, to October, 1834,* 3 vols. (London: John Murray, 1835); James Silk Buckingham, *The Slave States of Ameria,* 2 cols. (London: Fisher, Son, [1842]); George Combe, *Notes on the United States of North America during a Phrenological Visit in 1838–9–40,* 2 vols. (Philadelphia: Carey and Hart, 1841); Charles Lyell, *A Second Visit to the United States of North America,* 2 vols. (London: John Murray, 1849); Frederick Marryat, *A Diary in America, with Remarks on Its Institutions* (New York: Knopf, 1962; orig. pub. 1839); and John Melish, *Travels through the United States of America, in the Years 1806 & 1807, and 1809, 1810, & 1811* (London: George Cowie, 1818).

Of the enumerating of the other works there would be no end once the process was begun. Consequently, the wisest course is not to start. It must suffice to note that I have examined innumerable histories of individual cities, of neighborhoods, of institutions, and of organizations. To these must be added dozens of dissertations and other specialized monographs and a mass of materials on as wide a spectrum of topics as my mind was capable of imagining, ranging in format from obscure pamphlets to multivolume sets of records and annals. These items are so diverse and extensive that I can do no more than suggest that readers peruse the voluminous documentation to this study contained in the notes. Even there they will find but a meager sampling of the sources consulted.

List of Initial Citations

Given below is the location of the initial citation of each source cited in this volume. The number preceding the colon indicates the chapter and that following the colon designates the note number. The letter P is used for notes in the preface and the letters A, B, C, and D for notes in the appendixes. All city directories are listed under "City Directories."

Abdy, *Journal* 2:22

Adams, "Disfranchisement of Negroes in New England" 5:22

African Methodist Episcopal Church, *Centennial Budget* 11:10

African Observer 10:47

Albany Board of School Commissioners, *Report, 1852* 10:34

Allen, *Negro in New York* 5:26

American Convention of Abolition Societies, *Minutes, 1800* 10:10

——, *Minutes, 1801* 10:11

——, *Minutes, 1804* 10:11

——, *Minutes, 1805* 10:11

——, *Minutes, 1806* 7:3

——, *Minutes, 1812* 10:21

——, *Minutes, 1816* 10:10

——, *Minutes, 1817* 10:10

——, *Minutes, 1818* 10:11

——, *Minutes, 1821* 10:11

——, *Minutes, 1823* 2:25

——, *Minutes, 1825* 10:10

——, *Minutes, 1828* 10:11

——, *Minutes, 1829* 13:32

Andrews, *History of the New-York African Free-Schools* 10:11

Anti-Slavery Record 2:54

Appeal on Behalf of a House of Refuge for Colored Juvenile Delinquent 5:28

Aptheker, *Documentary History of the Negro People* 5:4

Augustin, *Digest of Ordinances of New-Orleans* 5:27

Bacon, *Statistics of the Colored People of Philadelphia* 2:20

Baldwin, *Pittsburgh* 5:27

Baltimore, *Ordinances, 1830* 8:3

——, *Ordinances, 1831* 5:23

——, *Ordinances, 1832* 7:7

——, *Ordinances, 1833* 8:3

——, *Ordinances, 1834* 8:3

——, *Ordinances, 2835* 8:3

——, *Ordinances, 1836* 7:7

——, *Ordinances, 1837* 7:7

——, *Ordinances, 1839* 5:28

——, *Ordinances, 1840* 5:12

——, *Ordinances, 1841* 7:7

——, *Ordinances, 1842* 7:7

——, *Ordinances, 1843* 7:7

——, *Ordinances, 1844* 7:7

——, *Ordinances, 1845* 5:24

——, *Ordinances, 1846* 7:7

——, *Ordinances, 1847* 7:7

——, *Ordinances, 1848* 7:7

——, *Ordinances, 1849* 7:7

——, *Ordinances, 1850* 7:7

——, *Ordinances, 1851* 7:7

Baltimore, City Health Department, *First Thirty-Five Reports* 4:9

Baltimore, Trustees for the Poor, *Report, 1828* 8:3

Bardolph, "Social Origins of Distinguished Negroes" 10:12

Barker, "Philadelphia in the Late 'Forties" 6:20

Barnard, "Special Report of the Commissioner of Education, D.C." 6:7

Bartlett, *Slave to Citizen* 6:16

Clark, *Communication from the Mayor*
6:12

Clark, "Samuel Nicholls Smallwood" 5:3

———, "William Winston Seaton" 5:30

Clarke, *Present Condition of the Free Colored People* 2:54

Clephane, "Slavery in the District of Columbia" 5:27

Combe, *Notes on the United States* 2:31

"Condition of the Coloured Population of Baltimore" 10:17

Crawford, *Report on Penitentiaries of the United States* 7:11

Cromwell, "First Negro Churches in the District of Columbia" 11:20

Curry, *New-York* 5:3

Dabney, *Cincinnati's Colored Citizens* 3:18

Dabney, *Schools for Negroes in D.C.* 10:17

Daniels, *In Freedom's Birthplace* 4:31

Davis, *History of Freemasonry among Negroes* 12:31

Davis, *Noah Davis* 10:19

Dawson and DeSaussure, *Census of Charleston, 1848* 1:12

DeBow, *Statistical View* 1:1

Degler, "Labor in the Economy and Politics of New York City, 1850–1860" 2:24

Delany, *Condition of the Colored People* 2:35

———, *Origin and Objects of Ancient Freemasonry* 5:5

Dennison, *Dorr War* 13:17

Dickens, *American Notes* 5:28

Dix, *Review of the State Penitentiary of Kentucky* 8:1

Doggett, *The Great Metropolis* 8:28

Douglass, *Annals of the First African Church* 10:14

Douglass, *My Bondage and My Freedom* 2:27

Drake, *Picture of Cincinnati* 5:2

Drake and Mansfield, *Cincinnati in 1826* 6:22

Drew, *North-Side View of Slavery* 2:28

Drowne, *Commemorative Discourse* 11:44

DuBois, *Economic Cooperation among Negroes* 12:4

———, *The Negro Artisan* 2:7

———, *The Negro Church* 11:1

———, *Philadelphia Negro* 4:10

Dunbar-Nelson, "People of Color in Louisiana" 10:22

Eaton, "Dangerous Pamphlet in the Old South" 13:26

Elliot, *Historical Sketches of D.C.* 11:51

Elliot, *Washington Guide* 9:10

Ellis, *Lancastrian Schools in Philadelphia* 10:8

Emerson, "Medical Statistics of Twenty Years" 9:2

———, "Medical Statistics, 1821–30" 9:3

———, "Vital Statistics, 1831–40" 9:3

Everest, *Journey through the United States* 8:19

———, "Pauperism and Crime" 7:19

Everett, "Emigres and Militiamen" 1:5

Farrison, "William Wells Brown in Buffalo" 12:19

Fearon, *Sketches of America* 5:27

Feldberg, "Philadelphia Riots of 1844" 6:25

Fenner, *Raising the Veil* 4:31

Ferguson, *Methodism in Washington* 11:19

Fisher, *Diary* 2:39

Fleming, *History of Pittsburgh* 8:1

Foote, *Schools of Cincinnati* 11:21

Ford, *Census of Charleston, 1861* 3:6

Ford and Ford, *History of Cincinnati* 6:24

Forten, *Address Delivered before the Ladies' Anti-Slavery Society of Philadelphia* 13:22

———, *Letters from a Man of Colour* 5:4

Fossier, *New Orleans* 5:26

Foster, *New York in Slices* 2:41

———, "Philadelphia in Slices" 4:2

Fox, *American Colonization Society* 13:41

Fox, "Negro Vote in Old New York" 5:22

Freeman, "Free Negro in New York City" 2:14

Frichett, "Status of the Free Negro in Charleston" 12:10

Funke, "Negro in Education" 10:7

Furman, *Views of the Baptists Relative to the Coloured Population* 5:3

Gaillard, "Sanitary Condition of Charleston" 1:12

Garrison, *Thoughts on Colonization* 13:41

Geffen, "Violence in Philadelphia in the 1840s and 1850s" 6:20

George, *Segregated Sabbaths* 10:14

Gibson, *Public Career of W. H. Gibson* 10:27

Gill, *Selections from the Court Reports* 5:31

Gillard, *Catholic Church and the Negro* 11:48

Goldin, *Urban Slavery in the American South* P:4

Gordon, *Negro Life and History in South Carolina* 10:3

Greene and Woodson, *Negro Wage Earner* 2:51

Greenleaf, *History of the Churches of New York* 11:12

Greve, *History of Cincinnati* 5:19

Griffith, *Annals of Baltimore* 2:31

Grimshaw, *Freemasonry among the Colored People* 12:29

Griscom, *Sanitary Condition of the Laboring Population of New York* 4:13

Hall, *Two-Fold Slavery* 2:8

Hardie, *Census of New Buildings* 7:8

———, *Description of New York* 7:8

Hardy, *Manual of New York (1870)* 8:31

Harris, *Negro as Capitalist* 12:2

Hazard's Register of Pennsylvania 6:26

Hazard's U.S. Register 6:27

Headley, *Great Riots of New York* 6:13

Hershkowitz, "New York City, 1834–1840" 2:14

Hesseltine, "Four American Traditions" 10:5

Hickok, *Negro in Ohio* 2:22

Hill, *Municipality of Buffalo* 11:30

Hirsch, "Negro in New York, 1783–1865" 5:26

History of American Methodism 11:11

History of the Ohio Falls Cities 11:19

Homans, *History of Boston* 11:31

———, *Sketches of Boston* 10:41

Horton, "Black Activism in Boston" 4:2

Hough, *Statistics of Population of New York* 5:22

Howard, *Public Health Administration in Baltimore* 9:3

Savage, *History of the Boston Watch* 6:11

Savage, *Presbyterian Church in New York City* 11:36

Scharf, *History of Baltimore* 10:3

———, *History of St. Louis* 3:20

Scharf and Wescott, *History of Philadelphia* 2:39

Schneider, "Mob Violence and Public Order in the American City" 5:21

Schoolcraft, *Letters on the Condition of the African Race* 2:19

Series of Letters and Documents Relating to the Late Epidemic 4:9

Shattuck, *Bills of Mortality of Boston* 9:5

———, *Census of Boston for the Year 1845* 5:22

Shaw, *Description of Boston* 10:14

Sheeler, "Struggle of the Negro in Ohio" 6:22

Shepard, *Early History of St. Louis* 6:5

Sherer, "Negro Churches in Rhode Island" 11:21

Shotwell, *History of the Schools of Cincinnati* 10:4

Silcox, "Negro Public Education in Antebellum Philadelphia" 10:37

Smith, *History of Buffalo* 11:21 ·

Smith, *Philadelphia As It Is in 1852* 8:13

Smyth, *Discourses on the Great Fire in Charleston* 1:12

Snow, *Census of Providence, 1855* B:6

Snow, *History of Boston* 10:42

Society for the Reformation of Juvenile Delinquents in the City and State of New-York, *Tenth Annual Report* 7:17

———, *Eleventh Annual Report* 7:18

———, *Twelfth Annual Report* 7:18

———, *Thirteenth Annual Report* 7:18

———, *Fourteenth Annual Report* 7:18

———, *Fifteenth Annual Report* 7:18

"Some Letters of Richard Allen and Absalom Jones" 11:41

Spaulding, "Coloured People of Boston" 2:23

Staples, *Annals of Providence* 6:18

Statistical Inquiry into the Condition of the People of Colour of Philadelphia 1:7

"Statisticks of Destitution in Baltimore" 10:45

Staudenraus, *African Colonization Movement* 13:38

Stavisky, "Negro Artisan in the South Atlantic States " 2:9

Steele, "Buffalo Common Schools" 10:34

Sterkx, *Free Negro in Louisiana* 1:5

Sterling, *Martin Robinson Delany* 6:9

Stiles, *History of Brooklyn* 10:35

Still, "New York City in 1824" 2:31

Stone, *History of New York* 6:13

Taeuber and Taeuber, *Negroes in Cities* 4:16

Taylor, *Recollections of the Early Days of the National Guard* 6:13

Teale, *Municipal Register of Brooklyn* 12:20

Teeters, "Early Days of the Philadelphia House of Refuge" 5:28

———, *They Were in Prison* 7:11

Thorpe, *Federal and State Constituions* 5:15

Townsend, *South Carolina Baptists* 11:30

Trexler, *Slavery in Missouri* 5:21

Turner, *Negro in Pennsylvania* 5:5

———, *Slavery in Pennsylvania* 1:2

Tyson, *Life of Elisha Tyson* 11:49

Ullman, *Martin R. Delany* 6:9

U.S., Census Office, *Census, 1800* 1:1

———, *Census, 1810* A:1

———, *Census, 1820* 1:6

———, *Census, 1830* 1:6

———, *Census, 1840* 3:7

———, *Census, 1850* 1:1

———, *Historical Statistics* 1:1

———, *Mortality Statistics, 1850* 1:18

———, *Statistics of the U.S. in 1860* 9:6

U.S., Commissioner of Education, *Schools for the Colored Population* 5:21

U.S., Congress, House of Representatives, Committee for the District of Columbia, "Report of Grand Jury" 5:16

Valentine, *Manual, 1844–45* 7:8

———, *Manual, 1845–46* 7:8

———, *Manual, 1847* 7:8

———, *Manual, 1848* 9:3

———, *Manual, 1850* 10:40

———, *Manual, 1854* 13:5

———, *Manual, 1856* A:4

Van Heusen, "Albany Lancaster School" 4:7

Varle, *Complete View of Baltimore* 10:15

Viles, "Population in Missouri before 1804" 1:1

Wade, "Negro in Cincinnati" 4:6

———, *Slavery in the Cities* P:3

Walker, *Appeal* 13:23

Notes

Preface

1. Carl Bridenbaugh, *Cities in the Wilderness: The First Century of Urban Life in America, 1625–1742* (New York: Ronald Press, 1938); Carl Bridenbaugh, *Cities in Revolt: Urban Life in America, 1743–1776* (New York: Knopf, 1959).

2. Blake McKelvey, *The Urbanization of America, 1860–1915* (New Brunswick, N.J.: Rutgers University Press, 1963); Blake McKelvey, *The Emergence of Metropolitan America, 1915–1966* (New Brunswick, N.J.: Rutgers University Press, 1968).

3. Richard C. Wade, *Slavery in the Cities: The South, 1820–1860* (New York: Oxford University Press, 1964).

4. Claudia D. Goldin, *Urban Slavery in the American South, 1820–1860: A Quantitative History* (Chicago: University of Chicago Press, 1976).

Chapter 1

1. U.S., Census Office, *Return of the Whole Number of Persons within the Several Districts of the United States,* [1800] (Washington: William Duane and Son, 1802), pp. 14, 38, 39, 44, 49, 57, 68, 77, 84; Wilhelmus B. Bryan, *A History of the National Capital* (New York: Macmillan, 1914–16), 2:136n; J. B. D. DeBow, *Statistical View of the United States* (Washington: A. O. P. Nicholson, 1854), p. 192; Jonas Viles, "Population and Extent of Settlement in Missouri before 1804," *Missouri Historical Review* 5 (July 1911): 208; U.S., Census Office, *The Seventh Census of the United States: 1850* (Washington: Robert Armstrong, 1853), pp. 52, 67, 92, 96, 99, 102, 158, 179, 221, 234, 339, 474, 612, 662, 830; U.S., Bureau of the Census, *Historical Statistics of the United States: Colonial Times to 1957* (Washington: Government Printing Office, 1960), pp. 8, 14.

2. George H. Moore, *Notes on the History of Slavery in Massachusetts* (New York: D. Appleton, 1866), pp. 210–14; Edward R. Turner, *Slavery in Pennsylvania* (Baltimore: Lord Baltimore Press, 1911), pp. 78–79; William D. Johnson, *Slavery in Rhode Island, 1755–1776* (Providence: Rhode Island Historical Society, 1894), p. 164; Edgar J. McManus, *A History of Negro Slavery in New York* (Syracuse: Syracuse University Press, 1966), pp. 174–75; Jeffrey R. Brackett, "The Status of the Slave," in J. Franklin Jameson, ed., *Essays in the Constitutional History of the United States in the Formative Period, 1775–1789* (Boston: Houghton Mifflin, 1889), pp. 287–95, 297–99; DeBow, *Statistical View,* p. 63.

3. DeBow, *Statistical View,* p. 63; U.S., Bureau of the Census, *Historical Statistics,* p. 13.

4. U.S., Census Office, *Census, 1800,* pp. 14, 38, 39, 44, 49, 57, 68, 77, 84; Viles, "Population in Missouri before 1804," p. 208; Bryan, *National Capital* 2:136n; DeBow, *Statistical View,* p. 192.

5. Herbert E. Sterkx, *The Free Negro in Ante-Bellum Louisiana* (Rutherford, N.J.: Fairleigh Dickinson University Press, 1972), pp. 91–93; Donald E. Everett, "Emigres

and Militiamen: Free Persons of Color in New Orleans, 1803–1815," *Journal of Negro History* 38 (October 1953): 381–83.

6. U.S., Census Office, *Census, 1800,* pp. 39, 44; *Census for 1820* (Washington: Gales and Seaton, 1821), pp. 9*, 13; *Fifth Census; or, Enumeration of the Inhabitants of the United States, 1830* (Washington: Duff Green, 1832), third pagination, pp. 36–37, 50–51.

7. Jesse Chickering, *A Statistical View of the Population of Massachusetts, 1760–1840* (Boston: C. C. Little and J. Brown, 1846), pp. 128, 153, 155; Jesse Chickering, *Report of the Committee Appointed by the City Council; and Also a Comparative View of the Population of Boston in 1850, with the Births, Marriages, and Deaths, in 1849 and 1850, by Jesse Chickering, M.D.* (Boston: J. H. Eastburn, 1851), p. 25; Charles Cist, *Cincinnati in 1841: Early Annals and Future Prospects* (Cincinnati: For the Author, 1841), pp. 34, 37; *A Statistical Inquiry into the Condition of the People of Colour, of the City and Districts of Philadelphia* (Philadelphia: Kite and Walton, 1849), p. 10.

8. *Miscellaneous Remarks on the Police of Boston* (Boston: Cummings and Hilliard, 1814), p. 32; Carter G. Woodson, *Free Negro Heads of Families in the United States in 1830* (Washington: Association for the Study of Negro Life and History, 1925), pp. xlii–xliii. Immigration from the Caribbean into New Orleans had been very large in the first decade of the nineteenth century, causing a doubling of its number of free persons of color. The large number of free blacks that the 1850 census enumerators listed as having been born in the West Indies suggests that this immigration continued after 1810. See Everett, "Emigres and Militiamen," pp. 381–82, 385; Sterkx, *Free Negro in Louisiana,* pp. 191–94.

9. The concomitant of this conclusion is that the growth of the native black population in these cities was eroded by low birth rates, high mortality, out-migration, increasingly inaccurate enumeration, or some combination of these.

10. DeBow, *Statistical View,* p. 63.

11. Chickering, *Population of Massachusetts, 1760–1840,* pp. 135–53. Chickering estimated that Boston's black population was the same in 1840 as in 1830, but he appears to have overestimated the census error in ward two.

12. P. C. Gaillard, "Report on the Sanitary Condition of Charleston, South Carolina," American Medical Association *Transactions* 2 (1849): 579; Thomas Smyth, *Two Discourses on the Great Fire in Charleston* (Charleston: J. P. Beile, 1838), passim; Charleston, *Year Book—1880* (Charleston: News and Courier Book Press, 1880), pp. 257, 274–76; J. L. Dawson and H. W. De Saussure, *Census of the City of Charleston, South Carolina, for the Year 1848* (Charleston: J. B. Nixon, 1849), pp. 1–2; U.S., Census Office, *Census, 1830,* pp. 94–95.

13. DeBow, *Statistical View,* p. 63. Connecticut, New Hampshire, Vermont, and Mississippi also reported losses in their free black populations in the 1840s.

14. It was accepted axiomatically in the mid-nineteenth century that males were more aggressive, assertive, and prone to violence than females. Consequently, masters were less fearful that female slaves might be moved to abscond or rise in revolt. Additionally, slave women were often "chained" to their place of bondage by the presence of small children.

15. Cf. table A-10, and DeBow, *Statistical View,* p. 66. The exceptions were Washington in 1820; Buffalo in 1830, 1840, and 1850; Pittsburgh in 1840; and St. Louis in 1850. In the case of Pittsburgh the difference was minute—a ratio of 110.06 females to each 100 males in the city as compared with 110.33 in the state.

16. The federal censuses were taken in the summer months with a presumed effective date of June 1. During this season some considerable portion of free black males (and some white males as well) may have been absent from the city while employed in such seasonal and largely rural occupations as canal and railroad construction. Additionally,

although persons temporarily absent from their residences were supposed to be reported, it is by no means certain that this was uniformly done. See DeBow, *Statistical View,* p. 41n.

17. Boston, New Orleans, and New York were excluded because the city and the county (or parish) boundaries were either identical or substantially the same.

18. U.S., Census Office, *Mortality Statistics of the Seventh Census of the United States, 1850* (Washington: A. O. P. Nicholson, 1855), p. 13. See also table A-16.

19. See tables A-10 and A-15. The proportion of children was, of course, much lower in the urban centers than in the country as a whole for all three population elements, though the differential was much greater for the slave component than for the other two (see table A-16). When New Orleans and Charleston are excluded, the rank-order correlation (Spearman) for the percentages of females and children in the free black urban populations was −.46 in 1820, −.55 in 1830, −.23 in 1840, and +.26 in 1850.

20. See tables A-10 and A-16.

21. U.S., Census Office, *Census, 1850,* pp. 52, 67, 92, 96, 99, 102, 158, 179, 221, 234, 339, 474, 612, 662, 830; DeBow, *Statistical View,* pp. 45, 63. The free black population had, of course, been disproportionately urban throughout the half-century. In 1800 roughly one-eighth of all free Negroes resided in these cities. See. U.S., Census Office, *Census, 1800,* pp. 14, 38, 39, 44, 49, 57, 68, 77, 89; Bryand, *National Capital* 2:136n; Viles, "Population in Missouri before 1804," p. 208; DeBow, *Statistical View,* pp. 45, 63, 192.

Chapter 2

1. F. J. Kingsbury, "The Tendency of Men to Live in Cities," *Journal of Social Science* 33 (November 1895): 18.

2. Louisville, City Council, *A Collection of the Acts of Virginia and Kentucky, Relative to Louisville and Portland: With the Charter of Louisville and the Amendments Thereto* (Louisville: Prentice and Weissinger, 1839), pp. 69, 128.

3. St. Louis, City Council, *The Revised Ordinances of the City of St. Louis,* ed. Wilson Primm (St. Louis: Missouri Argus Office, 1836), pp. 143–46; Charleston, City Council, *A Digest of the Ordinances of the City Council of Charleston. From the Year 1783 to Oct. 1844,* comp. George B. Eckhard (Charleston: Walker and Burke, 1844), pp. 219–55; John C. Hurd, *The Law of Freedom and Bondage in the United States* (Boston: Little, Brown, 1859–62), 2:98.

4. Washington, City Council, *Laws of the Corporation of the City of Washington,* [1837] (Washington: Jacob Gideon, Jr., 1836 [should be 1837]), p. 176. It will be noted that the laws and ordinances cited were enacted in the years immediately following the Nat Turner uprising.

5. Hurd, *Law of Freedom and Bondage* 2:19–25, 156–69; Sterkx, *Free Negro in Louisiana,* p. 162; James M. Wright, *The Free Negro in Maryland, 1634–1860* (New York: Columbia University Press, 1921), p. 97.

6. Jeffrey R. Brackett, *The Negro in Maryland* (Baltimore: Johns Hopkins University, 1889), pp. 211–12; Louisville, *Acts (1839),* pp. 151–52; St. Louis, *Ordinances (1836),* pp. 143–46.

7. Brackett, *Negro in Maryland,* pp. 209–10; W. E. Burghardt Du Bois, *The Negro Artisan* (Atlanta: Atlanta University Press, 1902), p. 15.

8. Brackett, *Negro in Maryland,* p. 209; Wright, *Free Negro in Maryland,* p. 97. There is no evidence to support Marshall Hall's oft-repeated assertion, "In Baltimore, a person of colour, however said to be free, may not drive a dray." See Marshall Hall, *The Two-Fold Slavery of the United States* (London: Adam Scott, 1854), p. 137. The federal census of 1850 listed 373 free men of color employed as draymen and 240 as carters.

See Manuscript Returns of the Seventh Census of the United States (1850), Population Schedules, Record Group 29, Microfilm Pub. 432, National Archives, Washington, D.C., Reels 281–87; hereafter cited as Mss. Census (1850).

9. Charleston, City Council, *Ordinances of the City of Charleston, from the 19th of August 1844, to the 14th of September 1854,* comp. H. Pickney Walker (Charleston: A. E. Miller, 1854), p. 28; Leonard P. Stavisky, "The Negro Artisan in the South Atlantic States, 1800–1860: A Study of Status and Economic Opportunity with Special Reference to Charleston," Ph.D. Diss., Columbia University, 1958, p. 132. The Charleston councils did pass legislation in 1843 (perhaps as a sop to the white petitioners) that made it slightly more difficult for Negroes to obtain cart licenses than it was for whites. The former were thereafter required to produce certificates of good character signed by "three respectable inhabitants of the city." See Charleston, *Ordinances (1783–1844),* pp. 41–42.

10. Sterkx, *Free Negro in Louisiana,* p. 221.

11. Louisville, *Acts (1839),* p. 120.

12. Washington, *Laws (1837),* pp. 176, 180–81.

13. Mss. Census (1850), Reels 56–57, 850.

14. Herman D. Block, *The Circle of Discrimination: An Economic and Social Study of the Black Man in New York* (New York: New York University Press, 1969), p. 28; Rhoda G. Freeman, "The Free Negro in New York City in the Era before the Civil War," Ph.D. Diss., Columbia University, 1966, pp. 291–94; Leo Hershkowitz, "New York City, 1834–1840: A Study in Local Politics" Ph.D. Diss., New York University, 1960, p. 326. The quotation is from the last-named source.

15. Mss. Census (1850), Reels 534–59; John Doggett, Jr., *Doggett's New-York City Directory, for 1846 and 1847* (New York: John Doggett, Jr., 1846), passim.

16. Mss. Census (1850), Reels 334–39 (Boston), 471–72 (Albany), 501–2 (Buffalo), 517–20 (Brooklyn), 534–59 (New York City), 687–91 (Cincinnati), 745–46 (Pittsburgh), 812–17 (Philadelphia), 844–45 (Providence).

17. Mss. Census (1850), Reels 56–57 (Washington), 206–7 (Louisville), 235–38 (New Orleans), 281–87 (Baltimore), 415–18 (St. Louis), 850 (Charleston).

18. Quoted in "Letters to Anti-Slavery Workers and Agencies," *Journal of Negro History* 10 (July 1925): 408–19.

19. [Mary H. Schoolcraft], *Letters on the Condition of the African Race in the United States* (Philadelphia: T. K. and P. G. Collins, 1852), p. 7.

20. Benjamin C. Bacon, *Statistics of the Colored People of Philadelphia* (Philadelphia: T. Ellwood, 1859), p. 15.

21. *Register of Trades of the Colored People in the City of Philadelphia and Districts* (Philadelphia: Merrihew and Gunn, 1838), pp. 1–8.

22. Charles T. Hickok, *The Negro in Ohio, 1802–1870* (Cleveland: Western Reserve University, 1896), p. 114; Ohio Anti-Slavery Society, *Condition of the People of Color in the State of Ohio* (Boston: Isaac Knapp, 1839), pp. 8–9; Benson J. Lossing, *History of New York City* (New York: Perine, 1884), pp. 221–22; Edward S. Abdy, *Journal of a Residence and Tour in the United States of North America, from April, 1833, to October, 1834* (London: John Murray, 1835), 1:121–22.

23. Charles Stimpson, Jr., *Stimpson's Boston Directory* (Boston: Charles Stimpson, Jr., 1835), passim; R. Spaulding, "Coloured People of Boston," *African Repository* 13 (March 1837): 89.

24. Carl N. Degler, "Labor in the Economy and Politics of New York City, 1850–1860: A Study of the Impact of Early Industrialization," Ph.D. Diss., Columbia University, 1952, p. 140; John R. Young, ed., *Memorial History of the City of Philadelphia* (New York: New York History Company, 1895–98), 2:223; Ellis P. Oberholtzer, *Philadelphia: A History of the City and Its People* (Philadelphia: S. J. Clarke, [1912]), 2:288.

25. American Convention of Abolition Societies, *Minutes of the Eighteenth Session of the American Convention for Promoting the Abolition of Slavery, and Improving the Condition of the African Race, [1823]* (Philadelphia: Daniel Neall, 1823), p. 13.

26. Quoted in "Letters to Anti-Slavery Workers," pp. 408–9.

27. Frederick Douglass, *My Bondage and My Freedom* (New York: Miller, Orton and Mulligan, 1855), pp. 311–12; Wright, *Free Negro in Maryland,* pp. 173–74 (quotation from p. 173); Ira Berlin, "Slaves Who Were Free: The Free Negro in the Upper South, 1776–1861," Ph.D. Diss., University of Wisconsin, 1970, pp. 363–64. Latrobe's comment was made with particular reference to unskilled employment.

28. Benjamin Drew, *A North-Side View of Slavery* (Boston: John P. Jewett, 1856), pp. 240–41.

29. Charles Lyell, *A Second Visit to the United States of North America* (London: John Murray, 1849), 2:160–61; Frederick L. Olmsted, *A Journey in the Seaboard Slave States, with Remarks on Their Economy* (New York: Mason Brothers, 1859), pp. 587–90; Sterkx, *Free Negro in Louisiana,* pp. 221–22. See also, Charles B. Rousseve, *The Negro in Louisiana* (New Orleans: Xavier University Press, 1937), pp. 46–47.

30. *City Characters; or, Familiar Scenes in Town* (Philadelphia: George S. Appleton, 1851), pp. 15, 36, 82–84, 98–100.

31. John T. Prince. "Boston in 1813, Reminiscences of an Old School-Boy," *Bostonian Society Publications* 3, 1st Ser. (1906): 82; Bayard Still, ed., "New York City in 1824: A Newly Discovered Description [by Samuel H. Jenks]," *New York Historical Society Quarterly* 46 (April 1962): 149; George Combe, *Notes of the United States of North America during a Phrenological Visit in 1838–9–40* (Philadelphia: Carey and Hart, 1841), 1:93, 328; Abdy, *Journal* 1:66; Thomas W. Griffith, *Annals of Baltimore* (Baltimore: William Wooddy, 1833), p. 292.

32. Charles H. Wesley, *Negro Labor in the United States, 1850–1925* (New York: Vanguard Press, 1927; repr. Russell and Russell, 1967), p. 76.

33. E.g., William Chambers, *Things As They Are in America* (London: William and Robert Chambers, 1854), p. 189.

34. Mss. Census (1850), Reels 56–57, 415–18, 471–72, 501–2, 534–59, 687–91, 812–17. The percentage figures were: Buffalo—16.48%, Cincinnati—17.42%, St. Louis—20.13%, Washington—20.77%, Albany—22.44%, New York—24.76%, Philadelphia—25.95%. In Baltimore, Brooklyn, Buffalo, Louisville, and Providence the figure was between 11.15% and 11.93% and in Pittsburgh was 14.91%. See ibid., Reels 206–7, 281–87, 501–2, 517–20, 745–46, 844–45. The very low percentages of free men of color employed as servants, waiters, and stewards in Charleston (0.69%) and New Orleans (1.99%) appear to represent a continuation of past employment patterns in these cities. See ibid., Reels 235–38, 850; George W. F. Howard, Earl of Carlisle, *Travels in America [in 1841]* (New York: G. P. Putnam, 1851), p. 61; and pp. 20–21, above. Ousting of Negroes from these occupations by new immigrants (especially Irish) appears to have been most pronounced in Boston, where only 6.16% of black males were so employed in 1850. Data drawn from earlier city directories suggest that this figure represents a substantial decline in the number of blacks following these vocations. See Mss. Census (1850), Reels 334–39; *Stimpson's Boston Directory (1835),* passim; Charles Stimpson, Jr., *Stimpson's Boston Directory* (Boston: Charles Stimpson, Jr., 1840), passim; Charles Stimpson, *Stimpson's Boston Directory* (Boston: Charles Stimpson, 1845), passim.

35. Martin R. Delany, *The Condition, Elevation, Emigration, and Destiny of the Colored People of the United States* (Philadelphia: King and Baird, 1852), pp. 110–12; *Niles' National Register,* June 13, 1848, p. 384; Mss. Census (1850), Reel 537, p. 43, ln. 13; Reel 537, p. 123, ln. 24; Reel 541, p. 39, ln. 24; Reel 687, p. 318, ln. 21; Reel 688, p. 639, ln. 39; Reel 817, p. 834, ln. 2; and passim.

36. C. S. Williams, *Williams' Cincinnati Directory and Business Advertiser, for 1850–*

1851 (Cincinnati: C. S. Williams, 1850), pp. 313–14; *McElroy's Philadelphia Directory, for 1852* (Philadelphia: Edward C. and John Biddle, 1852), pp. 164, 200; Mss. Census (1850), Reel 812, p. 404, ln. 29; Reel 814, p. 213, ln. 42, and passim.

37. *McElroy's Philadelphia Directory, for 1852*, pp. 185, 390; Mss. Census (1850), Reel 812, p. 270, ln. 33; Reel 813, p. 691, ln. 10; Daniel A. Payne, *History of the African Methodist Episcopal Church* (Nashville: A.M.E. Sunday School Union, 1891), 1:85. This situation was common elsewhere as well. The Cincinnati census marshal recorded John Hall as a Baptist preacher, but the directory compiler listed him as a bricklayer. See Mss. Census (1850), Reel 687, p. 118, ln. 18; *Williams' Cincinnati Directory, for 1850–1851,* p. 120.

38. Mss. Census (1850), passim. The figure is 29.69%.

39. Mss. Census (1850), passim; Jane Campbell, "Old Philadelphia Music," *Philadelphia History* 2 (1926): 189; Sidney G. Fisher, *A Philadelphia Perspective: The Diary of Sidney George Fisher Covering the Years 1834–1871,* ed. Nicholas B. Wainwright (Philadelphia: Historical Society of Pennsylvania, 1967), pp. 70, 73; J. Thomas Scharf and Thompson Wescott, *A History of Philadelphia* (Philadelphia: L. H. Everts, 1884), 2:993.

40. Mss. Census (1850), passim.

41. [George G. Foster], *New York in Slices* (New York: W. F. Burgess, 1849), pp. 93–95; Lossing, *History of New York City,* pp. 97, 100; Henry Wilson, *The Directory of the City of New-York, for 1852–1853* (New York: John F. Trow, 1852), p. 182; Thomas Longworth, *Longworth's American Almanac, New-York Register, and City Directory* (New York: Thomas Longworth, 1835), p. 358; Carter G. Woodson, "The Negroes of Cincinnati Prior to the Civil War," *Journal of Negro History* 1 (January 1916): 21–22.

42. Mss. Census (1850), Reels 334–39.

43. Ibid., passim.

44. Ibid., Reels 206–7, 235–38, 334–39, 534–59, 812–17, 850. All of these statements are based on analyses which exclude census entries for agricultural entrepreneurial activity from the category totals. Hence, wherever the term entrepreneurial is used, it should be understood to mean nonagricultural entrepreneurial activity.

45. Obviously, it is not suggested that latitude can be viewed as influencing black occupational patterns. But some conditions (such as the strength and persistence of the slave system and accompanying attitudes) are tightly tied to geographic location while others (such as city size or rapidity of urban growth) are not.

46. DeBow, *Statistical View,* pp. 272–73, 278–79, 399. Because city figures are not available, county figures were used for Brooklyn (Kings County) and Pittsburgh (Allegheny County).

47. Ibid., p. 192.

48. U.S., Census Office, *Census, 1850,* pp. 52, 67, 92, 96, 99, 102, 158, 179, 221, 234, 339, 474, 612, 662, 830.

49. DeBow, *Statistical View,* pp. 202–5, 242–59, 266–83, 290–307. County figures were used for this analysis because city figures are not available.

50. U.S., Census Office, *Census, 1850,* pp. x–xii.

51. If the 1830 figures on free black employment in Boston published by the *African Repository* are correct, it would appear that occupational patterns for this segment of the population improved slightly over the next two decades. The total increase, however, was only about .0500 on the index of occupational opportunity scale (from .0919 to .1421) and still left Boston's blacks in a deplorably depressed employment situation. See Lorenzo J. Greene and Carter G. Woodson, *The Negro Wage Earner* (Washington: Association for the Study of Negro Life and History, 1930), p. 5.

52. DeBow, *Statistical View,* pp. 202–5, 242–59, 266–83, 290–307.

53. Such a relationship is, of course, suggested by the moderately large negative

coefficient of correlation between black occupational opportunity and the per capita annual value of manufactured product. See p. 30.

54. Lyell *Second Visit*, 2:98–99; *Anti-Slavery Record* 3 (December 1837): 14? See also James F. Clarke, *The Present Condition of the Free Colored People of the United States* (New York: American Antislavery Society, 1859), p. 16. One of the most unexpected and startling results of the analyses upon which much of this chapter is based was the discovery that the employment pattern of Charleston's slaves was more favorable than that of free blacks in one Upper South and five northern cities. The index of occupational opportunity was .1694 for the male slaves of Charleston and ranged from .1366 to .1678 for free black males in Pittsburgh, Boston, Providence, New York, Albany, and St. Louis. See Dawson and De Saussure, *Census of the City of Charleston, 1848*, p. 34; Mss. Census (1850), Reels 334–39, 415–18, 471–72, 534–59, 745–46, 844–45.

55. Marshall Hall, it is true, spoke of "that prejudice which subsists against him [the Negro] in the northern States, a prejudice unknown in the south, where the domestic relation between the African and the European are so much more intimate." But it is clear that Hall was speaking specifically about the manifestation of prejudice in the form of occupational distribution. See Hall, *Two-Fold Slavery*, p. 17.

56. Ben Casseday, *The History of Louisville from Its Earliest Settlements to the Year 1852* (Louisville: Hull and Brother, 1852), pp. 228–30; Mss. Census (1850), Reels 206–7. Whites constituted approximately 97.24% of the employed males in Louisville.

Chapter 3

1. Wesley, *Negro Labor in the United States*, p. 53; A Merchant of Philadelphia, *Memoirs and Autobiography of Some of the Wealthy Citizens of Philadelphia, with a Fair Estimate of Their Estate* (Philadelphia: Booksellers, 1846), p. 58.

2. Additionally, erroneous entries can, in some instances, have a substantial impact on the gross value figures. In Albany and Louisville, for example, there are listings of real estate holdings of $15,000 for a restorer and $25,000 for a boatman. These are both very low opportunity occupations. If (as appears likely) the entries should have been $1,500 and $2,500, the total value of all black-owned real estate would be reduced by more than thirty percent in Albany and by almost twenty-five percent in Louisville. See Mss. Census (1850), Reel 206, p. 37, ln. 23, and Reel 471, p. 376, ln. 16.

3. DeBow, *Statistical View*, pp. 103, 191.

4. This is somewhat higher than the ratio of averages for the four New York cities (1.45:1) but not more so than would be anticipated as a result of the impact on the analysis of the disproportionately low percentages of black landowners in Philadelphia, Boston, and Baltimore—all older and heavily built-up cities. The ratio of black real estate owners to landowners in the whole population should not be misunderstood. The measure used here (and in table C-3) is the ratio of percentages, not the ratio of the number of owners. Hence a ratio of 2:1 does not mean that one-half of all owners in the whole population were black, but rather that the *percentage* of real estate owners in the black population was one-half that in the whole population.

5. E.g., Clarke, *Present Condition of the Free Colored People*, p. 14.

6. Charleston, *List of the Tax Payers of the City of Charleston, for 1859* (Charleston: Walker, Evans, 1860), pp. 383–405; Frederic A. Ford, *Census of the City of Charleston, South Carolina, for the Year 1861* (Charleston: Evans and Cogswell, 1861), passim.

7. Providence, Board of Assessors, *A List of Persons Assessed in the City Tax of Sixty-five Thousand Dollars, Ordered by the City Council, June, 1840* (Providence: H. H. Brown, 1840), pp. 59–60; U.S., Census Office, *Sixth Census or Enumeration of the Inhabitants of the United States, As Corrected at the Department of State, in 1840* (Washington: Blair and Rives, 1841), pp. 52–53.

8. Mss. Census (1850), Reels 56–57, 206–7, 235–38, 281–87, 334–39, 415–18, 471–72, 501–2, 517–20, 534–59, 687–91, 745–46, 812–17, 850. The 1840 Providence tax list showed 88.1% of the black real estate holdings (excluding estates of deceased property holders) assessed at $1,000 or less and none with a value as great as $3,000. See Providence, *List of Persons Assessed, 1840,* pp. 59–60.

9. See Mss. Census (1850) sources cited in note 8. The Louisville case was probably an error. See note 2.

10. Mss. Census (1850), Reel 813, p. 757, ln. 23. Smith's holdings were listed at $70,000.

11. Mss. Census (1850), New Orleans, vol. 5, p. 299, ln. 21; vol. 5, p. 741, ln. 35; vol. 5, p. 780, ln. 1; vol. 5, p. 791, ln. 8; vol. 7, p. 237, ln. 10. This reference is to the original copies of the manuscript census, which were used in a few cases when the microfilm copies were illegible.

12. Mss. Census (1850), Reel 850, p. 197, ln. 18; p. 210, ln. 20; p. 270, ln. 3.

13. Charleston, *List of Tax Payers, 1859,* pp. 383–405. This statement rests on an analysis of the white taxpayers listed (pp. 3–379), excluding corporate, partnership, firm, and joint holdings and all property held as part of estates.

14. Ibid., pp. 383–405; Leonard Mears and James Turnbull, *The Charleston Directory* (Charleston: Walker, Evans, 1859), passim; Ford, *Census of Charleston, 1861,* passim.

15. See, for example, Providence, *List of Persons Assessed, 1840,* passim; Charleston, *List of Tax Payers, 1859,* passim.

16. Merchant of Philadelphia, *Wealthy Citizens of Philadelphia,* pp. 12, 24, 50, 58. Martin R. Delany, in his highly impressionistic *Condition . . . of the Colored People,* pp. 94–95, identified Casey (or Cassey) as a "money broker."

17. Samuel M. Welch, *Home History. Recollections of Buffalo during the Decade from 1830 to 1840, or Fifty Years Since* (Buffalo: Peter Paul and Brother, 1891), p. 191.

18. Clarke, *Present Condition of the Free Colored People,* p. 10; Delany, *Condition . . . of the Colored People,* pp. 97–98; Wendell P. Dabney, *Cincinnati's Colored Citizens: Historical, Sociological and Biographical* (Cincinnati: Dabney, 1926), p. 71.

19. *Statistical Inquiry into the Condition of the People of Colour of Philadelphia,* p. 14. See also Wright, *Free Negro in Maryland,* p. 197; Freeman, "Free Negro in New York City," p. 274.

20. J. Thomas Scharf, *History of Saint Louis City and County* (Philadelphia: Louis H. Everts, 1833), 1:192–93; Providence, *List of Persons Assessed, 1840,* pp. 59–60; Wright, *Free Negro in Maryland,* p. 185. The total assessments were : $134,516 in St. Louis in 1811; $17,195,701 in Providence in 1840; and $127,899,370 in Baltimore in 1860.

21. See Robert C. Reinders, "The Free Negro in the New Orleans Economy, 1850–1860," *Louisiana History* 6 (Summer 1965): 281; Robert C. Reinders, *End of an Era: New Orleans, 1850–1860* (New Orleans: Pelican, 1964), pp. 167–68.

22. See Mss. Census (1850) sources listed in note 8.

23. Carter G. Woodson, *Free Negro Owners of Slaves in the United States in 1830* (Washington: Association for the Study of Negro Life and History, 1924), p. vii; N. Webster Moore, "John Berry Meachum (1789–1854), St. Louis Pioneer, Black Abolitionist, Educator, and Preacher," *Bulletin of the Missouri Historical Society* 29 (January 1973): 99.

24. Woodson, *Free Negro Owners of Slaves, 1830,* p. 7.

25. See Mss. Census (1850), Reels 57, 225, 245, 300, 862.

26. Charleston, *List of Tax Payers, 1859,* pp. 383–405.

27. See appendix C, p. 270.

Chapter 4

1. Isabella Lucy Bishop, *An Englishwoman in America* (London: John Murray, 1856), pp. 382–83.

2. James O. Horton, "Black Activism in Boston, 1830–1860," Ph.D. Diss., Brandeis University, 1973, p. 21; George G. Foster, "Philadelphia in Slices," ed. George R. Taylor, *Pennsylvania Magazine of History and Biography* 93 (January 1969): 62.

3. *Register of Trades of the Colored People in Philadelphia,* pp. 3–8.

4. *Matchett's Baltimore Directory . . . for 1835–6* (Baltimore, 1835), passim; *The Providence Directory* (Providence: H. H. Brown, 1832), pp. 130–33; *The Providence Directory* (Providence: H. H. Brown, 1836), pp. 129–34; *The Providence Directory* (Providence: H. H. Brown, 1841), pp. 181–87; *The Providence Directory* (Providence: H. H. Brown, 1844), pp. 193–202; Charles Cist, *The Cincinnati Directory, for the Year 1843* (Cincinnati: R. P. Brooks, 1843), pp. 391–99; *Stimpson's Boston Directory* (1845), pp. 543–50. Directory listings doubtless underreported the number of persons living in alleys, courts, and rear buildings, for these were precisely the locations that the agents of the directory compilers were least likely to canvass thoroughly.

5. William J. Brown, *The Life of William J. Brown, of Providence, R.I.* (Freeport, N.Y.: Books for Libraries Press, 1971; orig. pub. 1883), pp. 32–33.

6. Richard C. Wade, "The Negro in Cincinnati, 1800–1830," *Journal of Negro History* 39 (January 1954): 44–45.

7. Theodore V. Van Heusen, "The Albany Lancaster School," *Transactions of the Albany Institute* 11 (1887): 128.

8. New York City, Inspector, *Annual Report of the Interments in the City and County of New-York, for Year 1842* (New York: James Van Norden, 1843), p. 165; William M. Bobo, *Glimpses of New-York City* (Charleston: J. McCarter, 1852), pp. 123–25.

9. Charleston, City Council, *Report Containing a Review of the Proceedings of the City Authorities From the 4th September, 1837, to the 1st August, 1838* (Charleston: Thomas C. Eccles, 1838), pp. 24–26; *A Series of Letters and Other Documents Relating to the Late Epidemic [of] Yellow Fever* (Baltimore: William Warner, 1820), pp. 45–48; Baltimore, Board of Health, *Report for 1849* (unpaged), in Baltimore, City Health Department, *The First Thirty-Five Annual Reports, 1815–1849* (Baltimore: Baltimore Commissioners of Health, 1953).

10. W. E. B. DuBois, *The Philadelphia Negro: A Social Study* (Philadelphia: University of Pennsylvania, 1899), p. 37.

11. *Statistical Inquiry into the Condition of the People of Colour of Philadelphia,* pp. 36–37.

12. Ibid., p. 38.

13. John H. Griscom, *The Sanitary Condition of the Laboring Population of New York, with Suggestions for Its Improvement* (New York: Harper and Brothers, 1845), p. 18.

14. Wilson, *Directory of New-York, for 1852–1853,* passim; *Stimpson's Boston Directory* (1845), pp. 543–50; L. G. Hoffman, *Hoffman's Albany Directory and City Register, for the Years 1850 '51* (Albany: L. G. Hoffman, 1850), passim; *The Providence Directory* (1844), pp. 192–202; Mears and Turnbull, *The Charleston Directory* (1859), passim. Unfortunately, available data do not permit an examination of this aspect of black urban housing with the precision one might wish. Only in city directories were the addresses of free blacks consistently listed in most major cities. But such listings were, unhappily, in varying degrees, partial in nature and probably underreported the blacks in high-density areas more heavily than those in low-density areas. Moreover, directory compilers differed greatly in the proportion of black (or other, for that matter) entries that they pinpointed by street number, and without such data it is not possible to determine the number of listed Negroes who resided in the same building. The New York directory of 1852 reported numbered addresses for well over ninety-five percent of the

blacks listed, while the figure fell to below eighty percent in the 1845 Boston directory, to only a little over fifty percent in the Charleston directory for 1859, and to as low as one-eighth in the Providence directory of 1844. In some directories addresses by street number are never, or rarely, given. Nevertheless, it is likely that an examination of those listings for which a specific address is recorded may produce a rough approximation of the prevalence of black multiple-family housing structures in the respective cities.

Specific addresses were listed for 222 of the Philadelphia blacks included in the 1838 *Register of Trades* (excluding duplicate listings). Fewer than one-half (101) lived at addresses not listed for at least one other of the included artisans, though a number of the multiple listings for single addresses obviously reflected familial relationships. The ratio of listings to addresses was 1.48:1, and it must be remembered that the Negroes included in this list constituted Philadelphia's black economic elite. See *Register of Trades of the Colored People in Philadelphia*, pp. 3–8.

15. *Report and Tabular Statement of the Censors Appointed by the Board of Mayor and Aldermen, to Obtain the State Census of Boston, May 1, 1850* (Boston: John H. Eastburn, 1850), pp. 30, 32; Stimpson, *Stimpson's Boston Directory* (1845), pp. 543–50.

16. Karl E. Taeuber and Alma F. Taeuber, *Negroes in Cities: Residential Segregation and Neighborhood Change* (New York: Atheneum, 1969), pp. 235–38.

17. The extent of this differential is indicated by indices of dissimilarity computed for two cities for 1950 from different data bases. The use of wards and whole populations yields indices of 27.0 for Charleston, South Carolina, and 44.7 for Jacksonville, Florida, but when block data for heads of household are employed the figures rise dramatically to 60.1 for Charleston and 94.3 for Jacksonville. See Taeuber and Taeuber, *Negroes in Cities*, pp. 40, 41, 47, 52.

18. U.S., Census Office, *Census, 1820*, pp. 5*, 9*, 13, 17*, 21*, 35*; *Census, 1830*, third pagination, 22–23, 24–25, 36–37, 50–51, 64–65, 68–69, 80–81, 94–95, 105–6, 126–27, 160–61; *Census, 1840*, pp. 46–47, 52–53, 82–83, 88–89, 114–15, 118–19, 150–51, 160–61, 194–95, 226–27, 256–57, 306–7, 412–13; *Census, 1850*, pp. 52, 67, 92, 96, 99, 102, 158, 179, 221, 234, 339, 474, 662, 830; John B. Jegli, *Louisville Directory, for 1848–1849* (Louisville: John C. Noble, 1848), p. 11. For a number of the cities in 1820, a few in 1830, two in 1840, and one in 1850, the population was not reported by wards (or any other division) and, as a result, no index figure can be computed. At no time during the half-century did the census marshals report Louisville's population by wards. Hence, the only available Louisville index figure has been calculated from a local census of 1845, which grossly (by about fifty percent) under-reports the number of free persons of color and overstates the number of whites (by more than 13%). All other indices were computed from federal census data. For a discussion of the measurement of residential segregation and the index of dissimilarity, see Taeuber and Taeuber, *Negroes in Cities*, pp. 194–245. The calculations for table 4-1 have employed whole populations rather than households because the Census Office did not provide data on the number of households during these years.

19. Taeuber and Taeuber, *Negroes in Cities*, pp. 32–34.

20. U.S., Census Office, *Census, 1850*, pp. 52, 102, 158, 178–79, 474, 662, 830.

21. Ibid., pp. 52, 67, 158, 179, 221, 234, 339. On the basis of the 1845 Louisville data no ward in that city had a free black percentage as much as double that for the whole city population, and only in Ward One was the percentage of free Negroes less than one-half the figure for the whole city. See Jegli, *Louisville Directory, for 1848–1849*, p. 11.

22. See table 4-1. See also U.S., Census Office, *Census, 1820*, p. 21*.

23. It should be understood that to raise the question (as in the preceding paragraphs) as to whether or not a rise in the index of dissimilarity reflects an actual increase in

residential segregation does not imply that the degree of racial residential concentration is *less* than that indicated by the index. In fact, it is doubtless, in every case, greater. Rather, the intention is to suggest the likelihood that an analysis of the earlier population figures, if broken down into a larger number of reporting units, would have shown an equally high level of residential segregation.

24. U.S., Census Office, *Census, 1850,* p. 339.

25. *Stimpson's Boston Directory* (1845), pp. 543–50; Wilson, *Directory of New-York, for 1852–1853,* passim; Edward Waite, *The Washington Directory, and Congressional, and Executive Register, for 1850* (Washington: Columbus Alexander, 1850), passim; U.S., Census Office, *Census, 1850,* pp. 52, 102, 234. Also proportionately underreported by the directory compilers were Boston's twelfth ward (South Boston) and Washington's extreme eastern (sixth) and southwestern (seventh) wards.

26. Wilson, *Directory for New-York for 1852–1853,* passim; Waite, *Washington Directory for 1850,* passim; U.S., Census Office, *Census, 1850,* pp. 102, 234.

27. See entry for Newport Sands in *Providence Directory* (1844), p. 200.

28. U.S., Census Office, *Census, 1850,* p. 52. The returns for the twelfth ward (South Boston) have been excluded from this calculation.

29. Judah Delano, *The Washington Directory, Showing the Name, Occupation, and Residence of Each Head of a Family and Person in Business* (Washington: William Duncan, 1822), passim; *The Washington Directory, Showing the Name, Occupation, and Residence of Each Head of a Family & Person in Business* (Washington: S. A. Elliot, 1830), passim; E. A. Cohen and Company, *A Full Directory of Washington City, Georgetown, and Alexandria* (Washington: W. Greer, 1834), passim.

30. Gabriel Collins, *The Louisville Directory, for the Year 1836* (Louisville: Prentice and Weissinger, 1836), passim; Gabriel Collins, *The Louisville Directory for the Year 1841* (Louisville: Henkle, Logan and Company, 1841), passim.

31. John Daniels, *In Freedom's Birthplace: A Study of the Boston Negroes* (Boston: Houghton Mifflin, 1914), p. 17; *Boston Directory* (1818), pp. 252–54; *Stimpson's Boston Directory* (1835), pp. 390–95.

32. The five wards (across which there was a fairly general distribution of black residences) were the fourth, fifth, sixth, eighth, and fourteenth. The lower fifteenth ward might also be included.

33. The area of heaviest black residential concentration in the second ward was in the triangle between Fulton, Main, and Front streets.

34. Until 1840 the city was divided into two ranks of rectangular wards—the eastern rank fronting on the Delaware River and the western on the Schuylkill—divided by a single north-south line. No ward lines were altered before 1825, and throughout the entire half-century the only change in the boundaries of the twelve wards lying north of Spruce Street was the 1825 shift of the north-south dividing line from Fourth Street to Seventh Street. South of Spruce Street, New Market Ward was subdivided (by Pine Street) into two wards—New Market and Pine—in 1825, and Cedar Ward was subdivided (by Twelfth Street and Schuylkill Seventh) into three wards—Cedar, Lombard, and Spruce—in 1846. But the data for these new wards can be aggregated to correspond to the two original Cedar and New Market wards, and the boundaries of fourteen reporting units can thus be held constant for the entire fifty years except for the single change of the north-south dividing line in 1825.

35. Berlin, "Slaves Who Were Free," pp. 388–89; Mss. Census (1850), Reel 281, pp. 226–244.

36. Van Heusen, "The Albany Lancaster School," p. 128; Providence Committee on Riots, *History of the Providence Riots, From Sept. 21 to Sept. 24, 1831* (Providence: H. H. Brown, 1831), p. 7.

37. *New Orleans in 1805* (New Orleans: Pelican Gallery, 1936; orig. 1805), passim.

38. Ford, *Census of Charleston, 1861,* passim.

39. Mss. Census (1850), Reel 538, pp. 159–60.

40. [Foster], *New York in Slices,* p. 23; Freeman, "Free Negro in New York City" p. 219.

41. John Doggett, Jr., *Doggett's New York City Street Directory for 1851* (New York: John Doggett, Jr., 1851), passim. The city's heavily segregated black residential pattern was, however, clearly indicated by these data. Just over a tenth of the streets contained as many as four black residences, and well over one-half of all the Negro listings were located on only fifteen streets.

42. *Report and Tabular Statement of the Censors Appointed to Obtain the State Census of Boston, 1850,* p. 23. A number of the native-born whites, however, were doubtless children of immigrants.

43. Ibid., pp. 19–29; *Doggett's New York City Street Directory for 1851,* passim.

Chapter 5

1. Frederick Marryat, *A Diary in America, With Remarks on Its Institutions,* ed. Sydney Jackman (New York: Knopf, 1962; orig. pub. 1839), pp. 149–50.

2. Daniel Drake, *Natural and Statistical View; or, Picture of Cincinnati and the Miami Country* (Cincinnati: Looker and Wallace, 1815), pp. 171–72.

3. [Daniel Curry], *New York: Historical Sketches of the Rise and Progress of the Metropolitan City of America* (New York: Carlton and Phillips, 1853), p. 176; DeBow, *Statistical View,* pp. 45, 63; Moore, *Notes on Slavery in Massachusetts,* p. 238; Richard Furman, *Rev. Dr. Richard Furman's Exposition of the Views of the Baptists, Relative to the Coloured Population of the United States* (Charleston: A. E. Miller, 1823), p. 23; Massachusetts General Court, House of Representatives, Committee on the Admission to the State of Free Negroes and Mulattoes, *Free Negroes and Mulattoes* (n.p., 1822); Allen C. Clark, "Samuel Nicholls Smallwood, Merchant and Mayor," *Records of the Columbia Historical Society* 28 (1926): 59–60.

4. Herbert Aptheker, ed., *A Documentary History of the Negro People in the United States* (New York: Citadel Press, 1951), p. 27; James Forten, *Letters from a Man of Colour, on a Late Bill before the Senate of Pennsylvania* ([Philadelphia, 1813]), pp. 2, 4. It will be noted, however, that the blacks chose their words carefully, acknowledging their status, but not its legitimacy.

5. Edward R. Turner, *The Negro in Pennsylvania: Slavery—Servitude—Freedom, 1639–1861* (Washington: American Historical Association, 1911), pp. 144, 146; Abdy, *Journal* 1:46–47; Hall, *Two-Fold Slavery,* pp. 17–18; Martin R. Delany, *The Origin and Objects of Ancient Freemasonry; Its Introduction into the United States, and Legitimacy among Colored Men* (Pittsburgh: W. S. Haven, 1853), p. 28n; Thomas L. Nichols, *Forty Years of American Life,* 2 vols. (London: John Maxwell, 1864), 2:228–34.

6. Curry, *New York,* p. 308.

7. James Silk Buckingham, *The Slave States of America* (London: Fisher, [1842]), 1:355–56.

8. Brown, *The Life of William J. Brown,* p. 88.

9. James D. Burn, *Three Years among the Working-Classes in the United States during the War* (London: Smith, Elder, 1865), p. xiv.

10. Combe, *Notes on the United States,* 1:252.

11. Hurd, *Law of Freedom and Bondage* 2:97; Stavisky, "Negro Artisan in the South Atlantic States," p. 176; George C. Rogers, *Charleston in the Age of the Pinckneys* (Norman: University of Oklahoma Press, 1969), pp. 145–46; *Niles' Weekly Register,* July 17, 1824, p. 336.

12. Brackett, *Negro in Maryland,* p. 176; Wright, *Free Negro in Maryland,* pp. 112–14;

Hurd, *Law of Freedom and Bondage* 2:21; Baltimore, City Council, *The Ordinances of the Mayor and City Council of Baltimore . . . , 1840* (Baltimore: Joseph Robinson, 1840), pp. 59–60.

13. Sterkx, *Free Negro in Louisiana,* pp. 92, 94, 117; Hurd, *Law of Freedom and Bondage* 2:161–64; *Niles' National Register,* June 22, 1839, p. 261; Buckingham, *Slave States* 1:376. It was stated that the court case reported in *Niles' Register* was "the first trial of the kind."

14. Moore, *Notes on Slavery in Massachusetts,* pp. 231–36; Boston Registry Department, *A Volume of Records Relating to the Early History of Boston Containing Minutes of the Selectmen's Meetings, 1799 to, and Including, 1810* (Boston: Municipal Printing Office, 1904), pp. 77, 93; Massachusetts, General Court, House of Representatives, Committee on Free Negroes and Mulattoes, *Free Negroes and Mulattoes,* pp. 1–3.

15. Francis N. Thorpe, *The Federal and State Constitutions[,] Colonial Charters, and Other Organic Laws of the States, Territories, and Colonies Now or Heretofore Forming the United States of America* (Washington: Government Printing Office, 1909), 4:2154; Missouri, General Assembly, *The Laws of the State of Missouri, Passed at the First Session of the Twelfth General Assembly, Begun and Held at the City of Jefferson, on Monday, the Twenty-first Day of November, Eighteen Hundred and Forty-two, and Ended Tuesday, the Twenty-eighth Day of February, Eighteen Hundred and Forty-three* (Jefferson: Allen Hammond, 1843), pp. 66–68. The act of February 23, 1843, did not specifically prohibit all free blacks from entering Missouri, but it had that practical effect by forbidding county courts to issue licenses to reside in the county to any free black who subsequently came into the state. Free black immigration was specifically prohibited by the act of February 16, 1847. See Missouri, General Assembly, *The Laws of the State of Missouri, Passed at the First Session of the Fourteenth General Assembly, Begun and Held at the City of Jefferson, on Monday, the Sixteenth Day of November, Eighteen Hundred and Forty-six, and Ended on Tuesday, the Sixteenth Day of February, Eighteen Hundred and Forty-seven* (City of Jefferson: James Lusk, 1847), pp. 103–4.

16. U.S., Congress, House of Representatives, Committee for the District of Columbia, *Report* (March 3, 1830), 26 Cong., 1 Sess., Ho. Rept. 269 "Report of Grand Jury," J. Kurtz (foreman), January 8, 1829, p. 55; Carter G. Woodson, *A Century of Negro Migration* (Washington: Association for the Study of Negro Life and History, 1918), p. 42; DuBois, *The Philadelphia Negro,* p. 27; Richard W. Pih, "Negro Self-Improvement Efforts in Ante-Bellum Cincinnati, 1836–1850," *Ohio History* 78 (Summer 1969): 180.

17. Washington, City Council, *Laws of the Corporation of the City of Washington,* [*1821*] (Washington: Way and Gideon, 1821), pp. 109–16.

18. E.g., Washington, City Council, *Laws of the Corporation of the City of Washington,* [*1824*] (Washington: Way and Gideon, 1824), p. 54; *Laws of the Corporation of the City of Washington,* [*1849*] (Washington: John T. Towers, 1849), p. 31; *Laws of the Corporation of the City of Washington,* [*1851*] (Washington: John T. Towers, 1851), pp. 89–90.

19. St. Louis, *Ordinances (1836),* pp. 75–76; Russell M. Nolen, "The Labor Movement in St. Louis Prior to the Civil War," *Missouri Historical Review* 34 (October 1939), p. 34; *Niles' National Register,* August 1, 1840, p. 347 [misprinted as p. 147]; Frank U. Quillin, *The Color Line in Ohio* (Ann Arbor: George Wahr, 1913), pp. 21–23; Charles T. Greve, *Centennial History of Cincinnati and Representative Citizens* (Chicago: Biographical Publishing Company, 1904), 1:593.

20. Hurd, *Law of Freedom and Bondage,* vol. 2, passim; Samuel Breck, *Recollections of Samuel Breck with Passages from His Note-Books (1771–1862),* ed. H. E. Scudder (Philadelphia: Porter and Coates, 1877), p. 302; Quillin, *Color Line in Ohio,* p. 52. The quotation is from the latter source. Black testimony was admissible in Ohio courts after 1849.

21. Harrison A. Trexler, *Slavery in Missouri, 1804–1865* (Baltimore: Johns Hopkins

Press, 1914), pp. 180–82; St. Louis, *Ordinances (1836)*, pp. 124–25; *The Revised Ordinances of the City of St. Louis, Revised and Digested by the City Council, in the Year 1850*, ed. John M. Krum (St. Louis: Chambers and Knapp, 1850), pp. 297–299; Stavisky, "Negro Artisan in the South Atlantic States," p. 152; Wright, *Free Negro in Maryland*, pp. 122–24; Louisville, City Council, *Revised Ordinances of the City of Louisville, Including the Charter of 1851* (Louisville: Louisville Courier, 1854), pp. 86–87; Washington, City Council, *Acts of the Corporation of the City of Washington*, [1809] (Washington: A. and G. Way, 1809), p. 24; Washington, City Council, *Laws, 1821*, p. 115; Washington, City Council, *Laws of the Corporation of the City of Washington, 1827* (Washington: Way and Gideon, 1827), p. 69; John C. Schneider, "Mob Violence and Public Order in the American City, 1830–1865," Ph.D. Diss., University of Minnesota, 1971, p. 37; Scharf, *History of Saint Louis* 1:666; Charleston, *Ordinances (1783–1844)*, p. 170; Buckingham, *Slave States* 1:569; Earl of Carlisle, *Travels in America*, p. 53; Olmsted, *Journey in the Seaboard Slave States*, pp. 592–93; U.S., Commissioner of Education, *History of Schools for the Colored Population* (New York: Arno Press, 1969; orig. pub. 1871), p. 316.

22. Hurd, *Law of Freedom and Bondage*, vol. 2, passim; Brackett, *Negro in Maryland*, pp. 186–87; John H. B. Latrobe, "Memoir of Benjamin Banneker," *Maryland Historical Society Publications* 1 (1845): 6; DuBois, *Philadelphia Negro*, pp. 22, 30; [Robert Purvis], *Appeal of Forty Thousand Citizens, Threatened with Disfranchisement, to the People of Pennsylvania* (Philadelphia: Merrihew and Gunn, 1838); Oberholtzer, *Philadelphia*, 2:279; Franklin B. Hough, *Statistics of Population of the City and County of New York* (New York: New York Printing Company, 1866), pp. 63, 67; Dixon R. Fox, "The Negro Vote in Old New York," *Political Science Quarterly* 32 (June 1917): 252–75; Freeman, "Free Negro in New York City," pp. 119–22; James T. Adams, "Disfranchisement of Negroes in New England," *American Historical Review* 30 (April 1925): 543–47; Brown, *Life of William J. Brown*, pp. 156–74; Lemuel Shattuck, *Report to the Committee of the City Council Appointed to Obtain the Census of Boston for the Year 1845* (Boston: John H. Eastburn, 1846), p. 44; *Niles' Weekly Register*, December 13, 1834, p. 237.

23. Charleston, *Ordinances (1783–1844)*, pp. 24–25, 70, 82–83, 173, 219–25, 280; Washington, City Council, *Acts of the Corporation of the City of Washington*, [1811] (Washington: A. and G. Way, 1811), pp. 29–30; Louisville, *Acts (1839)*, pp. 128–29; Baltimore, *Ordinances, 1840*, Appendix, pp. 120–25; Baltimore, City Council, *The Ordinances of the Mayor and City Council of Baltimore . . ., 1831* (Baltimore: Lucas and Deaver, 1831), p. 83; Brackett, *Negro in Maryland*, p. 216; Christoval Morel and Thomas W. Collens, *A Digest of the Ordinances in Force in Municipality No. One, on the 13th. May 1846* (New Orleans: Auguste Bruslé, 1846), pp. 91–92; Washington, City Council, *Laws of the Corporation of the City of Washington*, [1829] (Washington: Way and Gideon, 1829), pp. 39–40; U.S., Commissioner of Education, *Schools for the Colored Population*, p. 315; Missouri, General Assembly, *Laws, 1846–1847*, p. 103. For discrimination in employment, see pp. 20–22, above.

24. Brackett, *Negro in Maryland*, pp. 211, 218–20, 229; Charleston, *Ordinances, 1783–1844*, p. 281, passim; *Niles' Weekly Register*, May 2, 16, 1829, pp. 149, 181; Baltimore, City Council, *The Ordinances of the Mayor and City Council of Baltimore . . ., 1845* (Baltimore: James Lucas, 1845), pp. 113–14; Louisville, *Acts (1839)*, pp. 155–56.

25. Clarke, *Present Condition of the Free Colored People*, pp. 3–4.

26. Leo H. Hirsch, Jr., "The Negro in New York, 1783–1865," *Journal of Negro History* 16 (October 1931): 425; Mary H. Ovington, *Half A Man: The Status of the Negro in New York* (New York: Longmans, Green, 1911), pp. 21–23; Schoolcraft, *Letters on the Condition of the African Race*, p. 8; James E. Allen, *The Negro in New York* (New York: Exposition Press, 1964), p. 22; Albert E. Fossier, *New Orleans: The Glamour Period, 1800–1840* (New Orleans: Pelican Press, 1957), pp. 38–39; Clarke, *Present Condition of the Free Colored People*, p. 14.

27. Charleston, *Ordinances (1783–1844)*, pp. 11–12; Hickok, *Negro in Ohio*, p. 133; William S. Rossiter, ed., *Days and Ways in Old Boston* (Boston: Stearns, 1915), opp. p. 119; Walter C. Clephane, "The Local Aspect of Slavery in the District of Columbia," *Records of the Columbia Historical Society* 3 (1900): 246–47; Sterkx, *Free Negro in Louisiana*, pp. 68–69, 245; Donatien Augustin, *A General Digest of the Ordinances and Resolutions Passed by the City Council of New-Orleans* (New Orleans: Jerome Bayon, 1831), pp. 365–71; Henry B. Fearon, *Sketches of America* (London: Strahan and Spottiswoode, 1819), p. 87; Leland D. Baldwin, *Pittsburgh: The Story of a City* (Pittsburgh: University of Pittsburgh Press, 1937), p. 264; Edwin Olson, "Social Aspects of Slave Life in New York," *Journal of Negro History* 26 (January 1941): 72; Thomas M. Marshall, ed., "The Journal of Henry B. Miller," *Missouri Historical Society Collections* 6 (1931): 251; Nichols, *Forty Years of American Life* 2:229–30.

28. Turner, *Negro in Pennsylvania*, pp. 146, 148; Negley Teeters, "The Early Days of the Philadelphia House of Refuge," *Pennsylvania History* 27 (April 1960): 177; *An Appeal to the Public on Behalf of a House of Refuge for Coloured Juvenile Delinquents* (Philadelphia: T. K. and P. G. Collins, 1846), pp. 1–9; *Philadelphia As It Is* (Philadelphia: George S. Appleton, 1845), p. 143; *The Picture of New-York and Stranger's Guide to the Commercial Metropolis of the United States* (New York: A. T. Goodrich, 1828), pp. 304–5; Augustin, *Digest of Ordinances of New-Orleans*, p. 171; Baltimore, City Council, *The Ordinances of the Mayor and City Council of Baltimore . . ., 1839* (Baltimore: John D. Toy, 1839), Appendix, p. 39; Charles Dickens, *American Notes for General Circulation* (London: Chapman and Hall, 1850; orig. pub. 1842), p. 57; Washington, City Council, *Laws of the City of Washington,* [1847] (Washington: John T. Towers, 1847), p. 107.

29. Charles Lyell, *Travels in North America; With Geological Observations on the United States, Canada, and Nova Scotia* (London: John Murray, 1845), 2:324–25; Baltimore, City Health Department, *First Thirty-Five Reports,* Report for 1818 (unpaged); Louisville, *Acts (1839),* p. 131; Washington, City Council, *Acts of the Corporation of the City of Washington,* [1807] (Washington: A. and G. Way, 1807), pp. 18–20; Charleston, *Ordinances, 1783–1844,* pp. 126–28; New Orleans, City Council, *A Digest of the Ordinances, Resolutions, By-Laws, and Regulations of the Corporation of New-Orleans, and a Collection of the Laws of the Legislature Relative to the Said City* (New Orleans: Gaston Bruslé, 1836), pp. 67–71.

30. Freeman, "Free Negro in New York City," pp. 98–100; Allen C. Clark, "Colonel William Winston Seaton and His Mayoralty," *Records of the Columbia Historical Society* 29–30 (1928): 49–51; Oberholtzer, *Philadelphia* 2:302; Campbell, "Old Philadelphia Music," p 187; Scharf and Wescott, *History of Philadelphia* 3:1906–7.

31. Ball Fenner, *Raising the Veil; or, Scenes in the Courts* (Boston: J. French, 1856), p. 121; Thomas Gill, *Selections from the Court Reports Originally Published in the Boston Morning Post, From 1834 to 1837* (Boston: Otis, Broaders, 1837), pp. 92–93; Brown, *Life of William J. Brown,* pp. 90–91, 126–27; Turner, *Negro in Pennsylvania,* p. 145; *Niles' Weekly Register,* November 26, 1825, p. 195; *Niles' National Register,* June 22, 1839, p. 262. See also pp. 100–101.

32. Washington, *Laws (1827),* p. 57. See also pp. 90, 166–67.

33. Fearon, *Sketches of America,* pp. 167–68.

Chapter 6

1. *Niles' Weekly Register,* September 19, 1835, pp. 34–35; Henry C. Castellanos, *New Orleans As It Was* (New Orleans: L. Graham and Son, 1895), pp. 289–90; the quotation is from the first source.

2. Stavisky, "Negro Artisan in the South Atlantic States," p. 148.

3. This particular assemblage constituted the initial element in a series of violent mob actions that eventually resulted in the murder of General James Lingan. See Maryland,

House of Delegates, Committee of Grievances and Courts of Justice, *Report of the Committee of Grievances and Courts of Justice of the House of Delegates of Maryland, on the Subject of the Recent Mobs and Riots in the City of Baltimore, Together with the Depositions Taken before the Committee* (Annapolis: Jonas Green, 1813).

4. Ibid., p. 3.

5. Elihu H. Shepard, *The Early History of St. Louis and Missouri from Its First Exploration by White Men in 1673 to 1843* (St. Louis: Southwestern, 1870), pp. 122–25; Benjamin G. Merkel, "The Abolition Aspects of Missouri's Anti-Slavery Controversy, 1819–1865," *Missouri Historical Review* 44 (April 1950): 239–40.

6. Joel Munsell, *The Annals of Albany* (Albany: Munsell and Rowland, 1858), 9:248.

7. *Niles' Weekly Register,* August 15, 1835, p. 410; William T. Steiger to Elizabeth Shriver, August 11, 1835, William T. Steiger to Andrew Shriver, August 13, 14, 1835, in William D. Hoyt, Jr., ed., "Washington's Living History: The Post Office Fire and Other Matters, 1834–1839," *Records of the Columbia Historical Society,* 46–47 (1947): 61–64; Bryan, *National Capital* 1:143, 146; Clephane, "The Local Aspect of Slavery in the District of Columbia," p. 245; Harry Barnard, "Special Report of the Commissioners of Education [of the] District of Columbia," *American Journal of Education* 19 (1870): 201; Washington, City Council, *Laws of the Corporation of the City of Washington, [1836]* (Washington: Jacob Gideon, Jr., 1836), pp. 90–91. All these accounts differ in some details; the chronology followed is that outlined in the Steiger letters and confirmed by the dates of city council resolutions printed in the *Laws of the Corporation.*

8. *Niles' Weekly Register,* August 22, 1835, p. 439. Apparently there was a very minor outbreak of anti-Negro violence on a Sunday morning a month later. This may have resulted from smoldering resentments having their origin in the Snow Riot. See ibid., September 19, 1835, p. 33.

9. Woodson, *Century of Negro Migration,* p. 47; Frank G. Rollin, *Life and Public Services of Martin R. Delany* (Boston: Lee and Shepard, 1883), p. 44; Dorothy Sterling, *The Making of an Afro-American: Martin Robinson Delany, 1812–1885* (Garden City, N.Y.: Doubleday, 1971), p. 58; Victor Ullman, *Martin R. Delany: The Beginnings of Black Nationalism* (Boston: Beacon Press, 1971), pp. 29–31.

10. Edward H. Savage, *A Chronological History of the Boston Watch and Police, From 1631 to 1865* (Boston: By the author, 1865), p. 66; *Boston Courier,* July 15, 17, 1826. The antiblack mob is not mentioned in the contemporary newspapers. See also, *Boston Daily Advertiser,* July 14–20, 1826.

11. Savage, *History of the Boston Watch,* p. 82; *Boston Daily Advertiser,* August 28, 29, 30, 1843. It is noteworthy that no accounts of these antiblack mobs are to be found in the multivolume histories of either Pittsburgh or Boston.

12. E.g., Lossing, *History of New York City,* p. 242; Aaron Clark, *Communication from His Honor the Mayor, In Relation to the Precautionary Measures Adopted by Him to Secure the Public Peace at the Recent Election in This City* (New York: Common Council, 1839), p. 299.

13. Clark, *Communication from the Mayor,* pp. 300–302; William L. Stone, *History of New York City* (New York: Virtue and Yotston, 1872), pp. 462–63; Hirsch, "The Negro and New York, 1783–1865," pp. 456–57; James G. Wilson, ed., *The Memorial History of the City of New York* (New York: New-York History Company, 1892–93), 2:341–43; Joel T. Headley, *The Great Riots of New York, 1712–1873* (New York: E. B. Treat, 1873), pp. 89–95; Asher Taylor, *Recollections of the Early Days of the National Guard, Comprising the Prominent Events in the History of the Famous Seventh Regiment, New York Militia* (New York: J. M. Bradstreet, 1868), pp. 148–58; Linda K. Kerber, "Abolitionists and Amalgamationists: The New York Race Riots of 1834," *New York History* 48 (January 1967): 30–33. The houses and businesses of white abolitionists and white churches whose ministers were identified with the abolitionist cause were also extensively damaged.

14. Headly, *Great Riots,* p. 93.

15. It has been suggested that the unsegregated intermixing of whites and blacks at an abolitionist meeting in Chatham Street Chapel on July 4 contributed to building tensions that broke into violence three days later. See Clark, *Communication from the Mayor,* p. 300.

16. Irving H. Bartlett, *From Slave to Citizen: The Story of the Negro in Rhode Island* (Providence: Urban League of Greater Providence, 1954), pp. 27–30; Henry Mann, ed., *Our Police: A History of the Providence Force from the First Watchman to the Latest Appointee* (Providence: [J. M. Beers], 1889), p. 36; the quotations are from the first source.

17. Providence, Committee on Riots, *History of the Providence Riots, 1831,* p. 7.

18. Ibid., pp. v, 7, 9, 18–19; Bartlett, *Slave to Citizen,* pp. 31–33; Mann, *Our Police,* pp. 37–39; William R. Staples, *Annals of the Town of Providence from Its First Settlement, to the Organization of the City Government, in June, 1832* (Providence: Knowles and Vose, 1843), pp. 397–99; *The Providence Directory* (Providence: H. H. Brown, 1832), passim; Providence, Board of Assessors, *A List of Persons Assessed in the City Tax of Forty Thousand Dollars, Ordered by the City Council, June, 1833* (Providence: J. S. Ham and Company and S. R. Weeden, 1833), p. 5. Staples, the author of the *Annals of Providence,* was the owner of one of the houses destroyed.

19. The imprecision of this statement illustrates the unreliability of the materials dealing with anti-Negro riots. One of the outbreaks—a moderately substantial one sparked by the murder of a Southwark watchman by a black escapee from Blockley Asylum—is, in different sources, given the dates of 1836 (probably a typographical error), 1839, 1840, and (by implication) 1838. See Joseph Jackson, *Encyclopedia of Philadelphia* (Harrisburg: National Historical Association, 1931), 1:86; Oberholtzer, *Philadelphia* 2:287; Young, *History of Philadelphia* 2:222.

20. Jackson, *Encyclopedia of Philadelphia* 1:84; DuBois, *The Philadelphia Negro,* p. 27; *Niles' Weekly Register,* October 5, 1839, p. 83; Charles R. Barker, "Philadelphia in the Late Forties," *Philadelphia History* 2 (1931): 264–65; Oberholtzer, *Philadelphia* 2:288–89; Elizabeth M. Geffen, "Violence in Philadelphia in the 1840s and 1850s," *Pennsylvania History* 36 (October 1969): 388.

21. Woodward was alleged to have mistreated two women patients, and the mulatto proprietor of the California House had committed the cardinal sin of marrying a white woman.

22. Wade, "Negro in Cincinnati," pp. 50–55; Abdy, *Journal* 2:382–83; Woodson, "Negroes of Cincinnati," pp. 6–7; John Malvin, *North into Freedom: The Autobiography of John Malvin, Free Negro, 1795–1880,* ed. Allan Peskin (Cleveland: Western Reserve University, 1960), pp. 38–44; J. Reuben Sheeler, "The Struggle of the Negro in Ohio for Freedom," *Journal of Negro History* 31 (April 1946): 212–13. The assertion that one-half of Cincinnati's black population—or, alternatively, about 1,000–1,200 Negroes—migrated to Canada is doubtful in the extreme, and appears to rest solely on a statement made at a meeting of the Ohio Antislavery Society six years later. Actually, the roughly 1,100–1,200 free persons of color in Cincinnati in 1830 and 1831 represents an increase of well over one hundred percent during the decade of the 1820s and is in line with local counts taken during the decade. See U.S., Census Office, *Census, 1820,* p. 35; Harvey Hall, *The Cincinnati Directory for 1825* (Cincinnati: Samuel J. Browne, 1825), p. 114; Greve, *History of Cincinnati* 1:546–47; Benjamin Drake and E. D. Mansfield, *Cincinnati in 1826* (Cincinnati: Morgan, Lodge, and Fisher, 1827), p. 57; U.S., Census Office, *Census, 1830,* pp. 126–27. The figures given for the Cincinnati free black population are: 1820—433, 1824—528, 1826—690, 1830—1,090, 1831—1,194.

23. *Niles' Weekly Register,* May 26, 1838, p. 195; Woodson, *Century of Negro Migration,* pp. 46–47; Turner, *Negro in Pennsylvania,* pp. 162–63; Eli K. Price, *The History of*

the Consolidation of the City of Philadelphia (Philadelphia: J. B. Lippincott, 1873), pp. 111–12. The destruction of the white-owned Pennsylvania Hall caused, naturally, considerable agitation. Eventually (in 1847), after an extensive court fight, the Philadelphia county commissioners paid the proprietors $47,940 to indemnify them for the property damage caused by the mob. See *Niles' National Register,* July 10, 1847, p. 293. I have found no evidence that any payment was ever made by any governmental body for the destruction of black-owned property by mob action.

24. Jackson, *Encyclopedia of Philadelphia* 1:85–86; Young, *History of Philadelphia* 2:215; Turner, *Negro in Pennsylvania,* pp. 161–62; Price, *History of Consolidation,* p. 111; Greve, *History of Cincinnati* 1:597; Henry A. Ford and Kate B. Ford, *History of Cincinnati, Ohio* (Cleveland: L. A. Williams, 1881), p. 87; G. M. Roe, *Our Police: A History of the Cincinnati Police Force, From the Earliest Period until the Present Day* (New York: AMS Press, 1976; orig. pub. 1890), p. 31. Roe specifically asserts that the cause of the defeated white boy in Cincinnati was taken up "by those who wanted to rid the community of the negro."

25. *Niles' National Register,* August 6, 1842, p. 356; Oberholtzer, *Philadelphia* 2:288–89; Turner, *Negro in Pennsylvania,* pp. 163–64; Price, *History of Consolidation,* p. 112. The white assailants were said to have been almost entirely Irish. See Fisher, *Diary,* p. 135; Michael J. Feldberg, "The Philadelphia Riots of 1844: A Social History," Ph.D. Diss., University of Rochester, 1970, pp. 49–51.

26. *Niles' Weekly Register,* August 23, 1834, pp. 435–36; Abdy, *Journal* 3:316–33; Oberholtzer, *Philadelphia* 2:282; Turner, *Negro in Pennsylvania,* pp. 160–61; John Runcie, "'Hunting the Nigs' in Philadelphia: The Race Riot of August 1834," *Pennsylvania History* 39 (April 1972): 187–218; *Hazard's Register of Pennsylvania,* August 23, 1834, pp. 126–28; ibid., September 27, 1834, pp. 200–203.

27. The exact nature of the actions taken by the Negroes after the cannon was brought up are unclear. Contemporary accounts state that the fire on the mob was continued, but at a much-reduced level because many of the blacks "fled to the hills." Blacks later claimed, however, that it was impossible for them to "flee to the hills," because their path was blocked by "Billy Goat Hill," an Irish settlement from which Negroes were rigorously and violently excluded. The firing diminished, they asserted, because they made a flank movement against the cannon and eventually captured it. There is no mention in contemporary accounts of such a capture. See *Hazard's United States Commercial and Statistical Register,* September 22, 1841, pp. 179–81; Dabney, *Cincinnati's Colored Citizens,* p. 70.

28. It was later revealed that the boys had first attacked the Negroes. See *Hazard's U.S. Register,* September 22, 1841, p. 181.

29. Ibid., p. 179; *Niles' National Register,* September 11, 1841, p. 32.

30. *Hazard's U.S. Register,* September 22, 1841, pp. 179–81; *Niles' National Register,* September 11, 1841, p. 32; Dabney, *Cincinnati's Colored Citizens,* pp. 48–55; Greve, *History of Cincinnati* 1:750–52.

31. Quoted in Runcie, "'Hunting the Nigs' in Philadelphia," p. 216.

32. See chapter 2.

33. By no means all opponents of abolitionism were lacking in self-confidence or social and economic status, of course. Many opposed abolitionist agitation for political, economic, constitutional, legal, social, or philosophical reasons, and some of these doubtless condoned (and, on rare occasions, participated in) antiabolitionist violence. But they were rarely, if ever, to be found among those assaulting the black population. For a contrary view, see Leonard L. Richards, *"Gentlemen of Property and Standing": Anti-Abolition Mobs in Jacksonian America* (New York: Oxford University Press, 1970).

34. A close student of the 1834 New York riot also argues that the Irish were notably absent from the antiblack mobs that assembled on that occasion. See Kerber,

"Abolitionists and Amalgamationists," pp. 34–35. For an analysis of the prevalence of Irish among the Philadelphia rioters of the same year, see Runcie, "'Hunting the Nigs' in Philadelphia," pp. 194, 198–202. I do not suggest, obviously, that the increase in immigration was a *cause* of the reduced incidence of antiblack rioting in the 1840s and 1850s, but only that there was no positive correlation between the frequency of such outbreaks and the size of the urban foreign-born populations.

Chapter 7

1. Quoted in Furman, *Views of the Baptists Relative to the Coloured Population,* p. 23.
2. Quoted in Donald M. Jacobs, "A History of the Boston Negro from the Revolution to the Civil War," Ph.D. Diss., Boston University, 1968, p. 52.
3. American Convention of Abolition Societies, *Minutes of the Proceedings of the Eleventh American Convention for Promoting the Abolition of Slavery, And Improving the Condition of the African Race* (Philadelphia: Kimber, Conrad, 1806), p. 13.
4. Foster, "Philadelphia in Slices," p. 62.
5. Washington, City Council, *Laws of the Corporation of the City of Washington,* [1838] (Washington: Jacob Gideon, Jr., 1838), p. 342; *Laws of the Corporation of the City of Washington,* [1846] (Washington: John T. Towers, 1846), p. 337; *Laws of the Corporation of the City of Washington,* [1848] (Washington: John T. Towers, 1848), p. 129; *Laws of the Corporation of the City of Washington,* [1850] (Washington: John T. Towers, 1850), pp. 448–50.
6. Mss. Census (1850), Reel 57, pp. 292–93.
7. These data are derived from the annual reports of the "Visiters [*sic*] and Governors of the Jail," as published in the following volumes: Baltimore, City Council, *The Ordinances of the Mayor and City Council of Baltimore . . ., 1832* (Baltimore: Joseph Robinson, 1832), Appendix, p. 60; *The Ordinances of the Mayor and City Council of Baltimore . . ., 1836* (Baltimore: Lucas and Deaver, 1836), Appendix, pp. 88–91; *The Ordinances of the Mayor and City Council of Baltimore . . ., 1837* (Baltimore: Lucas and Deaver, 1837), Appendix, pp. 58–64; Baltimore, *Ordinances (1839),* Appendix, p. 26; Baltimore, *Ordinances (1840),* Appendix, p. 35; *The Ordinances of the Mayor and City Council of Baltimore . . ., 1841* (Baltimore: Joseph Robinson, 1841), Appendix, p. 30; *The Ordinances of the Mayor and City Council of Baltimore . . ., 1842* (Baltimore: Lucas and Deaver, 1842), Appendix, p. 48; *The Ordinances of the Mayor and City Council of Baltimore . . ., 1843* (Baltimore: Lucas and Deaver, 1843), Appendix, p. 74; *The Ordinances of the Mayor and City Council of Baltimore . . ., 1844* (Baltimore: Lucas and Deaver, 1844), Appendix, p. 103; Baltimore, *Ordinances (1845),* Appendix, p. 196; Baltimore, City Council, *The Ordinances of the Mayor and City Council of Baltimore . . ., 1846* (Baltimore: James Lucas, 1846), Appendix, pp. 122–23; *The Ordinances of the Mayor and City Council of Baltimore . . ., 1847* (Baltimore: James Lucas, 1847), Appendix, pp. 124–25; *The Ordinances of the Mayor and City Council of Baltimore . . ., 1848* (Baltimore: James Lucas, 1848), Appendix, pp. 156–57; *The Ordinances of the Mayor and City Council of Baltimore . . ., 1849* (Baltimore: James Lucas, 1849), Appendix, pp. 144–45; *The Ordinances of the Mayor and City Council of Baltimore . . ., 1850* (Baltimore: James Lucas, 1850), Appendix, pp. 120–21; *The Ordinances of the Mayor and City Council of Baltimore . . ., 1851* (Baltimore: James Lucas, 1851), Appendix, pp. 46–47. The figures in the text exclude persons imprisoned for debt, for safekeeping, and as runaways.
8. *Niles' Weekly Register,* January 20, 1821, p. 352; ibid., February 22, 1823, p. 386; ibid., January 30, 1829, p. 366; James Hardie, *A Census of New Buildings Erected in this City, In the Year 1824, Arranged in Distinct Classes, According to Their Materials and Number of Stories* (New York: S. Marks, 1825), p. 21; James Hardie, *The Description of the City of New-York* (New York: Samuel Marks, 1827), p. 205; David T. Valentine,

Manual of the Corporation of the City of New York, for the Years 1845–6 (New York: Levi D. Slamm and C. C. Childs, 1846), pp. 190–93; David T. Valentine, *Manual of the Corporation of the City of New York, for the Years 1844–5* (New York: J. F. Trow, 1844), p. 172; David T. Valentine, *Manual of the Corporation of the City of New York, for the Year 1847* (New York: Casper C. Childs, 1847), p. 227.

9. Shattuck, *Census of Boston for the Year 1845,* p. 117.

10. Abigail F. Mott, *Biographical Sketches and Interesting Anecdotes of Persons of Color; with a Selection of Pieces of Poetry* (New York: M. Day, 1839), pp. 234–35.

11. Negley K. Teeters, *They Were in Prison: A History of the Pennsylvania Prison Society, 1787–1937* (Philadelphia: John C. Winston, 1937), pp. 82–83; *Philadelphia in 1824* (Philadelphia: H. C. Carey and I. Lea, 1824), pp. 143–44; DuBois, *The Philadelphia Negro: A Social Study,* p. 239; Pennsylvania Society for the Promotion of the Abolition of Slavery, *The Present State and Condition of the Free People of Color, of the City of Philadelphia and Adjoining Districts* (Philadelphia: By the Society, 1838), p. 17; *Statistical Inquiry into the Condition of the People of Colour of Philadelphia,* pp. 28–29; Turner, *Negro in Pennsylvania,* p. 156n; William Crawford, *Report of William Crawford, Esq., on the Penitentiaries of the United States, Addressed to His Majesty's Principal Secretary of State for the Home Department* (Montclair, N.J.: Patterson Smith, 1969; orig. pub. 1835), Appendix, p. 21.

12. Mss. Census (1850), Reel 339, pp. 746–53, Reel 520, pp. 720–21, Reel 690, pp. 903–5; ibid. (New Orleans), vol. 5, pp. 474–79; *Hazard's U.S. Register* 3 (July 1840): 58.

13. These generalizations are based on an examination of annual returns from the Baltimore jail for the period 1838–50. See the references to Baltimore ordinances (1839–51) in footnote 7, above. Records of commitments (for more serious offenses) to the Eastern Pennsylvania State Prison in Philadelphia between 1829 and 1848, however, show a slightly larger percentage of blacks than whites incarcerated for crimes against persons and a much larger percentage of blacks than whites guilty of the use of violence in committing property crimes. See *A Statistical Inquiry into the Condition of the People of Colour of Philadelphia,* pp. 28–29.

14. See the references to Baltimore ordinances in note 7, above. See also, Hardie, *Description of New–York,* p. 205; Hardie, *Census of New Buildings,* p. 21; *Niles' Weekly Register,* January 20, 1821, p. 352; ibid., February 22, 1823, p. 386; ibid., January 31, 1829, p. 366; Valentine, *Manual (1844–45),* p. 172; Valentine, *Manual (1845–46),* pp. 189–93; Valentine, *Manual (1847),* p. 227; *Philadelphia in 1824* (Philadelphia: H. C. Carey and I. Lea, 1824), pp. 143–44; Mss. Census (1850), Reel 284, pp. 911–14; Crawford, *Report on Penitentiaries of the United States,* Appendix, p. 21.

15. Turner, *Negro in Pennsylvania,* p. 156n.

16. Mss. Census (1850), Reel 57, pp. 292–93, Reel 285, pp. 914–19, Reel 844, pp. 169–71.

17. The Society for the Reformation of Juvenile Delinquents in the City and State of New-York, *Tenth Annual Report* (New York: Mahlon Day, 1835), p. 15.

18. The Society for the Reformation of Juvenile Delinquents in the City and State of New-York, *Eleventh Annual Report* (New York: Mahlon Day, 1836), pp. 44–45; *Twelfth Annual Report* (New York: Mahlon Day, 1837), p. 51; *Thirteenth Annual Report* (New York: Mahlon Day, 1838), pp. 6–7; *Fourteenth Annual Report* (New York: Mahlon Day, 1839), pp. 4–5; *Fifteenth Annual Report* (New York: Mahlon Day, 1840), p. 3. In fact, the number of black children admitted to the house of refuge was never as many as fifty in any one year in the first half of the nineteenth century.

19. *A Statistical Inquiry into the Condition of the People of Colour of Philadelphia,* p. 27; Robert Everest, "Pauperism and Crime—White and Colored—Native and Foreign," *DeBow's Review* 19 (September 1855): 273. These comments were based on data relative to imprisonment in the Eastern Pennsylvania State Prison in Philadelphia, established in 1829.

20. Valentine, *Manual (1845–46)*, pp. 192–93; Hardie, *Census of New Buildings*, p. 21; Hardie, *Description of New York*, p. 205; *Niles' Weekly Register*, January 20, 1821, p. 352; ibid., February 22, 1823, p. 386; ibid., January 31, 1829, p. 366.

21. See the references to Baltimore ordinances in note 7, above. See also, Alexander Hunter, *Report on Persons Imprisoned for Debt in the District of Columbia*, 24 Cong., 2 Sess., Ho. Exec. Doc. No. 24, passim.

22. *Niles' National Register*, September 12, 1840, pp. 19–20; Foster, *New York in Slices*, p. 23.

23. Sterkx, *Free Negro in Louisiana*, pp. 230–31; Ira Berlin, *Slaves without Masters* (New York: Pantheon, 1974), p. 265.

24. Edward Whitely, *The Philadelphia Directory and Register, for 1820* (Philadelphia; M'Carty and Davis, [1820]), unpaged. Girard was also listed as colored.

25. Mss. Census (1850), Reel 339, pp. 746–53.

26. See the references to Baltimore ordinances in note 7, above.

27. Persons imprisoned for debt have also been excluded except for that portion of the chapter dealing solely with debtors.

28. See chapter 5.

29. E.g., Charleston, City Council, *A Report Containing a Review of the Proceedings of the City Authorities from First September, 1838, to First August, 1839* (Charleston: W. Riley, 1839), pp. 46–47.

Chapter 8

1. George T. Fleming, *History of Pittsburgh and Its Environs* (New York: American Historical Society, 1922), 3:570; Ford and Ford, *History of Cincinnati*, p. 202; J. N. Larned, *A History of Buffalo, Delineating the Evolution of a City* (New York: Progress of the Empire State Company, 1911), 2:82; Evelyn C. Beven, *City Subsidies to Private Charitable Agencies in New Orleans* (New Orleans: School of Social Work, Tulane University, 1934), pp. 12–16; Dorothea L. Dix, *A Review of the Present Condition of the State Penitentiary of Kentucky, With Brief Notices and Remarks upon the Jails and Poor-Houses in Some of the Most Populous Counties* (Frankfort: A. G. Hodges, 1845), p. 35.

2. Although one or two slaves were occasionally to be found in the almshouses of the southern cities, it clearly was not intended that any but free persons should be admitted. E.g., Washington, *Laws (1847)*, p. 110.

3. Baltimore Trustees for the Poor, *Report*, [1828] (n.d.), Appendix C; Baltimore, City Council, *Ordinances of the Mayor and the City Council of Baltimore . . . , 1830* (Baltimore: Bailey and Francis, 1830), Appendix, p. 49; Baltimore, *Ordinances (1832)*, Appendix, p. 42; Baltimore, City Council, *Ordinances of the Mayor and City Council of Baltimore . . . , 1833* (Baltimore: Sands and Neilson, 1833), Appendix, p. 43; *Ordinances of the Mayor and City Council of Baltimore . . . , 1834* (Baltimore: James Jucas and E. K. Deaver, 1834), Appendix, p. 43; *Ordinances of the Mayor and City Council of Baltimore . . . , 1835* (Baltimore: Lucas and Deaver, 1835), Appendix, p. 41; Baltimore, *Ordinances (1836)*, Appendix, p. 39; ibid. (1837), Appendix, p. 44; ibid. (1839), Appendix, p. 32; ibid. (1840), Appendix, p. 41; ibid. (1842), Appendix, p. 34; ibid. (1843), Appendix, p. 108; ibid. (1844), Appendix, p. 131; ibid. (1845), Appendix, p. 184; ibid., (1846), Appendix, p. 175; ibid. (1847), Appendix, p. 165; ibid. (1848), Appendix, p. 199; ibid. (1849), Appendix, p. 170; ibid. (1850), Appendix, p. 137; ibid. (1851), Appendix, p. 62.

4. Baltimore, *Ordinances (1832)*, Appendix, pp. 42, 53.

5. Washington, *Laws, 1850*, pp. 443, 446–47; Mss. Census (1850), Reel 57, pp. 171–72. Though admissions varied more erratically, the inmate population (both black and white) of almshouses, rather naturally, tended to increase during the fall and winter,

reaching its highest point in the December-to-March period, and to decline in the spring and summer. E.g., Baltimore, *Ordinances (1839),* Appendix, p. 32.

6. *Niles' Weekly Register,* June 15, 1816, p. 263 [misnumbered as p. 363]; ibid., January 20, 1821, p. 352; ibid., March 9, 1822, p. 32; ibid., February 22, 1823, p. 386; Hardie, *Census of New Buildings,* p. 205; *Niles' Weekly Register,* January 31, 1829, pp. 365–66; "Letters to Anti-Slavery Workers," p. 463; J. F. Richmond, *New York and Its Institutions, 1609–1871* (New York: E. B. Treat, 1871), pp. 439–40; DeBow, *Statistical View,* p. 162; New York City, Comptroller, *Annual Statement of the Funds of the Corporation of the City of New-York, For the Year Ending December 31, 1847* (New York: William Osborn, 1848), pp. 9–10. The quotation is from the last-named source. The amount of the city's support for paupers in the colored home was sixty cents per week per inmate.

7. *Niles' Weekly Register,* July 14, 1827, p. 326; Turner, *Negro in Pennsylvania,* p. 154; *Appeal on Behalf of a House of Refuge for Colored Juvenile Delinquents,* p. 4; *A Statistical Inquiry into the Condition of the People of Colour of Philadelphia,* p. 23; Everest, "Pauperism and Crime," p. 284.

8. Munsell, *Annals of Albany* 8:158; Mss. Census (1850), Reel 472, pp. 457–65.

9. *Miscellaneous Remarks on the Police of Boston,* p. 5; *Niles' Weekly Register,* June 1, 1833, p. 223; Mss. Census (1850), Reel 435, pp. 379–87.

10. See pp. 260–61, 268. Occupational opportunities for, and real estate ownership by, blacks were not notably greater in Albany. The British traveler Robert Everest asserted that blacks were excluded from the Boston almshouse in the early 1850s. Everest, "Pauperism and Crime," p. 284.

11. Washington, *Laws, 1846,* p. 337; ibid. (1851), pp. 234–36; Mss. Census (1850), Reel 57, pp. 171–72, Reel 844, pp. 206–7.

12. Data for these statements are drawn from sources previously cited in this chapter. The figures are based on reports of the number of inmates in residence on a specific date in single years for all cities except Baltimore. The Baltimore figure is derived from the average of the published monthly averages of inmates in residence for the years 1846–50. For population figures, see chapter 1, for all cities except Philadelphia. Philadelphia population figures are those of Philadelphia County. See U.S., Census Office, *Census, 1850,* p. 179. For the method of calculating population in intercensus years, see appendix D, note 3.

13. Abdy, *Journal* 1:186–87; Raymond H. Mohl, *Poverty in New York, 1783–1825* (New York: Oxford University Press, 1971), pp. 86, 93; Mss. Census (1850), Reel 594; Washington, City Council, *Laws, 1847,* p. 107; Turner, *Negro in Pennsylvania,* p. 146; Baltimore, *Ordinances (1839),* Appendix, p. 24; R. A. Smith, *Philadelphia As It Is in 1852* (Philadelphia: Lindsay and Blakiston, 1852), p. 143; Baltimore, *Ordinances (1841),* Appendix, p. 99.

14. See sources listed in note 3, above.

15. Mohl, *Poverty in New York,* p. 87.

16. See sources cited in note 3, above. For population figures see chapter 1.

17. Mohl, *Poverty in New York,* p. 87.

18. Baltimore, *Ordinances (1842),* Appendix, p. 34. For population figures, see chapter 1. Though the incidence of inmates per thousand of population can be used for a single city, it is not a measurement that can be applied to different cities because of the variation in the method of reporting data. In New York in 1820, for instance, the incidence of almshouse inmates was 13.9 per 1,000 population for adult whites, 15.1 per 1,000 for adult blacks, 14.7 per 1,000 for white children, and 14.4 per 1,000 for black children. But the Baltimore figures are derived from the average of inmate censuses taken at the end of each month, while those for New York rest on a single census taken at the end of the year, when almshouse populations were usually at their highest level. See Mohl, *Poverty in New York,* p. 87.

19. Robert Everest, *A Journey through the United States and Part of Canada* (London: John Chapman, 1855), pp. 85–86.

20. Freeman, "Free Negro in New York City," p. 234.

21. Ibid., pp. 234–35; Everest, "Pauperism and Crime," p. 283. For population figures, see chapter 1.

22. Purvis, *Appeal of Forty Thousand Citizens*, p. 11; Abdy, *Journal* 3:163–64; *Statistical Inquiry into the Condition of the People of Colour of Philadelphia*, pp. 23–24, 31–32.

23. *Statistical Inquiry into the Condition of the People of Colour of Philadelphia*, pp. 24–25.

24. Munsell, *Annals of Albany* 2:295.

25. Baltimore, *Ordinances (1843)*, Appendix, p. 98; Baltimore, *Ordinances (1850)*, Appendix, p. 131; Mss. Census (1850), Reel 283, pp. 705–6; Valentine, *Manual, 1844–5*, p. 172; ibid. (1845–6), p. 190; ibid., (1847), p. 228.

26. Eugene P. Link, "The Civil Rights Activities of Three Great Negro Physicians," *Journal of Negro History* 52 (July 1967): 171; Mss. Census (1850), Reel 335, pp. 632–36.

27. Sterkx, *Free Negro in Louisiana*, p. 88; *Cohen's New Orleans and Lafayette Directory* (New Orleans: The Daily Delta, 1852), p. 37; Mss. Census (1850), Reel 282, pp. 711–13, Reel 537, pp. 289–94. It should be noted, however, that during the last dozen years of the half-century black patients in the New Orleans Charity Hospital constituted less than one percent of the whole number of patients admitted. See DeBow, *Statistical View*, p. 110.

28. John Doggett, Jr., *The Great Metropolis; or Guide to New-York for 1846* (New York: Directory Establishment, [1846]), pp. 83–84; *Statistical Inquiry into the Condition of the People of Colour of Philadelphia*, p. 24; *Gibson's Guide and Directory of the State of Louisiana, and the Cities of New Orleans & Lafayette* (New Orleans: John Gibson, 1838), p. 176; Julianna L. Boudreaux, "A History of Philanthropy in New Orleans, 1835–1862," Ph.D. Diss., Tulane University, 1961, pp. 183–84; Wright, *Free Negro in Maryland*, p. 250. Assistance provided by black beneficial societies is discussed in chapter 12.

29. Lossing, *History of New York City*, pp. 469–70.

30. Freeman, "Free Negro in New York City," pp. 243–44.

31. Richmond, *New York and Its Institutions*, pp. 302–5; Curry, *New-York*, pp. 251–52; Freeman, "Free Negro in New York City," pp. 243–49; Valentine, *Manual (1844–5)*, pp. 251–52; N.Y.C., Comptroller, *Report, 1847*, pp. 9–10; John Hardy, *Manual of the Corporation of the City of New York*, [1870] (New York, 1871), p. 762. The quotation is from Richmond, p. 302. The orphanage was destroyed in the riots of 1863.

32. Curry, *New-York*, p. 251.

33. Smith, *Philadelphia As It Is in 1852*, p. 276.

34. Charles Cist, *Sketches and Statistics of Cincinnati in 1851* (Cincinnati: William H. Moore, 1851), p. 151; Dabney, *Cincinnati's Colored Citizens*, pp. 357, 394; Mss. Census (1850), Reel 689, pp. 280–81. The quotation is from Cist.

35. Richard M. Bayles, *History of Providence County, Rhode Island* (Providence: W. W. Preston, 1891), 1:427; *The Providence Directory* (Providence: H. H. Brown, 1847), p. 257; Mss. Census (1850), Reel 844, p. 245.

36. It is possible that there may have been an equal proportion of indigents among the most recently arrived immigrants, but it is not possible to separate this group from the much larger foreign-born population in general. In 1850 black inmates of the colored home comprised more than five percent of the city's Negro population, while the foreign-born inmates of the almshouse constituted about $1\frac{1}{8}$ percent of that segment of the white population. See DeBow, *Statistical View*, pp. 162, 399.

Chapter 9

1. Amasa Walker, *Ninth Report to the Legislature of Massachusetts, Relating to the Registry and Return of Births, Marriages and Deaths, in the Commonwealth, for the Year Ending December 31, 1850* (Boston: Dutton and Wentworth, 1851), p. 15; DeBow, *Statistical View*, pp. 102, 254.

2. *Report of the Joint Special Committee on the Census of Boston, May, 1855, Including the Report of the Censors, with Analytical and Sanitary Observations, by Josiah Curtis, M.D.* (Boston: Moore and Crosby, 1856), p. 68; Gouverneur Emerson, "Medical Statistics: Being a Series of Tables, Showing the Mortality in Philadelphia, and Its Immediate Causes, during a Period of Twenty Years," *American Journal of Medical Sciences* 1 (1827–28): 123; New York City, Inspector, *Annual Report . . . of the Number of Interments in the City of New-York, for the Year 1841* (New York: Bryant and Boggs, 1842), pp. 165–66.

3. William T. Howard, Jr., *Public Health Administration and the Natural History of Disease in Baltimore, Maryland, 1797–1920* (Washington: Carnegie Institution, 1924), pp. 508–9 (see also appendix D, note 3); Dawson and De Saussure, *Census of the City of Charleston, 1848*, pp. 240, 248; Freeman, "Free Negro in New York City," p. 447; *Niles' Weekly Register*, February 22, 1823, p. 86; ibid., March 4, 1826, p. 3; *Picture of New-York*, pp. 178–80; New York City, Inspector, *Annual Report of the Interments in the City and County of New-York . . . for the Year 1837* (New York: T. Snowden, 1838), pp. 474–79; New York City, Inspector, *Annual Report of the Interments in the City and County of New York, for the Year 1839* (New York: Bryant and Boggs, 1840), p. 504; ibid. (1841), p. 451; ibid. (1842), foldout sheet 9; New York City, Inspector, *Annual Report of the City Inspector of the City of New-York for the Year 1844* (New York: J. F. Trow, 1845), pp. 685–86; *Annual Report . . . of the Number of Deaths and Interments in the City of New York, During the Year 1948* (New York: McSpedon and Baker, 1849), p. 786; *Annual Report . . . of the Number of Deaths and Interments in the City of New York, During the Year 1849* (New York: McSpeden and Baker, 1850), p. 398; *Annual Report . . . of the Number of Deaths and Interments, in the City of New York, During the Year 1850* (New York: McSpedon and Baker, 1851), p. 346; Valentine, *Manual, (1845–6)*, p. 238; ibid. (1847), pp. 274–75; David T. Valentine, *Manual of the Corporation of the City of New York, for the Year 1848* (New York: William Osborn, 1848), p. 286; Gouverneur Emerson, "Medical Statistics; consisting of estimates relating to the population of Philadelphia, and its changes as influenced by the Deaths and Births, during a period of ten years, *viz.* from 1821 to 1830 inclusive," *American Journal of Medical Sciences* 9 (November 1831): 42; Gouverneur Emerson, "Vital Statistics of Philadelphia, for the decenial period from 1830 to 1840," *American Journal of Medical Sciences* 16 n.s. (July 1848): 18. Decennial averages are computed by dividing the average number of deaths by the average population. See appendix D, note 3 for an explanation of the computation of annual population. Since the area covered by the Philadelphia statistics does not conform to any political jurisdiction, census data do not provide usable population figures. Annual populations have been computed from figures given in Emerson, "Medical Statistics of twenty years," pp. 136–37; Emerson, "Medical Statistics, 1821–1830," p. 42; and Gouverneur Emerson, "Vital Statistics, 1830–1840," p. 18.

4. See sources listed in note 3.

5. Lemuel Shattuck, *Bills of Mortality, 1810–1849, City of Boston, with an Essay on the Vital Statistics of Boston, From 1840 to 1841* (Boston: Registry Department, 1893; essay orig. pub. 1841), p. xlii; Boston, City Registrar, *Report by the City Registrar, on the Births, Marriages, and Deaths, in the City of Boston, for the Year 1855* (Boston: Moore and Cosby, 1856), pp. 13, 17; *Report by the City Registrar, of the Births, Marriages, and Deaths, in the City of Boston, for the Year 1856* (Boston: George C. Rand and Avery, 1857), pp. 17, 26; *Report by the City Registrar, of the Births, Marriages, and Deaths, in the*

City of Boston, for the Year 1857 (Boston: George C. Rand and Avery, 1858), pp. 16, 23; *Report by the City Registrar, of the Births, Marriages, and Deaths, in the City of Boston, for the Year 1858* (Boston: George C. Rand and Avery, 1859), pp. 14, 52; *Report by the City Registrar, of the Births, Marriages, and Deaths, in the City of Boston, for the Year 1859* (Boston: George C. Rand and Avery, 1860), pp. 20–21; *Providence Directory* (1841), p. 210; ibid. (1844), p. 226; *The Providence Directory* (Providence: H. H. Brown, 1847), p. 238; *The Providence Directory* (Providence: H. H. Brown, 1850), p. 241; *Hazard's U.S. Register,* January 19, 1842, p. 44; Washington, Board of Health, *Report . . . for the Year Ending July 1, 1849* (n.p., n.d.), pp. 6–11; Washington, *Laws (1850),* p. 547; *DeBow's Review* 9 (August 1850): 230. The 1840 figure for Boston has been computed on the basis of estimated black population (see p. 6). The Washington and Providence figures include stillbirths, while the data for Boston and (apparently) New Orleans do not. The higher white death rate in New Orleans in 1849 was probably largely the result of the yellow fever epidemic. This disease was deadly to whites but rarely fatal to blacks. In Charleston, for instance, between 1822 and 1848, there were only fourteen reported Negro deaths from yellow fever, out of a total of 948 deaths attributed to this cause. See Dawson and De Saussure, *Census of the City of Charleston, 1848,* p. 252.

6. See table 9-1; U.S., Census Office, *Statistics of the United States, (Including Morality, Property, &c.,) in 1860* (Washington: Government Printing Office, 1866), p. 280.

7. Howard, *Public Health in Baltimore,* pp. 508–9; Baltimore, City Health Department, *First Thirty-Five Reports,* reports for 1832 and 1849 (unpaged); Baltimore, *Ordinances (1830),* Appendix, p. 22; ibid. (1832), Appendix, p. 18; ibid. (1846), Appendix, p. 150; Washington, Board of Health, *Report, 1849,* Appendix 1.

8. Shattuck, *Bills of Mortality of Boston,* p. xiii.

9. DeBow, *Statistical View,* p. 110.

10. E.g., Emerson, "Medical Statistics . . . of twenty years," p. 123; Baltimore, City Health Department, *First Thirty-five Reports,* report for 1849 (unpaged); William Elliot, *The Washington Guide* (Washington: Franck Taylor, 1837), p. 50; David B. Warden, *A Chronological and Statistical Description of the District of Columbia* (Paris: Smith, 1816), p. 19.

11. *Niles' Weekly Register,* August 25, 1832, p. 451; ibid., September 1, 1832, p. 2; Philadelphia, Board of Health, *Statistics of Cholera* (Philadelphia: King and Baird, 1849), p. 46; Washington, *Laws, 1850,* p. 519; N.Y.C., Inspector, *Report, 1844,* p. 693; Hardie, *Description of New-York,* p. 161.

12. Emerson, "Medical Statistics . . . of twenty years," p. 133n; Washington, *Laws (1850),* pp. 518–19.

13. It must also be noted that the validity of any analysis of causes of death is severely limited by the extremely unsatisfactory medical nomenclature of the period. One is at a loss, for example, to know what disorder caused the deaths attributed to dropsy, convulsions, fits, or teething. The analysis that follows deals, perforce, with the data as reported at the time.

14. Dawson and De Saussure, *Census of the City of Charleston, 1848,* pp. 249–54; N.Y.C., Inspector, *Report, 1837,* pp. 474–79; New York City, Inspector, *Annual Report of the Interments in the City and County of New York for the Year 1838* (New York: T. Snowden, 1839), pp. 70–88; ibid. (1839), pp. 499–504; ibid. (1841), pp. 446–51; ibid. (1842), pp. 140–48; Washington, Board of Health, *Report, 1849,* pp. 6–11; Washington, *Laws (1850),* pp. 522–27; Washington, Board of Health, *Report . . . for the Year Ending July 1, 1851* (n.p., n.d.), pp.12–18. The relatively (in some cases, dramatically) low Negro death rates for some childhood diseases may, at least in part, result from the unusually low percentage of children in the black population and from a tendency not to report the deaths of infants or to inter their remains.

15. U.S., Census Office, *Mortality Statistics, 1850,* p. 303. See also sources listed in note 13.

16. Dawson and De Saussure, *Census of the City of Charleston, 1848,* pp. 216–17; N.Y.C., Inspector, *Report, 1838,* pp. 88–89; ibid. (1842), pp. 148, 151; ibid. (1844), pp. 698–708, 730–40, 762–72, 794–804. In Charleston the number of deaths of children under ten made up a remarkably small proportion of the total mortality, averaging less than one-third. This may have been, in part, a result of inadequate reporting of such deaths, but the more significant reason was doubtless a very high adult mortality rate. In the 1840s, for example, the proportion of children in the total deaths increased by more than six percentage points over the previous decade, despite the fact that the average annual number of such deaths decreased slightly. This anomaly was created by a much larger drop in adult mortality.

17. Dawson and De Saussure, *Census of the City of Charleston, 1848,* p. 211; N.Y.C., Inspector, *Report, 1838,* p. 88; ibid. (1839), p. 504; ibid. (1841), p. 451; ibid. (1842), p. 148, ibid. (1844), pp. 685–86; Valentine, *Manual (1845–6),* p. 238; ibid. (1847), pp. 274–75; ibid. (1848), p. 236; Washington, Board of Health, *Report, 1849,* p. 11; ibid., 1851, p. 18; Washington, *Laws (1850),* p. 546; *DeBow's Review* 9 (August 1850): 230.

18. U.S., Census Office, *Mortality Statistics, 1850,* p. 27; DeBow, *Statistical View,* pp. 49, 66, 86.

19. See sources listed in note 16 for white male/female mortality figures.

20. Howard, *Public Health of Baltimore,* pp. 508–9; U.S., Census Office, *Census, 1820,* p. 21*; ibid. (1830), third pagination, pp. 80–81; ibid. (1840), pp. 194–95; ibid. (1850), p. 221.

21. See sources listed in note 20.

22. *Niles' Weekly Register,* January 21, 1826, p. 325; Warden, *Description of the District of Columbia,* p. 19.

Chapter 10

1. Boston, Registry Department, *Minutes of the Selectmen's Meetings, 1799–1810,* p. 14.

2. Allen, *Negro in New York,* p. 119; Turner, *Negro in Pennsylvania,* pp. 128–29; Erasmus Wilson, ed., *Standard History of Pittsburg [sic], Pennsylvania* (Chicago: Goodspeed, 1898), p. 514; U.S., Commissioner of Education, *Schools for the Colored Population,* pp. 376–77; Freeman, "Free Negro in New York," pp. 318–19. The blacks in New York and Philadelphia at the beginning of the eighteenth century were, of course, overwhelmingly slaves, and Neau's school, at least, was designed to prepare slaves for baptism in the Anglican church. See Arthur Zilversmit, *The First Emancipation: The Abolition of Slavery in the North* (Chicago: University of Chicago Press, 1969), p. 8.

3. Charles H. Wesley, *Richard Allen: Apostle of Freedom* (Washington: Associated Publishers, 1935), pp. 91–92; Asa H. Gordon, *Sketches of Negro Life and History in South Carolina* (Columbia: University of South Carolina Press, 1971; orig. pub. 1929), p. 84; J. Thomas Scharf, *History of Baltimore City and County* (Philadelphia: Louis H. Everts, 1881), p. 225n.

4. U.S., Commissioner of Education, *Schools for the Colored Population,* p. 383; Charles H. Wesley, "The Negro's Struggle for Freedom in Its Birthplace," *Journal of Negro History* 30 (January 1945): 68; Bryan, *National Capital* 2:137; Rousseve, *Negro in Louisiana,* pp. 42–43; Berlin, "Slaves Who Were Free," pp. 141–42; John B. Shotwell, *A History of the Schools of Cincinnati* (Cincinnati: School Life Company, 1902), p. 447; Brown, *The Life of William J. Brown,* p. 49; Rossiter, *Days and Ways in Old Boston,* p. 128; Carter G. Woodson, *The Education of the Negro Prior to 1861* (New York: G. P. Putnam, 1915), pp. 128–29, 224.

5. William B. Hesseltine, "Four American Traditions," *Journal of Southern History* 27 (February 1961): 3–32.

6. Wilson, *History of Pittsburg*, p. 514; Brown, *Life of William J. Brown*, pp. 44–45; Donnie D. Bellamy, "Free Blacks in Antebellum Missouri, 1820–1860," *Missouri Historical Review* 67 (January 1973): 222–23; Ohio Anti-Slavery Society, *People of Color in Ohio*, p. 11; Abdy, *Journal* 2:400–402; U.S., Commissioner of Education, *Schools for the Colored Population*, p. 371; Arna W. Bontemps and Jack Conroy, *They Seek a City* (Garden City, N.Y.: Doubleday, Doran, 1945), pp. 56–57.

7. Ford and Ford, *History of Cincinnati*, p. 169; Betty Porter, "The History of Negro Education in Louisiana," *Louisiana Historical Quarterly* 25 (July 1942): 731–32; Sterkx, *Free Negro in Louisiana*, pp. 270–71; American Convention of Abolition Societies, *Minutes, 1806*, p. 22; Boston Society for the Religious and Moral Instruction of the Poor, *Eighth Annual Report* (Boston: Crocker and Brewster, 1824), pp. 23–24. The Bostonians' ambivalent attitude toward blacks is indicated by their wistful observation that Negro education was particularly important because it "may enable individuals to stamp the features of morality, science and religion on Africa, Hayti, or other countreis to which Providence may call them." In the pre-Revolutionary period the Society for the Propagation of the Gospel in Foreign Parts maintained a mission school in Charleston employing two Negro instructors. See Loretta Funke, "The Negro in Education," *Journal of Negro History* 5 (January 1920): 3.

8. *Statistical Inquiry into the Condition of the People of Colour of Philadelphia* (Philadelphia: Kite and Walton, 1849), pp. 19–20; James Mease, *The Picture of Philadelphia* (Philadelphia: B. and T. Kite, 1811), pp. 262–63; Charles C. Ellis, *Lancastrian Schools of Philadelphia* (n.p., [1907?]), p. 8.

9. Mease, *Picture of Philadelphia*, pp. 263–64; George F. Bragg, *History of the Afro-American Group of the Episcopal Church* (Baltimore: Church Advocate Press, 1922), pp. 68–69; Daniel Bowen, *A History of Philadelphia* (Philadelphia: D. Bowen, 1839), pp. 118–19. The Infant School Society also operated facilities for white children. When donations slumped following the 1837 panic, the society, in a desperate plea for support, noted, "The Funds for the support of the white and colored schools, are kept entirely separate. Any contributors having a preference will please to designate it." Bowen, *History of Philadelphia*, p. 119.

10. U.S., Commissioner of Education, *Schools for the Colored Population*, p. 379; American Convention of Abolition Societies, *Minutes of the Proceedings of the Sixth Convention of Delegates from the Abolition Societies Established in Different Parts of the United States* (Philadelphia: Zachariah Poulson, 1800), p. 7; American Convention of Abolition Societies, *Minutes of the Proceedings of the Fourteenth American Convention for Promoting the Abolition of Slavery, and Improving the Condition of the African Race* (Philadelphia: W. Brown, 1816), pp. 8–9; *Minutes of the Proceedings of the Fifteenth American Convention for Promoting the Abolition of Slavery, and Improving the Condition of the African Race* (Philadelphia: Merritt, 1817), p. 10; *Minutes of the Nineteenth Session of the American Convention for Promoting the Abolition of Slavery, and Improving the Condition of the African Race* (Philadelphia: Atkinson and Alexander, 1825), p. 13; Pennsylvania Society for Promoting the Abolition of Slavery, *Free People of Color of Philadelphia*, p. 29; *Statistical Inquiry into the Condition of the People of Colour of Philadelphia*, pp. 20–21.

11. Charles C. Andrews, *History of the New-York African Free-Schools* (New York: Mahlan Day, 1830), pp. 7–45, 85–87, 97, 114, 116; Samuel L. Mitchell, *The Picture of New-York; or the Traveller's Guide* (New York: I. Riley, 1807), pp. 113–14; William O. Bourne, *History of the Public School Society of the City of New York* (New York: William Wood, 1870), pp. 95, 164, 670–74; U.S., Commissioner of Education, *Schools for the Colored Population*, pp. 364–66; American Convention of Abolition Societies, *Minutes, 1800*, p. 13; American Convention of Abolition Societies, *Minutes of the Proceedings of the Seventh Convention of Delegates from the Abolition Societies Established in Different Parts*

of the United States (Philadelphia: Zachariah Poulson, 1801), pp. 6–7; *Minutes of the Proceedings of the Ninth American Convention for Promoting the Abolition of Slavery, and Improving the Condition of the African Race* (Philadelphia: Solomon W. Conrad, 1804), p. 5; *Minutes of the Proceedings of the Tenth American Convention for Promoting the Abolition of Slavery and Improving the Condition of the African Race* (Philadelphia: Kimber, Conrad, and Company, 1805), pp. 7–8; ibid. (1806), pp. 6–7; ibid. (1816), pp. 13–16; ibid. (1817), p. 7; American Convention of Abolition Societies, *Minutes of the Proceedings of a Special Meeting of the Fifteenth American Convention for Promoting the Abolition of Slavery, and Improving the Condition of the African Race* (Philadelphia: Hall and Atkinson, 1818), p. 13; *Minutes of the Seventeenth Session of the American Convention for Promoting the Abolition of Slavery, and Improving the Condition of the African Race* (Philadelphia: Atkinson and Alexander, 1821), p. 6; ibid. (1823), p. 6; American Convention of Abolition Societies, *Minutes of the Twentieth Session of the American Convention for Promoting the Abolition of Slavery, and Improving the Condition of the African Race* (Baltimore: Benjamin Lundy, 1827), pp. 34, 37.

12. Richard Bardolph, "Social Origins of Distinguished Negroes, 1770–1865," *Journal of Negro History* 40 (July 1955): 244, 248; Allen, *Negro in New York,* p. 53.

13. Bourne, *History of the Public School Society,* pp. 614, 670. In the pre-Revolutionary period some slight support for the education of Negroes had been supplied by the Society for the Propagation of the Gospel in Foreign Parts and by the Bray Associates. See Freeman, "Free Negro in New York City," p. 318.

14. William Douglass, *Annals of the First African Church, In the United States of America, Now Styled the African Episcopal Church of St. Thomas, Philadelphia* (Philadelphia: King and Baird, 1862), pp. 110–11; Wesley, *Richard Allen,* p. 91; Carol V. R. George, *Segregated Sabbaths: Richard Allen and the Emergence of Independent Black Churches, 1790–1840* (New York: Oxford University Press, 1973), p. 76; Payne, *History of the AME Church.* 1:143, 176–77; Charles Shaw, *A Topographical and Historical Description of Boston* (Boston: Oliver Spear, 1817), p. 270; Wright, *Free Negro in Maryland, 1634–1860,* p. 205.

15. Wright, *Free Negro in Maryland,* pp. 202–5; U.S., Commissioner of Education, *Schools for the Colored Population,* pp. 205–6; Funke, "Negro in Education," p. 3; Charles Varle, *A Complete View of Baltimore* (Baltimore: Samuel Young, 1833), p. 33. Some educational opportunities had been provided (probably intermittently) for black Catholics prior to the establishment of St. Francis Academy.

16. Wright, *Free Negro in Maryland,* p. 202.

17. Munsell, *Annals of Albany* 7:185, 187; Wade, "Negro in Cincinnati," p. 17; Bellamy, "Free Blacks in Missouri," p. 222; Brown, *Life of William J. Brown,* p. 40; Lorenzo D. Johnson, *The Churches and Pastors of Washington, D.C.* (New York: M. W. Dodd, 1857), p. 129; U.S., Commissioner of Education, *Schools for the Colored Population,* p. 221; James P. Wesberry, *Baptists in South Carolina before the War between the States* (Columbia, S.C.: R. L. Bryan, 1966), p. 70; Lillian G. Dabney, *The History of Schools for Negroes in the District of Columbia, 1807–1947* (Washington: Catholic University of America Press, 1949), p. 12; "The Condition of the Colored Population of the City of Baltimore," *Baltimore Literary and Religious Magazine* 4 (April 1838): 169–70; Wilson, *Standard History of Pittsburg,* p. 926; Boston Society for the Religious and Moral Instruction of the Poor, *Fifth Annual Report* (Charlestown, Mass.: S. Ethridge, 1821), p. 10.

18. Dabney, *Schools for Negroes in D.C.,* p. 12.

19. Munsell, *Annals of Albany* 7:194, 8:167; Sterkx, *Free Negro in Louisiana,* p. 260; U.S., Commissioner of Education, *Schools for the Colored Population,* p. 221; Greve, *History of Cincinnati* 1:575; Johnson, *Churches of Washington,* p. 133; William J. Catto, *A Semi-Centennial Discourse, Delivered in the First African Presbyterian Church. Philadelphia, on the Fourth Sabbath of May, 1857: With A History of the Church from Its First*

Organization (Philadelphia: Joseph M. Wilson, 1857), p. 111; Noah Davis, *A Narrative of the Life of Rev. Noah Davis, A Colored Man* (Baltimore: John F. Weishampel, Jr., 1859), p. 84.

20. Wesley, "Negro's Struggle for Freedom," pp. 68–69; Scharf, *History of Baltimore,* p. 225n; C. W. Birnie, "The Education of the Negro in Charleston, South Carolina, Prior to the Civil War," *Journal of Negro History* 12 (January 1927): 19; Ralph F. Weld, *Brooklyn Village, 1816–1834* (New York: Columbia University Press, 1938), p. 327.

21. Birnie, "Education of the Negro in Charleston," p. 15; Young, *History of Philadelphia* 2:313; Aptheker, *Documentary History of the Negro People,* pp. 72–73; American Convention of Abolition Societies, *Minutes of the Thirteenth American Convention for Promoting the Abolition of Slavery, and Improving the Condition of the African Race* (Hamiltonville: John Bouvier, 1812), p. 7; Freeman, "Free Negro in New York City," pp. 352–55, 369–70; Andrew Murray, *Presbyterians and the Negro–A History* (Philadelphia: Presbyterian Historical Society, 1966), pp. 96–97; Dabney, *Schools for Negroes in D.C.,* pp. 6–11; Wilson, *History of Pittsburg,* p. 514.

22. Alice Dunbar-Nelson, "People of Color in Louisiana—Part II," *Journal of Negro History* 2 (January 1917): 65; Sterkx, *Free Negro in Louisiana,* pp. 268–69; Porter, "History of Negro Education in Louisiana," p. 733–34; U.S., Commissioner of Education, *Schools for the Colored Population,* pp. 352–53; Woodson, *Education of the Negro,* p. 143.

23. Hickok, *Negro in Ohio,* p. 88.

24. American Convention of Abolition Societies, *Minutes, 1812,* p. 7; Thomas Boese, *Public Education in the City of New York: Its History, Condition and Statistics* (New York: Harper and Brothers, 1869), p. 57.

25. Pennsylvania Society for Promoting the Abolition of Slavery, *Free People of Color of Philadelphia,* pp. 29, 39; *Statistical Inquiry into the Condition of the People of Colour of Philadelphia,* pp. 19–22.

26. U.S., Commissioner of Education, *Schools for the Colored Population,* pp. 370–71; Shotwell, *History of the Schools of Cincinnati,* pp. 447–56; Bontemps and Conroy, *They Seak a City,* pp. 56–57; Hickok, *Negro in Ohio,* pp. 82–83.

27. Woodson, *Education of the Negro,* p. 142; "Condition of Colored Population of Baltimore," p. 171; Mss. Census (1850), Reel 286, p. 300, ln. 41, p. 301, lns. 1–4; William H. Gibson, Sr., *Semi-Centennial of the Public Career of W. H. Gibson, Sr.,* Part II of *History of the United Brothers of Friendship and Sisters of the Mysterious Ten* (Louisville: Bradley and Gilbert, 1897), pp. 4–5, 38; Henry C. Weeden, *Weeden's History of the Colored People of Louisville* (Louisville, 1897), p. 31; George D. Wilson, "A Century of Negro Education in Louisville," Unpublished report on W.P.A. Project 665-43-3-77-2, copy in University of Louisville Library, Louisville, Kentucky, pp. 8–9.

28. U.S., Commissioner of Education, *Schools for the Colored Population,* pp. 195–214; Dabney, *Schools for Negroes in D.C.,* pp. 5–13.

29. Porter, "History of Negro Education in Louisiana," p. 734; Henry Rightor, ed., *Standard History of New Orleans, Louisiana* (Chicago: Lewis, 1900), p. 234; John A. Paxton, *The New-Orleans Directory and Register* (New Orleans: Benj. Levy, 1822), p. 16; Reinders, "Free Negro in the New Orleans Economy," p. 277; Woodson, *Education of the Negro,* pp. 217, 219; Payne, *History of the A.M.E. Church* 2:394; Bierne, "Education of the Negro in Charleston," pp. 18–19.

30. *Niles' Weekly Register,* January 10, 1849, p. 32; Sterkx, *Free Negro in Louisiana,* p. 269.

31. Bryan, *National Capital* 2:388–89; U.S., Commissioner of Education, *Schools for the Colored Population,* p. 215.

32. Aptheker, *Documentary History of the Negro People,* pp. 19–20; American Convention of Abolition Societies, *Minutes, 1806,* p. 22.

33. Shotwell, *History of the Schools of Cincinnati,* pp. 447, 455–57; Woodson, *Educa-*

tion of the Negro, pp. 326–28; *Niles' National Register,* January 27, 1844, p. 343; ibid., February 21, 1849, p. 122; U.S., Commissioner of Education, *Schools for the Colored Population,* pp. 371–72; U.S., Census Office, *Census, 1830,* third pagination, pp. 126–27.

34. Albany, Board of School Commissioners, *Report of the Board of School Commissioners of the District Schools of the City of Albany, to the Common Council, made July 12, 1852* (Albany: Franklin Office, 1852), pp. 8–9, 12–18, 20; Oliver G. Steele, "The Buffalo Common Schools," *Publications of the Buffalo Historical Society* 1 (1879): 418–23; Horatio N. Walker, *Buffalo City Directory: Containing a List of the Names, Residences and Occupations of the Heads of Families, Householders, &c. on the First of May, 1840* (Buffalo: Faxon and Graves, 1840), p. 23.

35. Weld, *Brooklyn Village,* p. 327; Henry R. Stiles, *A History of the City of Brooklyn* (Brooklyn: By Subscription, 1867–70), 2:230; Archie E. Palmer, *The New York Public School; Being a History of Free Education in the City of New York* (New York: Macmillan, 1905), pp. 213–16.

36. Woodson, *Education of the Negro,* pp. 315–16; U.S., Commissioner of Education, *Schools for the Colored Population,* p. 383; Staples, *Annals of Providence,* pp. 508–14; Wilson, *History of Pittsburg,* pp. 514–18; Isaac Harris, *Harris' General Business Directory, of the Cities of Pittsburgh and Allegheny* (Pittsburgh: A. A. Anderson, 1841), p. 112; Isaac Harris, *Harris' Business Directory of the Cities of Pittsburgh & Allegheny* (Pittsburgh: A. A. Anderson, 1844), p. 59.

37. Henry C. Silcox, "Delay and Neglect: Negro Public Education in Antebellum Philadelphia, 1800–1860," *Pennsylvania Magazine of History and Biography* 97 (October 1973): 444, 448–52; Ellis, *Lancastrian Schools in Philadelphia,* p. 56; Oberholtzer, *Philadelphia* 2:73.

38. Silcox, "Delay and Neglect," pp. 452–59.

39. Ellis, *Lancastrian Schools in Philadelphia,* p. 56; Thomas Wilson, *Picture of Philadelphia for 1824* (Philadelphia: Thomas Town, 1823), p. 60; Philadelphia, Controllers of the Public Schools, *Sixth Annual Report* (Philadelphia: William Fry, 1824), p. 6; *Fifteenth Annual Report* (Philadelphia: n.p., 1833), pp. 3–4, 14–16; *Sixteenth Annual Report* (Philadelphia: n.p., 1834), pp. 3–4, 14–15; *Seventeenth Annual Report* (Philadelphia: n.p., 1835), pp. 3–4, 11–12; *Eighteenth Annual Report* (Philadelphia: William Stavely, 1836), pp. 3–4, 11–12; *Nineteenth Annual Report* (Philadelphia: A. Waldie, 1837), pp. 3–4; *Twenty-first Annual Report* (Philadelphia: J. Crissy, 1839), pp. 5–6; *Twenty-third Annual Report* (Philadelphia: J. Crissy, 1841), p. 10; *Twenty-seventh Annual Report* (Philadelphia: Crissy and Markley, 1846), pp. 15–57; *Thirty-second Annual Report* (Philadelphia: Crissy and Markley, 1850), pp. 19–66; Pennsylvania Society for Promoting the Abolition of Slavery, *Free People of Color of Philadelphia,* p. 29; *Statistical Inquiry into the Condition of the People of Colour of Philadelphia,* pp. 19, 21.

40. Bourne, *History of the Public School Society,* pp. 674–78; U.S., Commissioner of Education, *Schools for the Colored Population,* p. 366; Freeman, "Free Negroes in New York," p. 336; David T. Valentine, *Manual of the Corporation of the City of New–York, for the Year 1850* (New York: McSpedon and Baker, 1850), pp. 298–326; Doggett, *The Great Metropolis,* pp. 92–93.

41. I. Smith Homans, *Sketches of Boston, Past and Present* (Boston: Phillips, Sampson, 1851), p. 215.

42. Josiah Quincy, *A Municipal History of the Town and City of Boston, During Two Centuries. From September 17, 1630, to September 17, 1830* (Boston: Charles C. Little and James Brown, 1852), pp. 20–27; Caleb H. Snow, *A History of Boston* (Boston: Abel Bowen, 1828), pp. 348–52; Daniels, *In Freedom's Birthplace,* pp. 446–47; Joseph M. Wightman, *Annals of the Boston Primary School Committee, From Its First Establishment in 1818, to Its Dissolution in 1855* (Boston: George C. Rand and Avery, 1860), pp. 68–70; Shattuck, *Census of Boston for the Year 1845,* pp. 43–44.

43. Daniels, *In Freedom's Birthplace,* pp. 447–49; Wightman, *Annals of the Boston Primary School Committee,* pp. 208–9, 212; Boston Registry Department, *A Volume of Records Relating to the Early History of Boston Containing Minutes of the Selectmen's Meetings from September 1, 1818, to April 24, 1822,* vol. 39 (Boston: Printing Department, 1909), p. 117; Aptheker, *Documentary History of the Negro People,* pp. 243–45, 297–99; Jacobs, "History of the Boston Negro," pp. 241–54.

44. Bacon, *Statistics of the Colored People of Philadelphia,* pp. 5–6; Azzie B. Koger, *History of the Negro Baptists of Maryland* (Baltimore: Jesse B. Clarke and Son, 1936), p. 11; Woodson, *Education of the Negro,* p. 144; Wilson, *History of Pittsburg,* p. 517.

45. Ohio Antislavery Society, *People of Color in Ohio,* p. 11; Boston Society for the Religious and Moral Instruction of the Poor, *Eighth Annual Report* (1824), pp. 23–24; American Convention of Abolition Societies, *Minutes, 1818,* p. 13; "Statisticks [*sic*] of Destitution in Baltimore," *Baltimore Literary and Religious Magazine* 3 (June 1837): 279.

46. U.S., Census Office, *Census, 1850,* pp. 48, 49, 56, 66, 70, 88, 90, 117, 154, 156, 191, 218, 219, 224, 232, 233, 236, 334, 335–36, 343, 466, 468–69, 479, 600, 604–5, 621, 646, 648–49, 672, 810, 813–14, 858. FPC designates free people of color. While the ages 5–16 might be a more usual conception of the school-age population, the published census figures do not divide the population in this manner. In any event, it was rare in antebellum America for children over fourteen years of age to attend school. It might be noted that the number of Negro girls attending school exceeded the number of boys in two-thirds of the cities. This was true among the white students in only Boston and New Orleans, despite the fact that the white school-age population was predominately female in two-thirds of the cities. The free black school-age population was female-dominant in every city except Providence.

47. *African Observer,* Seventh Month, 1827, p. 122.

48. Mss. Census (1850), Reels 56–57, 206–7, 235–38, 281–87, 334–39, 415–18, 471–72, 501–2, 517–20, 534–59, 687–91, 745–46, 812–17, 844–45, 850; Whitley, *Philadelphia Directory for 1820.* To conserve space the other directories examined will not be cited here. See appendix B, note 3 for a listing of about one-half of those whose content was analyzed.

49. James M. Bland to William McLain, July 3, 1848, "Letters to the American Colonization Society," *Journal of Negro History* 10 (April 1925): 227; Andrews, *History of the New-York African Free-Schools,* pp. 117–22. For an analysis of free black occupational trends, see chapter 2.

Chapter 11

1. W. E. B. DuBois, *The Negro Church* (Atlanta: Atlanta University Press, 1903), p. 30.

2. Wesley, *Richard Allen,* pp. 50–52; George, *Segregated Sabbaths,* pp. 41, 51, 55.

3. At a later date, of course, after racially separated churches became commonplace, prospective leaders were prepared to take a chance on a new venture with fewer adherents.

4. George, *Segregated Sabbaths,* pp. 22–32, 41–43, 48, 51; Wesley, *Richard Allen,* pp. 35, 41–44, 48–52. The opposition of the white churchmen probably sprang from the fact that a separate black congregation would doubtless have black officers, including trustees who would control (though not necessarily own) any property that might be acquired.

5. It is notable that at least three of the four blacks who favored the establishment of a separate black church were involved in this affair and that their entrance into the church coincided with a period of public prayer, which probably made it less likely that they would be carefully shepherded to the assigned seats.

6. Wesley, *Richard Allen*, pp. 52–53; George, *Segregated Sabbaths*, pp. 54–55; DuBois, *The Philadelphia Negro*, p. 19.

7. Wesley, *Richard Allen*, pp. 65–66, 68–72; George, *Segregated Sabbaths*, p. 57; Bragg, *History of the Afro-American Group of the Episcopal Church*, pp. 60–68.

8. Wesley, *Richard Allen*, pp. 75–88, 99; George, *Segregated Sabbaths*, pp. 66–67.

9. Wesley, *Richard Allen*, pp. 135–41; George, *Segregated Sabbaths*, pp. 60–71, 78–79; Richard R. Wright, Jr., *The Encyclopedia of the African Methodist Episcopal Church* (Philadelphia: Book Concern of the AME Church, 1947), pp. 330–34.

10. Wesley, *Richard Allen*, pp. 149–53; George, *Segregated Sabbaths*, pp. 56, 86–89; Wright, *Free Negro in Maryland*, pp. 212, 215–19; African Methodist Episcopal Church, *The Centennial Budget* (n.p., [1888]), pp. 272–75. The Philadelphia and Baltimore churches probably enrolled more than four-fifths of all AME members in 1816.

11. David H. Bradley, *A History of the A.M.E. Zion Church* (Nashville: Parthenon Press, 1956, 1970), 1:44–91; *The History of American Methodism* (New York and Nashville: Abingdon Press, 1964), 1:609–14, 625–29.

12. *History of American Methodism* 1:614–19. Asbury Church in New York—which was at various times affiliated with the regular Methodists, the AME body, and the Zionites—for a time also headed an independent black Methodist organization. See Hirsch, "Negro and New York, 1783–1865," p. 442; Jonathan Greenleaf, *A History of the Churches, of All Denominations, In the City of New York, From the First Settlement to the Year 1846* (New York: E. French, 1846), pp. 323–25.

13. Payne, *History of the AME Church* 1:33, 45, 50, 59. A number of Methodist free persons of color, after 1822, migrated from Charleston to Philadelphia, where their leaders continued their work in the AME Church. Most of the migrants, however, affiliated with the biracial Scotch Presbyterian Church. See *History of American Methodism* 1:609.

14. Payne, *History of the AME Church* 1:9–10; Bradley, *History of the AME Zion Church*, 1:76; Daniel A. Payne, *The Semi-Centenary and the Retrospection of the African Meth. Episcopal Church of the United States* (Baltimore: Sherwood, 1866), p. 23; George, *Segregated Sabbaths*, pp. 61, 99.

15. George, *Segregated Sabbaths*, p. 92; Bradley, *History of the AME Zion Church* 1:91.

16. *Niles' Weekly Register*, October 4, 1828, p. 86.

17. Payne, *History of the AME Church* 1:9–10, 154.

18. Ibid., 1:154; *Niles' Weekly Register*, August 17, 1844, p. 412. The AME figures are for 1842 and those for the regular Methodists are for 1843.

19. Wright, *Free Negro in Maryland*, p. 212n; Stiles, *History of Brooklyn* 3:704; Bradley, *History of the AME Zion Church* 1:48; *History of the Ohio Falls Cities and Their Counties* (Cleveland: L. A. Williams, 1882), 1:360; Homer E. Wickenden, "History of the Churches of Louisville with Special Reference to Slavery," M.A. thesis, University of Louisville, 1921, pp. 41–42; W. Martin Ferguson, *Methodism in Washington* (Baltimore: Methodist Episcopal Book Depository, 1892), p. 65; Luther P. Jackson, "Religious Instruction of Negroes, 1830–1860, with Special Reference to South Carolina," *Journal of Negro History* 15 (January 1930): 102.

20. Wright, *Free Negro in Maryland*, pp. 212–13; Wesley, *Richard Allen*, p. 83; DuBois, *Negro Church*, pp. 92–93; John W. Cromwell, "The First Negro Churches in the District of Columbia," *Journal of Negro History* 7 (January 1922): 65.

21. George R. Howell and Jonathan Tenney, eds., *History of the County of Albany, N.Y., From 1609 to 1886* (New York: W. W. Munsell, 1886), pp. 765–66; Arthur J. Weise, *The History of the City of Albany, New York, From the Discovery of the Great River in 1524, by Verrazzano, to the Present Time* (Albany: E. H. Bender, 1884), p. 501; *Hoffman's Albany Directory, 1850 '51*, p. 66; *Matchett's Baltimore Director for 1851*

(Baltimore: Richard J. Matchett, 1851), unpaged appendix; Scharf, *History of Baltimore*, p. 584; Payne, *AME Church* 1:57, 222, 232; Snow, *History of Boston*, pp. 417–18; Able Bowen, *Bowen's Picture of Boston, or the Citizens' and Strangers' Guide to the Metropolis of Massachusetts, and its Environs* (Boston: Lilly Wait, 1833), p. 176; Justin Winsor, ed., *The Memorial History of Boston, Including Suffolk County, Massachusetts, 1630–1880* (Boston: James R. Osgood, 1880–81), 3:440–41; [Edward Ruggles], *A Picture of New-York in 1846* (New York: Homans and Ellis, 1846), p. 74; Stiles, *History of Brooklyn* 2:275, 285, 702–8; H. Perry Smith, ed., *History of the City of Buffalo and Erie County* (Syracuse: D. Mason, 1884), 2:300; Cist, *Cincinnati in 1851*, pp. 80–81; *The Cincinnati Almanac for the Year 1846* (Cincinnati: Robinson and Jones, 1846), unpaged; John P. Foote, *The Schools of Cincinnati, and Its Vicinity* (Cincinnati: C. F. Bradley, 1855), p. 92; Gabriel Collins, *Louisville and New Albany Directory, and Annual Advertiser, for 1848* (Louisville: G. H. Monsarrat, n.d.), p. 244; Wilson, "A Century of Negro Education in Louisville," p. 10; Sterkx, *Free Negro in Louisiana*, pp. 259–60, 267; *Cohen's New Orleans and Lafayette Directory* (New Orleans: The Daily Delta, 1851), p. 222; E. Porter Belden, *New-York: Past, Present, and Future* (New York: Prall, Lewis, 1850), pp. 92–105; Smith, *Philadelphia As It Is in 1852*, p. 317; *A Statistical Inquiry Into the Condition of the People of Colour of Philadelphia*, pp. 29–30; *Harris' Directory of Pittsburgh* (1841), p. 105; Bradley, *History of the AME Zion Church*. 2:21; Robert G. Sherer, Jr., "Negro Churches in Rhode Island before 1860," *Rhode Island History* 25 (January 1966): 19–20; *Providence Directory* (1850), pp. 270–71; [T. H. Knox], *The St. Louis Directory for the Years 1854–5* (St. Louis: Chambers and Knapp, 1854), p. 32; William Hyde and Howard L. Conrad, eds., *Encyclopedia of the History of St. Louis* (St. Louis: Southern History Company, 1899), 3:1478; Cromwell, "First Negro Churches in D.C.," pp. 65–73, 83; Bryan, *National Capital* 2:378n. Absolute certainty would appear to be impossible in these matters. The affiliation of some congregations is extremely difficult to determine, the date of the establishment of others is highly uncertain, and a few were very short-lived. Doubtless a number never appeared in any listing. Additionally some churches changed their denominational affiliation (sometimes more than once), and the dates of (as well as the reasons for) such shifts are often obscure. Nevertheless, I believe the statements in the text to be substantially correct.

22. Brown, *The Life of William J. Brown*, p. 46.

23. Wesley, "The Negro's Struggle for Freedom in its Birthplace," p. 68; Abdy, *Journal* 1:134.

24. Abdy, *Journal* 1:133–35.

25. Wickenden, "Churches of Louisville," pp. 41–42; Lyell, *A Second Visit* 1:293; Hickok, *Negro in Ohio*, p. 133.

26. Howell and Tenney, *History of Albany*, p. 765; Julian Rammelkamp, "The Providence Negro Community, 1820–1842," *Rhode Island History* 7 (January 1948): 24–25; Barnard, "Special Report of the Commissioner of Education, D.C.," p. 219. In at least one instance blacks were openly barred from membership in a religious body. The 1820 constitution of Charleston's Beth Elohim Congregation prohibited the admission to membership of black converts to Judaism, though at least one was allowed to attend services. See Charles Reznikoff and Uriah Z. Engleman, *The Jews of Charleston* (Philadelphia: Jewish Publication Society of America, 1950), p. 78.

27. Murray, *Presbyterians and the Negro*, p. 36; Lyell, *Second Visit* 1:211–12; AME Church, *Centennial Budget*, pp. 298–99.

28. Cromwell, "First Negro Churches in D.C.," pp. 65, 83; Ralph F. Weld, *Brooklyn Is America* (New York: Columbia University Press, 1950), pp. 159–60; AME Church, *Centennial Budget*, p. 296. Even a third of a century later, shouting during religious services was not uncommon among both black and white Methodists in many congregations. See Lyell, *Second Visit* 2:284. The Sands Street pastor, Alexander McCaine, later

held pastorates in the slave area and in 1842 published a pamphlet entitled *Slavery Defended from Scriptures, Against the Abolitionists.*

29. Walter N. Brooks, "The Evolution of the Negro Baptist Church," *Journal of Negro History* 7 (January 1922): 19; DuBois, *Negro Church*, p. 111.

30. Weise, *History of Albany*, p. 494; Koger, *History of Negro Baptists of Maryland*, pp. 10–11; *Matchett's Baltimore Director, or Register of Households, Corrected up to June, 1842* (Baltimore: Baltimore Director Office, 1842), Appendix, pp. 5–7; Brooks, "Evolution of the Negro Baptist Church," pp. 11–17; Horton, "Black Activism in Boston," p. 41; Winsor, *Memorial History of Boston* 3:424; Snow, *History of Boston*, p. 342; Stiles, *History of Brooklyn* 2:279; *Hearnes' Brooklyn City Directory, 1851–1852* (n.p., n.d.), Appendix, p. 49; Henry W. Hill, ed., *Municipality of Buffalo, New York: A History, 1720–1923* (New York: Lewis, 1923), 2:604; Walker, *Buffalo City Directory,* (1840), p. 26; *The Commercial Advertiser Directory, for the City of Buffalo* (Buffalo: Jewett, Thomas, 1851), p. 52; Dabney, *Cincinnati's Colored Citizens*, p. 370; C. S. Williams, *Williams' Cincinnati Directory and Business Advertiser, for 1851–1852* (Cincinnati: C. S. Williams, 1851), p. 308; Weeden, *History of the Colored People of Louisville*, p. 45; *The Louisville Directory for the Year 1832* (Louisville: Richard W. Otis, 1832), p. 142; Wilson, "Century of Negro Education in Louisville," p. 10; William E. Paxton, *A History of the Baptists of Louisiana, From the Earliest Times to the Present* (St. Louis: C. R. Barns, 1888), pp. 121–22; Freeman, "Free Negro in New York City," pp. 400–401; Belden, *New-York*, pp. 92–105; Scharf and Wescott, *History of Philadelphia* 2:1311; Smith, *Philadelphia As It Is in 1852*, pp. 312–13; *Philadelphia in 1824* (Philadelphia: H. C. Carey and I. Lea, 1824), p. 56; Mott, *Biographical Sketches of Persons of Color*, p. 234; Samuel Fahnestock. *Fahnestock's Pittsburgh Directory, for 1850* (Pittsburgh: George Parkin, 1850), pp. 115–16; Staples, *Annals of Providence*, pp. 489–91; *Providence Directory* (1850), pp. 270–71; Sherer, "Negro Churches in Rhode Island," pp. 19–20; Scharf, *History of Saint Louis* 2:1682; Lewis G. Jordon, *Negro Baptist History, U.S.A., 1750–1930* (Nashville: Sunday School Publishing Board, NBC, n.d.), pp. 106–7; Barnard, "Special Report of the Commissioner of Education, D.C.," p. 219; Cromwell, "First Negro Churches in D.C.," pp. 76, 81. Because of the absence of any significant Baptist organizational structure and the ease with which legitimate Baptist churches could be gathered and supplied with ministers, it is almost certain that at least some black Baptist congregations existed in these cities without being included on any list so that no reference to their existence has survived. The black membership in the early Baptist Church at Charleston seems to have been substantial and it is not unlikely that separate services were held for the Negro communicants. See Leah Townsend, *South Carolina Baptists, 1670–1805* (Baltimore: Genealogical Publishing Company, 1978; orig. pub. 1935), p. 257.

31. Snow, *History of Boston*, p. 342; Weise, *History of Albany*, p. 494; Allen, *Negro in New York*, p. 19; Hardie, *Description of New-York*, p. 162; Isaac S. Homans, *History of Boston, From 1630 to 1856* (Boston: F. C. Moore, 1856), pp. 62–65.

32. Sterkx, *Free Negro in Louisiana*, pp. 263–64; Wickenden, "Churches of Louisville," pp. 19–20; Cist, *Cincinnati in 1851*, p. 80; Gibson, *Public Career of W. H. Gibson*, pp. 17–18.

33. Ruggles, *Picture of New York in 1846*, pp. 140–48; *Hearnes' Brooklyn Directory, 1851–1852*, p. 49; Johnson, *Churches of Washington*, p. 20.

34. Staples, *Annals of Providence*, pp. 491, 641; Greenleaf, *History of the Churches of New York*, pp. 273, 330; Pennsylvania Society for Promoting the Abolition of Slavery, *Free People of Color of Philadelphia*, pp. 32, 40; Davis, *Noah Davis*, p. 83; John B. Meachum, *An Address to All the Colored Citizens of the United States* (Philadelphia: King and Baird, 1846), p. 5; Collins, *Louisville Directory for 1848*, p. 244. The quotation is from *A Call upon the Church for Progressive Action, to Elevate the Colored American People* (n.p., [1848]), p. 6. There were doubtless many blacks associated with biracial, white-

controlled Baptist congregations in the southern cities. Hence, there may well have been far more Baptists among the free blacks (and slaves) of those cities than the enrollment in separate Negro churches would indicate.

35. Catto, *Semi-Centenary Discourse,* pp. 19–27, 60, 69–75, 110; Murray, *Presbyterianism and the Negro,* p. 35; Scharf and Wescott, *History of Philadelphia* 2:1284–85; William P. White and William H. Scott, *The Presbyterian Church in Philadelphia* (Philadelphia: Allen, Lane and Scott, 1895), pp. 33, 77; Pennsylvania Society for Promoting Abolition, *Free People of Color of Philadelphia,* p. 32. John Gloucester had been purchased (for his protection) by the Reverend Gideon Blackburne of Maryville, Tennessee, who accompanied him to Philadelphia and freed him. Goucester subsequently purchased his wife and four children, who were not held by Blackburne.

36. Murray, *Presbyterianism and the Negro,* p. 37; Theodore F. Savage, *The Presbyterian Church in New York City* ([New York]: Presbytery of New York, 1949), pp. 154–55; Greenleaf, *History of the Churches of New York,* pp. 152–54.

37. *Matchett's Baltimore Director* (1842), Appendix, pp. 5–7; James E. P. Boulden, *The Presbyterians of Baltimore; Their Churches and Historic Graveyards* (Baltimore: William K. Boyle and Son, 1875), p. 132; Murray, *Presbyterianism and the Negro,* p. 34; Stiles, *History of Brooklyn* 2:279; *Commercial Advertiser Directory for Buffalo* (1851), p. 51; Jackson, "Religious Instruction of Negroes," pp. 100–102; Cist, *Cincinnati in 1841,* p. 96; John B. Jegli, *John B. Jegli's Louisville, New Albany, Jeffersonville, Shippingport and Portland Directory, for 1845–1846* (Louisville: The Louisville Journal, 1845), p. 26; Wilson, "Century of Negro Education in Louisville," p. 10; Belden, *New-York,* pp. 92–105; *Harris' Directory of Pittsburgh,* (1844), p. 64; Cromwell, "First Negro Churches in D.C.," p. 80. The Cincinnati and Pittsburgh congregations appear to have been short-lived, since they are not included in listings at the end of the decade. See Cist, *Cincinnati in 1851,* pp. 78–79; *Fahnestock's Pittsburgh Directory, for 1850,* p. 116.

38. Catto, *Semi-Centenary Discourse,* pp. 82, 84–85, 88–92; *Matchett's Baltimore Director for 1851,* unpaged appendix; Murray, *Presbyterianism and the Negro,* pp. 34–35; Barnard, "Special Report of the Commissioner of Education, D.C.," p. 202; Scharf and Wescott, *History of Philadelphia* 2:1287.

39. Catto, *Semi-Centenary Discourse,* p. 110; Murray, *Presbyterianism and the Negro,* p. 37; Jackson, "Religious Instruction of Negroes," p. 100; Benjamin Quarles, *Black Abolitionists* (New York: Oxford University Press, 1969), pp. 80–81.

40. Wesley, *Richard Allen,* p. 73; Douglass, *Annals of the First African Church,* pp. 118–22; Bragg, *History of the Afro-American Group of the Episcopal Church,* pp. 59–71, 90.

41. Absalom Jones to Dorothy Ripley, June 3, 1803, in "Some Letters of Richard Allen and Absalom Jones to Dorothy Ripley," *Journal of Negro History* 1 (October 1916): 440–41; Douglass, *Annals of the First African Church,* pp. 107–11, 123–28, 139; Catto, *Semi-Centenary Discourse,* pp. 46, 107. Though organized as a black mission congregation, the Church of the Crucifixion had become predominantly white by the mid-1850s. In the late 1830s the Edinburgh traveler George Combe attended services at St. Thomas's and observed, with apparent surprise and an abundance of condescension, that there were no "ludicrous incidents." He noted with approval Douglass's "pure good English, equal to that of any of the other clergymen of the city." See Combe, *Notes on the United States* 1:251.

42. Greenleaf, *History of the Churches of New York,* pp. 79–81; Bragg, *History of the Afro-American Group of the Episcopal Church,* pp. 81–83.

43. Greenleaf, *History of the Churches of New York,* pp. 97–98. Both DeGrasse and Crummell were Negroes. DeGrasse had been ordained a deacon in 1838 and Crummell in 1842. See Bragg, *History of the Afro-American Group of the Episcopal Church,* pp. 187–88.

44. Bragg, *History of the Afro-American Group of the Episcopal Church,* pp. 90–96, 102, 105, 185; Staples, *Annals of Providence,* p. 641; T. Stafford Drowne, *A Commemorative Discourse Delivered on the Occasion of Celebrating the Completion of the Tower and Spire of the Church of the Holy Trinity, Brooklyn, L.I.* (New York: Hurd and Houghton, 1868), p. 54.

45. Jackson, "Religious Instruction of Negroes," p. 102; Mears and Turnbull, *Charleston Directory* (1859), p. 268; Stavisky, "Negro Artisan in the South Atlantic States," p. 148; Sterkx, *Free Negro in Louisiana,* p. 259; Bragg, *History of the Afro-American Group of the Episcopal Church,* pp. 64–68, 85, 102; Douglass, *Annals of the First African Church,* pp. 139–71; William Ferguson, *America by River and Rail* (London: James Nisbet, 1856), pp. 148–49.

46. Bragg, *History of the Afro-American Group of the Episcopal Church,* pp. 62–63, 76–78, 85, 97–98, 102; Drowne, *Commemorative Discourse,* p. 53.

47. Greenleaf, *History of the Churches of New York,* pp. 45, 367; Hardie, *Description of New York,* p. 176; John Jones to ?, January 30, 1839, in "Letters to the American Colonization Society," pp. 162–63; Pennsylvania Society for Promoting Abolition, *Free People of Color in Philadelphia,* p. 32; [Joseph Willson], *Sketches of the Higher Classes of Colored Society in Philadelphia* (Philadelphia: Merrihew and Thompson, 1841), p. 16; Belden, *New-York,* pp. 92–105; Cist, *Cincinnati in 1851,* p. 80; *Williams' Cincinnati Directory, for 1850–51,* p. 309.

48. John N. Boucher, ed., *A Century and a Half of Pittsburg [sic] and Her People* (Lewis Publishing Company, 1908), 2:267; John T. Gillard, *The Catholic Church and the American Negro* (Baltimore: St. Joseph's Society Press, 1929), pp. 15, 39. The Catholic church in the South seems to have been remarkably free from any hint of segregation. Not only was seating mixed and access to the communion table open in New Orleans churches, but there are references to racially intermixed choirs and first communion classes. See Rousseve, *Negro in Louisiana,* pp. 40–41; Nichols, *Forty Years of American Life* 1:188.

49. Bragg, *History of the Afro-American Group of the Episcopal Church,* pp. 50, 82, 94; Douglass, *Annals of the First African Church,* p. 115; Brown, *Life of William J. Brown,* pp. 47–48; Charles Shaw, *Description of Boston,* p. 269; Scharf, *History of Baltimore,* pp. 567–68; [John S. Tyson], *Life of Elisha Tyson, The Philanthropist* (Baltimore: B. Lundy, 1825), p. 57; Weeden, *History of the Colored People of Louisville,* pp. 14–16, 45.

50. Catto, *Semi-Centenary Discourse,* p. 59; Wesley, *Richard Allen,* p. 143; Payne, *History of the AME Church* 1:46; Weeden, *History of the Colored People of Louisville,* pp. 14–16.

51. Bragg, *History of the Afro-American Group of the Episcopal Church,* pp. 50–51, 82; Hardie, *Description of New York,* pp. 161–81; Jonathan Elliot, *Historical Sketches of the Ten Miles Square Forming the District of Columbia* (Washington: J. Elliot, 1830), pp. 193–94; Ruggles, *Picture of New York in 1846,* p. 174; Pennsylvania Society for Promoting Abolition, *Free People of Color in Philadelphia,* p. 32.

52. Catto, *Semi-Centenary Discourse,* p. 59; Bragg, *History of the Afro-American Group of the Episcopal Church,* pp. 68, 102; Scharf, *History of Baltimore,* pp. 525–26; Weeden, *History of the Colored People of Louisville,* p. 18; Douglass, *Annals of the First African Church,* p. 137; *Matchett's Baltimore Director, Corrected up to June, 1829* (Baltimore, 1829), passim; A. G. Stevens and William H. Marschalk, *Brooklyn Directory, for the Years 1838–39* (Brooklyn: Arnold and Van Anden, 1838), pp. 26, passim; *The Commercial Advertiser Directory for the City of Buffalo* (Buffalo: Jewett Thomas, 1850), pp. 51, passim; *Commercial Advertiser Directory of Buffalo* (1851), pp. 49–51, passim; Gabriel Collins, *The Louisville Directory, for the Year 1838–39* (Louisville: J. B. Marshall, 1838), passim; *Jegli's Louisville Directory, for 1845–1846,* passim; James Hardie, *The Philadelphia Directory and Register* (Philadelphia: James Hardie, 1794), passim; Thomas

Stephens, *Stephens's Philadelphia Directory, for 1796* (Philadelphia: Thomas Stephens, [1796]), passim; *[Philadelphia] Census Directory for 1811* (Philadelphia: Jane Aitken, 1811), passim; *The Philadelphia Directory and Register for 1821* (Philadelphia: M'Carty and Davis, 1821), passim; *Desilver's Philadelphia Directory and Stranger's Guide, for 1833* (Philadelphia: Robert Desilver, 1833), passim; *Providence Directory* (1844), passim. See also Norman J. Johnston, "The Caste and Class of the Urban Form of Historic Philadelphia," *Journal of the American Institute of Planners* 32 (November 1966): 338–39. The Baptist and Presbyterian positions appear to be reversed on the chart on p. 339.

53. Smith, *Philadelphia As It Is in 1852*, pp. 281–324; George Adams, *The Boston Directory, for the Year 1851* (Boston: George Adams, 1851), Appendix, p. 49; *Hearnes' Brooklyn Directory, 1851–52*, Appendix, pp. 49–51; Belden, *New–York*, pp. 92–105; Cist, *Cincinnati in 1851*, pp. 80–81; *Providence Directory* (1850), pp. 270–71. In the cities without significant Negro residential concentrations, such as Louisville and Washington, the black churches were widely scattered across the settled area of the city. See Collins, *Louisville Directory, for 1848*, p. 244; Johnson, *Churches of Washington*, pp. 19–20.

54. Stavisky, "Negro Artisans in the South Atlantic States," p. 152; Louisville, *Revised Ordinances* (1854), pp. 86–87; Scharf, *History of St. Louis* 1:666; St. Louis, *Ordinances (1850)*, p. 298; Washington, *Laws* (1837), p. 177; Bradley, *History of the AME Zion Church* 1:65–66; *Niles' Weekly Register*, November 26, 1825, p. 195. See also chapter 6.

55. Munsell, *Annals of Albany* 7:194, 8:167; Payne, *History of the AME Church* 1:157; Davis, *Noah Davis*, p. 41; Bacon, *Statistics of the Colored People of Philadelphia*, p. 10; Bradley, *History of the AME Zion Church* 1:65; Wilson, *Standard History of Pittsburg*, p. 429.

56. *History of American Methodism* 1:276; Murray, *Presbyterianism and the Negro*, p. 60; Stiles, *History of Brooklyn* 2:23n; Brown, *Life of William J. Brown*, pp. 40–41; Boston Society for the Religious and Moral Instruction of the Poor, *Ninth Annual Report* (Boston: Crocker and Brewster, 1825), pp. 21–22; Wesberry, *Baptists in South Carolina*, p. 70; Wilson, *Standard History of Pittsburg*, p. 926; Andrew Rothwell, *History of the Baptist Institutions of Washington City* (Washington: W. Ballantyne, 1867), p. 10; "Condition of the Colored Population of Baltimore," pp. 169–72.

57. Lyell, *Second Visit* 2:324–25; Douglass, *Annals of the First African Church*, p. 123; Freeman, "Free Negro in New York City," pp. 410–12; Berlin, "Slaves Who Were Free," p. 430; Baltimore, City Health Department, "Report for 1818," in Baltimore, City Health Department, *First Thirty-five Reports;* Charleston, *Ordinances, 1783–1844*, pp. 129–30. Almost all churches in this era, of course, had burial grounds for their members.

58. Shaw, *Description of Boston*, p. 270; Bragg, *History of the Afro-American Group of the Episcopal Church*, pp. 68, 94–95; Murray, *Presbyterianism and the Negro*, pp. 32–34; Payne, *History of the AME Church* 1:143; Koger, *History of Negro Baptists in Maryland*, p. 11.

59. George, *Segregated Sabbaths*, pp. 95–97.

60. Rammelkamp, "Providence Negro Community, 1820–1842," p. 26; "Statisticks of Destitution in Baltimore," p. 279; Spaulding, "Coloured People of Boston," p. 89.

61. Wesley, "Negro's Struggle for Freedom in Its Birthplace," p. 68; Allen, *Negro in New York*, p. 18; Bardolph, "Social Origins of Distinguished Negroes, 1770–1865," pp. 219–30. See also Quarles, *Black Abolitionists*, pp. 68–69.

Chapter 12

1. See chapters 2, 3, and 8, above.

2. Abram L. Harris, *The Negro as Capitalist* (Philadelphia: American Council of

Political and Social Sciences, 1936), p. 20; Aptheker, *Documentary History of the Negro People,* p. 113; Pennsylvania Society for Promoting the Abolition of Slavery, *Free People of Color of Philadelphia,* pp. 26–27. See also, p. 176, above.

3. Boudreaux, "History of Philanthropy in New Orleans, 1835–1862," p. 115; James B. Browning, "The Beginnings of Insurance Enterprise among Negroes," *Journal of Negro History* 22 (October 1937): 421, 423–24; Aptheker, *Documentary History of the Negro People,* pp. 38–39. One reason for the almost simultaneous development of multiple beneficial associations in Charleston was the exclusion of persons with more than one-half Negro ancestry from membership in the Brown Society. The Free Dark Men of Color was organized, in part, to protest this discrimination.

4. Daniel Perlman, "Organizations of the Free Negro in New York City, 1800–1860," *Journal of Negro History* 56 (July 1971): 185; Wright, *Free Negro in Maryland,* p. 250; Brown, *Life of William J. Brown,* pp. 81–83; Howell and Tenney, *History of Albany County,* p. 726; Mott, *Biographical Sketches of Persons of Color,* p. 240; Bryan, *National Capital* 2:312n.

5. Perlman, "Organizations of the Free Negro in New York City," pp. 182–84; W. E. B. DuBois, *Economic Co-operation among Negro Americans* (Atlanta: Atlanta University Press, 1907), pp. 96–97.

6. Perlman, "Organizations of the Free Negro in New York City," p. 184; C. W. Birnie, "Education of the Negro in Charleston," p. 15; Pennsylvania Society for Promoting Abolition, *Free People of Color in Philadelphia,* pp. 26–27; Aptheker, *Documentary History of the Negro People,* p. 113.

7. Pennsylvania Society for Promoting Abolition, *Free People of Color of Philadelphia,* pp. 26–27; Brackett, *Negro in Maryland,* p. 204; Browning, "Beginnings of Insurance among Negroes," pp. 423–24, 428–29; Birnie, "Education of the Negro in Charleston," pp. 15–16; Boudreaux, "History of Philanthropy in New Orleans," p. 116; Sterkx, *Free Negro in Louisiana,* p. 283; Perlman, "Organizations of the Free Negro in New York City," pp. 186–87; Howell and Tenney, *History of Albany County,* p. 726; Donald M. Jacobs, "History of the Boston Negro," pp. 58, 104, 144; Daniels, *In Freedom's Birthplace,* p. 452; Brown, *Life of William J. Brown,* pp. 130–31; [National Negro Convention], *Minutes of the National Convention of Colored Citizens; Held at Buffalo, On the 15th, 16th, 17th, 18th, and 19th of August, 1843, For the Purpose of Considering Their Moral and Political Condition as American Citizens* (New York: Piercy and Reed, 1843), p. 38.

8. Pennsylvania Society for Promoting Abolition, *Free People of Color of Philadelphia,* pp. 26–27; Aptheker, *Documentary History of the Negro People,* pp. 113–14; "The Condition of the Coloured Population of Baltimore," p. 174; Birnie, "Education of the Negro in Charleston," p. 15; Browning, "Beginnings of Insurance among Negroes," pp. 421–22; Perlman, "Organizations of the Free Negro in New York City," p. 187.

9. Pennsylvania Society for Promoting Abolition, *Free People of Color of Philadelphia (1838),* pp. 26–27; "Condition of the Coloured Population of Baltimore," p. 174; Freeman, "The Free Negro in New York City," pp. 239, 241, 302; Brown, *Life of William J. Brown,* p. 130.

10. Perlman, "Organizations of the Free Negro in New York City," p. 184; Browning, "Beginnings of Insurance among Negroes," p. 423; E. Horace Frichett, "The Status of the Free Negro in Charleston, South Carolina, and His Descendents in Modern Society," *Journal of Negro History* 32 (October 1947): 441n; "Condition of the Coloured Population of Baltimore," p. 174; Pennsylvania Society for Promoting Abolition, *Free People of Color of Philadelphia (1838),* pp. 26–27.

11. *Matchett's Baltimore Directory for 1824* (Baltimore: R. J. Matchett, 1824); Collins, *Louisville Directory, for the Year 1838–39; The Saint Louis Directory For the Year 1842* (St. Louis: Chambers and Knapp, 1842); Knox, *St. Louis Directory, for the Years 1854–5; Alfred Hunter, *The Washington and Georgetown Directory, Strangers' Guide-Book for*

Washington, and Congressional and Clerks' Register (Washington: Kirkwood and McGill, 1853); Dawson and De Saussure, *Census of the City of Charleston, 1848*, pp. 34–35. The Charelston census (pp. 29–30) shows women constituting just over one-ninth of all employed whites. The same census (pp. 6–7) reported that females comprised roughly sixty-three percent of the free black population and about sixty-seven percent of those ten years of age and older.

12. Pennsylvania Society for Promoting Abolition, *Free People of Color of Philadelphia*, pp. 26–27; Aptheker, *Documentary History of the Negro People*, pp. 113–14; "Condition of the Coloured Population of Baltimore," p. 174; Browning, "Beginnings of Insurance among Negroes," pp. 428–29.

13. Pennsylvania Society for Promoting Abolition, *Free People of Color of Philadelphia*, pp. 26–28, 40; Aptheker, *Documentary History of the Negro People*, pp. 113–14, 131–32; *A Statistical Inquiry into the Condition of the People of Colour of Philadelphia*, pp. 22; Browning, "Beginnings of Insurance among Negroes," p. 419.

14. "Condition of the Coloured Population of Baltimore," pp. 174–85; Brackett, *Negro in Maryland*, p. 204n; Browning, "Beginnings of Insurance Among Negroes," p. 437.

15. Freeman, "Free Negro in New York City," p. 241; Brown, *Life of William J. Brown*, pp. 130–31; Birnie, "Education of the Negro in Charleston," p. 15; Boudreaux, "Philanthropy in New Orleans," p. 115; Sterkx, *Free Negro in Louisiana*, p. 283; Mott, *Biographical Sketches of Persons of Color*, p. 240.

16. Weld, *Brooklyn Village*, p. 327; Birnie, "Education of the Negro in Charelston," p. 15; Dabney, *Schools for Negroes In D.C.*, pp. 6–11; Freeman, "Free Negro in New York City," pp. 369–70.

17. Young, *History of Philadelphia* 2:313; Freeman, "Free Negro in New York City," pp. 352–53; American Convention of Abolition Societies, *Minutes, 1812*, p. 7; Arnett G. Lindsay, "The Economic Condition of the Negroes of New York Prior to 1861," *Journal of Negro History* 6 (April 1921): 193; Andrews, *History of the New–York African Free–Schools*, p. 105; Pennsylvania Society for Promoting Abolition, *Free People of Color of Philadelphia*, p. 26; Rollin, *Martin R. Delany*, p. 43.

18. Sterkx, *Free Negro in Louisiana*, p. 283; Aptheker, *Documentary History of the Negro People*, pp. 38–39, 131–32.

19. Douglass, *Annals of the First African Church*, pp. 113–14; W. E. B. DuBois, *The Philadelphia Negro*, pp. 119n, 237; Hardie, *Description of New–York*, pp. 296–97; "Condition of the Coloured Population of Baltimore," pp. 168, 175; Payne, *History of the AME Church* 1:142; Rammelkamp, "Providence Negro Community, 1820–1842," p. 28; William E. Farrison, "William Wells Brown in Buffalo," *Journal of Negro History* 39 (October 1954): 303–4; Isaac Harris, *Harris' Pittsburgh Business Directory, for the Year 1837* (Pittsburgh: Isaac Harris, 1837), pp. 126–38; Mott, *Biographical Sketches of Persons of Color*, p. 240; [National Negro Convention], *Minutes and Proceedings of the Third Annual Convention, For the Improvement of the Free People of Colour in These United States* (New York: Published by Order of the Convention, 1833), p. 16.

20. Jacobs, "History of the Boston Negro," pp. 58, 104; Thomas P. Teale, *Municipal Register of the City of Brooklyn, and Manual of King's County, From the Earliest Period Up to the Present Time* (Brooklyn: E. B. Spooner, 1848), p. 56; Dorothy B. Porter, "The Organized Educational Activities of the Negro Literary Societies, 1828–1846," *Journal of Negro Education* 5 (October 1936): 557, 564–65; Birnie, "Education of the Negro in Charleston," p. 16; Freeman, "Free Negro in New York City," pp. 430–31.

21. Porter, "Organized Educational Activities of Negro Literary Societies," pp. 558, 560–61, 565–68; Aptheker, *Documentary History of the Negro People*, pp. 138–39; Willson, *Colored Society In Philadelphia*, pp. 96–100; National Negro Convention, *Minutes, 1833*, p. 24; Pennsylvania Society for Promoting Abolition, *Free People of Color of Philadelphia*, p. 30.

22. Porter, "Organized Educational Activities of Negro Literary Societies," pp. 557–58, 568; Perlman, "Organizations of the Free Negro in New York City," p. 191.

23. Willson, *Colored Society in Philadelphia*, pp. 101–8; DuBois, *Philadelphia Negro*, p. 45; Porter, "Organized Educational Activities of Negro Literary Societies," pp. 557, 561–62; Pennsylvania Society for Promoting Abolition, *Free People of Color of Philadelphia*, p. 30.

24. Porter, "Organized Educational Activities of Negro Literary Societies," pp. 558, 570–71; Jacobs, "History of the Boston Negro," pp. 145, 223–25.

25. Porter, "Organized Educational Activities of Negro Literary Societies," pp. 558, 572, 573; "Condition of the Coloured Population of Baltimore," p. 174; [National Negro Convention], *Minutes of the Fifth Annual Convention for the Improvement of the Free People of Colour In the United States* (Philadelphia: William H. Gibbons, 1835), p. 6.

26. Porter, "Organized Educational Activities of Negro Literary Societies," pp. 557–58, 571, 572; National Negro Convention, *Minutes, 1843*, pp. 37–38; *Harris' Directory of Pittsburgh* (1844), p. 69; Willson, *Colored Society in Philadelphia*, pp. 109–11.

27. Porter, "Organized Educational Activities of Negro Literary Societies," p. 563; Foster, "Philadelphia in Slices," p. 61.

28. Pennsylvania Society for Promoting Abolition, *Free People of Color of Philadelphia*, p. 30; Allen, *Negro in New York*, p. 51; National Negro Convention, *Minutes, 1843*, pp. 37–38; Willson, *Colored Society in Philadelphia*, pp. 101–11.

29. Olmsted, *Journey in the Seaboard Slave States*, pp. 14–15.

30. William H. Grimshaw, *Official History of Freemasonry among the Colored People of North America* (New York: Broadway Publishing Company, 1903), pp. 69–87, 104; Daniels, *In Freedom's Birthplace*, p. 21; DuBois, *Economic Co-operation among Negro Americans*, p. 22.

31. Grimshaw, *Freemasonry among the Colored People*, pp. 111–15; Scharf and Wescott, *History of Philadelphia* 3:2070; Harry E. Davis, *A History of Freemasonry among Negroes in America* ([Philadelphia]: United Supreme Council, Ancient and Accepted Scottish Rite of Freemasonry, Northern Jurisdiction, U.S.A., Prince Hall Affiliation, 1946), pp. 82–84, 94.

32. Grimshaw, *Freemasonry among the Colored People*, pp. 124–25, 132–39, 165.

33. Ibid., pp. 201–4; William A. Muraskin, *Middle-Class Blacks in a White Society: Prince Hall Freemasonry in America* (Berkeley: University of California Press, 1975), pp. 37–38; Gibson, *Public Career of W. H. Gibson*, pp. 42–43. The anti-Masonic agitation of the late 1820s and early 1830s seems not to have affected black lodges. Whites were apparently incapable of perceiving any assemblage of blacks as an elitist threat to democratic egalitarianism. See Muraskin, *Middle-Class Blacks in a White Society*, p. 36.

34. Grimshaw, *Freemasonry among the Colored People*, pp. 336–45, 356.

35. Ibid., pp. 110–12, 132; Delany, *Origin and Objects of Ancient Freemasonry*, passim; Muraskin, *Middle-Class Blacks in a White Society*, pp. 26–27, 33–38. In Philadelphia, New Orleans, and, probably, other cities, a number of the founders of black freemasonry had been initiated into the fraternity in Europe (especially England) and the West Indies. See Grimshaw, *Freemasonry among the Colored People*, pp. 112, 233; Scharf and Wescott, *History of Philadelphia* 3:2070; Weeden, *History of the Colored People of Louisville*, p. 54.

36. DeBois, *Economic Co-operation among Negro Americans*, pp. 115–17; Browning, "Beginnings of Insurance among Negroes," p. 422; Freeman, "Free Negro in New York City," pp. 430–31; Howell and Tenney, *History of Albany County*, p. 726; Perlman, "Organizations of the Free Negro in New York City," pp. 195–96; Charles H. Brooks, *A History and Manual of the Grand United Order of Odd Fellows in America* (Philadelphia, 1893), pp. 19–26.

37. Brooks, *History of the G.U.O.O.F.*, pp. 31, 33, 36, 45–47, 55, 64, 99. There were

also Odd Fellows lodges in such smaller cities as Alexandria, Hartford, Newark, Troy, and Wilmington.

38. Ibid., pp. 11, 20, 31.

39. Muraskin, *Middle-Class Blacks in a White Society*, p. 26; Brown, *Life of William J. Brown*, pp. 82, 127–30; Perlman, "Free Negro Organizations in New York City," pp. 187, 190.

40. E.g., Brown, *Life of William J. Brown*, pp. 82, 128–30.

41. In addition, the first five annual conventions (attended by 182 persons) drew two delegates from Maine and one each from Ohio and Virginia.

42. Howard H. Bell, *A Survey of the Negro Convention Movement, 1830–1861* (New York: Arno Press, 1969), pp. 1–37, 275; [National Negro Convention], *Constitution of the American Society of Free Persons of Colour, for Improving Their Condition in the United States; for Purchasing Land; and for the Establishment of a Settlement in Canada, Also the Proceedings of the Convention, with Their Address to the Free Persons of Colour in the United States* (Philadelphia: J. W. Allen, 1831), p. 12; [National Negro Convention], *Minutes and Proceedings of the First Annual Convention of the People of Colour* (Philadelphia, 1831), p. 10; *Minutes of the Third Convention for Improvement of Free People of Colour (1833)*, p. 24; *Minutes of the Fourth Annual Convention, for the Improvement of the Free People of Colour, in the United States* (New York, 1834), pp. 16, 35; *Minutes of the Fifth Convention for Improvement of Free People of Colour* (1835), pp. 4–5, 9; Porter, "Organized Educational Activities of Negro Literary Societies," pp. 562–63, 565–68, 574; Charles S. Johnson, "The Rise of the Negro Magazine," *Journal of Negro History* 13 (January 1928): 10; Perlman, "Free Negro Organizations in New York City," pp. 191–92.

43. Perlman, "Free Negro Organizations in New York City," pp. 188–89; E. Delorus Preston, "William Syphax, a Pioneer in Negro Education in the District of Columbia," *Journal of Negro History* 20 (October 1935): 456.

44. Bell, *The Negro Convention Movement*, pp. 35–68.

Chapter 13

1. Adams, "Disfranchisement of Negroes in New England," p. 545; Shattuck, *Census of Boston for the Year 1845*, Appendix, pp. 34–35.

2. *Niles' Weekly Register*, December 13, 1834, p. 237; Shattuck, *Census of Boston for the Year 1845*, p. 44, Appendix p. 36; Richard P. McCormick, *The Second American Party System* (New York: W. W. Norton, 1973; orig. pub. 1966), pp. 37–38.

3. DeBow, *Statistical View*, p. 395. The proportion of females in Boston's adult white population was two percentage points less than in the black component.

4. Fox, "Negro Vote in Old New York," pp. 257, 263; Block, *Circle of Discrimination*, p. 157; Hirsch, "Negro and New York, 1783–1865," p. 423. There was a procedural requirement applicable only to blacks established in 1814. Black voters were required to present to election officers copies of the registration forms required for all free blacks by the same statute. The ostensible purpose of the legislation was to prevent slave voting. See Fox, "Negro Vote in Old New York," p. 257. In the New York cities the Negroes' political loyalties were doubtless strongly influenced by the fact that Federalists were prominent in support of the elimination of slavery in that state and, in their attempt to preserve a property qualification for all voters, led the unsuccessful fight against discriminatory suffrage requirements for blacks. This latter position was also supported by a number of prominent Whigs in later years. See Fox, "Negro Vote in Old New York," pp. 262–66.

5. Fox, "Negro Vote in Old New York," pp. 257, 264; Block, *Circle of Discrimination*, p. 157; Hirsch, "Negro and New York," pp. 417–18; Freeman, "Free Negro in New York City," pp. 119, 122–24; David T. Valentine, *Manual for the Corporation of the*

City of New-York for 1854 (New York: McSpeden and Baker, 1854), pp. 486–96; *Census of the State of New York, for 1835* (Albany: Crosswell, Van Benthuysen and Burt, 1836), p. 27; New York, Senate, *Journal of the Senate of the State of New-York; At their Forty-ninth Session* (Albany: E. Crosswell, 1826), Appendix L. The eighth ward was usually Democratic after 1838. Freeman (p. 122) gives the number of qualified black voters in New York City as ninety-one in 1845.

6. Hirsch, "Negro and New York," pp. 422–23.

7. *Census of the State of New York, for 1835*, pp. 2, 14, 21; *Census of the State of New York, for 1845* (Albany: Carroll and Cook, 1846), unpaged.

8. Adams, "Disfranchisement of Negroes in New England," pp. 545–46.

9. Rammelkamp, "Providence Negro Community, 1820–1842," pp. 31–33; Brown, *The Life of William J. Brown*, pp. 157–74; Providence, *List of Persons Assessed, 1840*, pp. 59–60; *Providence Directory* (1841), p. 209; ibid. (1844), pp. 193–202. Brown (p. 156) estimated the number of black voters in the state at 300–400. In 1840 more than forty percent of Rhode Island's free men of color over twenty years of age resided in Providence. See U.S., Census Office, *Census, 1840*, p. 52.

10. Thorpe, *Federal and State Constitutions* 5:3084, 3096; Hurd, *Law of Freedom and Bondage* 2:67–72; DuBois, *Philadelphia Negro*, p. 30; Turner, *Negro in Pennsylvania*, pp. 169–71, 190; Oberholtzer, *Philadelphia* 2:279; Edwin Wolf II and Maxwell Whiteman, *The History of the Jews of Philadelphia from Colonial Times to the Age of Jackson* (Philadelphia: Jewish Publication Society, 1956), p. 209; Breck, *Recollections*, p. 302. The vote in the constitutional convention to restrict suffrage to whites was 77 to 45.

11. Thorpe, *Federal and State Constitutions* 3:691; Brackett, *Negro in Maryland*, pp. 186–87; Wright, *Free Negro in Maryland*, p. 119n; Scharf, *History of Baltimore*, pp. 169–70. The quotations are from the latter source.

12. DeBow, *Statistical View*, p. 63; Thorpe, *Federal and State Constitutions* 3:1691, 1705; Wright, *Free Negro in Maryland*, p. 119; Brackett, *Negro in Maryland*, p. 187; Latrobe, "Memoir of Benjamin Banneker," p. 6.

13. Thorpe, *Federal and State Constitutions* 3:1269, 1278, 1382; 4:2152; 5:2907; 6:3258–59; Samuel Burch, comp., *A Digest of the Laws of the Corporation of the City of Washington, to the First of June, 1823* (Washington: James Wilson, 1823), p. 5; Sterkx, *Free Negro in Louisiana*, pp. 165–66; U.S., Census Office, *Census, 1800*, p. 84.

14. Purvis, *Appeal of Forty Thousand Citizens*, pp. 2, 14–15, passim.

15. Allen, *The Negro in New York*, pp. 22–23; Aptheker, *Documentary History of the Negro People*, pp. 164–65; Block, *Circle of Discrimination*, pp. 158–60; *The Whig Almanac and the United States Register for 1847* (New York: Greeley and McElrath, [1847]), p. 44.

16. Brown, *Life of William J. Brown*, pp. 85–86; Adams, "Disfranchisement of Negroes in New England," p. 546; Providence, Board of Assessors, *List of Persons Assessed, 1840*, pp. 59–60. The total tax assessed on the Providence blacks in 1840 was actually slightly over $135.

17. George M. Dennison, *The Dorr War: Republicanism on Trial* (Lexington: University of Kentucky, 1976), pp. 42–43, 62–63, 98, 220, passim; Brown, *Life of William J. Brown*, pp. 171–74; Rammelkamp, "Providence Negro Community," pp. 31–32; Adams, "Disfranchisement of Negroes in New England," pp. 546–47.

18. Quarles, *Black Abolitionists*, pp. 12–28; Freeman, "The Free Negro in New York City," pp. 195–96; Horton, "Black Activism in Boston," p. 135.

19. Quarles, *Black Abolitionists*, p. 29; Daniels, *In Freedom's Birthplace*, pp. 36, 46; Perlman, "Organizations of the Free Negro in New York City," p. 194; Brown, *Life of William J. Brown*, p. 131; *Harris' Directory of Pittsburgh* (1844), p. 69; Boudreaux, "History of Philanthropy in New Orleans," p. 116.

20. Aptheker, *Documentary History of the Negro People*, p. 51.

21. Ibid., p. 52.

22. James Forten, *An Address Delivered Before the Ladies' Anti-Slavery Society of Philadelphia, on the Evening of the 14th of April, 1836* (Philadelphia: Merrihew and Gunn, 1836), pp. 4–5, 12–13.

23. Berlin, *Slaves without Masters,* p. 65; Aptheker, *Documentary History of the Negro People,* pp. 90–93; David Walker, *Walker's Appeal, in Four Articles, together with a Preamble, to the Coloured Citizens of the World, but in Particular, and Very Expressly, to Those of the United States of America, Written in Boston, State of Massachusetts, September 28, 1829,* 3d ed. (Boston: David Walker, 1830), pp. 24, passim.

24. Walker, *Appeal,* pp. 14, 29–30.

25. Ibid., p. 19.

26. Clement Eaton, "A Dangerous Pamphlet in the Old South," *Journal of Southern History* 2 (August 1936): 325–33.

27. *Niles' Weekly Register,* March 27, 1830, p. 87. Otis noted that the *Appeal* had not been circulated in Boston.

28. Aptheker, *Documentary History of the Negro People,* pp. 226–33.

29. National Negro Convention, *Minutes,* 1843, pp. 17–19, 23–24; Bell, *The Negro Convention Movement,* pp. 76–77. The vote on reconsideration was nine to fourteen.

30. National Negro Convention, *Minutes, 1843,* pp. 11, 18–19, 23–24. The black communites in the other ten major cities were not represented at this convention. Theodore S. Wright of New York supported the "Address" on the first vote but opposed it on the second.

31. Fred Landon, "The Negro Migration to Canada after the Passing of the Fugitive Slave Act," *Journal of Negro History* 5 (January 1920): 24–26; Wilson, *Standard History of Pittsburg,* p. 820.

32. Berlin, "Slaves Who Were Free," p. 433; American Convention of Abolition Societies, *Minutes of the Adjourned Session of the Twentieth Biennial American Convention for Promoting the Abolition of Slavery, and Improving the Condition of the African Race* (Philadelphia: Samuel Parker, 1828), p. 53; New York Committee of Vigilance, *First Annual Report of the New York Committee of Vigilance, for the Year 1837* (New York: Piercy and Reed, 1837), passim; Joseph A. Boromé, "The Vigilant Committee of Philadelphia," *Pennsylvania Magazine of History and Biography* 92 (July 1968): 320–52; Rollin, *Martin R. Delany,* p. 43; Horton, "Black Activism in Boston," pp. 142–43.

33. Daniels, *In Freedom's Birthplace,* pp. 57–58; Hirsh, "Negro and New York," p. 408; Wilson, *Standard History of Pittsburg,* p. 821. See also Olmsted, *Journey in the Seaboard Slave States,* p. 15.

34. *Niles' Weekly Register,* September 11, 1824, p. 32.

35. Horton, "Black Activism in Boston," pp. 139–41; Wilson, *Standard History of Pittsburg,* pp. 817–20.

36. Stanley W. Campbell, *The Slave Catchers: Enforcement of the Fugitive Slave Law, 1850–1860* (New York: W. W. Norton, 1972; orig. pub. 1968), pp. 117–32, 148–51, 199–207. It is, however, perhaps worth remembering that twelve of the fourteen delegates from the major cities opposed Henry Highland Garnet's "Address to the Slaves of the United States" at the 1843 National Convention of Colored Citizens. See pp. 228–29.

37. Bowen, *Picture of Boston,* p. 214; Hirsch, "Negro and New York," p. 395; National Negro Convention, *Minutes,* 1834, p. 14; Berlin, *Slaves without Masters,* pp. 314–15; *Niles' National Register,* August 5, 1843, p. 368; Wilson, *Standard History of Pittsburg,* p. 822; Thomas Cole to ? Johnson, August 7, 1840, "Letters to Anti-Slavery Workers," pp. 355–56.

38. Aptheker, *Documentary History of the Negro People,* pp. 102–3; *Niles' Weekly Register,* October 23, 1824, p. 114; Griffith, *Annals of Baltimore,* p. 254; Freeman, "Free Negro in New York City," pp. 27–29. Apparently some hundreds—perhaps

thousands—of free blacks emigrated to Haiti in the mid-1820s. It should also be noted that Daniel Coker of Baltimore, James Forten of Philadelphia, and Peter Williams of New York had, in 1812, supported Daniel Cuffee's ill-fated effort to encourage the migration of American blacks to the British crown colony of Sierra Leone. See P. J. Staudenraus, *The African Colonization Movement, 1816–1865* (New York: Columbia University Press, 1961), pp. 9–11.

39. Sterkx, *Free Negro in Louisiana,* pp. 289–90; *Niles' Weekly Register,* January 17, 1829, p. 330; U.S., Congress, House of Representatives, Committee for the District of Columbia, *Report,* "Report of the Grand Jury," pp. 54–55; Brackett, *Negro in Maryland,* pp. 238–39.

40. Staudenraus, *African Colonization Movement,* pp. 28–29.

41. Early Lee Fox, *The American Colonization Society, 1817–1840* (Baltimore: Johns Hopkins Press, 1919), pp. 46–51; Staudenraus, *African Colonization Movement,* pp. 38, 71, 73; William L. Garrison, *Thoughts on African Colonization: or an Impartial Exhibition of the Doctrines, Principles and Purposes of the American Colonization Society. Together with the Resolutions, Addresses and Remonstrances of the Free People of Color* (Boston: Garrison and Knapp, 1832), second pagination, pp. 9–13; Oberholtzer, *Philadelphia* 2:279–80. The quotations are from Garrison (p. 9) and Oberholtzer (p. 280).

42. Staudenraus, *African Colonization Movement,* pp. 36–93, 97–149; Berlin, "Slaves Who Were Free," pp. 217–18; Garrison, *Thoughts on Colonization,* second pagination, pp. 52–57, 63–67; quotations are from pp. 55–56, 67.

43. Staudenraus, *African Colonization Movement,* pp. 193–96; Garrison, *Thoughts on Colonization,* second pagination, pp. 13–28, 34–35, 44–45; quotations are from pp. 14, 19, 21, 22, 23, 25, 35, 45.

44. National Negro Convention, *Proceedings, 1831,* p. 10; *Minutes,* 1831, pp. 5, 15; [National Negro Convention], *Minutes and Proceedings of the Second Annual Convention, for the Improvement of the Free People of Color In these United States* (Philadelphia: Martin and Boden, 1832), pp. 8, 18, 33; *Minutes and Proceedings of the Third Annual Convention, For the Improvement of the Free People of Colour In these United States* (New York, 1833), pp. 23, 26–28, 34–36; *Minutes of the Fourth Annual Convention of the Free People of Colour,* pp. 4–6, 30–31; *Minutes of the Fifth Annual Convention For the Improvement of the Free People of Colour In the United States, 1835,* pp. 17, 21–25. The quotations are from the minutes of the 1833 (p. 35) and 1834 (p. 5) conventions. The preponderance of urban residents among the delegates to successive national conventions does not necessarily indicate that they occupied similar degrees of dominance in their state conventions (where those existed) or that their views were overwhelmingly supported by blacks in their home states. For, as Howard H. Bell observes, "There was no consistent pattern followed in choosing delegates. . . . The ideal was the election of local representatives to state or national conventions, but in few cases was the rule followed rigidly. Once present, a man had a good chance of being accredited as a delegate, especially if he had come from an unrepresented area." Bell also points out that the convention managers "allowed easy accreditation for those interested in promoting a given cause, but refused recognition to anyone in the opposition." See Bell, *The Negro Convention Movement,* p. 5.

45. Bourne, *History of the Public School Society,* p. 679; *Call Upon the Church for Progressive Action,* p. 3. See also Horton, "Black Activism in Boston," p. 129.

Appendix A

1. U.S., Census Office, *Census, 1800,* pp. 14, 38, 39, 44, 49, 57, 68, 77, 84; U.S., Census Office, *Aggregate Amount of Each Description of Persons Within the United States of America, and the Territories Thereof, Agreeable to the Actual Enumeration Made According to Law, in the*

Year 1810 ([Washington, 1811]), pp. 7, 23, 28, 33, 44, 53, 62, 72, 79, 82, 89; *Census, 1820,* pp. 5*, 8, 9*, 11, 13, 15*, 17*, 21*, 26, 31*, 33*, 35*, 40*; ibid. (1830), third pagination, pp. 22–23, 24–25, 36–37, 38–39, 50–51, 64–65, 68–69, 80–81, 94–95, 105–6, 114–15, 126–27, 160–61; ibid. (1840), pp. 46–47, 52–53, 82–83, 88–89, 114–15, 118–19, 150–51, 160–61, 194–95, 226–27, 256–57, 280–81, 306–7, 412–13, 470–71; ibid. (1850), pp. 52, 67, 92, 96, 99, 102, 158, 179, 221, 234, 339, 474, 612, 662, 830; Scharf, *History of Saint Louis* 2:1015; Bryan, *National Capital* 2:136n; DeBow, *Statistical View,* p. 192; Viles, "Population in Missouri before 1804," p. 208.

2. Mss. Census (1850), Reels 56–57, 206–7, 235–38, 281–87, 334–39, 415–18, 471–72, 501–2, 517–20, 534–59, 687–91, 745–46, 812–17, 844–45, 850.

3. U.S., Census Office, *Census, 1820,* pp. 21*, 26, 31*, 33*; ibid. (1830), third pagination, pp. 80–81, 94–95, 105–6, 114–15, 160–61; ibid. (1840), pp. 194–95, 226–27, 256–57, 280–81, 412–13, 470–71; ibid. (1850), pp. 221, 234, 339, 474, 612, 662. The census returns before 1820 did not divide either slaves or free blacks by sex or age. The 1820 figures for the three northern cities with one hundred or more slaves were:

	White	Slave
Albany	1.0810	1.1800
Brooklyn	.9009	.7925
New York	1.0397	1.9266

See *Census, 1820,* pp. 9*, 13.

4. DeBow, *Statistical View,* pp. 55–57, 69, 73, 91–92. Birth statistics are difficult to obtain for the first half of the nineteenth century and truly comparable data are impossible to come by. It is perhaps worth noting, however, that the New York City Inspector reported in 1855 a ratio of only .8230 females to each male among free Negro births. The figure given by the Washington Board of Health in 1850 was .7667 females to each male, and the Charleston census of 1848 reported .8065 females to each male. See David T. Valentine, *Manual of the Corporation of the City of New-York for 1856* (New York: McSpedon and Baker, 1856), p. 208; Washington, *Laws (1850),* p. 529; Dawson and De Saussure, *Census of the City of Charleston, 1848,* p. 180.

5. DeBow, *Statistical View,* pp. 49, 67, 87; tables A-9 and A-10.

6. U.S., Census Office, *Census, 1850,* pp. 67, 92, 96–97, 99–100, 158–59, 178–79, 220–21, 234, 388–39, 611–12, 655, 662, 830. The use of the county data would reduce the average female-to-male ratio for free blacks in these fifteen cities from 1.2463:1 to 1.2005:1. In 1850, of course, the suggested impact of economic segregation on free black housing patterns would have been greater than in the earlier decades (except in the case of Charleston, which had extended its boundaries in 1849).

7. U.S., Census Office, *Census, 1820,* pp. 21*, 26, 31*, 33*; ibid. (1830), third pagination, pp. 80–81, 94–95, 105–6, 114–15, 160–61; ibid. (1840), pp. 194–95, 226–27, 256–57, 280–81, 412–13, 470–71. The 1800 and 1810 census returns did not show age or sex for the slave or the free black population. The 1850 census did not disaggregate the population data by age for the cities and counties. Such data for thirteen of the cities were provided by the superintendent of the census in another publication, however. See DeBow, *Statistical View,* pp. 397–98. The 1820 figures for the three northern cities with one hundred or more slaves were:

	White	Slave
Albany	39.65%	36.70%
Brooklyn	36.06%	31.05%
New York	37.36%	37.60%

See U.S., Census Office, *Census, 1820,* pp. 9*, 13.

8. DeBow, *Statistical View,* pp. 54, 73, 91–92; tables A-14 and A-15.

Appendix B

1. DeBow, *Statistical View,* pp. 80–81. The census office aggregation of black male occupations in New York City, for instance, shows more than half of the free blacks following unskilled occupations; my aggregation (including over two hundred more entries than that of the census office) places that figure at slightly under forty percent.

2. Mss. Census (1850), Reels 56–57 (Washington), 206–7 (Louisville), 235–38 (New Orleans), 281–87 (Baltimore), 334–39 (Boston), 415–18 (St. Louis), 471–72 (Albany), 501–2 (Buffalo), 517–20 (Brooklyn), 534–59 (New York), 687–91 (Cincinnati), 745–46 (Pittsburgh), 812–17 (Philadelphia), 844–45 (Providence), 850 (Charleston).

3. Charles Keenan, *The Baltimore Directory for 1822 and '23* (Baltimore: J. Matchett, 1822); *Matchett's Baltimore Director, Corrected Up to June 1831* (Baltimore, 1831); *Matchett's Baltimore Director, 1842; Matchett's Baltimore Director for 1851; Boston Directory* (1818); *Stimpson's Boston Directory* (1835); ibid. (1840); ibid. (1845); Stevens and Marschalk, *Brooklyn Directory, 1838–39;* Thomas Leslie et al., *Brooklyn Alphabetical Street Directory, and Yearly Advertiser, for 1843 & 4* (Brooklyn: Stationer's Hall Works, 1843); *Hearnes' Brooklyn Directory, 1851–1852;* Daniel J. Dowling, *The Charleston Directory; and Register, for 1835–6* (Charleston: Daniel J. Dowling, 1835); Mears and Turnbull, *Charleston Directory* (1859); *Gibson's Directory of New Orleans* (1839); *Cohen's New Orleans Directory* (1852); John Doggett, Jr., *The New York City Directory for 1842 and 1843* (New York: John Doggett, Jr., 1842); ibid., *for 1846 and 1847;* Wilson, *Directory of New-York, for 1852–1853; Providence Directory* (1832); ibid. (1841); ibid. (1844); *The Saint Louis Directory, For the Year 1842* (St. Louis: Chambers and Knapp, 1842); Knox, *St. Louis Directory, for 1854–5;* Delano, *Washington Directory* (1822); Hunter, *Washington Directory* (1853). Some directory data for Cincinnati and Philadelphia were used for subregional comparisons. This material has not, however, been used in the analysis of directory data across time because black entries in the directories of these two cities are not identifiable (or are not sufficiently numerous) late enough in the half-century. See Cist, *Cincinnati Directory, for 1843;* [*Philadelphia*] *Census Directory for 1811;* Whitley, *Philadelphia Directory for 1820.*

4. The number of free black males for whom occupations were recorded in each of the directory listings comprised the following perentages of the number of free black males whose occupations were listed in the 1850 manuscript census enumeration in the same cities:

Baltimore	44.92%
Louisville	32.50%
Brooklyn	32.46%
New York	29.58%
Washington	29.54%
New Orleans	6.36%

5. Pearson's *r* is an unsatisfactory statistical instrument in this case. Nor have I been able to locate any other that will deal adequately with an effective N of three (the aggregated groupings) or even eight (the occupational categories). The search for a serviceable statistical instrument is further complicated by the fact that we do not wish to measure the extent to which two sets of data conform to (or deviate from) a "line of best fit" between the two, but, rather, the extent to which the directory data conform to the census data. In addition, it is desirable that the statistical analysis should yield an index figure readily comprehensible to the uninitiated (e.g., located on a scale of -1 to $+1$, or 0 to 1).

6. Dawson and De Saussure, *Census of the City of Charleston, 1848,* pp. 31–35; Shattuck, *Census of Boston for the Year 1845,* pp. 39–43; New York, Secretary of State, *Census of the State of New-York, for 1855* (Albany: Charles Van Benthuysen, 1857), pp. 178–95; Edwin M. Snow, *Census of the City of Providence, Taken in July, 1855* (Provi-

dence: Knowles, Anthony, 1856), pp. 37–39; Cist, *Cincinnati in 1851,* pp. 49–51; Casseday, *History of Louisville,* pp. 228–30.

7. Dawson and De Saussure, *Census of the City of Charleston, 1848,* pp. 31–35. The percentages in the horizontal rows do not always equal 100 because of rounding.

Appendix C

1. Mss. Census (1850), Reels 84–85.

2. Ibid., Reels 56–57, 206–7, 235–38, 281–87, 334–39, 415–18, 471–72, 501–2, 517–20, 534–59, 687–91, 745–46, 812–17, 850. As previously noted, no real estate holdings were reported for Providence.

3. In addition to the sources cited in note 2, data employed in the construction of this table were obtained from U.S., Census Office, *Census, 1850,* pp. 52, 92, 96, 99, 102, 158, 179, 221, 234, 339, 474, 612, 662, 830.

4. New York, Secretary of State, *Census of the State of New-York, for 1855,* pp. 1, 5, 7, 8; table C-2.

5. Boston, Assessing Department, *List of Persons, Copartnerships, and Corporations Who Were Taxed Twenty-five Dollars and Upwards, in the City of Boston, in the Year 1845* (Boston: J. H. Eastburn, 1846), passim; *Stimpson's Boston Directory* (1845), pp. 543–50.

6. The tax rate in 1845 was $.57 per $100, which would result in a tax of $25 on an estate of $4,385.96. The 1850 federal census enumerators located only three Boston Negroes with real estate holdings over $4,000. See Boston, Assessing Department, *List of Persons Taxed, 1845,* passim; Mss. Census (1850), Reels 334–39.

7. Reinders, "Free Negro in the New Orleans Economy," p. 281.

8. *Statistical Inquiry into the Condition of the People of Colour of Philadelphia,* pp. 12–14.

9. Woodson, "Negroes of Cincinnati," p. 9.

10. Wright, *Free Negro in Maryland,* p. 184; *Statistical Inquiry into the Condition of the People of Colour of Philadelphia,* pp. 12–15.

11. See Mss. Census (1850) sources listed in note 2. See also, U.S., Census Office, *Census, 1850,* pp. 52, 92, 96, 99, 102, 158, 179, 221, 234, 339, 474, 612, 662, 830. FPC designates free persons of color; FWC designates free women of color.

12. Woodson, *Free Negro Owners of Slaves, 1830,* pp. 2–3, 5, 9–15, 16–17, 27–30; U.S., Census Office, *Census, 1830,* pp. 80–81, 94–95, 105–6, 114–15, 160–61. There were no black slaveholders listed in St. Louis.

13. Woodson, *Free Negro Owners of Slaves, 1830,* pp. 2–3, 5, 9–15, 16–17, 27–30; Woodson, *Free Negro Heads of Families, 1830,* pp. 17–20, 28, 31–38, 43–52, 155–57.

14. Woodson, *Free Negro Owners of Slaves, 1830,* pp. 2–3, 5, 9–15, 16–17, 27–30.

15. Ibid.; U.S., Census Office, *Census, 1830,* pp. 80–81, 94–95, 105–6, 114–15, 160–61. A source of potential error in these figures is the circumstance (previously noted) that the 1830 census does not list slaveholders by name. Hence, some or all of the slaves recorded as owned by a woman head-of-household might have been owned by other "family" members—perhaps male—or by whites.

Appendix D

1. U.S., Census Office, *Mortality Statistics, 1850,* pp. 13, 303; U.S., Census Office, *Census, 1850,* pp. 52, 67, 92, 96, 99, 102, 158, 178–79, 221, 234, 339, 473, 612, 662, 830; DeBow, *Statistical View,* pp. 45, 63, 82, 95.

2. U.S., Census Office, *Mortality Statistics, 1850,* p. 303; U.S., Census Office, *Census, 1850,* pp. 52, 67, 92, 96, 99, 102, 158, 178–79, 221, 234, 339, 473, 612, 662, 830.

3. U.S., Census Office, *Mortality Statistics, 1850,* p. 303; Howard, *Public Health Administration in Baltimore,* p. 509; New York City Inspector, *Report, 1850,* p. 346. Howard

is cited as a convenient source for the Baltimore death figures. His entries have been spot-checked against the original sources and found to be accurate. Unfortunately, the same cannot be said of his population figures (p. 178), which are demonstrably inaccurate in census years by as much as eighteen percent. Population figures for computation in this appendix (and in chapter 9) are based on federal census data (see chapter 1) and assume an equal distribution of the intercensus change to each of the ten intercensus years. Since the growth of most of these urban populations was heavily influenced by in-migrations (which are sometimes wildly erratic), no assignment by formulae of portions of the intercensus growth to given years has any necessary relationship to reality. Consequently, it is believed that the simpler, arithmetic method of assigning population increments is likely to create no more distortions than more complex approaches.

Index

Since the fifteen cities comprising the research universe (see p. 5) for this work are mentioned hundreds of times and usually in a comparative context, index entries have been prepared for these individual cities only in cases of more extensive treatment of conditions or events in a single city, e.g.,"Washington, antiblack riots in (1831)." For somewhat similar reasons, the reader will find no index entries under "cities," "urban," "black," or "free black" because the whole of the work deals with these matters. Tables, maps, and figures are not separately indexed; the reader is directed to the lists following the table of contents. To facilitate the location of cited material, the few index entries for the notes are identified by chapter rather than by page, e.g., chap. 1, n.8.